*"While awaiting the Grand Jury prize announcement, Claire wondered if the anxiety she felt at maxing out 5 credit cards to finish her film was as great as the anxiety her competitor felt investing $50 million to make his."*

Hollywood Reporter advert, Cannes Market Guide 2004



## So you want to know more about film financing?

If you are reading this, you must be at least partly interested in making films. Or financing them. Or perhaps both. It may be that you already have a string of Oscar winning hits behind you, but need just need clarification on the proposed new "20% UK tax credit", or the new minimum contribution criteria for a UK-France co-production. Alternatively, you may be just about to embark on your first attempt at producing a short film, and wondering where on earth you can get your money from. You've heard that there are funds available for filmmakers, but have no idea where they are, what you need to do in order to access them, or how to keep your budget low enough to avoid having to put in ten times as much money yourself. Or perhaps, despite being in the game for a while now, you're still not quite sure how a Sale & Leaseback actually works, or what the difference is between gapping and bridging, and are too embarrassed to ask your colleagues. Maybe you are one of those colleagues and, having just been asked, don't actually know the answer.

Whatever the case may be, hopefully we can help. Having been involved with or advised on the production, financing and/or sales of nearly 200 films between us (ranging from £20 shorts to features costing nearly US$100m), we have written this Handbook for anyone and everyone who wishes to understand the mechanics of the financing process, and who needs specific information about where the money comes from. Basically, we want to provide you with your own comprehensive guide to all the ins and outs of production financing for independent films.

And although the Handbook may be written from a UK perspective, the same tools of the trade apply throughout the world. Most of the information and explanations we provide are equally as relevant to foreign producers, financiers and industry executives as they are to those in the UK. Many films are financed by sources from more than one country, and those that aren't will go through very similar procedures to those that are financed solely within our shores. The idea is that any person in any country who wishes to source production funding for his/her picture should find this Handbook an essential tool for getting to grips with the many concepts involved.

The Handbook is not limited to feature films either. Much of the information provided can be applied to documentaries, short films and films made for TV.

Whatever your reason for buying this book, we trust you find it enjoyable and useful.

**Adam P Davies & Nic Wistreich**

## This Second Edition

For this Second Edition, we have split the Handbook into four main areas, the Main Text (Chapters 1 to 5), the Funding Organisations (Chapter 6), the Directory (Chapter 7), and a small Reference Section.

The **Main Text** includes the theory and practice relating to all aspects of film finance. Each Chapter ends with a number of case studies and interviews with high-level experienced producers, financiers, directors and other industry executives, who each give their personal or corporate views on various aspects of the financing process. Taking each Chapter in turn:

**Chapter 1** gives an *overview* of the film industry in the UK and internationally, a background to financing, issues such as neogtiating and business plans, and first hand advice from experienced practitioners.

**Chapter 2** looks predominantly at *lower* and *"microbudget"* films, and demonstrates over a hundred basic and inventive ways to keep the budget down in order to get maximum production value on screen, alongisdde sample micro budgets and case studies.

**Chapter 3** discusses in depth all the various aspects of production financing. This includes the types of entity that provide funding, why financiers make it available, what they want in return, and how they interconnect to (hopefully) provide the entire budget. We look step by step at the entire range of finance available in the industry, including *Soft Money, Equity, Deferments, Pre-Sales, Gap, Sales Advances, Negative Pick-ups, EIS and Venture Capital, Sponsorship* and *Product Placement*. We also illustrate the roles of the various other companies in the mix who, although not technically financiers themselves, are integral to the financing process. These include *Sales Companies, Distributors, Discounting Banks,* and *Completion Guarantors.*

**Chapter 4** takes a closer look specifically at the UK-based tax incentives, present (*sections 48 and 42*) and future (the *20% tax credit*?!), and the various financing products they have brought about, such as *Sale & Leaseback* and *Production Funds*.

**Chapter 5** explores the financial merits of *international co-production*, how to qualify under the *Treaties* and the *European Convention*, and what you might get for your troubles. It includes a brief look at the incentives available in 20 or so countries around the world.

**Funding Organisations** does "exactly what it says on the tin", providing a full breakdown of private, public and international funds available to UK film producers. We give information on each of the available *funding bodies* within the UK, including details on their criteria, objectives and the amounts they are willing to provide. We also identify a number of relevant international film bodies and funding institutions.

**The Directory** is a comprehensive listing of financing companies, public bodies, funds, organisations and film companies involved in production and funding within the film industry, a "Who's Who" of the production and financing world. It also contains contact details for organisations referred to in previous chapters.

**Reference Section** contains a few sample documents and resources to compliment the contents of the previous Chapters, including an in-depth legal explanation of copyright and other intellectual property rights issues, a table of common financing contracts, sample agreement schedules, useful websites and further reading list.

## Preface - Financing in the current environment

You're at a bar, a party, a function or just out with friends, and you get introduced to someone who asks what you do for a living. "*You're in the film industry?!*" they respond (usually a little too loud for comfort). "*Wow. That must be great. Especially with British Films doing so well right now.*" And then you ask yourself, "Actually, how well *are* British Films doing right now?". Our population might be one quarter the size of the Untied States', but do we really produce a proportionate amount of successful films? Did we really answer the call back in 1982, when *Chariots of Fire* writer and Oscar® winner Colin Welland proclaimed "The Brits are coming!"? If you were to ask your friends if they could name just ten British films that became international hits in the last few years, they would probably find it impossible. The headline titles *Four Weddings and a Funeral, Brassed Off, Shallow Grave, Shooting Fish,* and *Trainspotting* are all at least nine or ten years old now. None of *Love Actually, Jonny English, Calendar Girls, Lara Croft, Shakespeare in Love, Bridget Jones, Chicken Run, Harry Potter, About a Boy* or *Gosford Park* were really British produced or financed, and certainly would never have seen the light of day had it not been for the strong involvement of a Studio from day one. Britfilms *Human Traffic, Mike Bassett, Little Voice, Bloody Sunday, Kevin & Perry, Iris, East is East, Ali G Indahouse, Girl with a Pearl Earring* and *Saving Grace* all did well on home turf but didn't quite "break out" internationally. And without mentioning the celebrated flops, that pretty much leaves *Lock Stock and Two Smoking Barrels, Billy Elliot, The Full Monty,* and *Bend It Like Beckham*, only one of which was financed this decade. With UK production falling 40% over the last year alone, you could end up painting a picture of pure doom and gloom, and be tempted to just give up on the whole thing.

But there is no need to despair, as the news is not all bad. UK admissions are still rising steadily. This means that people in Britain want to pay to watch films on the big screen. And an ever increasing number of people are getting involved in film production; widening and deepening the reservoir of talent from which the next big hits will come. The Relph Report reminded us that films made in the UK were, on average, almost the most expensive in the world. The industry has quickly taken heed, and the subsequent explosion of microbudget filmmaking, using techniques and equipment costing a fraction of what they did just a few years ago, has caught the eye of the mainstream industry and simply can't be ignored. *Batman Begins* director Christopher Nolan was himself making microbudget pictures only three films ago.

The disastrous implosion of the financing industry that took place at the turn of the decade also finally seems to have stabilised. After suffering the dot.com crash, Neur Markt closure, withdrawal of insurance-backed gap finance, departure of many traditional lending banks from the sector, reduction in pre-sale values and the aftermath of the Studio mergers and consolidation, we were left wondering where the next financing penny was going to come from, and whether it would stay around long enough for the ink on the funding documents to dry. But the vacuum was soon filled by the "Super" sale & leaseback, which swooped in like any "Super" hero to save the damsel producer in distress. Of course, the future of Sale & Leaseback itself now looks fairly bleak, but that void is likely to be filled partly by the proposed 20% UK tax credit, and partly by alternative new forms of soft money available around the world. A few more banks, new and old, are gingerly dipping their toes in the gap financing pool again, pre-sale values seem to have stopped plummeting, and the speculative high-risk investor is slowly returning to the table, having recovered from the loss in value of his/her information technology stocks.

So what we are saying, basically, is that there *is* money out there and available for the right project. If you know which sources to approach, and understand what you should be asking for and offering in return, there are deals to be made. This Handbook should arm you with that information, and hopefully give you a little edge over any other Producer who might be vying for that same production dollar. If we can help at least one deserved project get made that otherwise wouldn't have, we've done our job. And if we can spread a little extra knowledge around those supposedly already in the know, well that's a bonus. Good luck, and enjoy.

**Adam P Davies**

April 2005

## NOTES FOR THE READER

To try to make things easier, when referencing '**Producers**' throughout this Handbook, we refer to them as *human beings* (**s/he**, **his/her**, etc), mainly to help distinguish them in the text from any other entity (company, partnership, fund, etc), which we will always refer to as an "**it**". We acknowledge that in practice this will not always be correct (the Producer, for financing purposes, will nearly always be a limited company or specialist partnership), but we felt that it would make it easier to differentiate between the various parties when describing multi-party transactions. Most people reading this Book will probably relate mostly to the Producer, and so we are allocating to you the privilege of humanity!

We also do not mean to intimidate by continually referring to the "**£10m Film**" example. We're all too aware of the shortage of independent films of this size in the real world. But £10m is an easy number to use for the purposes of illustration, and so we use it where possible. We can all live in hope!

Lastly, in many cases, we sometimes use capitalised terms for specific "entities" (the Distributor, the Bank, the Sales Agent, etc), again to try to help you pick out which one we are discussing at any particular moment. Those of you who have read production or financing contracts will be familiar with this style of labelling.

# Preface - digital democracy

Could UK cinema be about to turn the corner? In 2004, the top 20 British films took £176m at the box office between them, an increase of more than 45% on the previous year. Meanwhile the opportunities for film production in the UK has exploded.

The new generation of HI-Def cameras are available for less than £3,000, while the latest desktop editing packages allow you to edit this 35mm equivalent tape on your home computer for less than a grand. If you can't afford a camera and edit system, there's probably never been a better time to apply for public money with over £60m available across the UK. If you can't afford film school, then books such as the Guerilla Moviemakers' Blueprint tell you everything you need to know about the process. And if you weren't lucky enough to have a relative working in the industry to help you get your foot in the door, networks such as Shooting People can connect you with an incredible number of keen, driven and like-minded people. And if you can't afford any of the above, a new breed of film workshops such as the Engine Room in Bridgewater are acting like public libraries, allowing members of the public to come in and use their kit for free.

The barriers that have kept cinema production (as opposed to consumption) from the masses seem to be falling down, while the recent successes of mini-majors such as Focus (*Eternal Sunshine of the Spotless Mind*, *Lost in Translation*) and Pixar (valued higher on the stock market than MGM after just 6 films) have again shown that audiences are hungry for original and thought-provoking entertainment.

But here's the rub - Focus and Pixar have the distribution might of Universal and Disney behind them. Could a UK producer, whether at the microbudget end (as covered in chapter 2) or the mainstream budget end (chapter 3) confront the market forces that define who sees what, and win? Films such as Ben Hopkins' *Nine Lives of Thomas Katz*, Steven Soderbergh's *Schizopolis* (his self-financed microbudget feature) or Ken Loach's *The Navigators* have never received a proper release in the UK. And even fully financed mainstream independents are struggling against the mini-majors who invest up to five times as much money in a film targeted at the same market as a £3m indie film, and with guaranteed distribution from the parent company built in. But this too may be changing - the Internet allows anyone to run a global TV station from their bedroom to those with broadband; affordable DVD pressing and print-on-demand has allowed producers such as Luke Morris or Warp Films to become best-selling video distributors, while the Film Council's planned Digital Screen Network will install some 250 digital screens across the UK, potentially offering low cost and low risk entry to any 'distributor' with a digital version of their film.

At the 2004 Leeds Film Festival panel '*Never Mind the Celluloid*', Laurence Boyce questioned if, with the entry barriers to film production stripped away, 'the UK is on the verge of a new punk film revolution in cinema'. The technology, resources and communities are in place. The distribution problems may be beginning to get resolved though technology. What remains to be seen, though, is exactly what sorts of stories and techniques will emerge from this period of greater creative freedom. It could be an exciting ride.

Nic Wistreich, April 2005

# 1. GETTING GOING



# 2. LOW AND MICROBUDGET FILMMAKING 35

## 3. PRODUCTION FINANCING 73

# Acknowledgements

Many thanks to the book's sponsors Avid, UK Film Council and Skillset. Also to Andrew Phillips at Trask, Zahir Noorani, Neil McCartney at McCartney Media, Cyndee Barlass and Patrick Roe at Kristian Stad who have helped tirelessly to bring the book to fruition; and all those who have been interviewed for this edition of the book - Nik Powell, David Thompson, Paul Trijbits, Jenny Borgars, Libby Saville, Becky LLoyd, Pippa Mitchell, Kerry Appleyard and Farah Abushwesha.

Further thanks to all the organisations and companies who have provided us with information and been helpful in pulling together and updating a large amount of data, especially Samantha Bell - Great British Films; Pippa Best - Cornwall Film; Angela Blackburn - Arts Council Of Wales; Davina Christmas - Croydon Council; Isabella Edgar - Scottish Screen; Sarah Hardie - Awards For All; Lorena Herbert - Screen Yorkshire; Sally Hudgson - EM Media; Anneli Jones - Arts Council of Wales; Nicky Wade - Screen East; Dan Lawson - Screen West Midlands; Bennett McGhee - Working Title; Jessica Nugent - UnLtd; Jacqui Rafferty - North West Vision; Hannah Raybould - Sgrîn; Paul Ryan - Edinburgh Mediabase; David Smith - Cineworks; Melvyn Singer - Random Harvest; Jo Smith - DNA Films; Honnie Tang - Film London; Ian Thomson - Film Council; Gaby Topalian - Screen South; Anna Webster - Sarah Radclyffe Productions Ltd.

Special thanks to Caroline Hancock and Jess, Cath and everyone else at Shooting People for helping make the first edition such a success, and to Stephen Salter for planting the initial seeds for the book with the Netribution funding guide back in 2001.

Big thanks finally to friends and family for continued support and patience - and to everyone else who we may have forgotton!


Please do let us know if there is anything we've missed or got wrong in the funds directory - info@ukfilmfinance.com many of the interviews in this book can be read in full at

**WWW.NETRIBUTION.CO.UK**

and many of those from chapter 2 are online at

**WWW.SHOOTINGPEOPLE.ORG/WIDESHOT**

# CHAPTER ONE
# GETTING GOING

Commerce and creativity. Film and finance. The pairs have often made ugly bedfellows.

On one side lies a creative person or team with a story, a vision, an image, that they wish to bring to life for audiences to enjoy. On the other side is a multi billion dollar business, filled to the brim with financiers, executives and experts seeking their cut as expert gamblers on the illusive nature of art and success.

At every step of the way, the producer or filmmaker dances a duet between the integrity of the project, and the profit motive of those financing, selling, distributing and promoting it – and of course his or her own needs to see a return and make some form of a sustainable living.

There are no wrong or right paths. As William Goldman famously said decades ago about Hollywood, 'nobody knows anything'. Jonathan Caouette used iMovie to cut his first feature *Tarnation* for $216, propelling him to Cannes in 2004 with a wide international release in 2005. New York couple Chris Kentis and Laura Lau (interviewed in Chapter 2) used $120,000 of savings to shoot *Open Water* in their weekends, which went on to open on 2,700 screens in the US grossing $31m there alone. Chris Nolan shot *Following* for a reported £5,000 and after the UK industry passed on his follow-up *Memento*, he went to Hollywood, returning two features later to shoot *Batman Begins* at Pinewood for Warner Bros. First time writer John Hodge met first time producer Andrew Macdonald and joined with first time feature director (but seasoned TV director) Danny Boyle to get FilmFour to back *Shallow Grave* to the tune of £1m, launching the careers of all involved. Interviewed in this chapter are first time writer-directors Nicole Kassell (*The Woodsman*) and Patty Jenkins (*Monster*), who both got films with difficult subject matters fully financed independently and a big name cast attached, and subsequent critical and commercial success.

But then, of course, for every *Following* or *Open Water*, festivals such as Sundance receive thousands of micro-budget features that they reject. And the knowledge, expertise (and bank accounts) of distributors, financiers, public film funds and sales agents can be incredibly valuable in producing a film that will have an audience when complete.

Before deciding the right financing approach for your project, one exercise that can be useful is asking yourself what exactly you want to achieve from the whole process. Getting your film financed and released, no doubt. But at what cost? Are you looking to build a business that can support you and those you work with over a number of years? Are you wanting to enjoy the filmmaking process as much as possible without being tied down with bureaucracy, market demands or delivery requirements? Are you looking for complete control over your work, or the security of having fully financed employment?

Ultimately, it is about finding the finance and business model that most suits your project, your intended audience, and the way you want to live and work. This chapter, and indeed this book, does not try to present one foolproof route to do this, for there are perhaps as many ways to get a film made as there are filmmakers to make them. But by combining the advice of those who have already navigated the industry with the practical facts regarding the nature of the business and law as it currently stands, as well as detailing the opportunities available to you, we hope to provide an armoury of tools to protect your vision and help bring your project to light.

**This chapter** begins by giving a background to the UK and international film industry and the basic elements of funding and budgets. We then look at certain business issues underlying raising finance - writing a business plan, talking with investors, negotiating. Finally we present a collection of advice, tips and interviews with those who've been there already.

# Where are we now?

## Background to the UK Film Industry

It's more than 23 years since Colin Welland infamously declared that the British were coming as he collected his Oscar for *Chariots of Fire* in 1982. For a brief moment it looked like he might be right - the following year Britain won 10 Oscars, while Goldcrest was financing international hits such as *Gandhi*, the *Killing Fields* and *The Mission*. But in 1984 the Thatcher government abolished the Eady Levy, which had channelled a share of box office receipts into domestic production, and ended tax breaks for production. The industry all but collapsed. Much of Britain's leading directing and producing talent migrated to the United States with great success and Goldcrest, after 24 films, ran out of capital and was sold off. Other than the then newly-launched British Screen, which supported non-commercial work from the likes of Mike Leigh and Ken Loach, British production came to a near standstill.

Stephen Frears' 1985 *My Beautiful Launderette* signalled a change in direction for the industry, in that TV-backed film investment started to feed local productions. The Channel 4 film encouraged the broadcaster to increase investment in filmmaking over the late 80s and also launched Working Title, initially run by Tim Bevan and Sarah Radcliffe (who left in 1992 to run her own company) and later Eric Fellner, with whom Bevan runs the company today. Video distributor and producer, Palace Pictures, run by Nik Powell and Stephen Woolley, followed the success in 1985 of Neil Jordon's *Company of Wolves*, with *Mona Lisa* in 1986. The British Film Commission was launched in 1991, and in 1992 Section 42 tax relief was launched offering tax relief on film investment over three years. Palace Picture's 1992 release *The Crying Game* was a massive global success yet the company collapsed and Powell and Woolley set-up Scala Productions. In 1993, newcomers Danny Boyle, writer John Hodge and producer Andrew MacDonald made *Shallow Grave* for Channel 4's film division FilmFour, and provided inspiration to a generation of young British filmmakers. The following year Rank released *Four Weddings and a Funeral*, grossing over £27m at the UK box office and heralding the start of a new wave of popular British filmmaking.

London-based PolyGram Filmed Entertainment (PFE), part of Philips-owned PolyGram, was behind both *Shallow Grave* and *Four Weddings*. During the mid-90s, PFE supported and nurtured British talent; financing, acquiring and distributing Working Title projects such as *Bean*, *Elizabeth* and *Notting Hill*, and dozens more British films such as *Backbeat*, *Trainspotting* and *Lock Stock and Two Smoking Barrels*. In May 1998, however, PolyGram was sold for £6.5bn to Canadian drinks and media conglomerate Seagram who were mainly interested in merging the group's music library with Universal Music. A sale for the film division was not secured after a bid from EMI was pulled at the last minute, and it became merged into the Universal empire, with its pre-1996 film library sold to MGM. After the merger of Seagram with Vivendi in 2000, PFE's former activities continued almost solely through the financing of Working Title via Universal Pictures.

As with the collapse of Goldcrest and Palace Pictures before it, the UK film industry had lost its key driver. Focus now shifted to Channel 4's then independent film production, sales and distribution arm FilmFour, which had begun producing, acquiring and releasing higher budget films; and the Lottery Franchises. In 1997 three franchises - DNA Films, Pathé and The Film Consortium - had successful bids for almost £100m between them over a six year period, from the Arts Council to part-finance a slate of feature films with the intention of becoming self-sustaining 'mini-studios' at the end of the franchise period. Labour's election victory of 1997 injected further life into the UK film sector, with the launch of Section 48 tax relief reinstating 100% first year tax write-offs for British film, and new consultation within the industry. A Department of Culture Media and Sport (DCMS) commissioned policy document, The Bigger Picture, steered by former PolyGram International chief Stewart Till, had called for a new public film body and the need for a distributor-led approach to the industry.

In 2000 the Film Council formally took on the functions of a host of national film agencies with the target of directing funds at initiatives that will move the industry forward as a whole, making up for a lack of sector-wide structure and strategy that had dogged the UK in previous years. This came through investing not just in production, but also training, distribution, exhibition, development and – through industry consultation – new initiatives to address shortfalls as they arise.

In July 2002, Channel 4 announced the closure of FilmFour, bringing back the division's film operations in-house. In September of that year, Granada followed suit, closing its film arm which had been responsible for such hits as *Ghost World*, *House of Mirth* and *Bloody Sunday*.

In 2004, production spend in the UK fell a massive 40% in one year, to £800m from the record £1.15bn in 2003. The level of investment in UK films fell by almost 60% compared to 2003, which many blamed on uncertainty about the future of the UK tax situation as the Treasury closed loopholes in the law (see chapter 4), with further uncertainty about the lifespan and replacement of Section 48. In all, the UK was involved in only 132 films (those at £500,000 or higher budgets), which included 27 UK-only features, 20 inward investment films and 85 co-productions.

More encouraging, however, was the performance of British films at the UK box office in 2004, with the top 20 films taking £176m between them, an increase of 45% on the previous year. The number of British films taking more than £3m at the box office also doubled from eight in 2003 to 16 in 2004, while six out of the top ten films on TV were British, according to figures from the UK Film Council.

If the British industry was to be valued on Oscar wins, then perhaps Colin Welland would have been proven right, with the British taking 21% of all statues from 1991 to 2003. There is no doubt that the UK has the necessary talent, skills and ideas. What it has long lacked, though, is sustainable sources of finance, a coherent, stable infrastructure, and a distribution-centric approach to ensure that the only films being made are those which can – and will – be absorbed by the world market.

## The Global Perspective

After the lacklustre global cinema slump of the 80s, cinema admissions rose during the 90s and early 00s by a phenomenal amount. In the US, box office receipts skyrocketed from $5.3bn in 1994 to $9.5bn in 2004, while UK screen admissions in the same period rose from 100m to 171m. Between 2002 and 2004 box office admissions have stabilised slightly with a 0.5% dip in box office takings in the US in 2003 being followed by a 0.5% rise in 2004. This stabilisation in receipts actually masks a fall in total admissions, due to a rise in ticket prices (48% between 1994 and 2004), and the number of people going to the cinema in the US falling 4% in 2003 and 2.4% in 2004 to 1.54bn total admissions.

Total global non-US box office revenues rose a massive 20% to $9.6bn in 2002 (from 2001), while total non-US admissions were up 7.5% to 7.3 billion in the same period.

As film audiences have flocked in ever-greater numbers to the cinema, film producers have found an increasing number of potential platforms for exploiting their product, with the birth of DVD, video on demand (VoD), and the explosion in pay-TV. In the 1950s, ancillary media such as TV were a threat; nowadays, they make up the vast majority of a film's total return.

And yet this increase in the public's appetite for film hides a contraction in film production worldwide. In 2004, US box office receipts were more than 50% up on 1997. Yet during the same period, the number of studio films produced in the US annually fell from by more than 25%, from 767 to 611, and films theatrically released from 510 to 483. As outlined above, a similar paradox has occurred in the UK with a rise in box office receipts against a dramatic fall in production at the levels. These figures are monitored by the UK Film Council and Motion Picture Association of America. However, the UK is an exception within Europe where, during the first quarter of 2005, the majority of box office admissions fell over the previous year. In France, admissions were down by 13%, in Germany by 11%, in Spain static, while The Netherlands, Denmark, Poland and Australia also fell, and the UK rose by 13%.

At the same time as this contraction in fully financed projects, there has been a considerable (if unmonitored) rise in microbudget productions using affordable DV cameras (HD cameras now available at £3,000) and desktop edit systems that put the power of an Avid workstation onto a home computer.

Another recent trend is the dramatic rise in the costs of production, release and marketing, which has made distributors keener to bring fewer, more bankable, films to market with a greater marketing push per film. In the US, the average combined production budget and studio overheads ('negative' cost) and print and advertising (P&A) expenditure for a studio feature hit $98m in 2004, a 4.8% fall on the year before, but almost double that of 1994. On the other hand, however, the combined costs for studio affiliates, such as New Line or Miramax, fell by a sizeable 39.8% in 2004 to $39.6m, from $61.6m in 2003 – its lowest level since 2000, and perhaps signalling a change in the budgeting and marketing strategies of the 'mini-majors'.

Yet the major issue in the international production slowdown is a fall-out in new sources of film finance, which took place alongside the 'irrational exuberance' (per Alan Greenspan) of the late 90s stock market boom. The new funding options that, in the 90s, were briefly postulated as the saviour of international film finance, such as insurance backed gap financing and over-excitable German funds, have all since collapsed. In the late 90s, dozens of German media companies made an Initial Public Offering (IPO) on the Neuer Markt, using over-ambitious sales estimates to raise significant amounts of money for film investment. Many, such as Helkon and Kinowelt, filed for bankruptcy protection, and the short lived ambitions of the German sector to compete with Hollywood as a major financier, have come to epitomise the heady days of deal-making at the time. With an average drop of 96% in the value of media companies traded on the Markt, the index closed at the end of 2003.

This collapse of new funding sources has been accompanied by a significant reduction in the prices paid for free and pay-TV rights for feature films for all but the most high profile product, as the TV advertising market dried up. Meanwhile distributors and sales agents have grown more cautious about pre-sales, typically favouring slate deals from a smaller pool of established 'safe' producers, reducing the opportunities for producers to sell individual projects.

In the excitement of the dot.com boom, many decisions were made that the industry later came to regret, from the top of the chain with the mergers of AOL and Time Warner, through to a surge in half-baked Europe-backed high-budget product that was green lit before it was ready. In Variety's 2002 overview of independent financing, Alliance Atlantis CEO Peter Sussman says 'we went through a period where even if a film was going on five cylinders you could still do well. Today if you're not going on all eight cylinders, abandon it.' Paul Brooks of Gold Circle Films added 'essentially, the indie world has been financed by crazy money in the last few years, and there's no crazy money out there anymore.'

It would be easy to despair as a producer but this fallout has occurred alongside a big increase in global box office receipts and the emergence of countless new 'soft finance' sources (ie. public funds and tax incentives) from countries all over the world. Furthermore, any industry contraction should work to flush out the management whose profligacy led to the boom and bust in the first place, so while independent producers have rarely been as tightly squeezed, those that survive the downturn should be well placed to feed a constantly increasing consumer appetite for films.

But the days of doom and gloom may already be over, and the vacuum on financing options slowly easing. In the last year or so, an unprecedented number of countries have started offering new tax breaks and other incentives. Borders are opening up around the world with governments actively enticing the filmmaker to "come and produce". It perhaps adds more importance to the co-production method of financing than in the past, but the financing model has always been a moveable feast. The number of banks offering gap funding has, after a sharp decline, started to increase again, and the UK Sale & Leaseback industry has finally decided to put together a set of standard working practices (under the auspices of the new *Screen Financiers Association*) to provide producers more comfort and reliability. The worst effects of the stock market and dot.com crashes of the start of this decade seem to have taken their toll, and the hope is that a new breed of savvy equity players will now be ready to enter the market. The presale market also seems to have bottomed out last (could it have gone any lower?), and so hopefully the foundation for structuring production finance has finally started to stabilise, providing the producer with a more solid platform from which to fund his/her picture.

# Financing Basics

## Release cycles

The potential revenues for a completed feature film come from exploitation on different formats, which are distributed through a release cycle that would typically progress across each country of release (although nearly always behind any North American release) as follows:

| | |
|---|---|
| 0 months | Theatrical release |
| 3 months | Airline |
| 4-6 months | Hotel Pay-per-view (PPV) |
| 6 months | PPV/Video-on-demand (VoD) |
| 6 months | Video rental |
| 6-12 months | Video sale |
| 18 months | Pay-TV (eg FilmFour) |
| 36 months | Free-TV (eg BBC1) |

With the right project, further revenues are available from soundtracks, merchandise, sponsorship and long term library sales.

## Finance

Feature films are financed in one of a number of ways:

**100% financing.** A Studio or other backer gives 100% of the film's budget in return for full ownership of the film (and control over its production). The success in getting such deals, which are extremely rare, especially in the UK, is based on the strength of the project, the track record of the producer and any key 'named' talent attached. Single party financing is not really an option for a first or second-time feature producer unless they surrender up all control, and as such is not covered in this book other than at the microbudget level where financing will often come from a single private investor.

**Multi-party financing**. The independent producer typically raises finance from a host of sources – oversees distributors, TV pre-sales, deferments, private investors, banks, as well as "soft money" such as tax breaks and public funds.

### MULTI-PARTY FINANCING OPTIONS

*(These options are all covered in much more depth in chapter 3)*

**Pre-sales.** In advance of the film being completed, a distributor or broadcaster acquires an agreed set of rights to distribute or broadcast the film.

**Financing (co-)producer.** A partnering producer who makes an equity investment in a film, taking a share of future income, and sometimes certain distribution rights. Co-producers on the same Film are often based in different countries in order to access multiple local benefits (see below).

**Deferments.** Cast and crew part-financing the film out of their own wages.

**Gap financing.** Banks occasionally provide a gap loan to match a shortfall between a film's budget and other funds raised from elsewhere.

**Private equity**. Investment in return for ownership of a piece of the pie.

Tax-based Funds. EIS, Section 42 and Section 48 offer private investors income tax relief on investment in feature films.

**Sale & leaseback.** Using the tax breaks, these offer UK producers a minimum of 12% of their budget, at least until 2006. Super-sale-&-leasebacks offer additional production investment in return for an equity stake or distribution rights at the same time.

**Negative pick-up.** A distributor or Studio promises to pay an amount on delivery of a completed picture in return for all rights.

**The Film Council.** The three film council funds have a combined £20m annual pot for investing in British films and international British co-productions.

**Regional funds.** The location of both the production company office and the shooting allow producers to tap into extensive regional investment.

**Oversees incentives.** International co-productions allow UK producers to tap oversees sources of soft money such as tax breaks and public subsidies by partnering with foreign producers.

**Product placement and sponsorship.** Companies provide cash or in-kind services in return for screen-time or marketing associated with the film.

**Venture Capital**. VCTs and EIS financiers typically invest in high-risk, high-return products, and if convinced on the strength of the team and project, may get involved.

**Friends and family**. The first films from Stanley Kubrick, John Waters, Ed Burns and countless others where financed by close family.

**Inventive alternatives.** If all else fails there's always original funding sources that can be of greater publicity benefit than the money they raise, such as Robert Rodriguez allegedly offering himself for medical tests to finance *El Mariachi*. Rocliffe Productions invited friends and family to provide sperm to sell to a sperm bank to finance their short film *No Deposit, No Return* (see the case study at the end of chapter 2 for more information).

## Packaging

Packaging is – off the back of a polished script – the putting together of the key cast, the above-the-line production team and, of course, the money. One question often asked is '*In what order should I package my finance?*' and in all honesty, there is no right answer. Often people go for local soft money first, and try to attract an equity investor at about the same time. With luck, this could make up about a half of the budget. It then might be a time to approach a Sales Agent (although it's always better to have cast secured by this stage), who may be able to bring the rest in by way of pre-sales and gap (from its regular bank) and, if compatible with any other soft money already in place and not already part of the finance secured, maybe a Sale & Leaseback. But there is no 'correct' order, although certain financiers will require that other types of money are in place before they commit.

# Budgets & Structures

The first thing you need to know before approaching any financier is how much your Film is actually going to cost. For this, you need to prepare a **Budget**, probably together with an experienced '**line producer**'. The first budget you draw up should be a fully funded model that puts the Director, Producer, all crew and cast in at the appropriate fees and all post-production in at industry standard prices. Unless you are already an established producer, the chances are that you will then want to reduce this figure using all manner of favours and by forgoing or deferring some or all of your own fees and those of other key creatives (see chapter 2 for 101 tips how to do this). This will leave you with your **cash budget** – the money you need to actually shoot and finish the film, including creating the delivery materials needed to satisfy a sales agent or distributor.

It is worth noting that few films financed with budgets between £3m and £15m ever become profitable. Films under £3m are more likely to be able to recoup their budget through ancillary sales such as DVD, while films over £15m can afford to payer the higher salaries to well known directors or stars that increase the chance of box office returns.

### MICRO-BUDGET - £100,000 AND UNDER

*Example Finance Plan A: DigiBeta, ghost story, no named cast, inexperienced producer, director and writer all unpaid, intended to sell to DVD/Video*

| | | |
|---|---|---|
| *Development* | *Self-financed* | *nil* |
| *Production* | *Private Equity* | *£30,000* |
| | *Deferred Fees* | *£60,000* |
| *TOTAL* | | *£90,000* |

### ULTRA-LOW BUDGET - £500,000 AND UNDER

*Example Finance Plan B: super16mm, Horror, one named British actor, producer and director with micro-budget experience on productions which have sold to distributors and has sales agent on board - intended for worldwide TV and DVD/video release.*

| | | |
|---|---|---|
| *Development* | *Private Equity* | *£10,000* |
| *Production* | *Private Equity* | *£160,000* |
| | *Advanced TV Sale* | *£20,000* |
| | *Sales agent as Co-Producer* | *£160,000* |
| *TOTAL* | | *£350,000* |

### LOW BUDGET - £2M AND UNDER

*Example Finance Plan C: super16mm, Black Comedy, 2 x UK named cast, up-coming director and producer intended for print blow up for theatrical release*

| Development | Regional Lottery Funds | £10,000 |
|---|---|---|
| | Private Equity | £10,000 |
| Production | Isle of Man Film & TV Funds | £250,000 |
| | Lottery New Cinema Fund | £280,000 |
| | Bank loan based on distributor guarantees | £150,000 |
| | Private Equity | £200,000 |
| | Sale and leaseback | £100,000 |
| TOTAL | | £1,000,000 |

### MID BUDGET - OVER £2M AVERAGE £3.5M

*Example Finance Plan D: 35mm, Romantic Comedy, 1 x US named cast, 1 x UK named cast, experienced director and crew intended for theatrical release*

| Development | Lottery Development Funds | £10,000 |
|---|---|---|
| | Private Equity | £10,000 |
| | Foreign co-producer | £10,000 |
| Production | Lottery Premiere Fund | £1,070,000 |
| | Bank loan based on distributor guarantees | £540,000 |
| | UK TV Pre-sale (cash) | £250,000 |
| | UK TV Equity | £250,000 |
| | Sale & Leaseback | £320,000 |
| | Private Equity | £210,000 |
| | Foreign co-producer | £1,110,000 |
| TOTAL | | £3,780,000 |

# Business related issues

## Presenting to Investors

If you're looking to raise private finance you need to be able to present a coherent business plan. 'But the script is the business plan' many filmmakers argue. While the script is the basic vital asset in financing and packaging a successful film, any investor is going to want to see that you understand your market and that the numbers for your film add-up. Most individual private investors capable of providing money for your film will have made their fortune in industries where a business plan and long-term, financial strategy are vital for success. A good pitch and the promise of getting 'that guy from *East is East*' may grab their attention in the short term, but will never persuade them to take your project seriously as an investment vehicle.

At the most basic level, a business plan needs to convince the potential investor that your film, or slate of films, can comfortably make a return on the investment and provide a profit a certain number of years down the line. Making this argument to sound convincing requires you to prove that the creative team possess the skills and experience, the management team possess the know-how and contacts, and, most importantly, that the market displays the demand and the ability to pay.

To present a convincing argument, you need to be very honest about your film's strengths and weaknesses in relation to similar films that have successfully come to market. How does your company's creative and production skills match the film and its likely audience? Your project may be a moving personal story of the toils of childhood in a Scottish village in the 70s, and you could certainly point to *Ratcatcher's* success, but had NFTS graduate Lynne Ramsay not already established herself as an art-house auteur with two Cannes nominations and one Special Jury Prize for her short films, raising £1.8m to make a film destined for the festival circuit rather than multiplexes would have been near impossible.

Indeed if you are not planning to produce a mainstream commercial feature, it may well be worth factoring in the production of a series of shorts to gain an international festival reputation as part of the business plan. Janey de Nordwall, producer of BAFTA and TCM-winning short *About A Girl* part-financed her first three shorts by selling an equity stake in her company to individuals found through a business angel network. She pitched making shorts as 'research and development' expenditure, allowing her to form creative relationships, introduce herself to the industry and master the art of producing for a world cinema audience.

If you are looking to produce more straightforward commercial films, you will need to illustrate how similar films have succeeded and why your film is similar to those. Many filmmakers believe that their idea is commercial because 'it contains all the elements – sex, action, comedy' or because it is comparable to a breakout critical hit such as *Pi, Being John Malkovich* or, worse still, *Blair Witch* or *Four Weddings*. Steve Mackler of Bedford Entertainment points out "you can't take the anomaly and make that the rule, that just doesn't work. Everyone all of a sudden goes out and makes Blair Witch, there were probably 20 Blair Witch knock-offs that did nothing."

You will also need to indicate that – at the very least – you have talked with suitable distributors and sales agents about your project and feel confident that it will meet the criteria for the sorts of films they are looking to acquire. The process allows you to form a relationship with a distributor early, and get an assurance that you are not planning to produce something completely unsuited to the market's appetite, or that the way in which you wish to shoot will only hinder your success. If you plan to shoot in black and white, the success of *Schindler's List* should not form the basis of your argument, especially with two recent strong B&W independent British features, *One Life Stand* and *Nine Lives of Tomas Katz* failing to secure a UK distributor. Likewise if you plan to shoot on DV, the success of *28 Days Later* is not enough to prove that your film will be released theatrically. A proportion of sales agents and distributors refuse to look at DV-based projects, no doubt partly because of the vast number of them out there, but largely because they know it will be harder to sell. Theatrical exhibitors aren't yet equipped to deal with them, and many industry executives still feel (probably wrongly) that the quality is lacking when compared with film.

You will also need to find out how much similar films have actually sold for (not box office revenue, but sales to theatrical, TV, and video distributors). This information is not too easy to track down as it is not formally published, but a trawl through industry websites such as screendaily.com, indiewire.com, hollywoodreporter.com or variety.com and a working knowledge of internet search engines usually throws up the goods.

The business plan should illustrate that you have done all this research and are confident that the budget of your film, your company overheads and the costs of selling it once complete, are considerably less than its realistic potential value at market. This may mean rethinking the film's budget, or deciding to target straight-to-video, or TV sales instead.

## Writing the business plan

There are various models of business plan for film investment, which vary depending on the type of funding being sought and the projects on offer. Ideally, you should work through your business plan with an accountant, though if you can't afford this, the business support contacts in chapter 7 may provide some help. Louise Levison, who wrote the plan for the *Blair Witch Project* has written a good, albeit US-focused, book called *Filmmakers & Financing, Business Plans for Independents* (Focal Press, 2001).

To paraphrase her report, a typical plan should include:

**Executive summary.** Write this section last, as it should summarise the rest of the plan in a clear and concise manner. You should also state the amount of investment you are looking for and, if you wish, indicate the nature of your proposal and the amount of equity you are offering (see the section on Equity in chapter 3).

**Company background.** This should outline why the company has been formed, what its objectives are, and how it is placed to achieve those objectives, as well as describing the legal nature of the company and how long it has been running. You need also to provide details of your management team, illustrating the skills, experience and contacts of the core team. If any member of the team lacks substantial experience, it is vital to find other partners with experience, or at least form an advisory board of your best contacts to illustrate that your inexperience is compensated by the involvement of people who know what they are doing.

**The film(s).** As well as outlining the project(s) you are seeking finance for and their budgets, this is your opportunity to convince the investor that you have a hot property. If you own an option on a book, have the confirmed interest of a named actor or director, have crew attached with well-known credits, have the support of your regional film agency, or a foreign distributor, state this here. Testimonials from seasoned producers who have already read the script will help, as will a sensible budget illustrating how the film is being made inexpensively (never use the word "cheap"!) without sacrificing quality.

**The industry.** You should provide an overview of how the film industry operates, as many investors will not completely understand, and provide market data to illustrate its workings. Of course, we might suggest you recommend that they buy this Handbook! Likewise, the BFI Handbook provides useful figures for the UK industry, and the MPAA provides in-depth analysis of the US (www.mpaa.org). Describe each of the different exploitation opportunities – theatrical, video/DVD-rental & retail, pay-per-view, pay-TV, free-TV, and so on.

**The market.** Here you should describe why there is a market for your films. What films similar to yours have been released successfully and why is your film comparable to those. What similar films have failed, and what are you doing to ensure this won't happen to yours? How do you intend to bring your products to market, and why in such a competitive environment do they stand out? How will you find a distributor and/or sales company (unless you have one already – which would be great), and what would your/their distribution strategy be?

**Financing and forecasts.** You should list your planned sources of finance to fund start-up, development and production and, with a knowledgeable industry accountant (or lawyer). produce the meaty part that any investor will look most closely at; your projections, cash-flow forecasts and assumptions. List the budget and returns - across all platforms - of successful films similar to yours. Use these numbers as the basis for sales forecasts for your film(s) which should be broken down by territory/region and platform. Use this, combined with the film's budget to make a quarter-by-quarter cash-flow statement for the first three or five years of operation. The key is to show that the numbers balance and that the investor could make an X% profit over Y years, based on a number of assumptions (which you should identify).

If you can't get a sales agent to provide sales estimates to support your forecasts, then you should at least provide a table of worldwide returns of similar films across platforms (theatrical, video/DVD, TV-sales) and territories. A lot of this data is available online through sites such as www.showbizdata.com, www.variety.com, www.bfi.org.uk, and journals such as Screen International, Screen Finance and Screen Digest. However, be careful with quoting box office data – a film that grosses £100m does not equate to revenues of £100m for the producer: in the UK the exhibitor typically takes off 50-60% and a further 17.5% goes on VAT, while prints and advertising costs, and the distributor's share of net receipts (30% to 50%) come off before the producer sees a penny. Chapter 3 goes into this in much more detail.

## Selling to an investor, by Harry Hicks

Let's assume the producer is going to meet the investor, rather than just sending something through the post. I would have thought the investor would only have the meeting if he or she liked the script, which they will have read in advance. It is paramount that the script is well developed and polished with a good story and commercial potential.

The producer should lead the meeting, especially if the investor is not fluent in film investment. During the presentation, the producer should give a very clear idea of the tone of the film, the genre, it's place in the market, and how the producer sees the marketability of the film. After all, investors are going to be interested in what sort of return they are going to be getting. We all know in film that is a very difficult thing to predict, but the investor would need some idea.

What are the ambitions of the producer? For the director? For the top cast? What is the budget? I would suggest the producer turn up with a detailed budget from a good line producer, so the investor can take it away and have a look at it if they want to. Certainly the investor won't be impressed if no thought has been given to the budget. The producer should also be clear on their own role. Are they exec producing, or producing? The investor needs to understand who they are speaking to.

It would impress the investor if the whole funding package had been sorted out. What I mean by this is whether the producer has given thought to pre-sales and sources of soft money.

Have they been given a commitment from a Sale & Leaseback organisation with an offer of say 12%, 13%, or 14%? Has the producer got a commitment from a production partnership to finance 25% or 30% of the budget through soft money? Has the producer thought about regional funding? In short, has the producer culled the rest of the budget together and does the investor know precisely what gap he or she is being asked to fill?

The more back-up documents the producer can show the better: the script, a print out of the budget, letters of intent from the main cast, and from a good director, the director's filmography. The director doesn't have to be well known, but thought should have gone into it. I have to say that if a producer comes to me with a glossy package (I'm not an investor, but I know people who are), that in itself does not impress me. I would be more interested in the guts behind it.

The investor would want to know what sort of rights they would be getting, what sort of return, where they would stand in the pecking order, when the film is going to be finished, when they come out of the deal, and whether there is a recoupment corridor. The investor will also want to know what investment scheme is available to them, for example the Enterprise Investment Scheme, or Section 48. The producer should prepare all this in advance with an accountant and lawyer and maybe bring one of them along to the meeting depending on the financial and legal ability of the producer. The producer could also ask the director into the meeting.

Some general advice for new producers would be to try not to over cook the budget. It should be kept as low as possible, allowing for creative quality. The other thing is to keep an eye on what is more likely to sell in the market place. People can get carried away with a really good script which is unlikely to sell, which will at the end of the day be a harder sell for the producer.

*Harry Hicks is head of film & TV at WJB Chiltern, tax and film investment advisers. Interviewed by* Caroline Hancock

## Negotiating

Sooner or later you will come to the point of negotiation, be it with a financier, buyer, or even a key creative whose talents you wish to employ to help package the film. Negotiations are the make-or-break point of any deal, and are one of the most intense and nerve-wracking parts of financing, particularly for a first-timer. Experienced producer, lecturer and writer on media business affairs, Dorothy Viljoen, offers some good advice in handling them:

**Preparation**. Find out as much about the financier beforehand and the style they are likely to adopt. "*If they are known to be tough negotiators work out ways in which they might have the satisfaction of winning, without actually doing so; for example, by asking for a far higher fee than you expect to receive in order that they can be seen to bear you down.*"

**Establish deal parameters in advance.** You should identify for each of control of rights, production fee and profit share; the maximum you can ask for, the target value that you would hope for, and the minimum value that you are prepared to accept. Knowing this in advance helps you to approach the negotiation in the secure position of knowing the parameters of what you would accept and what you would ideally like. "*With these goalposts and lines firmly in place you can then play around with the various balls the other side may lob into the field.*"

**Don't go to the meeting alone.** Bringing in a lawyer too early in the deal-making process can appear heavy handed, instead go with a colleague who can "*take notes, confirm impressions or recollections and generally give moral support.*"

**Dress to impress.** Typically it is a lawyer or accountant that negotiates contracts who by nature of their training are often "*instinctively unwilling to grant monies/rights/ownership to someone wearing jeans, t-shirts and trainers and carrying papers in a carrier bag.*"

**Start with your dream deal and work down.** If the other party opens negotiations, remember that they will most probably be employing the same tactic, "*stay calm, don't accept the first thing that's offered (even if it exceeds your wildest dreams): you can almost certainly do better.*"

**Keep your nerve.** If your asking price isn't being met "*offer to drop certain terms which are not so important to you before you start negotiating down on the key provisions.*" Make sure you don't agree to parts of the deal or terms that you don't understand, and avoid being pressed into agreeing terms on the spot. "*It is very rare for there to be such urgency about a deal that it has to be settled there and then, and great caution should be taken in dealing with anyone who insists on an immediate decision.*"

**Follow-up.** Keep notes on all that is said and agreed and follow-up each meeting with an email or fax outlining what has been established and what remains to be resolved. If you realise that terms agreed are less favourable than you first thought don't try and renegotiate the deal, "*put it down to experience: don't keep going back and trying to tinker with a deal once it has been set. It looks unprofessional and can damage chances for more successful dealings in the future.*"

Quoted from the *Art of the Deal* (PACT, 2002) – strongly recommended for the shelves of any serious film producer (order via www.pact.co.uk).

# In Other's Words

Film is an industry with thousands of people with viable projects fighting to get in, and a relatively small and close-knit group of people acting as gatekeeper. It's easy for frustration to boil over at what can feel like an impenetrable old boys club, but more often than not it is just about getting noticed in a way that doesn't present yourself as a potential risk. If you're trying to raise a substantial amount of money for your first feature then you need to be in it for the long haul, present yourself seriously, and take the knock-backs as part of the training. Of course you would rather be making films than filling in forms, networking and making presentations, but proving that you can jump through hoops is what the market is looking for to feel confident you won't be a risky green light.

To help navigate the film finance circus and in the honoured tradition of self-help books, we've put together seven tips based on the advice of those who've been there before.

## 1 BUILD THE RIGHT TEAM

*"I was both the producer and the director, a situation I don't ever want to be in again. The conflicts between the artistic imperatives of the director and the financial and practical considerations of the producer are bad enough when they are fought between different people but when that battle is raging constantly in your own head, it's enough to drive you stark raving mad."* Owen Carey Jones – Baby Blues (£30,000 feature)

There are two drivers to a movie – the creative vision that makes a film good and the entrepreneurial energy that gets the film made. While some filmmakers successfully combine both producer and director roles this is generally the exception. At one extreme the film gets made and is sold, but suffers artistically; or at the other end the film is a creative success, but is never sold, runs out of money or is not finished. Building the right creative team is the prime factor behind success in raising finance, production and eventual sales. The situation is made more difficult by a shortage of good producers in proportion to writers/directors, which has led some, such as Guerrilla Filmmaker Handbook authors Chris Jones and Genevieve Jolliffe, to partner and take it in turns to produce each other's movies. Also remember that relationships take time to build up and that if someone seems too good to be true, they probably are.

*"I don't mean to be cynical, but when it comes to any kind of business, you can't really trust anyone, so check them out and try them out. The minute someone lets you down or doesn't keep a promise then be very wary. If it happens again, drop them immediately."* Piotr Szkopiak, director, Small Time Obsession

## 2 KNOW YOUR AUDIENCE

*"People think they can make anything and it will find an audience. This is not the case. You have to be really honest about your film. Go to the video store and hire five successful films like yours and ask yourself how does yours stack up? Too many new filmmakers are so wrapped up in the excitement and glamour they forget about the end purpose of a film."* David Nicholas Wilkinson, Guerrilla Films

The 'if I build it they will come' philosophy is a way of putting off facing the unpleasant realities of the film business until the end of post-production, when the filmmaker hopes that their skill and imagination will be sufficient to attract a magical distributor and sales agent who will sign up their film and whisk them away to a studio to start work on their next project. This never happens. The rare low-budget success stories were still made with a focus on who would want to see that film at the end of the process. Robert Rodriguez knew that there would, at the least, be a video audience for his $7,000 *El Mariachi* especially if he got a few 'money' shots to put into a trailer. *The Blair Witch Project* raised finance with a solid business plan that identified who would go and see the film once produced, backed up with a well-planned debut at Sundance.

Once you know who your audience is (clubbers, couples on dates, genre-hungry film-geeks, Guardian-readers), you can look at the films competing for that audience's attention and see what your project has to offer that will make it stand out. Find out as much as you can about the audience, and make sure that your film is better than anything else they are currently being offered. This also gives you an idea of how much your film could expect to make, which in turn allows you to figure out how much money you can spend making it.

*"If you know there are millions of teenagers out there desperate to see your film then go online, do your research and get your statistics. So many independent filmmakers have the passion but not the interpretation that convinces those with the money that there is some commercial, and I don't mean formulaic, but financially sound reason to make it and that you are trying to reach a certain audience."* Amanda Posey, producer Fever Pitch

## 3 EMBRACE DEVELOPMENT

*"Don't rush development, and don't abandon the script the moment it looks like your funding has fallen into place. It can always be made better"* Working Title executive

Before showing the script for *Four Weddings and a Funeral* to anyone, Richard Curtis wrote five drafts working closely with his script editor and wife Emma Freud. Then came further rewrites for his producer, for Working Title, for the director, and more for budget cuts, subsequent budget cuts, responses after the first read-through – a total of 17 re-writes in all. And this from a screenwriter who had already proved his skills in writing some of the most successful British TV comedy of the last 20 years. As Curtis says in the introduction to the screenplay *"don't resent the rewrites – the awful painful truth is that the script probably did get a bit better each time."*

The development process is a mixture of reworking a film until it's at the best possible place creatively and from an audience's perspective; and making sure that the main people involved with the project – financiers, producer, director and even key cast if a named actor is on board – are happy enough with the script to put their name, time and money behind it. It has been said that a successful screenwriter is not only one with a good script, but one who is able to rewrite and stay on board the project at every step of the development process.

*"The producer's job is to end up with a script that will attract talent, the talent attracts the money, that's how it works, there aren't any real shortcuts."* Nik Powell, producer

## 4 NETWORK WISELY

*"I think another common mistake people make is to tire the contacts they make or approach people the wrong way - they think they have to pitch to everyone all the time. I think that when making contacts you need to be as natural as possible, not harassing them with phone calls."* Pikka Brassey, Wanton Muse.

The nature of the British film means that the gatekeepers – be they financiers, festival chiefs, journalists or successful producers – are in constant demand. Try to remember that you are only one of many people attempting to get as much as you can out of them. Few successful people in the industry are purely altruistic, so always consider what a contact is getting in return from you. Networking is too often seen as the process of convincing everyone in a room that you are great, when in fact making friends with a few people at a party can set-up useful long-term relationships. It is not the quantity of contacts, but the quality of the relationships. And once you've got a bursting contact book, think before using it – there's only so much you can ask for before needing to give something in return.

*"Let the work speak for itself; don't try too hard to convince anybody that it's any good (it can easily sound like desperation). I've gone to a lot of festivals now and seen how other filmmakers operate. Some cruise the jury, some even buy them presents. I like to keep out their way until after the adjudication. Best strategy is be yourself and meet as many people as you can."* Irvine Allen, director Daddy's Girl (winner short Palme D'Or 2001)

## 5 SEE THE BIGGER PICTURE

*"Filmmakers may make wonderful films, but know nothing about distribution, so they can shoot themselves in the foot, quite unintentionally. You have to approach the market very carefully to get as much out of it as you can."* David Nicholas Wilkinson, Guerrilla Films

While developing and promoting your project it is very easy – almost inevitable – to be caught up only in the part of the industry relating to where you are, be it development or fundraising. Taking a step back to address the bigger picture can help in understanding why you may not be moving forward with your project as you would hope.

The production executive who isn't returning your calls is beholden to their management and must field dozens of potential projects at any one time. Their management is in turn dependent on the company's backers, and the company as a whole is investing vast sums of money in product that they must be able to sell on the international market to survive. The distributors and sales agents they sell to in turn need to acquire a certain number of hits to ensure their survival. The studios and corporations that own these distributors are accountable to their shareholders. At every step of the way the success of your project is dependent on an awful lot of people believing that backing you won't risk them their job.

That's the bottom line and while it can feel like you're a Kafkaesque cog at the bottom of a giant machine, film is a $60bn a year industry and until you are a proven safe bet with a commercial or critical hit under your belt, it's not going to be any other way. You may have the best script in the world, but as far as the gatekeepers are concerned, you're just as much a risk as anyone else until you've proven otherwise.

*"The key issue about making a feature is that politics plays a huge part. I had to get constant approval from three executives, not just the basic costs and crewing but on everything. They were all supportive but I had to constantly communicate to them that they were all being treated equally well. I didn't handle that too well but I've since realised that that is a principle element of producing."* **Gavin Emerson, producer Ratcatcher**

## 6 BE READY FOR A LONG RIDE

*"There was always that nagging question in my head about how long would I wait and what would I do if it didn't come together. But every time that doubt got really strong, we would have a breakthrough and that's what kept me going. Every six months there would be something that just reminded me or encouraged me to believe in it and keep going. So I did."* **Nicole Kassell, director, The Woodsman**

Ambition and drive tends to come hand-in-hand with wanting success fast, which is usually followed by despair when success doesn't come. Filmmakers and producers with a long term game-plan are better equipped to cope with the constant let-downs of trying to get their project made than those expecting overnight recognition. How many short films do you realistically need to make to both get noticed, and equip yourself with the skills to make a feature? How long are you prepared to push your feature project forward for and how many compromises will you make on the way? Each new project that doesn't get finance or a release can be a useful learning experience if you are honest enough about the mistakes you made on the way.

By focusing solely on the end product you can also miss the chance to enjoy the process. It is an unfortunate irony that film, so often intended to give something positive to an audience can be an incredibly stressful experience for the producers and key players involved.

*"The thing that has kept me going every day, and that I would love for people to take away from the film is what happened at the test screening. After the film they asked, 'How many of you in the audience think she was vicious and did some horrible things?' 95% of the audience raised their hands. Then they said, 'How many of you felt tremendous compassion for this character?' 95% of them raised their hands. It just destroyed me. I burst into tears because if anything, what I care about the story for is shades of grey and compassion."* **Patty Jenkins, director, Monster**

## 7 STAY FOCUSSED

*"It's one of the most frustrating, irritating and problematic jobs around - especially working in Britain at this time. And one is constantly dispirited and crushed by the system in trying to get your film forward and struggling for the available funds. But there's always that possibility you will get to make your film. And once you're actually there standing in a field and the cameras are turning over and the actors are just doing what they're doing, there's nothing more exciting in the world and then it's all worth it."* **Ben Hopkins, director, Simon Magus/The Nine Lives of Tomas Katz**

Even in America, which employs half a million people in the film business, wanting to become a filmmaker has never been a sensible career path. In the UK, which is currently producing less than 50 locally financed mainstream theatrical features a year, it's even more uncertain. So it is worth knowing what you want to achieve from the start.

"*You're kind of living on the edge all the time, and there are these big highs and then these incredible lows when you don't want to have anything to do with this industry. The highs and lows are going to be a constant thing and you have to ask yourself, what do you want out of this? Is it kudos, is it awards, is it money? I want to achieve an emotion from an audience and that kind of makes it a lot easier than being motivated by money or fame.*" **Janey de Nordwall, Silver Films, producer About a Girl, Jump, Walking with Angels (shorts)**

If the process of making films and getting a strong positive reaction from an audience is pleasure enough, you are probably much better equipped to face the wilderness years of the development, fundraising and rejection circuit, than those whose understanding of success is a an oak panelled Wardour Street office and a cabinet of Oscars. As you keep hitting walls it is easy to lose faith and blame your woes on the Film Council, distributors or even your fellow filmmakers, bemoaning endlessly the state of British film. But if you enter the industry with your eyes open and a clear focus on what you want to achieve it is harder to get knocked off course.

"*Experience teaches you that there are no external forces capable of preventing you achieving what you've set your mind to. I've come up against some pretty intransigent forces in my time, but the only true obstacles are internal ones like self-doubt and pessimism. Once you've conquered these, the outside world is a relative pushover.*" **Omid Nooshin, director, Panic (short)**

# Roy Disney, *savedisney.com*
# Storytelling

The secret of Disney's success? - Great story telling I think. Great stories, great characters, great music - it's a lot of things, music is an amazing part of people's memories of film. When you play 'when you wish upon a star' it conjures up a whole movie for you and *The Lion King* is like that as well. We have such a tremendous tradition of what was done in the past, (uncle) Walt kinda looks over our shoulder and says 'this is what you have to live up to - be this good, be this good.'

I like comedy. I like to go into a theatre and sit back and relax, not to have too many heavy social messages crammed down my throat and if so I'd like to be entertained by that too. I'd like to understand that if people have problems that they have funny sides and sad sides, I want a picture with memorable characters in. I find a lot of disaster movies, shoot-em-ups and exploding planet movies don't really work that way for me, I'd rather be entertained by something small and charming than by someone blowing up the world - unless it's funny!

I found my way into the business by way of nature movies - turned out to be the greatest film school you could have gone to. We'd go out with a 16mm camera and an endless supply of film and literally shoot pictures of animals for months and months throughout the seasons. Many of the movies involved the birth and growing up of different animals, we'd take that back to the studio and they'd have to try to make a story out of it. The craft of story telling was implicit in everything we did. *NW*

photo by Doug Bolton

# Nik Powell *Virgin, Palace, Scala & National Film & TV School*

*When it comes to building media businesses, Nik Powell has an unprecedented record in the UK. Childhood friend of Richard Branson, Nik co-founded Virgin Records with him, and then took on the running of the Scala Cinema where he set up producer-distributor Palace Pictures with Stephen Woolley. Palace produced dozens of landmark UK features including Company of Wolves, Mona Lisa and The Crying Game, as well buying for the UK the first films from Lars von Trier, the Coen Brothers and Sam Raimi. When Palace ended, Powell launched Scala Productions with Woolley, and left recently to head up the National Film and Television school.*

**Is it more important for producers to focus on packaging their film as a sellable product, or in creating a good film?**

They're both key. You can be a creative producer if you're in partnership with an entrepreneurial style producer, and you can be a creative producer if you're employed by someone - at Working Title or whatever. But you can't be an independent producer and only creative. You also can't be an independent producer and only entrepreneurial. You know you have to have both sets of skills because they are both required. You need to create a script that will attract.

The producer's job is to create a script that will attract talent; the talent attracts the money. That's how it works; there aren't any real shortcuts. And there are certain kinds of money that are not cast-sensitive, so cast doesn't matter; certain kinds of money that are not director-sensitive, so therefore you can cast a first time director; there are certain kinds of money that are only really interested in tax deductions, so they only real care about you getting the film made - they don't care about quality or anything else.

So you need the different skills, but you need to be able to create things that attract interesting talent. What we're trying to do is make a film that stands up, gets released, and hopefully people go and see, and the critics like. We might not achieve all these things, but that is really our goal; everything else is just a means to get that. So the process in itself is geared to that, it's not geared to whether the distributors like it, whether financiers like it, any of those things. I'm saying the obvious, but we will not change things. Most of my producer colleagues will not change anything if it will lose our main audience, even if it will get us some money. But it can be tricky because you don't want to spend two years making a film that will go down the plug-hole; that no-one ever sees. We've all made those films of course - just look at my CV; quite a few of them - too many!

Sometimes a producer kind of treats it as an end - get the film made and that's all that counts. But it's not actually, its the least important thing. The most important thing is to get a film that the people who you make it for want to go and see.

**How did Shane Meadows attract Bob Hoskins for his first feature, Twenty-Four-Seven?**

We did it - because we'd had Bob in two films already, and I have done lots of business with his agent. So we spoke to Harriet Robinson, his agent, and arranged for Bob and Shane to meet, which wasn't difficult because Shane's work sold itself. If it was another director, with nothing like as impressive short films, they wouldn't have got to meet Bob. Of course when Shane did meet Bob they got on like a house on fire. They were the same kind of size and you'd seen them wondering around together like Tweedle Dum and Tweedle Dee, and they got on as me and Steve expected them too - they get on like that and its fantastic.

But that would never have happened if Shane had not made about five fantastic shorts. People think it has to do with contacts, but I think it helped me and Steve saying to Harriet this is a cool director, you've got to get Bob to look at these shorts. This is out of the ordinary. And then Harriet would look at them and she saw they were great and she told Bob he should bloody well watch them, and he did and of course. Bob loved it, because you know Bob's gonna like those kind of shorts. But we could have completely different type of shorts, wouldn't have been up Bob's ally, and there'd have been no meeting. So it's the work that sells itself, obviously people are a bit sensitive. But to me in my experience in general it's the work itself that sells itself, that you sell, and if you haven't got that, it's very hard.

**What was the first sale you made at a market or festival?**

*Company of Wolves* was the first one, and we took that to MIFED, which is a market not a festival, and we sold it to America, to Cannon. And they paid loads of money for it. It was a bit worrying because I did the whole deal with the famous partners at Cannon, Menahem [Golam] and Yoram [Globus], and at the end of the meeting Yoram said to Menahem, 'Don't you think you should see the film?'. Because we were number one at the British box office at the time, he was like 'Oh no it's number one in England, I'm sure it's fine', and Yoram said 'No, before you sign this I think you should go see the film'. And I thought 'fuck me, they're going to hate the film'. I had thought I was going to get away without having to show it to them. So they asked me when the screening was, and I said there's one tomorrow at 9am. I came in at quarter to 9 and I went off to get a coffee. When I came back and it was about ten past nine and I looked in the hall and there was no Menahem in there, where I was showing the film. So afterwards, I went down to the Cannon office and there was Menahem. I just assumed he'd hated it and walked out, and that was the end of it - my first fairly major international deal. I was about to say 'did you hate it?', but fortunately I didn't. He said, 'Ah Nik, we can close the deal now'. I said 'What do you mean? You've only seen like ten minutes of it' - he said 'Nik, my own films I only see ten frames, I seen ten minutes of your films, it's fine'. And the first ten minutes is just a Volvo driving, it's got nothing to do with the rest of the film.

So he signed. It's essentially an art film really, but they released it like a horror film. I remember Steve and I saw it in a house in New York, which was quite a downmarket horror house, and they definitely didn't like the film. But the critics loved it, and it was a big hit here in the UK.

**How do you deal with criticism?**

I don't care, because most people have lousy taste and judgement. It's like the good script syndrome - every successful film has a great script, but when I've been involved in some of those successful films and taken the script around, 90% of people hated the script. But suddenly its a great script because its a hit, so these things are subjective. There are people in this business whose opinions I take totally seriously, like my ex-partner Steve Woolley, or Jeremey Thomas - you know, heavyweights. But the majority of the industry - they've never made a film, they've never had a hit, it's 'What do they know?'. They may be great script development executives, but they don't have any kind of proven track record.

But if a film is not successful then I always look and analyse that to see where I've gone wrong. Maybe I didn't develop the script enough. Maybe I cast it wrong - or allowed the director to cast it wrong, or maybe it was the wrong story at the wrong time. Whatever. I like to take a good hard long look when things don't work. Maybe it was just the execution of the film and we cocked it up and did a bad job - but I don't need someone else to tell me that. But failure informs you.

And if it's a critical hit and a box office failure then I don't feel so bad because we've got a good film, and we've got it out there and for one or other reason it hasn't worked. People think it's a good film, it just hasn't caught fire.

But a general industry thing - the first screening I ever went to in the industry was a screening of *The Killing Fields*. So I went in and thought, fantastic film, playing *Imagine* at the end was a piece of genius. It's a difficult subject matter; but it really delivers. I couldn't find a single other person who was in that screening room - and it was all people from the industry - who liked the film. They've all got an axe to grind. They all hate Puttnam (I mean they would never say that to him, but they're all jealous of his success). And it was all, 'I don't think that was very good', and 'Playing *Imagine* at the end - what a sell out', and, 'Performance by Sam Waterston, ooh I don't know'. He went on to be nominated for an Oscar of course, and nine months later when all that happened they were all 'Yeah yeah. Thought it was fantastic. That Sam Waterston performance was outstanding.' and you think 'My God, these are people who have to really run to keep their jobs'. But to me, it was just a really fantastic piece of filmmaking and it had to be admired and liked. And it made an important statement about the world. I don't care about how untrendy someone is - Puttnam or whoever - the film speaks for itself. And so often I've been at screenings where 90% of people have walked out. Like my most famous example was *Blood Simple*, the Coen brothers movie. And that was distributors seeing it, not English industry people who would have hated it even more.

I went in with Joel and Ethan Coen, Sam Raimi and Bob Tappert. Sam Raimi had put me onto it and we'd done *Evil Dead* together already. Oh, and Paul Webster – who I had in distribution at the time. We sat down in this crowded screening. Because it was called *Blood Simple,* obviously all these distributors thought it was going to be a fantastic slasher movie, and of course it is a very slow paced movie. So when I woke up from the film at the end, there was only Joel and

Ethan, me and Paul, and Sam and Bob Tappert in the cinema. There were about three other people. It had been packed at the beginning, but I hadn't noticed because I'd been so involved in this incredible film. So I knew I could get the film for next to nothing, which I did.

And when I saw Lars von Triers' first film *Element of Crime* - most people have never seen it - I paid $5000 for that, in MIFED again. Very weird film - as one might expect from Lars von Triers' first film. I brought it back and I proudly showed it to all the staff at Palace; showed it to Daniel Battsek who was head of distribution at the time, who now runs Disney [Europe]. He and some of the staff came back to my office, and came to see me and said 'Nik, we've just watched this film, it's completely crap, and if you were not our boss, we'd fire you.' That's the advantage of being a boss - employees can't fire you. The banks can fire you, but they can't.

So Steve and I saw *Diva* - we saw *Diva* in LA - we flew from LA to Paris to make the deal because we thought it's gonna be a hit. It's a flash film about absolutely nothing. Beautifully paced, beautifully made, flash superficial film and it doesn't matter that it's in French, and it went onto do huge business. *Evil Dead* Steve saw by himself and just came back and said we had to buy it, and we met this young filmmaker and I decided the only reason Steve wanted to sign this film - I hadn't seen it myself yet - was because this young filmmaker Sam Raimi called Steve 'Sir'. Steve's a working class north London boy and Sam is a mid-western, more middle class. Of course they're trained in those manners - they call you 'Sir'. And so there's this 19-year old Sam calling 22-year old Steve 'Sir', and that was too much for Steve and he had to sign it. No, he loved it, and he thought the movie was fantastic, and he was right.

Very often you're alone and very often you're not. For *My Left Foot* and *Cinema Paradiso* we were up against Harvey Weinstein, who we were also making films for then, so that was kind of tricky. There was lots of double dealing involved, but we won out in the end.

**How have you developed your business partnerships**

I've been lucky in my partners. I've had the same number of partnerships as I've had marriages, but the partnerships lasted longer, tho they all ended at the end of the day because I'm not a believer that things need to last forever to be valuable. And you remain friends with your partners even when you stop being their partners. In fact I think one of the secrets of remaining friends with your partners - both in marriage and in business - is stopping them at the right time, and not getting to the point where you want to murder each other. So I've been lucky with Branson and Woolley - and I've always looked for people who are not the same as me, that are very complimentary to me, whom I deeply trust.

Specifically after [the partnership with] Richard ran out, I wanted someone who combined creativity and business and Steve had reprogrammed the Scala cinema (that Branson and I had bought and put some money up to kind of rescue it because it was going bankrupt). And our friend Jo Boyd, who was on the board of it, had recommended this little punk guy to run it. So I met Steve and he impressed Richard and me hugely about what he was going to do to turn it around. And a lot of people do that - they have the mouth, but then they don't actually turn it around. But Steve did, and he turned it around with a mixture of putting on the Clash and the Sex Pistols, who were unknown at the time, and throwing out all the European films and programming it with American absurdist films - early John Waters and suchlike -, good eastern European films, because Steve loves films from everywhere, and he turned it around putting us in profit within 12 months of him taking over. The cinema never made big money, but it was creative. You know, Steve knew the value of having midnight shows by the Sex Pistols. It's not easy to organise. So I thought 'That's my man', and when I sold out of Virgin I approached him because he had the qualities I want.

Stephen Woolley and I, and before that me and Branson - I think our very hiring practices were very different to our competitors. We were never very interested in experience, for instance.

First of all, we couldn't afford to pay what our competitors could pay, both at Virgin and at Palace, so we couldn't pay for experienced people. I learnt this off Richard really. We basically employed people who we figured were intelligent; had intelligence and insight and focus and ambition; and we didn't really care if they'd worked for a farm.

And that's what we required. So when [Daniel] Battsek came into my office, he had worked in the mailroom at Hoyts in Australia - and he was dead impressive, I sent him over to Paul [Webster]. Steve had brought Paul in because he'd programmed the Gate cinema and Steve was very impressed - and Steve was saying we did need someone who knew a little bit about distribution.

**What would you advise a producer in building a business?**

I never believed in this building your company up. I think Tim [Bevan, Working Title] has done it fantastically. But there's only a few. Film producers produce films, that's what we do for a living, and everything is simply to service that purpose. Other than the Working Title model - I think there's not a business model that works. And it's only the people who are on salaries who think that there is a business model that works. You can have 500 examples to show that they don't work, and you know producers should concentrate on producing, not on building businesses, and if they happen to have successful films they'll have lots of cashflow and there'll be a business there and if they don't, they don't.

So my advice to a producer is concentrate on producing, because that is your core business, and people should stick with their core businesses. It's not about building a business, unless you're a real entrepreneur, in which case you know, the Working Title or the Palace model (which could have worked). In that case you're an entrepreneur and your core business is distributing, and secondarily producing. And that can work, but that's a different thing. I don't believe a production company in itself is a viable business model. I think producing for yourself is a very viable life, a nice life.

*Nic Wistreich & Doug Bolton.*

# Laurence Boyce, *Leeds Film Festival* Planning for festivals

## PLANNING FOR FESTIVALS

There's no point spending months and months of scraping together funding, going through weeks of intensive shooting and then sweating for an a long period over the edit if – at the end of your long and winding road –you can't get your movie screened outside of your front room. Having a knack for getting money for your film is one thing. Getting people to actually come and see the damn thing is quite another. Most likely, you're planning to enter your film into every film festival that you can think of. But it's not as a simple process as it seems. With thousands of movies being sent into them every year, festival programmers have a lot to choose from. And, unless you've managed to create something special, then it's more than likely that your film could end up in the pile marked 'reject'. So even if your movie, be it feature or short, is a mere cinematic gleam in your eye then it would be best to heed some of the following advice. It could make the difference between making you the toast of the film festival circuit or just, well, toast.

## 1) WATCH OTHER FILMS.

One of the biggest complaints made by people who run Film Schools is that their pupils never seem to watch films made by other people. And - before you ask - popping down your local Art House Cinema once in a month of Sundays or renting the occasional French film from Blockbusters doesn't count. If there's a film festival in your area, go to it. Try and get to other festivals around the world. If you can't get to them, look at their programmes and try and get hold of copies of the movies that they show. Take note of the films that show at lots of festivals. Ultimately, your film will be judged alongside many others from across the world. If you don't measure up in terms of style, story or theme then you can forget it now.

## 2) THINK ABOUT WHY YOU'RE MAKING YOUR FILM.

Before you have illusions of walking up the red carpet in Cannes, you really need to think about who your film is aimed at. Is your student piece really worth sending in for consideration or are you, in a few years time, going to be chewing your fingers off in embarrassment knowing that someone has seen it (remember, most student films are like masturbation: Self indulgent abuse for which you'll hopefully never have an audience). Similarly, are you making the film to show off everything you know about using a camera? All well and good, but most festival programmers can spot a 'business card' movie miles off. Is it worth the effort of sending it in? Festival programmers – at least on a general basis – look for good stories that are being told because the filmmaker has a passion for telling it and a stylish way in which to do so. Anything else is window dressing.

## 3) KNOW WHERE YOU'RE GOING TO SEND YOUR FILM

It's so tempting just to grab a load of festival addresses from the net, get the entry forms and buy as many stamps as you can afford. But it's best to actually do a bit of research into the festivals that you apply for. If your film is a searing thriller full of sex and violence, it's a waste of time and energy – and, if they are charging an entry fee, money - sending it into a festival that specializes in children's films. Check the festival's website and try and get an understanding of what it's all about. Will your film really suit them? And, when you find the festival that you want, make sure you read the entry form. There's nothing more that annoys a Festival programmer than an entry form that you can't read, or an entry that has some components missing. If you're asked for a synopsis, stills or to use block capitals, then do it.

**4) IF YOUR FILM ISN'T SELECTED, DON'T BE DISHEARTENED**

Even if you follow all the previous instructions, there's a chance that your film still won't get chosen. With many festivals receiving thousands of films every year, there are many reasons why your film may not have been selected. Also, with many festivals employing only a few staff, it may be a difficult to find out why your work hasn't been picked. If you can get some feedback, be polite and be prepared to take on board the comments that are given.

**5) IF YOU FILM IS SELECTED, THEN MAKE THE FESTIVAL WORK FOR YOU**

After all that, and the festival has said yes. If they are offering flights and accommodation, then what are you waiting for? Hop on the plane and enjoy. But, even if they don't, try and find a way of getting there. Because, when you get there you can do a lot more than simply introduce your film. You can meet future collaborators, other festival programmers who may want to take your film or – once in a blue moon – an investor who wants to buy your work for distribution or put some money into your next film. And then you can start the entire process again.

As of writing there are more than 4,000 film festivals taking place across the world. Some are big, some are small, but many can give you the opportunity for people from all over the globe to actually see your film. And after that blood, sweat and tears of actually making your film, getting an audience for your movie is perhaps the sweetest thing. Well, that and actually getting some money for your effort.

*Laurence Boyce is short film programmer for Leeds International Film Festival and short film reviewer for Hotdog magazine.*

# Nicole Kassell *The Woodsman*

*After watching Steven Fechter's play, The Woodsman, first time writer/director Nicole Kassell wrote a screenplay adaptation on spec and sent it to the author, and on eventually finding a producer, insisted he could only have the script if she directed it.*

**What made you choose paedophilia, one of the last taboos, as the subject of your first film? Aren't first films difficult enough to make without putting further obstacles in your way?**

I really felt like the subject matter found me. I didn't search for the most difficult topic to make a film about [laughs]. But I saw Steven Fechter's play, *The Woodsman*, back in March 2000, and was so affected by it that I really felt it was a story that was important to tell. The more research I did, the more I discovered that there was an epidemic problem, and the more committed I came to it. So I knew I was raising the stakes against myself. But the odds of getting a film made period are so slim, and a first feature even harder, I figured why not? You have to be passionate about it and I was. I went for it."

**What was Steven Fechter's reaction when you sent him your screenplay adaptation of his play on spec?**

Well the first draft he saw, or when I showed him the first draft, he was impressed that I'd done it period, and liked where it was going. From that point on he was involved in every draft. We would sit down and discuss a draft in detail and I would sit down and write it. So he didn't get surprised in any big way through the writing phase. It was more when I went off to film the movie that he was not involved. But I know when he saw the final film he felt very proud and said the movie was true to the heart of the play."

**What kinds of reactions did you get when you sent the script out in search of finance?**

It took a very long time. The big break I got was winning the Slamdance screenplay competition in September 2001. At that point we started sending the script out and we got a lot of reactions of, 'We love the script but it's too dark, too hard to raise the money, too edgy,' so it was a full year before I found Lee Daniels, the producer. He came on in September 2002.

**Daniels, of course, produced *Monster's Ball* and seems attracted to dark and edgy material. Did he ask you to change anything?**

He was very happy. He didn't ask for any changes. In fact I kept re-writing it and he got irritated! I'm a compulsive re-writer. He supported the re-writing but he was happy with it as it was. Yeah, he loved the script. He said it was the best thing he'd read since *Monster's Ball*. After *Monster's Ball* he thought he'd get offered all these great projects but he was actually getting what he calls 'Leprechaun 3 in the Hood' type projects. So it's really a testament to him that he was interested in more complex material.

**And what do you think brought Kevin Bacon onboard?**

We sent it out. We went to a couple of people before Kevin got it and it was similar to the producers' reaction: 'It's a great character but . . . ' People did feel it would be putting their career on the line, I guess. Kevin's never been afraid and made choices based on that fear.

**Did you have any apprehension, as a first time director, about working with people like Kevin who have been making films for years?**

I did but it was also my dream. I got over the intimidation by focusing very much on the material. I had lived with it for three years at that point and that's where my confidence came from.

**Were you going to pursue this whatever? Were there occasions where you almost gave up?**

There was always that nagging question in my head about how long would I wait and what would I do if it didn't come together. But every time that doubt got really strong, we would have a breakthrough and that's what kept me going. Every six months there would be something that just reminded me or encouraged me to believe in it and keep going. So I did.

*Stephen Applebaum*

# Gus van Sant, *director, Elephant*

*Elephant was made for TV, and went on to win the Palme D'Or at Cannes in 2003. Covering the Columbine High School shootings, it was a difficult subject to get produced from the very beginning.*

**How hard was it for you to get *Elephant* off the ground?**

I just addressed it to people that were in the business of making TV movies. I didn't want to make a feature film or something that would be outside of the television realm. The idea was always for television. But I wanted to make a television movie in the sense of a CBS, NBC, ABC television movie, because that was the same forum, or at least the mainstream forum, where the journalistic articles were as well. So they all said no. HBO wasn't the same exact idea, but it was mainstream television.

Hollywood was way too frightened by the whole event. They were coming under scrutiny by the government for violence on television as being a cause for Columbine, specifically. The same week I was pitching the idea was the same week they were actually flying to Washington with the fear there was going to be actions against television violence. So the idea to even consider doing something about Columbine was so far outside their possibilities. And, apparently, HBO's. I mean HBO was a little later. It had been a little while and Colin Callendar [HBO president] had a way to think about it that was not addressing Columbine directly.

**Would you say this issue of conformity has become greater since you were at school?**

A lot of this is also influenced by my high school years. But when I went to high school it was the Sixties, 1968, '69, '70, and so it was very common to work against the system of conformity -- conformity was suspect, at least in my circle -- and people battled against it. But those same people, the hippie generation, for some reason became ultra conservative when they grew up. I can't figure out how that happened. People that are my age, I oftentimes ask them, 'Were you a hippie?' and a lot of them they were, sort of. But now they drive SUV's and they have very strict, rigid programmes for their children, and they want children to succeed beyond all expectations. They make their children feel that anybody that doesn't exist like they exist is somehow like cancerous or they're losers, to the point that they'd probably be proud of their children if they picked on their classmates who are 'losers'.

*Stephen Applebaum*

# Patty Jenkins, *writer/director, Monster*

*Written in seven weeks, financed in just eight, Patty Jenkins' debut feature Monster took a clutch of award nominations for her and star Charlize Theron for her portrayal of serial killer Eileen Wuarnos.*

**As a first-time filmmaker, what attracted you to Aileen Wuornos's story?**

I had always read crime stories since I was young, and when Aileen's story broke in 1989, I was in high school and I remember being really struck by the dichotomy of what I was seeing. People were saying, 'Man-hating, cold-blooded serial killer', but she had this defensive, wounded look in her eyes, and it just struck me as so uncharacteristic of a serial killer. She didn't seem like somebody who had bloodlust or enjoyed killing, which I thought was intriguingly heartbreaking. You know, to see this person who looked so victimised, who had killed her johns after being a beat-up prostitute for all these years, I remember just being struck sideways by the combination of things. As the years went by I followed her story, but I never, ever, really thought, 'I want to be a lesbian serial killer director,' which has always felt like what has stood in for whatever was the real story.

**How did you get in contact with her?**

I think she always wanted her story to be told in a film and I just contacted her and told her I had sympathy with her story, which I saw as a fascinating, classic story in the tradition of good people turning bad. There wasn't something genetic formed in her brain that turned her into a serial killer. It was purely that this series of events led her to this place, and that's a famous, classic tradition. You've got war stories, *Hamlet, Badlands, Taxi Driver*. So I just wrote her and told her, 'I'm not going to lie to you and make you look like a feminist hero, because I think you killed innocent people. But I also think the series of events that led you to that place are something that most people can't truly understand.

**How difficult was it get the film funded? A lot of the people who fund films are men.**

It wasn't difficult at all, probably for all the wrong reasons. I think a movie with the combination of lesbian and serial killer is easier to fund than one would think. And then it just so happened we were making the movie we were making. So I think the ball was already rolling. I decided to do the film a year-and-a-half ago, I wrote the script in seven weeks, and it was set up in two months. So it just went forward.

**What lessons do you hope can be learned from Aileen's story and that people will take away from your film?**

As I said, I don't like the idea of being an agenda filmmaker. Like I don't think you will see me doing another film like this. I think the thing that has kept me going every day, and that I would love for people to take away from the film, I mean it would be my greatest dream, is what happened at the test screening. After the film they asked, 'How many of you in the audience think she was vicious and did some horrible things?' 95% of the audience raised their hands. Then they said, 'How many of you felt tremendous compassion for this character?' 95% of them raised their hands. It just destroyed me. I burst into tears because if anything, what I care about the story for is shades of grey and compassion.

*Stephen Applebaum*

# Mark Herbert *Warp Films* DVD distribution

*Faced with late night only broadcasts of the Aphex Twin's Come to Daddy video, music label Warp decided to sell the video direct to Aphex Twin and Warp fans as a video. This was so successful that the strategy was repeated with the follow-up single Windowlicker. To date, the Come to Daddy and Windowlicker videos have accumulated sales of 90,000 units worldwide. Warp Films, headed by Mark Herbert, launched in 2002, producing Chris Morris' BAFTA winning first short film, My Wrongs 8245-8249 and 117 and produced Shane meadow's Dead Man Shoes for FilmFour in 2004.*

We got *My Wrongs 8245-8249 and 117* into the top ten of both HMV and Virgin, as a standalone DVD with some nice extras on it. By the end of March we'd sold 12,500 units, more than many British features. If you've got something quality enough it shouldn't matter that the film is a short. In all other arts things aren't judged on size: you get great paintings, small or big; albums of 30 and 90 minutes. Why should everything be a short or feature, it should suit whatever the artist wants to do? If its 15 minutes but good enough we think there's a market for it. Obviously Chris Morris and Warp have a fan-base, but both wholesalers and distributors have now seen that DVD is changing the market for shorts slightly – there's the Cinema 16 DVD which has shown there is a market for the right shorts.

We're at a time with a bit of a revolution happening in the industry, DV cameras are coming right down in price, Final Cut Pro is getting more advanced. The problem has always been distribution – self-produced DVD releases hopefully mean you won't have to get distribution. Apple has an authoring programme so you can do the whole lot in your bedroom: edit and press DVDs.

We got a NESTA grant to kick-start Warp Films of which we used a portion to make *My Wrongs*, we should recoup but it won't make a profit. The film cost more than £100,000 – the post-production took up the majority of that because of the talking dog. Most films we do will be for far less than that.

Right now we're working on a Shane Meadows feature, *Skull*. We've stripped it right down – stripped the crew right down. Budgets and particularly crew are too high and big in this country. It's fine for certain films because sometimes we need that, but in most cases why do you need 75 people to make a film? The Europeans and particularly the South Americans have proved you can do it on far less. This should cost less than three-quarters of a million, and will be shot on film. It's being financed by FilmFour, regional funding and private equity. *NW*

# Amanda Posey, *Fever Pitch*

*Like Paul Webster, Stephen Woolley, Robert Jones and Daniel Battsek, Amanda Posey started out at Palace Pictures. She oversaw films such as the Crying Game and Interview with a Vampire before becoming Head of Development at Scala. She went on to produce the profitable British feature Fever Pitch with Film Four through her production company Wildgaze and its US remake, directed by the Farrelly Brothers.*

*Fever Pitch* opened on about 220 screens, which is a big release, but the very big American movies will open on 350 - 400 screens. FilmFour tested it and that's what gave them the conviction to put a certain amount of money behind it. They spent nearly £1m promoting it and it cost £1.8m to make. You'll never recoup that theatrically but where they made that back was on video because they'd raised the profile so high theatrically. Meanwhile, they were effectively buying themselves a high profile TV broadcast - this was in the days before FilmFour channel. It's just a business; they have to make the pieces of the puzzle fit. That was all without international sales which they did well with too.

The problem comes with the big percentages that get taken off from commission. It has taken something like £3m in actual income but once you take off the commission that FilmFour International took from selling it abroad, and the advertising and promotional budget then it comes down and it's not officially in profit. In terms of the channel they've paid almost nothing for a television broadcast in comparative terms, so for them it's very successful.

Very few people on the creative side have the exposure to the marketing and distribution so they don't know what choices have to be made when putting out a trailer or devising a poster or deciding where to place the ad. I was lucky in that I started in Palace Pictures, which went under for all sorts of reasons, but it was then the biggest independent distributor and producer. You got to see the film from start to finish, so whether it succeeded or failed you learnt lessons throughout. I remember Steve Woolley having huge trouble with *The Crying Game*. No-one wanted to finance that film and he ended up using cash from the Scala cinema and the connected video shop just to live day to day.

You can't rely on anybody else to tell you how to make your movie or to tell you why your movie is going to be any good. If you expect other people to give you money, it's a lot of money and a lot of time and commitment, you have to convey to them that you know what your audience is even if they don't know. And you have to be able to back it up. If you know there are millions of teenagers out there desperate to see your film then go online, do your research and get your statistics. So many independent filmmakers have the passion but not the interpretation that convinces those with the money that there is some commercial, and I don't mean formulaic, but financially sound reason to make it and that you are trying to reach a certain audience. What's often levelled at British filmmakers is that they don't care who their audience is and I think that's something that should be focused on. *NW*

# Gavin Emerson, *Ratcatcher*

*A screening at the NFTS got Lynne Ramsay noticed by Gavin Emerson who over three years worked with her to make the short film Gasman, winner of the Special Jury Prize at Cannes, and then the award winning follow-up feature Ratcatcher.*

I met Lynne Ramsay at the graduation screenings at the NFTS in 1996 and saw *Small Deaths*. She graduated as a cinematographer and, I think for more political reasons, the school just wasn't pushing the film at all and it wasn't being sent to any festivals. She did it as part of the cinematography course but ended up directing it. I saw her film and thought it was absolutely astounding and revealed a unique talent. I went up to her afterwards and asked her if she wanted to work with me and gave her a small amount of money for a treatment for what turned out to be *Ratcatcher*. Really it was a three-year process and we were very lucky to be given the opportunity to work with a £1.8 million budget but at the time we didn't have a clue what we were doing.

You have to go through the short process. You have to make mistakes so, at the very least, they give you the opportunity to fuck up and learn from it in order to make a feature. The more short films the better, but when you think you've got something, build on it and think about future projects like feature length scripts or acquiring the rights for something. I say this because the chances are, once the short is finished you'll be in a really good position to go to someone with a feature script and to ask them what they think.

*Ratcatcher* was about building on the existing relationship we had with the BBC in that we were commissioned to make the short *Gasman* for Tartan Shorts. It was off the back of that that we managed to get the BBC to put the money into *Ratcatcher*. It was quite fortunate that Andrea Calderwood, who was head of BBC Scotland, moved over to Pathé and was already interested in the project. Also it was all about building awareness, attending film festivals and societies and so on. There was a key player called Jim Wilson who was at Fox Searchlight at the time and is now at Channel 4, he'd seen the shorts when we met up at Edinburgh and after Gasman played we just got chatting. We ended up sending him the script despite the confidentiality agreement with the Beeb and Pathé and he was really enthusiastic about it and started showing it around Fox Searchlight who'd probably never have noticed otherwise. But he was great at raising that awareness, saying to Searchlight that the BBC and Pathé had greenlit it, which they hadn't at that point. By getting involved in it he acted as the catalyst for Pathé to agree to finally commit to it. So my role really was the PR, you know, getting out there as a producer and raising awareness for the film.

I was pretty naive to be honest. What I really believed in was Lynne's talent and the talents of the group of people around her and I knew that if we planned it carefully and were judicious about it, we'd end up making a feature. I learnt that the key issue about making a feature is that politics plays a huge part. I had to get constant approval from three executives, not just the basic costs and crewing but on everything. They were all supportive but I had to constantly communicate to them that they were all being treated equally well. I didn't handle that too well but I've since realised that that is a principle element of producing, whether it should be like that is debatable but that was the reality. The other great thing I learnt from *Ratcatcher* is that it was always so possible. If you've got a good idea or a good short film planned properly it is so, so possible to get a feature made.

*Clifford Thurlow*

t

# Michael Lerman *Lerman and Co*
# Working with an accountant

**When should a film producer seek the advice of an accountant for their general business affairs (as opposed to film budgets?)**

Viewing your accountant as a business adviser, not just as a professional trained in traditional accountancy and tax compliance services, could greatly assist a film producer's business. In addition to performing routine accountancy duties, a large part of the professional accountant's duties are those of advising clients on their budgets, profitability improvement, and operational procedures - and performing other tasks not often associated with accountants. Always keep your long-term goals in mind. Running your business more cost-effectively can be achieved only if you have the vision to project your goals into the future. Frequent cash shortages, lack of a solid business plan to guide the business, and steady decreases in profitability are all warning signs that a business is heading towards a potential financial crisis. It is crucial to evaluate your business's structure, the projects undertaken and performance before it displays these danger signals.

An accountant can help you to boost your profitability by analysing all the elements of your business. Reporting on profitability is a standard procedure, but helping create it by providing intelligent, entrepreneurial advice is what an accountant strives for. Dealing with your accounts doesn't have to be a problem, even though it sometimes feels that way. For film producers, more important than making a huge profit, is controlling your finances and covering your costs. With control of those key elements of the business, the profits will flow!

Often, a film producer's accounting system will need to record transactions related to a number of projects, over a number of years. This is a complication that is a challenge and should be used to the producer's advantage for monitoring cash-flow and profitability.

The key to financial control is knowing what's happening. Therefore you need to monitor your financial situation at all times. The best way to monitor the financial success of your business is to regularly review elements such as:

- debtors
- creditors
- financial commitments
- cash balances and borrowings

Every bit of money that comes into or leaves your business should be documented. It is this documentation that will form the basis of your year-end accounts and your financial records. All sales should be receipted or invoiced, as should all costs and purchases. It is important to ensure that you have a working relationship with your accountant. When meeting prospective advisors, make sure you choose someone who you feel comfortable with and who gives you a feeling of confidence in their abilities. Items to consider, when choosing an accountant range from: -

1 Costs – most accountants today will consider quoting a fixed fee for the work being undertaken. Whilst costs will vary, the purchaser of accounting services must be sure that he/she is receiving "value for money".

2 Experience in the particular industry – this is not necessarily essential amongst professional accountants, it is a useful pointer to obtaining relevant and useful advice.

3 Accessibility – the cost of travelling to an accountant far away may be prohibitive. See if the prospective accountant will travel to you, to see your business as opposed to always expecting you to travel to him/her.

4 Qualification – A professional accountant will have the ability to advise you on most areas affecting your business. Many accountants who are not qualified under the many recognised institutes, will only have experience in limited areas of business.

## ANNUAL ACCOUNTS

All businesses should produce accounts on a regular basis. For management purposes, accounts will be in a format that is most useful to the owner, and produced at times most relevant to the running of the business (e.g. monthly, quarterly, or at the end of a particular production). Annual accounts are required for tax purposes and for submission to providers of finance and banks. In the case of Limited Companies and LLPs, annual accounts in a format governed by statute, must be prepared and submitted to companies house within a certain time limit.

Annual accounts will include: -

- a balance sheet,
- a profit and loss account,
- certain notes relating to the financial items in the accounts.

A balance sheet shows the financial position of the business as at the date to which the statement is prepared. It represents the balance of assets and liabilities at that moment and is presented on a historical cost basis. This means that no "valuations" are carried out on the figures (except in the case of land and buildings or certain other appreciating assets). The general format of the balance sheet is to start with "long term assets" such as cars, equipment and buildings. Then short term assets, such as bank balances and debtors and matched against short term creditors, for example overdrafts, loans, payables and taxation. Long term creditors (e.g. bank loans), are then deducted and you arrive at a figure for "net assets". Whilst this is not a value of the business, it measures, to a large extent, its financial health.

An asset is generally described in accounting terms as anything on a company's books considered to have a positive monetary value. Assets include holdings of liquid value (cash, debtors), less liquid items (stock, aging equipment), and other quantities (pre-paid expenses, goodwill) considered an asset by accounting conventions but possibly having no market value at all. Assets are shown on the balance sheet.

An asset that is utilised in the business for, generally, more than one year; is shown on the balance sheet as a "Fixed Asset". The costs of such assets are spread over their useful lives. Depreciation is the term given to the process of "writing off" the fixed asset over its lifespan.

*For more information see www.lermanandco.com*

# Rocliffe
## *No Deposit, No Return - sperm banking*

Sometimes it's easy to get caught up in the long and painful processes of raising capital for your latest project, and to forget that the film industry is primarily about creativity, and that this can be applied to gathering funds. Believing there is only one road to funding your short, is limiting, when really there are as many ways of raising money as there are stories to be made into films.

One funding success story is that of Rocliffe. Started by Farah Abushwesha in 2000, Rocliffe began as a new forum for un-represented writers who might ordinarily find their work put in the slush pile. Rocliffe provides what Michael Kuhn of Qwerty Films calls "a development workout", giving new scripts a vigorous testing before a live audience while guest co-chairs provide criticism and advice and in turn come into contact with new talent and scripts. The audience becomes a peer group, and networking opportunities arise as the members often retire to the bar downstairs afterwards.

This structure has been highly successful, and the Rocliffe staff has expanded to include Kerry Appleyard, an experienced development executive, and Pippa Mitchell, a full time film and television producer. Success stories now abound; writers presenting at Rocliffe have gone on to gain agents, and although it is too early to have seen any of the features optioned as a result of Rocliffe produced, several writers have gone on to write for radio and television. Rocliffe has also been a success story itself in developing working relationships, introducing writers to directors, producers and actors. But what happens after the forum is up to you. As Farah says, while they might help get Mohammed to the mountain there's still a lot of climbing to be done. The story doesn't end there.

It certainly hasn't for the ladies of Rocliffe. Some less creative people might have just expanded the forums, moving to a bigger venue and charging more to take cynical advantage of people's interest. Besides the fact that the ladies are very proud of the forum's intimacy, Rocliffe was established to help move projects into development and ultimately production. Through Rocliffe, they came across a short called "No Deposit, No Return" in 2002, and Kerry worked very hard with the writer, Jonathon Edwards, and the director, Dallas Campbell, to create a strong draft that would support Rocliffe's reputation.

However, it was due to an episode of Hollyoaks that they began their funding journey. "No Deposit, No Return" is the story of a desperate woman who holds up a sperm bank in her quest for a child, and is disarmed by a sympathetic security guard who is looking for love. And in Hollyoaks a storyline about poor students looking for ways of making quick cash caught Farah's eye. Instead of approaching the usual sources of film funding or putting themselves into hock on credit card after credit card, they decided to ask men for the financial proceeds of their sperm donations. Kerry wrote press releases asking men to put their hands in their pockets and "come up with the goods" and soon their story was being covered by the Irish press, and then the film business bible, Screen International.

In Cannes they continued their quest as "Sperm Angels" and ended up winning the "Best Pitch in Cannes, 2003" from the Times Newspaper. Their high profile also resulted in offers of help from Ealing Studios, Fuji Film, Lipsync Post, and individuals such as Chris Kenny ("Tomb

Raider"), who would provide the necessary experience they needed to help them actually make the short. After a year of dashing around as "The Sperm Angels", appearing in photos shoots holding turkey basters, they had £12,000 in cash, and £60,000 in total of sponsorship, in kind help, mentoring and product placement.

For the shoot in August 2003 they arranged to have on set mentors so that the amateur crewmembers working for expenses could benefit from contact with the HoDs. They also reduced their location costs by offering a drama day and a film career presentation to the school they shot at and several students were runners. The 3 day shoot also included cars breaking down with all the camera equipment inside and being forced to arrange shooting around catering problems (making four minute pasta on a BBQ is not advisable, it takes an hour and half!). But with help from the HoDs, Super 35 stock from Fuji, advanced Panavision cameras, sound and grading by Lipsync, and Soho Images spending two hours explaining post production to them, the film ended up with very high production values.

With shoot completed, and an almost final cut prepared, Rocliffe then decided to approach the UK Film Council. Farah believes that the key to approaching funding bodies is to realise that simply applying will not be enough, and that the funds are a business contract requiring good management skills and clear accounts. Rocliffe had failed to get money from two funds prior to production, but with all the work they had put into financing it themselves, the relationships they had developed with established people and the evidence they had of continued support, they received completion funding.

There was a lot of pressure on Rocliffe to make a short that lived up to the advance publicity their "Sperm Angels" approach had garnered. But response to the film was very good, it has been shortlisted for a BIFA Award and appeared in several festivals including Raindance and The Edinburgh Film Festival. It is a simple crowd pleaser with a strong theme: 'What is more important, the rights of a woman to have a child, or what is best for the child?' The ladies decided that love and not the need to reproduce should be the driving force. But that didn't stop the Casting Director, the Director's wife and the writer's wife feeling the creative process most keenly and deciding to join in with three little projects of their own during the course of making the film!

Rocliffe is now moving into features; one developed from a script that came via Rocliffe Forums, and the other an adaptation of a Spanish novel. Their reputation now precedes them, and helps them into meetings with agents and producers that they might have struggled to get before. But they still see that innovative approaches to funding; finding a hook in the story and marketing yourselves on the basis of that, will still be a large part of the independent producer's funding arsenal. By writing hundreds of letters to condom companies, sperm banks, and drug companies they were thinking laterally and taking advantage of funding methods that are not over subscribed. Even now when they return to Cannes, they are asked what their hook is this year. But their real hook, and what will ensure that they will continue to be the interesting and successful producers that they are, is their creativity.

*By Beth White, winner of the 2004 Re:Creation Award for writing and co-founder of Sensate Media, a script development and PR firm*

## CHAPTER TWO

# LOW AND MICROBUDGET FILMMAKING

### AN OVERVIEW BY JAMES MACGREGOR

Determining just what a low budget film is and where the boundary lines lie, is an almost fruitless exercise. Alan Parker's idea of low budget might represent almost limitless resources to some filmmakers; it all depends on perception. Generous or mean, budgets are ultimately judged by what appears on the screen and there are films that have produced astonishing results on meagre resources. In the final analysis, low budget production is governed by an attitude of mind rather than a pot of gold. It is that attitude of mind I set out to explore for the 2005 Film Funding Handbook.

# Cutting Budgets – The Relph Report

With a reduction in available funds for fully financed feature film production, the British industry has finally begun to look at ways to reduce the cost of shooting in the UK. The Film Council commissioned Simon Relph, film producer and chairman of BAFTA, to produce a major study into the financing structures and options for low-budget UK films, with an eye to helping bring down average budgets through a series of proposals. *The Relph Report*, was published at the end of 2002 and described by Alan Parker as 'the best industry report I've ever read.' Although Relph's report is mainly targeted at films currently costing between £2 and £4 million, he studied 26 'low budget' British films ranging from £76,000 to £7 million. His recommendations for cutting budgets is evidence of low budget film practice starting to make impact on the mainstream UK film industry.

The study compared the UK environment with the US and mainland European market, and concluded that Britain was one of the more expensive places in the world to shoot. In the US, 'enthusiasm for the work is as important as pay and conditions', allowing US indies to pay low wages in return for greater potential at the back-end, while mainland Europe typically employs smaller crews over longer periods with shorter hours. Ultimately, Relph concludes, the UK will need to follow one of these two models – big crews on lower wages and intense shooting schedule, or much smaller crews over shorter hours and a longer schedule.

The report blames many of the UK's current problems with the film finance mini-boom at the end of the 90s: 'Lottery money, tax breaks, bank finance and insurance deals coincided, making it easier to fund films and establishing a new and higher going rate. Now that production funding is less freely available, it is hard for the industry to return to the lower cost ways of working'. Central to the report is an ambition to bring the average cost of 'low budget films' down from £2.5m to £1.5m, largely through greater employee flexibility with the creation of an equivalent to the PACT/Equity low budget film agreement, for crew.

# Summary of Relph's Points

## DEVELOPMENT & PRE-PRODUCTION

- Cheaper films begin with writing to budget. The producer should have a realistic idea of the potential value of the film and with the director encourage the writer to work to that budget.

- Development is a vital stage, but the upfront cost of the script and options should be kept to a minimum until there is a clear idea of the size of the project and the investment it can attract.

- Long films cost more and can be harder to sell. Footage that ends up being cut in post production because the film is too long is a waste of money that should have been spent on the rest of the film.

- Maximum preparation time saves money. Ideally producers would confirm financing *at least three months before the start of shooting* to give enough time to creatively maximise the budget with the director and production manager. Too often money is confirmed – or even slashed - at the 11th hour.

- The director and producer must work hand-in-hand. Too many directors see the relationship as a battle where they must try and get away with as much as they can. In a good working relationship the director will be aware of budget limitations and search for creative alternatives. Storyboards, rehearsals and shot lists lengthen the lower-cost pre-production process and save time during the far more expensive shoot.

- Schedule in pick-ups. It can be cheaper to schedule pick-up days after the shoot rather than have a long shoot that tries to cover for every eventuality.

## PRODUCTION

- Cut crew numbers. The smaller the crew, the longer you can afford to shoot.

- The line producer is the most important factor in controlling the final cost of the film. Small production departments are possible where other departments take on a greater share of administration, while the line producer or production manager needs to have a hearty appetite for finding ways to produce the same effect for less money.

- Seasoned cinematographers can cause problems, in having greater expectations of equipment, crew size and speed of working. As the camera department's costs can be highly unpredictable, it's important that the DP is working closely with the production department to bring the film in on budget.

- Top line acting talent can be attracted to the right project by offering, rather than a deferred fee or profit share, a gross position, ie. a share of all film revenues from the first receipt.

- Crew can take the place of Film Artists Association (FAA) stand-ins, while large crowds of background artists can be gathered cheaply by offering prizes rather than paying each extra.

- DV and Super16mm offer advantages not just in cheaper kit and stock, but also in making the production quicker, allowing for smaller crews and less lighting.

- If shooting on 35mm, money can be saved by only developing and telecining the rushes, ie not printing until the film is cut.

- Finding a location where good quality sound can be recorded makes a huge difference to post-production costs, as can employing a sound recordist who will also mix and edit the film's sound in post.
- Studio sets are increasingly dressed to shoot in all directions, even when only one or two walls may end in the final cut. Better planning and more decisions on shots up front allow the art department to save resources in shooting. Working with what is found on the location rather than imposing a design can save costs and time massively.
- Basing locations close to each other and the production base can save massively on both time and transport costs. Reduce the number of drivers - electricians drive their own equipment vehicles, yet props, construction and camera departments very rarely do.
- Location caterers working from a van charge between £11 and £15 a day per person – getting a cook and providing equipment and ingredients is far more cost effective, although not all locations allow for this.
- Delivery costs have risen dramatically in recent years and tend to be the same for low budget films as higher budgeted work. Some sales agents have been persuaded to accept some of these costs as a distribution expense. Digital post production provides some savings in that the digital master replaces the interpositive and DVD/video copies can be easily run off that.

Full report available at www.ukfilmcouncil.org.uk/filmindustry/relphreport/

# Impact of Digital Technology

One of the keys to reducing budgets is digital technology. High budget productions have been taking advantage of what this technology offers in post-production for many years, but it is the independent filmmaker who has really embraced it, at the front end as well as in post. The digital video camera allows great freedoms for the filmmaker to experiment and create new filming parameters in areas that conventional film would rule out purely on grounds of cost.

Digital Video has encouraged new ways of thinking, lateral approaches to problem-solving and brings up new solutions, and it has done this across all low budget levels.

Cast size, the number of locations and their accessibility, and crew size all impact on budget. Anyone contemplating a low budget feature needs to keep all these elements small, and if they also shoot on DV, they will already have the elements that can keep costs down.

# Microbudget Movies 101

Looking back through the James MacGregor interview archives netted this collection of thoughts, ideas and expositions from seasoned practitioners of the low budget shoot. They may inspire low budget filmmakers to greater effort, or at the very least, inform them better on just what they are up against.

## THE BUSINESS

### 1) OK - HERE'S THE PUT DOWN

"The problem with new filmmakers is - quite naturally - they all think that their film is the best thing since sliced bread. Unfortunately, this gives them a false sense of security. They think that they are going to get more than it cost them to make the film from their first sale alone. This rarely happens. They need to talk to other producers to find out what the likely sales are."

David Nicholas Wilkinson. Distributor, Guerilla Films

### 2) REGISTER & CLAIM BACK VAT

"Form the business skills to put a company together and keep an accurate record of accounts. It forces you to be business-like, makes you put better preparation into your film, make a better account of all the numbers and overall you'll get a better result because of this. The other thing is of course, that you can claim back VAT if you are a registered company, which not all filmmakers will be aware of!"

Tom Swanston. Producer, The Ultimate Truth

### 3) KEEP IT SIMPLE

"The majority of the film is set in one location, a cottage. So much of the film visually was going to be in this one location that we looked for a very long time for the right place. We found a wonderful place in Northern Ireland and that happened to work for us and we found a great crew up there and we were able to access financial resources from the Northern Ireland Film & Television Commission."

Karl Golden. Director, The Honeymooners

### 4) PRODUCTION VALUE ON SCREEN

"Put production value in the film. Production value is, among other things, crowds, great locations, crane and tracking shots, sex, violence, nudity, special effects if you can do them convincingly, otherwise don't do SFX at all..., good costumes and make-up, and last but not least, good acting."

Sean Martin. Director, The Notebooks of Cornelius Crow

### 5) KNOW YOUR STUFF

"There a few factors that are essential, that excite backers. A filmmaker's passion and vision for a project. My dedication to it was total. I could tell you what colours the heist corridors should be, tell you how the characters walked or talked. Nobody will part with money if you go "eehhhhh" and you think about it. If they ask a question about the project, you have to KNOW what they will ask, before they know."

David Paul Baker. Director, Pasty Faces

## 6) YOU EXPECT AN ADVANCE?

"Most low budget British films do not even recoup their prints & advertising costs from the cinema AND video rental, sell-though and DVD, let alone pay back any of the film's investment. I have over 40 films. I have only paid an advance for one of them."

David Nicholas Wilkinson. Distributor, Guerilla Films

## 7) COST WRITE OUT

"Embarking on Rosetta meant writing to accommodate resources, locations, crew and facilities I knew I could access with a high degree of certainty. Without a budget, there was no point in trying to film elaborate -and expensive- extracts from operas to show Rosetta's early years. In fact, we never see Rosetta sing. My story is about Rosetta's life today, her feelings of loss, betrayal, regret and the repercussions of sacrifices she made."

Kenneth D Barker. Director, Rosetta: Prima Donna Assoluta

## 8) CONTAINING COSTS

"I offered deferral contracts but I did not PROMISE anything. I simply told it how it was and the people made their own decision whether or not to get involved."

Piotr Szkopiak. Director, Small Time Obsession

## 9) PITFALLS TO FAILURE

"SCRIPT, SCRIPT, SCRIPT...! The big problem is that new filmmakers think they know it all. They will not listen. So many films could be so much better if only more time was given to the script. Also names. There are very few real stars in the business but people with some profile will help. This means I can get free press coverage."

David Nicholas Wilkinson. Distributor, Guerilla Films

## 10) SHARE KNOWLEDGE

"One of the reasons we wrote The Guerilla Film Makers Handbook was because film makers were keeping the information to themselves and not getting it out there - we felt it was our mission to inform other film makers with the information at hand to help them make their movies."

Genevieve Jolliffe. Director, Urban Ghost Story

## 11) NO ACCOUNTING FOR TASTE

"Ours is an industry where normal rules do not apply. If you make a good suit, people will buy it. Go into any video store and see what people rent. Some really bad films do far, far better than some brilliant ones."

Davis Nicholas Wilkinson. Distributor, Guerilla Films

# DEVELOPMENT HELL

## 12) FATAL ATTRACTION

"I have always been attracted to romantic comedies; I think they make a great first feature film genre. Romantic comedy is something I feel very passionate about, but they are also very cheap to make because they don't necessarily require stars, or special effects."

Karl Golden. Director, The Honeymooners

## 13) I'LL DO IT MY WAY

"I tried to short-circuit the system. When you make a film here or in any western country it's all about rewrites and script editors, it becomes a collective effort but the more people get involved the more formulaic it becomes. So we just tried to get a small amount of money and make the film without getting other people involved."

Pawel Pawlikowsky. Director, The Last Resort

## 14) IN WHOM WE TRUST

"I have a couple of friends who are writers, whose opinion I really trust, and I will show them some work and let them really pull it apart. Apart from that the regional funding agency put on workshops where they brought in writers just to talk about our work and talk it through with you. It always helps to have a professional person come in and you can challenge each other and bash ideas out."

Sarah Walker. Director, Almost Strangers

## 15) BETTER THE EDGE YOU KNOW

"I find it hard to give advice in this area. It smacks of a formula. Formulaic films never work for me. It's like painting by numbers with the result looking like a cold, and poor, imitation of something that was original. Try to make the film as real as possible. Writing based on your own history or experiences will show and will give your film an edge."

David Nicholas Wilkinson. Distributor, Guerilla Films

## 16) WRITER-PRODUCER DEVELOPMENT

"From a creative point of view, the first thing is to make sure that you both want to tell the same story, that you both want it to go in the same direction. It may seem self-evident, but it is quite easy for people to have different emphases, even when working within a genre like comedy. People want to make different kinds of comedy or have got feelings about what kind of comedy works commercially. You need to understand what it is that you trying to do, trying to make, and to have a rapport with writers such that you trust each other in terms of the direction you want to take something. So, in terms of practicalities, I would be very hands on with expressing to the writer what I think is working/not working or when I think the story is hitting beats or missing beats."

Michael Duffy. Producer, AltoAtlantic Films

# SHOW ME THE MONEY

### 17) 50/50

"The film initially cost £40,000 to make. Half of that was my own money and the other half came from family and friends. My half of the money was savings from my working as a freelance AVID editor for three years. I could save this much because I remained living at home and my family waived the rent. I accepted the fact that no one I didn't know was going to give money to an unknown, first-time director who wanted to use an unknown cast."

Piotr Szkopiak. Director, Small Time Obsession

### 18) SHARE DEAL

"I formed a limited company and issued a certain number of shares. Then I went around seeking private investors. All in all, we had fourteen investors who bought shares and that raised the £30,000 to make the film."

Tom Swanston. Producer, The Ultimate Truth

### 19) FINANCIAL CREATIVITY

"I take the view that if you get the right people around you, not having any money can be a creative thing. You are not throwing money at problems, so you've got to find other ways to solve those problems. If you've got very young and very talented, very passionate people around you, on both sides of the camera, they find interesting creative solutions."

Karl Golden. Director, The Honeymooners

### 20) LOGICAL INVESTMENTS

When approaching money or facilities, ask yourself why YOU would part with the money or why YOU would help a project like this one. Put yourself in their shoes. Look at it logically. Why should I give you £500,000 to make your film if you have never made a film before? Would you give someone £500,000 if they had never made a feature before. I got my money and help from people that KNEW ME. They invested in ME and not the project.

Piotr Szkopiak. Director, Small Time Obsession

### 21) INFECTIOUS

"Our passion for it infected people. We believed we would make it, so they believed. They also liked the sound of it. They said it was something they would go and see. We were also honest with them. We told them this would be a flutter, don't give us your life savings as it's a long haul just getting a movie off the ground. Over that week we got around fifteen cheques that amounted to seven thousand. We were in Vegas two weeks later with another two actors and four of a crew."

David Paul Baker. Director, Pasty Faces

### 22) SAFETY NETS

"I said at the start that this was a film that I could do in eighteen days; really just studying the script and looking at each schedule day and having as many safety nets as you can and just having the sort of budget where you can ask, "Can we cover this? Can we cover that?" If you can't you, just have to find your way around it. We planned; we did an awful lot of advance planning, because having a lot of passion and drive gets your picture made, but you need to have the right logistics, particularly because you have to account for the money."

Karl Golden. Director, The Honeymooners

### 23) ALTRUISTIC ENTREPRENEURS

"The production finance for Rosetta came on stream several months after I committed to producing the film. Through contacts, I was introduced to a local business entrepreneur who was prepared to be fabulously altruistic and offered a small cash budget to fund Rosetta. Many sponsors saw their contribution as putting something back into the community. Others enjoyed the cachet of being involved in a film production, even at this minor level. Looking back now, it is almost frightening to contemplate the logistics and complexity of getting so many people to come together to produce this film."

Kenneth D Barker. Director, Rosetta: Prima Donna Assoluta

### 24) SEE YOU LATER...

"The film was done on deferred fees. Not ideal, I know, but it was the only way to get the film made in the time available, and with the available money. Everyone understood that and really threw themselves into it."

Sean Martin. Director, The Notebooks of Cornelius Crow

### 25) I CAN'T PROMISE..

"I think the worse thing you can do is promise people that they will definitely get their money back because that is not true. You cannot promise anything and the reality is that they will probably never get paid. Anyway, you are not making a first film to make money and neither are they, they do it for other reasons and it is those reasons you offer - not money. What you want is to start a career. You make your first film to show what you can do."

Piotr Szkopiak. Director, Small Time Obsession

## VALUE FOR MONEY

### 26) A GOOD INVESTMENT

"Before making London Voodoo, my wife and I went on the Chris Jones course. His book was our Bible and that course was the best money I ever spent in terms of getting the producing knowledge. Film school was all about the art and craft of making films, but this was all about production. The great thing about the Guerilla Filmmakers weekend course was you learned all about where you could get things cheap, things we hadn't encountered before, that sooner or later you would have come up against further down the line. It was fantastic value."

Robert Pratten. Director, London Voodoo

### 27) EXPRESS FILMMAKING

"Final Cut Pro, the home computer editing weapon of choice, has a little brother called Final Cut Express, which costs around £200. Now this is a bargain. Apart from having less sophisticated colour-correction tools, the only limitation compared to it's big brother is that it only captures from mini-DV."

Ben Hughes-Games. Director, A Slice of Life

### 28) LOOKS A MILLION DOLLARS

"I went against all the rules of making a first low budget film. They say set it in the one room and chop everybody up physically or psychologically. I agree with that, but I wanted a low budget film that looked like a movie, that had great locations. But you pay for it in another way, as we were doing a lot of set ups each day. I lost count of the amount of locations, there was a lot. The film constantly moves."

David Paul Baker. Director, Pasty Faces

### 29) DOUBLE VALUE

"Because money was so tight, I allowed myself one luxury when writing the project, which was the wax sculptures of human limbs which a professional sculptor generously allowed us to have extremely cheaply. This meant that all the locations and props written in to the script were ones that we all either had, or could borrow without paying the money. Since the majority of the shooting took place in either my house or my lead actor's house, whoever was hosting took care of catering. In fact, often the characters had to eat a meal in the scene so that was neatly taken care of. "

Ben Hughes-Games. Director, A Slice of Life

### 30) CUT THROAT OPERATIONS

"The film ends with a showdown in a mysterious chapel, and it originally had a hanging in it, but we cancelled it at the last minute and cut the character's throat instead, as it was quicker to do (and about £1500 cheaper!)."

Sean Martin. Director, The Notebooks of Cornelius Crow

## LOCATION, LOCATION, LOCATION

### 31) CHOOSING CAREFULLY

"Getting the right location is incredibly important. The typical balance a producer is trying to strike is between location fees and the production design costs if you had to construct the same location to get the look right for the film. It is usually more expensive to go for the studio design and construction route, so we spend a lot of time looking for the right location."

Michael Duffy. Producer, AltoAtlantic

### 32) PRAY FOR FORGIVENESS

"We had a bit of a problem with one scene, which we had wanted to shoot in the churchyard. The church wanted £800 and approval of the script to vet it for sex and violence. Unfortunately, the whole scene is about precisely these two things, and also features partial public nudity. We ended up shooting in the street, which was council property and therefore we would not have to give the church the best part of a grand to shoot."

Sean Martin. Director, The Notebooks of Cornelius Crow

### 33) SAVE CASH ON LOCATIONS

"If you have a good location you probably don't need to build a set, because sets can be expensive. A good location can add a lot of production value to your film. It adds more class.

Using someone's front room doesn't necessarily work, but to tell the right story well, you really do need top locations. They just have to look right within the frame. If you don't get good locations, you can devalue your film quite a lot."

Dean Fisher. Producer, Scanner-Rhodes Productions

### 34) RENT-A-WRECK AND WIN

"Inside, the farm had suffered the penetrating effect of forty Shetland winter weathers and looked it. Ceilings were coming down and in one part of the building the upper floor was coming down to meet the lower one. This did not trouble our production designer. Builders jacks came in to put the upper floor back to its rightful place, the roof that leaked was sheeted over to make it watertight and all the tiles the wind had stripped off into the garden were tidied away. Broken windows were reglazed and a balcony was erected from scrap wood right along the front of the old house. Finally, two false gravestones were constructed to make a family burial plot in the corner of the garden and then the garden, with its half-century of decay and neglect, was tidied and plants imported to shoot a January summer garden scene. Marvellous job Sarah!"

Leslie Lowes. Producer, Penultimate Films & Features

### 35) AIRPORT

"Manchester wasn't easy to deal with. I think they get large number of requests to film. There's lots of form-filling, lots of bureaucracy and they charge you lots of money.

But Leeds/Bradford Airport is after publicity! They were extremely nice and very friendly, as long as we didn't want to shoot in their busy peak May to October. We shot there at the end of last April when it was about 27 degrees and it looked like June."

John Williams. Producer, Diary of A Bad Lad

### 36) POSITIVE ATTITUDE

"The Americans take their filmmakers deadly serious. So they helped us a lot. They gave us a penthouse in the Stardust Hotel, let us shoot in the Stratosphere Tower, and even stopped the huge tower turning for us so a table in the restaurant could be in line with the Vegas strip way, way below. Again, kind of bizarre as we were looking around for free extras for the scene, but we could get the Tower stopped! It sounds like a big budget film, but believe me it was not."

David Paul Baker. Director, Pasty Faces

### 37) ATTITUDE COUNTS

" If you go at it with the right attitude, people are happy to help. I would be honest and say, "Nobody is paying me to do this production, I haven't got any money, and can I use your place?" - And most people would say "Yea, OK." Since then, I've made short films in LA, in places like coffee shops where they regularly charge big movies $5,000 a day and I got them for free. It is all a question of attitude."

Ian Vernon. Director, Actors

### 38) TIME RUNS OUT

"We were hampered by losing a couple of locations. Replacements had to be found almost immediately, and sometimes they weren't suitable but, as we were shooting, we had no choice but to go with things that were merely available rather than ideal. Had we stopped to find something more ideal, the film would have been sunk. Once you have started a tight shoot like this, every minute counts and you have to learn to think on your feet extremely fast.."

Sean Martin. Director, The Notebooks of Cornelius Crow

### 39) CLOSE PROXIMITY

"We knew that it would be a two-week shoot, and a decision was taken that we would have to shoot everything in the same area to avoid losing valuable shooting time by travelling between locations, so Doug started to look for locations in and around the immediate area: the Aldwych, Fleet Street, the Embankment and the Strand."

Sean Martin. Director, The Notebooks of Cornelius Crow

## PREPPING

### 40) GETTING IT RIGHT

"You only get one shot at prepping a film. If Production hasn't done the best job, you are not going to get the best shoot and the best film in the can. Plus, if you only have a budget of £20,000 you really need to get your deals and work on people - and that takes time. We had to get meeting people and getting deals even before our Heads of Department started. We spent a good two to three months working on this sort of stuff, even before pre-production started. That included planning the whole shoot, working out all the different areas that could cost us a lot of money, finding solutions and sorting out catering."

Dean Fisher. Producer, Scanner-Rhodes Productions

### 41) SIGN HERE PLEASE...

"After agreeing a price with whoever owns or controls the location, you must secure it by means of an agreement, that is a location contract. This will indemnify the owner of the property against accidental damage the shoot may cause and lays down the agreed daily or weekly fee and a date. The date should not be fixed, because schedules are known to change. The date needs to be on an "on or around" basis. It should also say when the owner will be paid his location fee, usually on the day it is used, or at the end of the first week if it is used for a number of days. Do not delay on getting signature on this agreement, because there is a danger of price escalation and you may by then be too close to shooting to go elsewhere. "

Leslie Lowes. Producer, Penultimate Films & Features

## CASTING

### 42) WHO DO YOU KNOW?

"The first step is to think very hard about who we know, that we like, who has done work which is good. It may be about 'how high can you go?' If you start with a big name and they tell you no, then you move down. Or, sometimes you see someone in a role on TV, someone not particularly well known, and you think that person could be absolutely perfect. So it starts with people you know; then you maybe work with a casting director. They will look further afield among people they know, or go wider, talking to other casting agencies. So, you start putting together a list of people and depending what level they are at, you either hold auditions or send out a contract."

Michael Duffy. Producer, AltoAtlantic Films

### 43) HOW I DO IT…

"One of the hardest things is to try to get people to come from London to Birmingham for auditions. Actors don't want to get on a train for two hours for an audition. Sometimes you see three people and you find the one you want as quickly as that, sometimes you see 25 and what you want just isn't there. Rather than have people coming in and having a quick cold reading, I send people pages in advance and when they come in for audition, I'll talk to them. It's usually by talking to them and discussing the character that I can figure out who's appropriate."

Sarah Walker. Director, Almost Strangers

### 44) WHY CASTING DIRECTORS?

"You get a better quality. Instead of being in a casting room and looking at hundreds of actors you get to see about 30. I've seen hundred of actors in castings before and never got anywhere, never found the people we needed. With a casting director, they bring a knowledge and a professionalism to the project. You get a corps of actors from whom to pick and choose, so you are not wasting tons of time on casting. Using their knowledge, a casting director knows who to bring in. Then they help you choose the ones you need to get the right balance, the right appeal on screen. Casting is very important. What is the point of spending six months hard on a project and then not getting the right cast? The cast is where you can live and die on your shoot."

Dean Fisher. Producer, Ten Minutes

### 45) LIVE-IN CASTING

"Al I had met relatively recently and had been trying to write material for him. On this project I managed to keep the number of his scenes down while keeping him a central character. While we shot the project we shared a house together, and a lot of the scenes were shot in this house. He was willing not only to put all of his feelings about events in his personal life into his preparation for this role, but to work for love rather than money.

The rest of the cast was made up of people whom I had met while studying drama at University and subsequently as a teacher. All of them were keen to appear in any film and also worked for free."

Ben Hughes-Games. Director, A Slice of Life

## CREWING

### 46) PERSUASION

"Well we have this wonderful Shooting People you know! I said this is going to be the project, it is going to be in India and if you can afford to pay your way and would not mind working four or five days for free and take a holiday afterwards, here's a script, read it and come along. I am pleased to say that holiday wasn't really the attraction for most people. They read the script and were very interested in it and that's what swayed them."

Ashvin Kumar. Director, The Road To Ladakh

## 47) YOU ARE IN SHOT!

" Two cameras, so two people on camera and one holding the microphone and the person with the microphone was usually playing in front of one of the lenses. And of course the cameras get in each other's shots. The cast absolutely loved it because they could act out whole scenes rather than do things in fragramentary fashion. We did not even need to go back and do cutaways because with two cameras running, we already had them!"

John Williams. Producer, Diary of a Bad Lad

## 48) A ONE MAN BAND....

" I did the DP, directed, did the camera work and I handled the sound because I have a recording studio and as a photographer as well, I set up all the lighting. But I did need people to help me, even just to carry stuff and for continuity..."

Ian Vernon. Director, Actors

## 49) DRIVEN BY HUNGER

"I picked everybody who was hungry. Some had worked on big budget films and some on other medium budget features, but a lot of films don't go anywhere. This was something fresh they were all excited about, so all the crew were so into it. Right down to the sparks, they went the extra mile."

David Paul Baker. Director, Pasty Faces

## 50) OPERATING ALONE

"As far as crewing was concerned, that was easy. I knew that I would be operating the camera myself, that I could not afford a professional sound recordist and, that in any case, we would have no time to give them the room to work they would need. I was very impressed with the on-camera mic of the old Nikon Hi-8 camera I had borrowed. Whenever possible, I shot the dialogue with the actors in close up. When this was not possible, I had them deliver their dialogue into the microphone in as similar a way as possible to the visual take, right next to the camera microphone. The ADR will be done using the Final Cut Express voice-over tool. Since I was lighting with natural light and practical bulbs, I was a one-man crew."

Ben Hughes-Games. Director, A Slice of Life

## 51) CHERRY-PICKING

"I handpicked a cast and crew of people I had seen both in Britain and in Ireland, who I felt were not getting the opportunity to express themselves in the film industry. You know, when you have people like that around you, they are hungry. They were able to express themselves and find ways around."

Karl Golden. Director, The Honeymooners

## 52) IF YOU NEED SHOOTING PEOPLE...

"I had worked with the DP before, but pretty well everyone else came thorough Shooting People. You get tons of CVs and you get the opportunity to pick the best. You will rarely get Heads of Department that have worked in that position on feature shoots for six or seven weeks, but you WILL get people below that position looking to gain some experience in the role they want to move into. When they have had solid experience on a feature shoot before, then you will get a professional crew together. We simply could not have made this film without Shooting People. I can't recommend them highly enough."

Dean Fisher. Producer, Ten Minutes

# ROLLING...

## 53) SACRED DAYS

"The typical working day was from nine to five each Monday to Friday. Weekends were religiously guarded as days off. In general I shot two scenes a day punctuated by a lunch break. This pace provided a good working compromise between getting the necessary coverage shooting from alternate angles, not out-staying our welcome in someone's property and respecting the cast/crews stamina."

Kenneth D Barker. Director, Rosetta: Prima Donna Assoluta

## 54) THE CLOCK IS TICKING...

"If you're shooting on low/no/micro budgets, even if you do have some kind of budget, you must be organised. If you have to get a scene in the can by noon, you HAVE to make sure that everything and everyone you need is there at the call time ready to shoot... There is no way we could have shot the film in two weeks without this thorough preparation. I visited every location with the AD and roughly blocked out each scene to ensure that we would not waste time in between set-ups wondering what shot was next."

Sean Martin. Director, The Notebooks of Cornelius Crow

## 55) SOUND ADVICE

"The thing that lets most low budget productions down is the sound quality; so if you do not know much about sound yourself, get somebody who is very good with sound. And if anybody uses radio mikes, make sure they switch off their mobile phones! There are lots of shots that get spoiled by bleeps caused by someone's mobile going off, even if it is set just to vibrate."

Ian Vernon. Director, Actors

## 56) SOUNDS HORRENDOUS

"Sound is so important to a movie. Many new film makers ignore it completely. We were very conscious to make sure that we had an extremely full soundtrack full of atmos. We wanted the tower block in the movie to be its own character so we gave it a constant breathing atmos. You can hardly hear it but it's there adding to the underlying tension. The pipes in the building would have their own throbbing atmos and we would search and search and search for strange animal sounds to add to the mix."

Genevieve Jolliffe. Director, Urban Ghost Story

### 57) RADIO, RADIO

" We were less fortunate with the sound gear. The DAT machine kept playing up and the radio mikes regularly let us down. If you're going to use radios a lot, make sure you hire expensive ones - the cheap ones are always more trouble than they're worth."

Sean Martin. Director, The Notebooks of Cornelius Crow

### 58) UNNATURAL LIGHT

"Every camera operator who has landed here has been surprised by how much stop-down is needed, yet they are still in the United Kingdom, not some tropic isle with overhead sun and cloudless skies. At these latitudes (about the same as Anchorage, Alaska) there is no atmospheric pollution, so Shetland light is exceptionally clear and bright. The sun's arc is fairly low, especially in winter. Everything it touches seems to be more uplit than downlit, giving an unusual not-of-this-world look to everyday features. It looks uncanny"

Leslie Lowes. Producer, Penultimate Films & Features

### 59) EGOTISTICS

"You also cannot afford to lose ANY time, so anything that will cause a delay - and over-inflated egos always cause delays - must be kept off the shoot, or kept in control. If you think that someone will be a prima donna on set, don't get them involved. Get someone else."

Sean Martin. Director, The Notebooks of Cornelius Crow

### 60) MORE IS BETTER

"Shoot far more than you need. Shoot other angles. A lot of people forget to shoot cutaways. In case they need an edit half way through a scene where half that scene's bad, but half is good and they need to use cutaways to slice two good halves together."

Ian Vernon. Director, Actors

### 61) HELLO DOLLY

"The dolly was so bad we had to take it back. It looked like something out of Bob the Builder, only wasn't yellow. You couldn't keep it in a straight line, and when someone got on it, it tilted under their weight. After getting shot of it, we had to improvise with the moving shots. For one shot, our dolly was actually a swivel chair as it was the only thing we could find that had wheels on it. It worked quite well, actually!"

Sean Martin. Director, The Notebooks of Cornelius Crow

## CLOSE-UPS

### 62) DIRECTOR'S STYLE

"One of the early mistakes I made was in trying to develop a style. I think that is something people out of film school and new filmmakers often try to do, but really, that's not something you can develop purposefully. It is something that just happens because you learn to trust the voice that is talking to you from inside you know. That's one of the things I learned on Road to Ladkh. Style is not something you can create. It either happens or it doesn't happen."

Ashvin Kumar. Director, The Road to Ladakh

## 63) SAFETY IN NUMBERS

"Even if you are not the most experienced person there (and I am assuming that people reading this will be directors or producers), make sure you have a crew who ARE. A novice director will be fine provided their DP is good, and also have a good 1st AD and Production Manager."

Sean Martin. Director, The Notebooks of Cornelius Crow

## 64) PRODUCER'S INSIGHT

"I had always wanted to direct, and producing was an amazing way to learn the ropes before actually being on set directing. It also gave me a good insight into having to work around shots that would be too expensive to do, and therefore it forced you to look for ingenious ways to get that shot you wanted."

Genevieve Jolliffe. Director, Urban Ghost Story

## 65) PICTURE THIS

"All that changeable weather does wonderful things to Shetland skies. The dawns and the sunsets will rank among the most spectacular you have ever seen. The clouds can pile up in huge billowing masses like stacks of enormous cream cakes. They can stratify and take on a streaky bacon appearance, or they can disappear and just leave miles and miles of blue, tinting the greens greener, enriching every colour around - and all free!"

Leslie Lowes. Producer, Penultimate Films & Features

## 66) WE'LL MOVE LOCATIONS...

"The movie storyline developed by accident. I was checking out locations in Scotland to shoot it cheaply and I got turned down by a big casino. I said "To hell with it, we'll shoot it in Vegas!" (They did!- JMc)

David Paul Baker. Director, Pasty Faces

## 67) SMELLERVISION

"By the time production starts, I know the characters intimately and how they will interlink in the completed film. The story's logic has to be robust - this gives me the confidence to say when something is wrong or right within that context. If you cannot smell your own film as a director on set, the cast will probably eat you alive!"

Kenneth D Barker. Director, Rosetta: Prima Donna Assoluta

## 68) POLITE NETWORK

"If you hit it off with someone (e.g. a producer or distributor), they will see you as someone who might have a great film inside them somewhere down the line, and will want to keep in touch with you. Once you have made those contacts, keep in touch. Let people know what you are doing. Be friendly, polite, chatty. Courtesy doesn't cost anything and it is always appreciated and remembered."

Sean Martin. Director, The Notebooks of Cornelius Crow

## 69) TRUST NO ONE

"I have been too trusting too often. There are excellent people out there who will help you unconditionally and then there are others who will try to take you for everything you've got.

They will smile at you, look you in the eye and LIE to you. Personally, I think it is very sad and totally unnecessary, but there are a lot of selfish people out there and, unfortunately, it's just the way it is. Use your gut feelings. Every time I didn't listen to mine, I regretted it."

Piotr Szkopiak. Director, Small Time Obsession

### 70) CLOSE HARMONY

"I needed very generous people because it was a pretty risky project. We didn't have much of a script so we would re jig certain scenes while we were shooting, if I'd been with normal British professionals it would have been a nightmare. They would have wanted a perfect script and just executed the plan whereas I had a tiny documentary group who all lived in one house and they were all very, very supportive. They all believed in me and the film and it was a great pleasure to work with them. I think it is reflected in the film because there is a chamber-like, organic feel to it."

Pawel Pawlikowsky. Director, The Last Resort

### 71) MURDER MOST FOUL

"Murder your darlings, especially during post. You need to cut your film as tightly and as pacily as possible."

Sean Martin. Director, The Notebooks of Cornelius Crow

### 72) QUESTION EVERYTHING

"Of course we all feel more comfortable having taken advice from more experienced people. But be careful. Making a film is your chance to express yourself in a creative way, so don't let anyone cramp your style. Especially don't just accept that you have to spend money. The exciting thing about the new home filmmaking technology is that it challenges you to use the tools it gives you and make a film. Your camcorder and editing programme will have all kinds of great features. They will also have a lot of completely useless ones to be avoided by all but makers of wedding videos. Find ways to use the good ones to express your ideas. On this film, I didn't have a problem ignoring advice because all the advice I received was delivered in such a patronising way. It made me just go out and shoot whatever I thought was cool and not listen to anyone else. "Can you really, feasibly, make a film of any merit for less than £100,000?" Watch me."

Ben Hughes-Games. Director, A Slice of Life

## WORKING WITH ACTORS

### 73) UNDERSTANDING CHARACTER

"With good actors you can get them to do amazing things, because they understand what the character could and should be doing. They bring so much to it, a huge percent already, so when I'm directing a scene and I say "OK I want to touch this a little more this way, or a little more that way", or "I want to make this a little less intense or a little more funny", or "Maybe this is a little too aggressive." I can give them just a few notes here and there and they will respond to that. They are like athletes - good actors will respond and come up with other things."

Alison Peebles. Director, Afterlife

### 74) IMPROVISATION

"The hard thing on a low budget film is finding space to afford a lot of improvisation without knocking things out of schedule. What I did not want, was to improvise the way a lot of people do; to improvise, turn that into script and give that back to the actors and then record that. I wanted the spontaneity of improvisation, which creates a different kind of naturalism. It can be quite fragile, because things can go wrong, but it is much more realistic to look at, especially if we are talking, as this is, about a black comedy; about things you would not normally associate with laughter."

Chris Cooke. Director, One For the Road

### 75) ALT WRITING TECHNIQUES?

"I have always shot on DV. You develop a technique working with actors which allows you to use a certain amount of improvisation; a certain structure of writing and working. I can't think of any other way to work to be honest. With my films there are three stages of writing; there's writing the script, then there's the shoot, where I start re-writing the script in terms of the improvisation. Finally, there's the edit, where working on DV means you can go out and get pickups or new sequences, which are not expensive to do if you structure and plan for them."

Chris Cooke. Director, One For The Road

### 76) NO PRESSURE

"Actors always want more rehearsal, especially if they are used to theatre. This was the whinge I always heard when I made my first film. Rehearsal is necessary. You need to let the actors play with the characters without the pressure of having to get fifty five shots by breakfast, or whatever. The ideal is that you have at least an idea of what your actors are like as actors. Some people don't feel confident committing to camera unless they've spent months discussing every psychological and physical aspect of the character with you and "workshopping", whatever that means. Others will learn their lines, find what interests them about the character and become bored if you do more than two takes of any line."

Ben Hughes-Games. Director, A Slice of Life

## MEALBREAK CALL

### 77) WHAT'S COOKING?

"The day I enjoyed most was the day in the garden. Everyone was having a good time and it was nice to be out in the open air all day, despite the fact that the food that day was awful. You know your catering is bad when the entire camera department go to McDonald's."

Sean Martin. Director, The Notebooks of Cornelius Crow

### 78) HOT TABLES FOR COLD DAYS

"Where at this location could you erect the hot table? That is the place where there's an urn always on the boil, coffee, chocolate, teabags, potnoodle, biscuits, fruit, mineral water and fruit juice available for tea-breaks or whenever someone needs a warming or cooling drink or snack. These things are essential after a few hours of intensive filming, but where would you plan to put them? And what about mealtimes? Where are your cast and crew going to eat their meal when dinner break is called?"

Leslie Lowes. Producer, Penultimate Films & Features

### 79) LIMITED MENU

"I spelled out very clearly the kind of conditions they would have to live in, in tents. Even though these were pretty luxurious tents, they were not five star hotels. The food situation had to be explained clearly; that there would be a very limited number of dishes."

Ashvin Kumar. Director, The Road To Ladakh

### 80) REMOTE CATERING

"Osla's Café, one of Shetland's favourite bistro bars, consistently came in on time and on budget with the hot nourishing meals our filmmakers needed. Good varied menus, making best use of local products and catering for everyone, from those of vegetarian persuasion, to the downright starving. Locally, there are no mobile film catering vans and dining buses of the kind that usually follow film shoots around, but Shetland does have its public hall network, with a modern hall in each community that has full catering and dining facilites for functions like weddings and dances, To that list of uses we have added feeding film crews and everyone agreed; the food was marvellous."

Leslie Lowes. Producer, Penultimate Films & Features

## GOING TO MARKET

### 81) SELF HARM

"It all boils down to this. The film market is complicated and not easy to work in. Crashing about in it, without a clear idea about what you are doing, may well cause you, and your project, harm. If you have not got a distributor, try and get one, or take the best distribution advice you can find, but don't just launch yourself into the market unprepared."

David Nicholas Wilkinson. Distributor, Guerilla Films

### 82) PRESENT YOUR PRODUCT WELL

"Originality makes for a good film, professionalism will sell it. You should have 20-25% of your budget allocated for marketing. put it together in a proper package, which has information about the filmmakers and the DVD is in a proper box and you can get a simple design done, it makes people pay attention and looks more professional."

Tom Swanston. Producer, The Ultimate Truth

### 83) SPECIFIC FOCUS

"We have been very specific about what we want to achieve with the release. We could have gone much wider but we would have lost a lot of money. This way we focused everyone into two cinemas, got our reviews and got out with great screen averages."

Chris Jones. Producer, Urban Ghost Story

### 84) DIGITAL COMES OUT

"It's up to all DV-filmmakers to get involved in shaping the future for digital exhibition. We are not against transferring DV to film, not in the least, provided that the maths add up. Top quality transfer costs around £50,000 or more, and after that there's the print costs. Now if you look at the chart in the Guerrilla Film Makers Blueprint detailing the UK box office gross for all UK films released in 2001, most of them would not have netted enough to recoup the transfer costs."

John Williams. Producer, Diary of a Bad Lad

### 85) SELFISH? MOI?

"You have to think of the marketing. There is this attitude that some people have, especially in personal films, "Oh I don't care if only one person sees it!" What's the point of that? We are in an industry that is there to entertain, or inform, inspire, it's a bit selfish to solely make it for yourself. A film is not a film without a room packed full of people."

David Paul Baker. Director, Pasty Faces

### 86) TROUBLE AHEAD

"Once a film is launched you have just 12 months before a whole raft of new films come along and your film becomes a back catalogue item in your Sales Agents portfolio. If you have announced completion to everyone and you do not have a sales agent after 12 months, then you are in trouble."

David Nicholas Wilkinson. Distributor, Guerilla Films

### 87) UNIMAGINATIVE DISTRIBUTORS

"Few, if any, UK distributors have the resources and imagination to acquire independent commercial material and find new sell-through markets. It is a buyers market and a lot of high quality independently produced British films never see light of day, for all the wrong reasons."

Kenneth D Barker. Director, Kingdom

### 88) PROOF OF THE PUDDING

"The thing is that, like it or not, filmmaking is a business and if you make someone money they will come back for more. If filmmakers want cinemas or video shops to take more small, independent UK films, they will have to prove that there is a market for these films. If no one goes to see these films in the cinema, no one rents them from the video shop and no one buys them on DVD, then why would the cinemas and the shops want another one."

Piotr Szkopiak. Director, Small Time Obsession

### 89) POSTCARD WHISPERS

"Even if you still have not got your film into a festival, register as a delegate and go to them all the same and start spreading the word about your film. Get postcards printed up. Do all you can to get the marketing campaign going, and learn how to talk your film up."

Sean Martin. Director, The Notebooks of Cornelius Crow

### 90) STREET WALKER

"I got situated around Soho in a 20-quid-a-night stinky bedsit, and captured a yellow pages with film company addresses. I pounded the streets, occasionally walking into soft porn production companies by accident. On my last day, I almost gave up. I then got a meeting with Victor Films. They gave me twenty minutes but most of the time it was hard to get people just to sit down and listen so I pitched it as if I was making Citizen Kane!"

David Paul Baker. Director, Pasty Faces

### 91) CREATING BUZZ

"Bucket loads of cash to create the demand always works. All the time. However, there are things you can do with the internet that can help. Look at the guys who did Blair Witch - that film was made on its internet marketing. There are several film makers who've made short films on crazy subjects such as George Lucas in Love, a ten minute short that you can see on the internet which caused such a buzz these guys now have a feature film deal. Talking in chat rooms and creating a buzz is always a good thing. And make sure you have a good website where you can view your movies, or clips - the US is now more or less constantly on DSL so it's very easy to tap in to the screen of some big movie exec if you create enough buzz."

Genevieve Jolliffe. Director, Urban Ghost Story

### 92) POT BOILING

"It is no use just sending the broadcaster a tape and hoping to sell your film to them. I like to get them excited about the film, so I get a nice piece in The Guardian and a couple of other nationals, to get the pot boiling. Then I can go to them with some publicity extracts that get them hooked. Get them interested, then we can talk business."

David Nicholas Wilkinson. Distributor, Guerilla Films

## OUCH!

### 93) STAYING ALIVE

"Staying alive is the hardest thing and I hope that in the next few years something will happen that will set us both up so that we can afford to develop projects over a number of years instead of always fighting to put food on the table."

Chris Jones. Producer, Urban Ghost Story

### 94) YOU ARE MY INSPIRATION

" I was trying to shoot a long scene like Woody Allen would. You know, you shoot a scene with no edits in it. You have four areas within a bar, where conversations are going on, so they are all choreographed and the trouble with this actor was, every time we came to her, she kept fluffing her lines up, so in the end we just had to call it a day and recast."

Ian Vernon. Director, Actors

### 95) STRESSBUSTER

"The worst moment? Probably the first day I had chest pains, when we weren't sure if the money was going to be in the bank by 5pm. If it was, we were shooting, if not, we were packing up and going home."

Sean Martin. Director, the Notebooks of Cornelius crow

## 96) GREAT EXPECTATIONS

"Expect everything to go wrong. People expect standard things to go wrong, but in India you must apply that to every single thing. If someone says he will be there at 2.00 o'clock, expect him at 3.30. Discount everything you hear by about one-and-a-half times. If someone says something will be ready, discount that by one-and-a-half times, because it will not be ready, not at the time you think it is going to be ready. Dubiously, it might be ready somewhat later."

Ashvin Kumar. Director, The Road To Ladakh

## 97) BEWARE OF THE BULL

"I found a private investor who said if we got the Glasgow side shot, he would finance the shoot in the States. We shot on digital betacam for three weeks, faking some US-style interiors where we could. I believed I had a really good script and I could have hawked it round companies, but we all believed we had to keep moving with it. So, if the money fell through, at least I would have some terrific scenes for trailer material. The money did fall through, at least on the States side, because the guy was basically a bullshitter."

David Paul Baker. Director, Pasty Faces

## 98) TRAVELLING SHOW

"Our unit base was in Glasgow, so that meant we had forty minutes there and forty minutes drive back and that took an hour-and-a-half out of our shooting day, every day, for two weeks."

Alison Peebles. Director, Afterlife

## 99) HEALTH & SAFETY

"Other hazardous places include windy cliff tops – we put cast and crew on out-of-shot waist ropes tied to 4x4s. The wind would have real problems blowing those over the cliffs!"

Leslie Lowes. Producer, Penultimate Films & Features

## 100) SPIRITED PERFORMANCE

" We lost two of our actors. They were living in a house we provided. We went there looking for them and they were in the Jacuzzi - in splendidly hospitable state, together with two women they had found the previous evening, all well in their cups. It seems they had been drinking all night. They were not exactly prepared for filming, but we just had to press ahead."

Tom Swanston. Producer, The Ultimate Truth

## 101) DIY DISTRIBUTION

"The big problem I had when I started distributing just my own films was that everyone - and I mean everyone - thought that I was having to do this because no one else would take the film, therefore it must be really bad. It is perception again. The only people who publish their own books are those that nobody else will take. Its called vanity publishing. The same assumption is made of self-distribution."

David Nicholas Wilkinson. Distributor, Guerrilla Films

# Case studies

## Transatlantic Experience – *Clerks; The Living End; El Mariachi*

In 1992, three young filmmakers proved that exceptional features can be made for less than the cost of a mediocre short. With plenty of creativity, ingenuity, determination and almost no money, these writers-directors made outstanding features that gained festival success, critical acclaim and US national distribution. *Laws of Gravity* ($38,000) and *El Mariachi* ($7,225) were first features that launched the careers of Nick Gomez and Robert Rodriguez spectacularly. *The Living End* ($22,769) was a third feature that boosted Gregg Araki to a new level of prominence and opportunity. Some shorts can cost $100,000 but these features were made for a fraction of that sum. Not only that, but these full length features had greater festival play and wider distribution than most successful shorts, while showcasing their directors' talents most effectively.

### KEVIN SMITH'S CLERKS

Clerks was the feature with the lowest budget in competition at the 1994 Sundance Film Festival. Its 23-year-old director- Kevin Smith made it for $27,575.

**BUDGET FOR CLERKS**

| | |
|---|---|
| **STOCK** | |
| 37 400ft rolls Kodak Double X Negative | $1600.00 |
| Nagra tapes | $200.00 |
| Camera expendables | $125.00 |
| **EQUIPMENT RENTALS** | |
| Insurance | $730.00 |
| Camera | $3400.00 |
| Sound and three lights | $1165.00 |
| **PROCESSING** | |
| Negative and work print | $3295.00 |
| Nagra rolls to mag stock transfers | $980.00 |
| **EDITING** | |
| Steenbeck/guillotine rental (3 months) | $940.00 |
| Editing expendables | $220.00 |
| Negative cut | $1830.00 |
| **MIXING** | |
| Slop print for mix | $900.00 |
| Sound mix and all sound related services | $7280.00 |
| **PRINT** | |
| Titles and animation | $800.00 |
| Optical | $990.00 |
| Screening print | $3120.00 |
| **Grand Total:** | **$27,575** |

## ARAKI'S THE LIVING END

Araki was experienced in making $5,000 features so his producers, Marcus Hu and Jon Gerrans of Strand Releasing, were confident that The Living End could be made for $20,000. Starting with a family loan, production began. Money was raised in bits and pieces along the way including some from a private investor. Toward the end of post-production Araki received a $20,000 American Film Institute grant which covered more than 85% of the budget.

### PRODUCTION EXPENSES

| | |
|---|---|
| Lights: Lowell lighting kit (rental) | $390 |
| Lenses: prime (rental) | $1200 |
| Props: guns (rental): | $150 |
| Food: | $1800 |
| sub-total: | $3540 |
| **STOCK** | |
| Film stock: 16mm color Kodak 7296. 12,000 ft = 30 rolls @ 5 106.5&- roll minus discount plus tax: | $2654 |
| Cassette tapes: production sound: | $50 |
| DAT tapes: post-production sound: | $50 |
| 1/2" tape: post-production sound: | $100 |
| sub-total: | $2854 |
| **POST-PRODUCTION EXPENSES** | |
| Editing supplies: | $50 |
| Dialogue editing, sound effects recording and editing, music recording and editing, ADR, looping and final sound mix, all done digitally with computer and 3/4" videotape, flat deal | $5000 |
| sub-total | $5050 |
| **SERVICES** | |
| Edge code: 24.000 ft x .0 15c -discount + tax | $326 |
| Negative cut. flat deal: | $1,000 |
| Film to 3/4" videotape transfer. Incl. stock. for post-prod sound mix: | $350 |
| DAT to mag transfer used to make optical from: | $400 |
| Optical Track: | $1500 |
| sub-total: | $3576 |
| **TITLES** | |
| Lithography | $150 |
| Processing and printing: | $50 |
| sub-total: | $200 |

LAB

| | |
|---|---|
| Workprint: (250c x 12,000 ft) | $3000 |
| 1st Answer print: (83c x 3240 ft) | $2689 |
| Release print: (37c x 3240: (wet gate made from original A x B roll negative) | $1277 |
| Check print: (18 c x 3,240 ft) | $583 |
| sub-total | $7549 |
| **Grand Total:** | **$22,769** |

## ROBERT RODRIGUEZ'S EL MARIACHI

El Mariachi 's financing (Rodriguez underwent medical tests to raise the money), micro budget and subsequent Hollywood success has become the stuff of legend.

STOCK

| | |
|---|---|
| 12 400 ft rolls-Kodak 7292 (indoor): | $1,140 |
| 13 400 ft roll-Kodak 7248 (outdoor): | $1,170 |
| 1 100 ft test roll (B+W): | $19 |
| sub-total: | $2,329 |

PROCESSING

| | |
|---|---|
| 25 400 ft roll, (13c per foot): | $1,300 |
| 1 100 ft test roll: | $23 |
| sub-total: | $323 |

EQUIPMENT

| | |
|---|---|
| 2 clip-on modeling lamps: | $60 |
| 7 bulbs: | $67 |
| sub-total: | $127 |

MISCELLANEOUS

| | |
|---|---|
| Acting fees: | $225 |
| Used guitar case: | $16 |
| 3 sheets diffuser gels: | $15 |
| 25 squibs: | $50 |
| Blanks (machine gun): | $50 |
| Fake blood, condoms (for squibs), gaffer tape, lens cleaner kit, extra bulb: | $122 |
| 4 rolls 35mm production still film: | $18 |
| 10 Maxell 11 audio cassettes: | $23 |
| 6 197 Ampex 3/4" BLA 60s: | $103 |
| sub-total: | $622 |

POST PRODUCTION

| | |
|---|---|
| Video transfer with overall color correction (28c per foot)* | |
| **Grand Total:** | **$7,225** |

# Chris Kentis & Laura Lau
# *Open Water*

*Writer/Director Chris Curtis and Producer Laura Lau took a based-on-true-events killer premise – a couple scuba diving in tropical waters is mistakenly abandoned – and turned it into a gripping thriller. Actors Blanchard Ryan and Daniel Travis spent 120 hours in the water and since prosthetic sharks were not an option at the $120,000 dollar level, the shark roles were played by the real thing.*

**How did the idea for this film come to you?**
CK: The initial idea was that because of the new DV technology that existed and was affordable, we were very excited about the idea that we could afford to make and finance films ourselves, and have total creative control. I guess we were very inspired by the Dogme 95 films and the success they were having. Now, at the same time, Laura and I we're married, we've been together many years, and we're recreational divers, we'd been divers for 10 or 11 years and we get all the diving newsletters and everything, and it was in the late 1990s [1998] that we heard about the very specific story that this film was based on, where a couple on vacation went out on a dive boat, and were accidentally left in the water. When I first read about that incident I had a very strong, upsetting, emotional response. Then, I guess around 2000/2001, we decided to make a digital film, and we thought this would be a story that worked very well in that format.

LL: You know digital imparts a very distinct look, a very distinct aesthetic, it gives a very strong sense of realism, so, first of all, we felt that making a digital feature and telling this story on that format would push the format into an area it hadn't been before. We live in New York and a lot of digital features are shot here, and we were thinking, 'What could we do that would be different?' So, once we decided that this story would be well suited to this medium, Chris wrote a script. Shooting in this format, we knew we were going to work with unknown actors, and we knew we were going to have to work with live sharks.

CK: And the reason behind the unknown actors is because we thought the way to make this story work was to make it as real as possible. That's why we used digital video. Working with recognisable stars would have shattered that illusion of reality, and, you know, at the same, we wanted to work out in the ocean, shooting in a documentary fashion. Pretty much everything you see that comes out of Hollywood today, the effects are all computer-generated, and everything in this film is real. We're working with real sharks, and there's a real difference; you're seeing something real on the screen interacting with the actors, and we thought the video format would drive that home even more.

**What expectations did you have when you were making it?**
CK: One of the challenges that appealed to us was that we were going to wear all the hats here and work without a crew and be doing everything ourselves. For 90% of the shoot it was just Laura and I and the two actors; occasionally her sister would be there as well. The exception was just the two out of six weeks we spent with the sharks, in which case we used professional shark experts that are used to working with sharks in film productions. We worked with them for two days. The bulk of the shoot was just us.

LL: It took us quite a few years to make this movie and since we came out with it, we finished it and we went to a couple of festivals, the response has been incredible. It has been fantastic and surprising to us.

CK: The reactions and comparisons have been surprising to us because we didn't want to do things in a way that we had seen done before. We tried to approach how we were going to structure this story a little bit differently and we didn't really have anything to lose. In a lot of ways we kind of saw this as a little bit more of an experiment.

LL: It's been so gratifying to hear the reactions from film festivalgoers, from divers, from the dive industry, from some of the general public. A lot still remains to be seen.

**Do you have clearly defined roles when you work together?**

CK: I'm listed as the writer and the director of the film and Laura's the producer, and, you know, one of the main reasons for that is I did write it and direct it, and I was the one who was very passionate about this story. It was my idea to make it, it was a vision of mine to do this; I don't think it was a story that Laura was terribly interested in telling. That said, as far as the process and how we worked, we did everything together. I wrote the first draft of this very quickly in six days, I went back and did a little polish, then I brought it to Laura and from that point on, we were working together. Getting that script to the point where it needs to be. We brought the actors on board, got to know them, then once we really understood who we had cast, and what we wanted to do with the characters, we went and wrote all the dialogue tailored for this cast. Then, in the production process, I was doing a lot of producing, Laura's doing a lot of directing, we both shot the film ourselves, and we both basically crewed the film ourselves, so it was interchangeable what we did there. Laura was directing the actors and getting a performance out of them as much as I was. So we really shared all duties. This is what's so special and wonderful about how we worked together.

LL: I think we had slightly different interests in what we wanted to focus on.

CK: Well I think that was great and that meant our different strengths were used here. One of the things that I was interested in had to do with structure and the challenges. Once again I didn't want to put in any side stories or sub plots, I just wanted to be in the water with these two people and keep it interesting. The challenge for me was to take two characters and put them in the ocean and stay with them, and hopefully not just hold the audience's attention but take them on this journey that would really be gripping and riveting and emotionally they'd have that same response that I had when I read the real story. In Laura's case, there was a lot of things as far as character, relationships and depth of those things that she brings to the table.

LL: There was an overlap but my focus would be more on the characters' journeys, their relationship, and what's happening to them psychologically and emotionally.

CK: As the director, because I'm an editor by trade, I have an understanding of what we needed coverage-wise to make sure that the film would cut together when we were done. But we're different individuals with a different aesthetic, and there was a definite overall aesthetic, a definite plan to how it should be shot that was appropriate to this story, but within that framework, it was great that we were both shooting because there were the shots that we had assigned so that we had coverage on the scenes, and then there were those extra shots that we needed to get texture. Certainly when we'd come back each day and look at the dailies, and especially when I sat down to edit, I was going, 'Oh God', I don't know how many times there was this amazing shot that Laura took and I wouldn't have thought of getting, that just brought the whole thing together and really rescued the moment. So, you know, I think we really complement each other. It takes so much time to make a movie and it can really overwhelm and become your life, so to be able to share that with your wife and your family is really special and important.

**Is it easy to separate your professional and your private life? If you have an argument about a professional matter can that spill over into your relationship, and vice versa?**

LL: I have to say we had so little conflict. I think because we're so in sync with each other, and because we respect each other so much, we really listen well. There's no real ego clashing going on. I can't even think of an incident where we didn't come to some agreement or some understanding about what the choice should be. Because it was spread out period of time, it wasn't like we were intensely in production for a continuous period of time. In fact I think we've worked more consistently hard on this film since Sundance, because of the release, because of the press, and everything else. It's taken over more now than it did before.

CK: In the same way that I was the driving force behind this film, a lot of projects that we're looking at now, a lot of opportunities have come our way and it's difficult to decide what we're going to do next, but certainly the one we're most excited about, if we can ever get time again, Laura is very close to finishing a script and her vision is very different to this film, in which case she would be the director/writer and I would take on the producing title. Hopefully that would be the next one, or the one after that.

**There's no way you could have made a film like this at a studio.**

CK: Yeah, I think if we went to the studio and said, 'Look, there has to be unknown actors, we have to shoot on digital video, we're shooting just in one location, with no back story, with no sub-plot, with nothing dramatic about them being revealed,' forget it. This is what was so ironic to us. I don't think anyone would have gone for this movie in a million years and now that it's done, it's like, 'Why didn't you come to us?' So we're thrilled that so many people are excited about it. We feel really honoured and lucky that that's the case and we don't take that for granted. Also, Laura and I have been working together for about 15 years, so this is not an overnight success story. This has been the result of a lot of long, hard work in educating ourselves. We didn't just come out of film school. It's been a process and it will continue to be a process. So as far as making this film in the studio system, I don't think it would have been possible. And certainly a lot of things we're interested in, we're definitely interested in working independently. But at the same time, we're going to rule anything out right now. We're ruling a lot of things out right now, but when an opportunity comes in we're open to looking at it. You know, if nothing comes in, we're just going to stick to the plan we have. If the movie bombs and nothing comes in, so be it. We're going to continue on our merry way to do what's important to us and work in a way that we had on this.

*Interview by Stephen Applebaum*

## ECONOMIES OF SCALE

Looking across the whole spectrum of low budget filmmaking, there appears to be little in principle separating low budget features from low budget short films, except length.

If a short can be shot over a week, a feature will take longer, but the budget increases in multiples of a week, give or take a few adjustments. The techniques that contain costs are common to both forms. The short film, overall, costs less, making shorts a good proving ground for tomorrow's talent to cut its filmmaking teeth without insolvency looming.

The short film is not a truncated feature, but a film form in its own right. Good low budget short filmmakers are aware of this and play to its strengths of brevity and surprise, while using ingenuity to keep costs down.

# Richard Heald &James Kibbey
# *In Absentia - no budget short*

*Heald and Kibbey were students at Nottingham University in a house-share and discovered they both had a yearning to make films. Their Opus One was, in their own words, crap. Undaunted, but somewhat chastened by their maiden effort they decided to make amends and make something far better, but with only the resources available to them. The 6-minute film that resulted was chosen from 4,000 other films to win the TriggerStreet film festival.*

In Absentia follows the last precious moments of a young person whose life has suddenly ended. The film is an innovative yet evocative study of suicide, but most of all it shows how love can transcend loneliness, fear and even death. The film was shot in reverse. Rather than be restricted by their lack of fancy equipment the two directors made a feature of it. Their iMac computer included iMovie, the basic editing package, which has a reverse button. This became the defining feature of In Absentia.

**How did you hit upon the idea of telling a story in reverse?**

JK A year earlier I had made a video for a friend's 21st birthday and had opened the film by setting the invitation alight and then playing this backwards so that the invitation arose from the ashes and 'unburned' to fill the screen. So, we knew backwards motion could be visually interesting and cost nothing to do. We also knew that we had to craft a script with minimal actors and locations. It gradually became the story of a man's suicide process shown backwards.

RH We made a list of what not to do, and what we had available. IMovie has a simple reverse effect button we started to play with, from which the concept of a suicide in reverse emerged. We limited the majority of the shoot to a single room to give us maximum control of how it looked, and also designed the story to unfold without dialogue. This was basically because we had no decent sound equipment, but we also turned it into an opportunity to learn more about telling a story with images alone.

**What equipment were you able to use and how did that effect the film?**

JK We knew we had access to a Canon XL1 and iMovie on a Mac. We already knew that it was easy to reverse footage on iMovie and this was obviously one of the main influences. We also had a smoke machine from a couple of house parties we'd thrown, which proved to be a crucial weapon in the look of the film.

RH We had a mate's bedroom that we confined ourselves to for the most part and put a lot of energy into making it look realistic. Pete Sciazza acted as a gaffer, lending us the lights he used for photography. The smoke machine was one of our best pieces of equipment. It was like adding instant atmosphere, and diffused that video look quite well. We also used a wheelchair to get tracking shots, they were a little shaky, but did the job.

**What technical issues did you feel you needed to be most aware of during shooting?**

RH Backwards continuity when you're filming things forwards is a nightmare. Just trying to discuss it caused a headache!

JK We had to constantly imagine what we were shooting would look like when it was played backwards to an audience, which was quite difficult at times. Also, a large part of the script revolved around matching cuts from the 'suicide process' scenes to the 'mental torture' scenes. As we had no experience on Final Cut in those days, we didn't have the ability to match up shots in the edit, so we had to do it on the shoot. This involved matching up two LCD monitors, one with the image we were currently shooting and the other with an image we'd already shot.

**The film reveals some distinctive visual images - tell us how they came about?**

JK We worked hard on creating strong visuals. We didn't want the fact that we were shooting on DV to be a limiting factor so, for the most part, we stuck to close ups. DV deals better with these than wideshots. Also, we knew that in a film with no dialogue, the visuals had to carry the story. To be honest, the roots of many of the distinctive visuals all stemmed from asking ourselves: "What looks cool backwards?"

RH It was an exercise for us in creating distinctive images. James and I were adamant In Absentia would come across well visually. One of the things about no-budget filmmaking is you can alienate your audience immediately if they see that the pictures aren't up to scratch. They instantly classify it as a low-quality film. I think this is changing, and DV is now starting to attain its own aesthetic, but we felt that high-quality visuals were a pre-requisite if In Absentia was to stand up well against shorts with bigger budgets.

**You have a six-minute film, but how much footage did you actually shoot?**

RH James will know for sure, but I'm guessing about 9 hours. Some will see this as a drawback to using cheap stock, but I think having the ability to capture anything and experiment was invaluable for us.

JK I think we actually used about five 1-hour tapes. That's another great thing about DV, you can have lots of stock. If we'd shot on film we'd probably only have had enough money to shoot about 5 seconds worth!

**The full interview with Richard Heald and James Kibbey can be found on-line in Shooting People's Wideshot resource http://shootingpeople.org/wideshot**

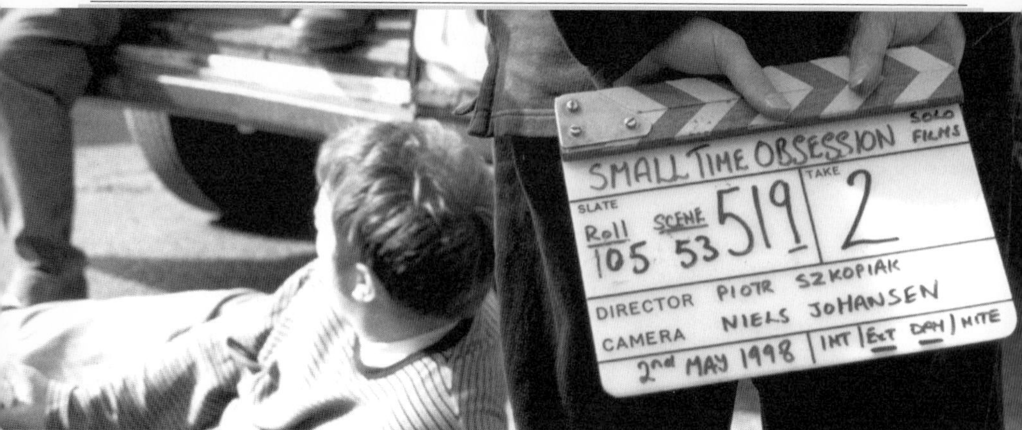


# Piotr Skopiak
# *Small Time Obsession*

*Piotr Szkopiak's story is a microcosm of the issues facing ultra-low- budget UK indie filmmakers – he self financed his feature for £40,000, shot on Super16 and had the good fortune to get the strong support of a distributor who brought in £150,000 completion funds taking him through to a limited theatrical release.*

Small Time Obsession initially cost £40,000 to make. Half of that was my own money and the other half came from family and friends. My half of the money was savings from working as a freelance Avid editor for three years. I could save this much because I remained living at home and my family waived the rent. I accepted the fact that no one I didn't know was going to give money to an unknown, first-time director who wanted to use an unknown cast.

I shot on Super16mm film, transferred everything to videotape, edited digitally on Avid and got a sound designer to do a TV quality stereo mix (with foley and everything). The beauty of editing digitally was that I did not have to cut my negative until I knew I had interest from a distributor. Why go to the expense of making a print unless you know you are going to get it shown? Anyway, I didn't have the money and Edinburgh does this great thing called Film UK. They list every UK film that has been made in the previous year, from a film like Notting Hill to the lowest of low budget video movies. They produce a booklet, which has all the films' details, and this is made available to all the buyers, sales agents and distributors at the festival. They then flick through the booklet and if there is something they like they can watch it in a special video viewing room, which stocks a couple of copies of every film. No pressure. This is where David Nicholas Wilkinson of Guerilla Films saw my film. He helped raise a further £150,000 to finish the film to 35mm print. All I had at this point was a virtual film if you like, it didn't exist in print form at all, just on Digibeta. The extra funding covered a re-cut, neg cut, blow-up, sound mix, music clearances, E&O insurance, telecines etc, etc, etc.

The £150,000 came from a private investment in the form of venture capital. This was a unique situation because I went to them with a finished film and with a UK distributor already attached. Normally, if you went to them for initial funding, you would not have a leg to stand on because you cannot prove you have a market for your film. Having a distributor can change that situation. When approaching money or facilities, ask yourself why you would part with the money or why you would help a project like this one. Put yourself in their shoes. Look at it logically. Why should I give you £500,000 to make your film if you have never made a film before? Would you give someone £500,000 if they had never made a feature before?"

## DISTRIBUTION

All you really have if you are a small, independent film is word-of-mouth. You don't have the benefit of a multi-million dollar advertising campaign like all the US films. So, in comparison, we did REALLY well. In fact, per print, we were actually doing a lot better than most US films. This is what people tend to forget when they look at box office takings. £1,000 on one print is actually a better return than £10,000 on 100 prints. Small Time Obsession was released on four prints in London and around the country through ABC Cinemas and Warner.

Its not that distributors do not want to spend money on distributing UK films, its just that they know they won't get their money back. That's a fact. Look at how you choose to go and see a film. When Small Time Obsession was released, there were about 25 other NEW films released that same month just in the cinema. Now, I love films but even I only see 3 or 4 films a month in the cinema. Furthermore, it costs the same amount of money to go see my film as it does Gladiator. Like it or not, you are in direct competition with Gladiator and, yes, you can offer something Gladiator doesn't but, again, without the advertising, you can't tell anyone what that is. All you have is word-of-mouth but that only spreads once people have seen the film.

Unfortunately, you have been kicked out of the cinema because not enough people knew about the film to come see it on the opening weekend because you didn't have the advertising spend. As a result, the film gets low box office figures and then the next UK film that comes along is told that it is not worth spending anything on advertising it because no one went to see the last UK film that came out and so the same thing happens. Catch 22. Now, no one can afford to take the risk.

When Small Time Obsession was released there was advertising on Shooting People, coverage on London Tonight, CNN and in the Evening Standard. Were you aware of it? I hope so but probably not. It gets lost. I say all this just to underline what you are up against and it's not pretty. It's competition and, most of the time, it is not fair but that's the reality and you have to know what you, and the distributors, are up against. Only when you know the truth can you do anything about it because I believe that, having said all this, it is possible to beat the system. Make a great film and do great marketing.

Unfortunately, that is what everyone is trying to do and there is no formula. All you can do is get stuck in. I tried and never thought I would get this far. But we have to work together. If everyone who reads Shooting People had gone to see my film when it opened, it would have blown the cinemas away. They weren't expecting anyone to come. As it is, I got a second week because it did so well. That is the first step. Make someone some money and they will come back for more.

*James MacGregor*

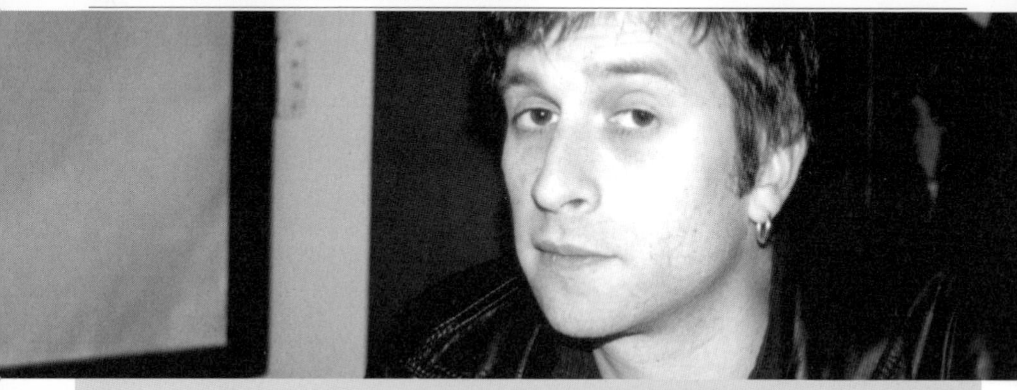

# Ben Hopkins *Nine lives of Thomas Katz*

*Ben Hopkins trod the path dreamt of by many – a graduation film from film school touring 30 festivals worldwide, scooping 14 awards and leading to a near £3m picture deal from British Screen. His debut feature Simon Magus with Ian Holm was critically acclaimed, yet landed on scarce few screens. His cult follow up, The Nine Lives of Tomas Katz, was shot on a ninth of that budget and cut every corner to create the mutant love child of Monty Python and Fritz Lang.*

Simon Magus cost £3m and was very carefully planned, very particular and very ornate. Tomas Katz was very cheap - shot in three weeks on a small budget - really knocked together. Shooting on such a tight budget was very enjoyable actually. As soon as you are over a certain level of funding, insurance companies and financiers have a much stronger element of control over you and more of a vested interest in what you are doing. It becomes important to make it look like money has been spent on it. Magus, like my short films, is very intricate and quite elegantly made and I got fed up with that so I thought I'd do something that looked like I'd just knocked it out for next to nothing. I shot Katz on 16mm, DV, High 8, Super16mm and Beta Cam.

One often feels that without much money you should concentrate on social realism and not light it properly with shit wallpaper. It's nonsense of course, you can be really imaginative with little money. Eraserhead is a fine example of how to create a entirely different universe with no money, that's inspiring. I'm just not very interested in daily life to be honest. I live in daily life and I don't need reminding of it every time I pay my money for a ticket, I'd much prefer to pay my money and be taken to another world!

I don't think we have any imaginative, creative and interesting distributors and I wonder why they bother spending good money on a product that is quite clearly shite. It's so stupid and a terrible waste of money. If you think of what could have happened to the celluloid that made up the 200 odd prints of Maybe Baby, why? What if the apocalypse happens tomorrow, all that's left is 200 prints of Maybe Baby in a warehouse somewhere.

You can make a masterpiece on a DV camera with a couple of unknown actors in a room and you can make a total piece of shit with $120m and all the help in the world. There's a magic thing in filmmaking, a sort of alchemical process where something is either working or it's not and it's very difficult to get into that realm - there's no formula to that. It either works or it doesn't." *Tom Fogg / NW*

# Owen & May Miles Thomas *Solid Air*

*Elemental Films, run by the husband and wife team of writer/director May Miles Thomas and producer Owen Thomas, are passionate advocates of digital cinema. They completed in 2000 one of the UK's first DV features, the multi-award-winning One Life Stand, shot on a micro-budget with a prosumer DV camera. The Glasgow-based company's follow-up feature Solid Air, was shot on HDCAM with full backing from Momentum Pictures, Scottish Screen and the Glasgow Film Fund.*

Crudely, there are two ways of getting a film made, but remember that nothing comes for free. One can attempt to produce a project that satisfies all established criteria, targeting the mid-ground of taste and pursuing a typical budget - all of which demands compromise. Alternatively one can be distinctive, look for less money, but retain one's editorial and creative freedom and a higher bite of recoupment. The trade-off is either psychological or physical exhaustion. Take your pick.

Some might say that a co-production deal with a larger, more established production company can help to move the project along, by providing access to the money. It's a reasonable option to consider, but be prepared to give away rights to your project and control of the budget and production. People don't steal scripts, they steal cash. At best, you'll get the film made - at worst, you'll get robbed blind.

By all means apply to the public funders - but again be prepared for compromise. Under certain existing schemes, you may be forced to have a completion bond. You may also be subjected to unwarranted cast and edit approvals and other concessions. Similarly with broadcasters, always be aware of the terms, and if you're making a film aimed at theatrical release, be sure that your film isn't killed at birth by being transmitted before release. A TX will tear up prospects for international sales.

While it's always possible to make a film on digital with very little resources, we found that unless you're visible, your film will be completely overlooked. In our case, the advantage of making a micro-budget film was to gain attention and a degree of credibility which we hoped would help to get a more ambitious project made. Making a no-budget movie worked for us to a certain extent - but we did it at a time when no-one else did. It seems there's a resistance to the no-budget DV movie now - ask any film festival director, who has to trawl through hundreds of submissions. Ask yourself why the EIFF is now charging 90 quid just to consider your film for screening.

We have an almost maniacal belief in what we do and the people we choose to do it with. We love making films, just as we believe that the audience in the UK deserves more intelligent, original and challenging pictures. This may sound idealistic, but so far we've never been motivated by money, or by taking the easy option. It also helps if overheads are kept to a minimum. One way to ensure this is to have the courage to make your own decisions, rather than defer to so-called 'executives'. British films can't make money because producers generally have to pre-sell the world to raise budgets, which erodes the prospect of profit participation. A lot of money is squandered in unnecessary offices, staff and facilities. If you're not in production, you're in hock, requiring the producer to chase his or her tail, giving away chunks of properties just to stay in business. As business models go, it's a non-starter because you'll always have to revisit the Lottery or source expensive money on a project-to-project basis, rather than attempt to generate real profit and reinvest in your future projects. *NW*

**www.elementalfilms.co.uk**

# Ken Russell
# *Moving to micro-budget*

The last studio film I did was *Dog Boys* which was a film for ShowTime. There was nothing of me in it - anyone could have made it. It would have looked exactly alike, the same. We had 21 days to shoot it, I went two days over schedule. Soon as it's done you send it to them, they send you three sheets of paper back the next day saying "change that, alter that, drop this, re-voice that person" and there's no one to talk to. In the old days, United Artists, you go in, there's two guys eating pastrami sandwiches and you can have a jolly good argument with them and usually you won it. They are all soft drinks salesmen anyway now, they know nothing about movies anyway. So it's to pay the rent.

You obviously get a bit depressed at times but then something comes along and well you have to drag yourself up by your boot straps and get on and do something, so I bought myself a video camera.

It started off as an economy thing but only because I'd seen how good it could get with these Danish films. I think film is fine - we all know what it looks like, but for me, video - especially for *The Fall of the Louse of Usher* - is ideal because it heightens the colour somehow or other. You can do tremendous things with it as you're shooting, much more than a normal camera, and you can see exactly what you've got and you can change all sorts. There are about 30 possibilities -you can alter the exposure, give it a certain effect, whatever. Marvellous stuff. I found that I love it - I love the colour of it, I love the texture of it. Well it's obvious the film's going to be finished sooner or later. Just a question of when.

*Stephen Applebaum*

# CHAPTER THREE
# PRODUCTION FINANCING

As touched upon in the previous chapters, there is no standard way to finance a very low budget feature film; it is mostly a question of pulling together whatever you can find. You might expect the 'mainstream' film finance market to be much more regimented, methodical or formulaic, but unfortunately that's not always true. The first, and probably only accurate, rule of independent film financing is often quoted as '**There Are No Rules**'. You can do almost any deal you like, so long as it is commercially acceptable to all concerned. At any given time, a film could be financed in a number of different ways, depending entirely on what can be negotiated at that moment between the specific parties involved. But then, with regular changes in the law (both at home and abroad), and with financing companies – and sometimes whole sectors – continually entering and leaving the market, the same film with an identical cast and budget could be financed in a completely different way, if made only a year or two later. That said, there would be no point in writing this chapter (or even this Handbook) if the industry was truly in a state of pure anarchy. There are in fact many 'rules of thumb' that can be used as guidance, if not gospel, and certain types of financier will always deal in a certain way. The purpose of this chapter is to discuss the range of options currently available in the mainstream independent market, and to see how they might be pieced together in a jigsaw-like fashion to obtain sufficient funds to get your script into the can.

The reason that film financing can be so complicated, when compared to other financing industries, is basically because in our business there are so many types of financier. Each has a different kind of interest in the film that it's financing, because each is putting in its money for a different reason. Some are more concerned with how or where the film is made (or at what cost), others with how much it can be sold for on the international market, or how well it may do at the box office in any particular territory or territories, or simply how passionate they are in wanting to see the film in question on the big screen.

A **lending bank**, for example, will only really be interested in its fee, and in receiving a fixed return (interest) on its loan, which it will always expect to be repaid – and usually before anyone else. So long as it is repaid in full, and quickly(!), it doesn't necessarily care how successful the film then goes on to be.

An **equity investor**, on the other hand, will sit and wait for other financiers to be paid back their contributions first, and will then (after being repaid its own investment) want to share in the profits of the film. It will therefore be very keen for the film to earn a lot of money worldwide for a long period of time, and thereby make a large profit.

A **rights-based financier**, such as a distributor or broadcaster, will put up funds in return for the right to keep the money it makes from distributing (or '**exploiting**') the film in its own territory. It will therefore not be as interested in how well the film does commercially anywhere else in the World (apart from perhaps in the United States), but it will want to be sure that the film is made in such a way as to have the greatest chance of being successful in its own territory.

Alternatively, **governments** that give grants or rebates, or offer tax incentives, will usually be keen for the film, or at least a large part of it, to be made within their jurisdiction so as to bring a benefit to their local economy.

Above are just a few, somewhat over-simplified, examples. Of course for the Producer, each dollar received goes directly into the production of his/her film, no matter where it comes from. The Producer must, however, understand that those putting up this money are looking to get very different, and often conflicting, benefits in return for their cash. It can be a difficult balancing act for the person who is engaged by the Producer to be responsible for pulling all the money together (such person is generally referred to as an '**executive producer**', although this term is regularly misused), to make sure that each of the financiers is happy with its individual deal.

## What is an 'Independent' film?

There is actually no single definition of the phrase 'an **independent**' film. The most common explanation is perhaps 'It's not a Studio picture'. But then what *is* a **Studio** picture? There are now currently only six remaining so-called Studios (also known as '**the Majors**'), being Warner Brothers, Disney, Paramount, Universal, Fox, and Sony (at the time of going to print, the ink was still drying on the contracts rolling MGM into the Sony empire), although some also class DreamWorks SKG as a Studio. These Studios are all located in the US, mostly around the Los Angeles area. Traditionally they have been based on their own, huge, production 'lots', where they have physically produced their own pictures on their own studio sound-stages (hence the term '**Studio**'). Over the years, the Studios became powerful enough to be able, without outside help, to develop, finance, produce, sell, distribute and even exhibit - although not in the US as this contravenes local competition laws - the films they made. However, more recently the Studios have been moving slowly away from this 'one-stop-shop' approach on some of their pictures. In order to share the risk on their films, some of which have truly massive budgets (regularly over $100m), they have begun to share some of the financing, production, distribution and exhibition elements both with other Studios, and with selected non-Studio companies within the mainstream sector.

In fact, many of the larger independent production and distribution companies (known sometimes as '**mini-majors**', such as Miramax, New Line, and Working Title) that originally began to partner with the Studios have since been bought out by them. Nevertheless, the Studios are continuing to seek outside financing partners for the pictures they are developing and producing.

An independent film could therefore be considered as one which is not developed and produced by a Studio. Even if it is, it would probably still be considered independent if it doesn't get sold and distributed around the world by the Studio that produced it. For our purposes, however, we will use the phrase 'independent' to relate to films whose financing has come, at least in part, from outside the Studio sector. I would imagine that for most of the readers of this Handbook, this will mean films that are produced outside the Studio sector too.

# 'Building' an Analogy

In this chapter, we have already touched on a few of the different categories of financier within the independent sector. However, before launching into an in-depth analysis of each type of finance, it may be useful to compare the various players with those in an alternative industry with which we may be a little more familiar, in order to understand better the varying roles in the financing process. As there are a large number of different players, we have chosen to use capitalised terms to help distinguish between them.

## The Players

Imagine the construction of a large, fifteen floor, apartment block costing £10m. Someone owns some land on which s/he would like the block to be built. A building Developer will buy the land, and then construct the building on it, based upon instructions given by an architect. At some point, an Estate Agent is appointed to sell off the various floors (usually by way of long lease) in order to bring in revenue. We could say that the land-owner is analogous to the owner of a film's underlying rights; the script or other property that is going to be used as the basis for creating the film. The Developer is the film's Producer; the person who actually puts the project together, engages the team, arranges the finance, and ultimately intends to own the finished product and earn money from it. The Architect could be seen as the film's Director, under whose guidance the vision is materialised. The Estate Agent, who may get involved surprisingly early in the process, can be compared to the film's Sales Agent, whose job it is to sell the film to international distributors, territory by territory, and so on. This analogy may not hold up 100% when analysed in minute detail, but it is a useful tool in helping to understand the basic 'Who's Who' in the film financing arena. We will therefore explore it a little further.

## Soft Money

So, once the building Developer has all its plans and designs finalised, and has obtained the necessary (albeit perhaps conditional) planning consents, and has identified the main department heads within the construction team, it will be in a position to go out looking for the finance required to pay for the construction of the Building. The first place the Developer may go in order to obtain some of the finance needed could be its local government. It may be eligible for a grant or other incentive available to those who create residential homes in the local area. We could, for the purposes of this example, assume the Developer is able to get a £1m contribution towards the project in this way. This is the equivalent of what we call '**soft money**' in the film industry because, although the money probably comes with restrictions as to how it may be spent, it is unlikely that it will have to be repaid in full.

## Pre-selling

The Developer may also, at this stage, try to pre-let some of the floors, usually by enlisting the services of an Estate Agent, in order to obtain further money to put towards the cost of construction. The prospective lessees (or tenants) of these floors would have to commit certain funds having only seen plans of the building, and would therefore probably obtain their leases at a lower price than if they had waited to see the finished article before committing to take possession. We could, for this example, assume three floors were sold off (by way of 25 year leases) at £1m each, thereby providing another £3m towards the construction costs. This is the equivalent of '**pre-selling**' a film to foreign distributors, whose '**territories**' could be considered the equivalent to the different floors (the penthouse probably being North America, and the other floors being equivalent to the UK, France, Germany, Japan, Scandinavia, Latin America, etc).

## Deferments

It may be that the Developer and Architect believe in the future commercial success of the project so much that they are willing to defer some of their own fees. Although there may be (say) £2m of such fees technically included as part of the budget for the construction, they may choose to defer half of these (£1m), and agree for them to be paid out of future income (obtained from selling off the remaining floors) rather than from funds raised to finance the Building. This will therefore reduce the amount that the Developer must find from elsewhere by £1m. Effectively, the Developer and Architect are themselves financing the construction to the tune of £1m. The analogy here would be the deferment by the Producers and/or Director or, for that matter, cast, of certain parts of their fees, a common (if often reluctant) sacrifice made by such 'above-the-line' personnel when 'passionate' about an independent film project.

## Equity

An Equity Investor may also believe in the long-term profitability of the apartment block. Despite realising that s/he is unlikely to see any money out of the pre-sold floors for some time (the amounts paid for those 25-year leases went straight into the construction of the building), s/he is comfortable that the remaining floors can be sold off at a level high enough to cover the remaining cost of construction, and make a profit on top. In return for any equity cash, the investor will require a share of the profit (if any) ultimately made by the Developer. If in our example s/he puts up another £3m, the Developer is left with a shortfall of £2m (the total budget was £10m, remember), having sold off three floors for £3m, received £1m soft money, and deferred £1m in fees.

## The Bank

Reluctantly, this is when the Developer probably needs to trot off to the Bank for a loan. It still has 12 floors to sell (including the penthouse), and only needs a further £2m to complete the financing for the block. The Estate Agent (whose projections the Bank trusts) confirms to the Bank that it thinks it should be able to sell the remaining floors for far in excess of this amount, even without selling the penthouse (and this is where our analogy is stretched a little as we have to imagine that penthouses – equivalent to the territory of North America – are notoriously and inherently difficult to sell, notwithstanding that if they are actually sold, they are likely to bring in the most money). So, ignoring any possible income from selling the penthouse, if the Bank thinks the potential receipts from selling the remaining floors outweigh by a huge margin the amount it is being asked to lend, it will consider lending the remaining £2m to the Developer. This will probably be on condition that a) the Bank gets its money repaid with interest (and an additional fee!), b) it is the first in the pecking order to be paid from any receipts generated from selling off the remaining floors, and c) it takes a security (in the form of charge or mortgage) over the building until such time as it is repaid in full. Naturally, there are many other conditions that the Bank will require, but these are the main ones for the purposes of our example. In the film industry, this type of plugging the hole in the finance is known as '**bank gap**' financing, and depends on the Bank's faith in the Sales Agent to sell the territories on behalf of the Producer at sufficiently high prices.

And so you have it. The Developer by hook or by crook (no pun intended) has managed to obtain the whole £10m needed to construct its building. Likewise, the independent film Producer is likely to need to approach a similar number and range of financiers in order to obtain the £10m needed to produce his/her film. The main outstanding issue still to be addressed is how, and in what order, each of the financiers gets paid back its contribution. That is down to the various financiers (and their respective lawyers) to agree, usually before one penny of construction (or, in our case, production) finance is actually spent. Now that we have illustrated (and simplified!) the main differences in the various types of financier, we can examine their respective typical deals, attributes and concerns in some more detail. We will revert back to our construction site analogy as and when appropriate, but for the time being, we can leave it and concentrate our minds back on the independent film industry.

# Recoupment and Profit

The term '**recoupment**' is just a film industry expression meaning repayment. As the film gets sold around the world, the buyers (being foreign Distributors) pay their respective purchase amounts into a '**Collection Account**' (sometimes fondly referred to as the '**pot**'), which is run by a specialist '**Collection Agent**'. The Collection Agent (often a bank) is charged with (i) collecting the proceeds of sale, (ii) paying the Sales Agent its commission for the sales it has made (and its expenses), (iii) repaying the financiers for their contributions to the financing of the film, and then (iv) distributing the profits to those entitled to participate in them.

Note that it is the amounts that the Distributors will pay for the film, known as '**MG**'s (see later), that go into the Collection Account 'pot', and are shared out between the producers and the various financiers. How well the film then does at the international box-offices is a matter for each Distributor, and not of immediate concern to the financiers. The way in which these sales are structured is discussed in more detail later in this chapter under the heading '**Pre-Sales**'. The point to note for now is that, in essence, repayment to financiers depends on the size of the MGs, and thus on the abilities of the Sales Agent to achieve good prices around the World.

As sales income is received, the Collection Agent will be obliged to repay the financiers strictly in accordance with a '**Recoupment Schedule**' (see an example in the Reference Section at the back of the book). This is a vital document as it sets out, as between the various financiers, the order of their recoupment, and must therefore be agreed by all of the financiers and profit participants at the time of financing the film. As receipts come in from each territorial sale, there is a specific order of entitlement spelling out exactly to whom each dollar received will go. Sometimes all the receipts will go to one financier until it is fully repaid, and then to the next (the order depending on who had the best bargaining power at the time the financing contracts are agreed). Alternatively, certain financiers might share out between them each dollar received, known as a '*pari passu*' distribution of income. Usually, as mentioned above, the Bank is the first to be paid off (even if, ultimately, it is only able to negotiate an entitlement to take, say, 90 cents of each dollar received on a *pari passu* basis), and all the other financiers have to fight amongst each other for their right to be next in line.

Ultimately, if the film is sold at high enough prices, sufficient money will flow into the Collection Account to repay all the financiers their respective contributions (together with interest, premiums, and/or whatever else they managed to negotiate at the time). At this point, the film is said to '**break even**'. This does not mean that the aggregate amount of sales equals the budget. In fact, unless there is a huge amount of soft money involved (see below), the receipts will usually far exceed the budget at this point, as the Sales Agent's commission and expenses, together with the financiers' interest and premiums (if any) also have to be paid out of sales income. However, once break-even is reached, there is nobody left to be repaid, and the film is therefore '**in profit**'. Any further receipts from sales after this point are usually referred to as '**Net Profits**' or '**back end**' and are distributed amongst the profit participants, again in accordance with the terms set out in the Recoupment Schedule. Certain types of financier are more likely to be entitled to a profit participation than others (the most obvious being 'equity' investors), and this is discussed more fully later in this chapter. The other main beneficiaries of Net Profits are usually the Producers themselves, and any cast or department heads who had enough power to be able to negotiate such an entitlement when being contracted to contribute their services to the film.

# Soft Money

The phrase '**Soft Money**' is often banded about to refer to all sorts of different types of finance. The common theme is that the providers of soft money generally take a less aggressive position in relation to recoupment. In fact, many types of soft money (such as grants, awards and rebates) do not have to be repaid at all. This kind of finance usually originates from a Government or public body, such as the UK Film Council. Alternatively, private individuals or entities can sometimes utilise various statutory regulations (such as so-called '**tax breaks**') whereby they obtain benefits outside the realms of financing the film itself, enabling them to take a much 'softer' approach when negotiating their recoupment position. For example, if a financier can somehow get a £4m reduction in his/her personal tax bill, simply by investing (say) £2.5m of his/her own money (which, believe it or not, has actually been possible in the UK until very recently), s/he will not be as concerned about how quickly the £2.5m gets repaid as would another financier who cannot benefit from such a scheme, such as (say) a lending bank. Likewise, a public body financed by a central government might not need (or wish) to be repaid its contribution quite as quickly as a Producer who has deferred his/her own hard-earned fee.

Soft money comes in all different shapes and sizes, and there are all sorts of ways to combine the various options available. Naturally, the more soft money you have in a budget, the better it is for the Producer and other financiers. This is because the less (or more slowly) you have to pay back to some financiers, the more money there is left in the 'pot' for everyone else to share, and thereby be repaid more quickly. And once everyone else has been repaid, the Producer can start sharing in the Net Profits. Although soft money sometimes does in fact need to be recouped by the entity providing it (albeit usually on weaker terms and at a later date than other finance), one often distinguishes between 'soft' finance and 'recoupable' finance when discussing how a budget is to be sourced, and we will keep to that distinction for present purposes.

## Co-Productions and International Soft Money

One way to minimise the amount of recoupable finance is to source as much soft money as possible from more than just one country. To access these benefits internationally, the film will normally (but not always) have to be set up as an official co-production between the relevant countries. To qualify as a co-production, the film will need to satisfy the requirements set out in the relevant *Co-Production Treaty* between the countries concerned (or, if produced substantially within Europe, the *European Convention on Cinematic Co-Production*). Different types of soft money are available in different countries, and chapters 5 (International Financing) and 6 (Funding Organisations) provide details, on a country by country basis, of many of the more popular international financing options, and how to qualify for them.

## UK Grants and Funds

As for the UK, there are two main avenues to go down. One of these is the purest (and most loved) of soft money options: the '**grant**'. This is the equivalent to the type of soft money obtained in our 'Building' analogy at the beginning of the chapter. Grants for film production are given by various bodies (usually quasi-governmental institutions or charitable organisations), and rarely have to be recouped at all. The largest such body, the UK Film Council (or 'UKFC', not to be confused with a high-street chain store), has several different pots of money to dish out from, depending on the type, budget, and commerciality of the film. It does, however, also have arguably the tightest qualification criteria, and also requires certain funds to be paid back from income derived from the film. There are numerous other institutions all over the British Isles offering an assortment of grants and awards of varying amounts, and subject to a huge range of conditions. chapter 6 (Funding Organisations) gives an in-depth explanation of what is available (at the time of going to press) throughout the country, and how it can be accessed.

## Tax Breaks

The other predominant source of soft money in the UK is so-called 'taxed-based' finance. Tax incentives are designed by a government to boost the local economy by attracting investment into a sector, such as the film industry. For producers, this is becoming an increasingly important source of film finance as other forms such as pre-sales and large 'gap' loans become harder to obtain. Broadly speaking, there are two kinds of tax incentives for the film industry; **tax credits** or offsets, and **tax allowances**.

Finance based on tax allowances comes mostly from people and companies who qualify for a reduction in their tax bill if they invest their income in films. The financiers are 'allowed' to write off some or all of their investment against their other taxable income. Producers and film financiers in countries offering this investment incentive can often benefit from specially constructed production funds, which utilise the tax allowances when they invest in a qualifying film. The system currently used in the UK is a **tax allowance** system, and has spawned many different types of financial product, from almost pure equity investment to the notorious niche 'UK Sale & Leaseback' industry. These schemes have typically provided a contribution of between 10% and 35% of a film's budget and, without them, it is claimed that most British films would never see the light of day. However, the workings of the UK tax system, to the extent it relates to film financing, is somewhat of a moveable feast, and the current tax regime is to come to an end shortly.

**Tax credits** (or offsets) are not yet available in the UK, but are available in other countries. chapter 5 (International Financing) covers where, internationally, they are available, and how they work. The basic idea is to encourage expenditure in a particular country by foreign and local producers, who will receive a form of rebate on amounts spent in that country. In making the film, the Producer will spend money locally on resources, infrastructure, locations and personnel, which can qualify him/her to receive a tax refund from the relevant governmental authority. Sometimes credits are limited to certain types of expenditure (such as a repayment of income tax spent in relation to the employment of local personnel), and sometimes they relate to the entire local spend. They are all direct rebates on money actually spent out of the budget by the Producer, rather than a tax incentive aimed specifically at the Investors in the project. Canada, Australia, Iceland and Malta are countries that have offered this type of incentive. The system proposed by the UK Government to replace the current tax allowance regime is also tax-credit based, and is due to come into force some time in 2006.

Both the current UK tax allowance system and its proposed replacement, the 20% tax credit (to the extent information is available at the time of going to press), are explored in full in chapter 4 (UK Tax-Based Money).

## Equity

The term '**equity**', for the purposes of film financing, basically means 'ownership'. An Equity Investor (or just 'Investor') will effectively be buying a piece of the film and will wish to share in the profits of it. It is investing in a similar way to a shareholder in a new company, taking a risk that the venture will ultimately become profitable, in the hope of participating in profits for as long as it owns a piece of the pie. As mentioned previously, a film goes into profit once all the financiers (other than those providing non-recoupable soft money) have been paid back their contributions plus, where relevant, any interest or premium to which they are entitled. The more soft money involved, the quicker the film goes into profit, and the sooner the Investor gets to share in those profits. This will, of course, be after the Investor has been repaid its own contribution (plus, as is often the case, a premium) as part of the recoupment process. However, because the Investor is entitled to share in the profits of the film, whereas other financiers generally are not, it will often be one of the last in line to be repaid as per the Recoupment Schedule. Any soft money providers that do in fact require repayment will normally sit behind the Investor. That said, once everyone has been repaid (and assuming the film is profitable), the Investor will share in proceeds for years to come as the film gets sold and resold during its life-cycle, particularly to television broadcasters.

An Investor, being effectively a 'part-owner' of the film, will often own a share in the copyright itself, and the film may therefore form part of its '**library**'. Going back to our 'Building' analogy at the beginning of the chapter, this is the equivalent to an investor jointly owning the building with the Developer, thereby continuing to share in the income from lease renewals once the other original financiers have been paid off. The obvious next question is, therefore, 'How much of the profit goes to the Investor, and how much goes to the Producers'?

## The Six Tenths Rule of Profit Share

The rule of thumb is often referred to as the '**Six Tenths Rule**', and this is how it works. Let's take an example of a £3m film where a single Investor will provide all the finance required to fund the entire picture. This is actually not as rare as you may think, particularly on lower budget films (successful British films to be financed in this way include *Human Traffic,* and *Stoned (The World of Brian Jones)*). In our example, the only people eligible to share in the profits of the film are the Producer (and possibly his/her cast and crew) who made the film, and the Investor who paid for it; otherwise known as the Creative people, and the Money people. The Six Tenths Rule, rightly or wrongly, says that Money is worth six tenths (60%), and Creative is worth four tenths (40%). Producers will argue that it should be closer to a 50/50 split, and some Investors will ask for 75%, or even more. But for argument's sake, let us assume 60/40 is appropriate in this example. This means that the film breaks even once the net revenues from sales (after deduction of the Collection Agent's fee, and the Sales Agent's commission and expenses) exceed £3m, assuming that the Investor – who paid for the whole £3m budget, remember - is not charging a premium. At this point, the Investor will have been paid back its investment, and any net income from further sales will be pure profit. For each dollar received after this point (film sales are actually calculated and quoted in dollars rather than pounds or Euros), the Investor would be entitled to 60¢, and the Producer to 40¢. To the extent that any other of the creative team (director, lead cast, heads of artistic departments) have negotiated an entitlement to Net Profits, this must come out of the Producer's share, because they are 'Creative', and not 'Money'. The Producer will agree the profit entitlements (if any) for its creative team at the time s/he engages them on the picture.

If, however, the Investor only financed half of the film's budget, the Six Tenths Rule would still apply, but only to half of the profits. In other words, the Investor would normally accept six tenths of half of the Net Profit, ie. a 30% profit participation, and the rest would be left for the Creative people (and/or other financiers). If it financed only a quarter of the film, it might expect to be given a 15% share of Net Profits, and so on. The Six Tenths Rule is not absolutely rigid, and where Equity Investors put up a smaller percentage of the budget (especially when they are the last financier to commit), the proportion may go up so that an Investor providing only 10% of the budget may get as high as an 8% (or even 10%) participation in the Net Profits rather than the 6% that the Six Tenths Rule might suggest. Naturally, the actual percentage agreed will depend on the respective bargaining powers, and on whoever else is trying to negotiate a profit share. Ultimately, the Producer will want to be left with at least a 40% share in the film s/he creates, even if s/he has to share some of this with his/her creative team.

It should be noted that many of the so-called 'Equity Funds' are in fact a hybrid of soft money (utilising the tax breaks referred to above and discussed more fully in chapter 4) and pure equity. This is why many of them take a 'softer' approach to Net Profit requirements than other Equity Investors who do not avail themselves of the tax breaks. Producers should try to avoid using any tax-based Equity Fund that applies the Six Tenths Rule in full. Examples of companies who, at the time of going to press, offer tax-based funding are identified later in chapter 6 (Funding Organisations).

# Pre-Sales and Distribution Deals

## Distribution Agreements

Before looking in any depth at pre-sales as a form of film financing, it is important to understand the basics behind standard sales agreements, otherwise known as 'distribution deals'.

To generate income to repay financiers, the Sales Agent is engaged (on behalf of the Producer) to sell the film to Distributors around the World. A large number of these sales occur at special industry 'markets' (such as the American Film Market in Los Angeles, or MIF in Cannes), and behind the scenes at the major festivals (such as Berlin, Sundance and Toronto), where the Sales Agent will give potential buyers private screenings of the films (or promotional trailers) that they are selling. Each sale made will be for a particular territory, usually a country or a geographically close group of countries (such as the Middle East, Central America, Eastern Europe, etc). The '**sale**' is really actually a licence, allowing the Distributor to distribute the film exclusively in its territory for a specified period of time (usually between seven and fifteen years). The Distributor will normally be granted the rights to exploit the film on all available formats, including **Theatrical** (cinemas), **Non-Theatrical** (airlines, ships, hotels, prisons, etc), **Television** (free, terrestrial, cable, digital, satellite, pay TV, Pay Per View, Video on Demand, etc) and **Home Video** (including DVD and any future formats). It may also acquire Internet rights, Merchandising rights (clothing, crockery, books, fast-food tie-ins, etc), Soundtrack rights and various other '**Ancillary**' rights. The Distributor might not itself be a specialist in each one of these fields, but it will know the relevant companies in its local territory, and will be permitted to sub-license to them the relevant rights as necessary. For example, the Distributor will book the film into the local cinemas, sell it to the national and local TV stations, and (unless it has the facilities in-house) engage a local video sub-distributor to manufacture and distribute videos and DVDs to appropriate outlets in its territory.

## The Minimum Guarantee

As mentioned earlier, the amount that the Distributor agrees to pay for this licence is known as a '**Minimum Guarantee**' (or '**MG**'). However, this MG is actually an advance against future revenues payable to the Producer pursuant to the Distributor's sale contract (or '**Distribution Agreement**'). This is because, in principle, every dollar received by the Distributor should be shared in an agreed proportion between the Distributor and the Producer, and the MG is just an advance paid to the Producer against his/her future share. The next few paragraphs explain how this works.

The Distributor, in deciding what level of MG it is prepared to pay, will need to consider how much it thinks it is likely to earn from exploiting the film in its territory. This will primarily be income derived from cinema exhibitors (assuming the film goes theatrical), television broadcasters, video distribution and, if relevant, associated merchandising.

When the Distributor and Producer agree the MG amount, they will also agree how the income received from the film's exploitation should be split notionally between them. These '**splits**', although roughly in accordance with industry norms, will actually vary from format to format, making distribution contracts more complex than you might initially think. For example, any income received by the Distributor from theatrical exploitation (after the cinemas have taken their cut, and after the Distributor has been reimbursed its costs of advertising, copying, dubbing and shipping the film) might get split 50/50 between the Producer and the Distributor - it will in fact be more complicated than this for the 'major territories', such as the USA, Germany, UK, France and Japan. For video, the Producer might only get a 12% or 15% royalty on all sales and rentals, leaving the Distributor with the lion's share (although it will be responsible for the costs of duplication, etc). Yet for TV, the split might be 70/30 the other way, with the Producer taking the majority of income from a sale to a broadcaster.

In calculating the level of MG it can afford, the Distributor should work out how much in total, during the life of its licence, it thinks it is likely to have to hand over to the Producer (based on the agreed splits). Then, rather than agreeing to make payments continually throughout the term of the licence, the Distributor agrees with the Producer an alternative amount to be paid up front. This is effectively a guaranteed minimum amount that the Producer will receive (hence the term '**Minimum Guarantee**') as its share of the Distributor's revenues earned from the exploitation of the film in the relevant territory. The MG is non-returnable, even if the Distributor miscalculates and doesn't end up achieving the level of receipts it had anticipated. However, if revenues turn out to be so high that the amount attributable to the Producer pursuant to the splits actually exceeds the advance (MG) paid at the time of the sale, the Distributor will have to start paying additional amounts (known as '**overages**') to the Producer in accordance with the agreed splits.

## Computing Sales Estimates and MGs using the Budget

Unfortunately, many Distributors do not go through the above calculation, and instead use a more arbitrary method to decide on how much they should be paying as an MG. In part, this is also due to the techniques used by some Sales Agents in calculating their Sales Estimates. The idea behind Sales Estimates is, of course, that they are a realistic estimate as to how much the Sales Agent (who prepares them) honestly thinks it can obtain for the sales it hopes to make to each country. Traditionally, the United States would bring in at least 50% of this revenue, although these days it is closer to 30% or 40% (assuming a US sale can be done at all). Likewise, certain other territories have also tended to generate a fairly steady, and therefore identifiable, percentage of the total worldwide revenue. Of course, it does actually fluctuate on a film-by-film basis, and will in each case be determined by how well the film in question is expected to do in the territory concerned. This in turn will depend on the film's genre, cast, subject matter, and so on.

However, sometimes what happens is that these 'predictable' proportions of worldwide income are used by the Sales Agent in generating their Sales Estimates. They are then re-calculated with direct reference to the film's budget. In other words, a Sales Agent may 'estimate' that, in its view, 10% (say) of the film's budget can be recovered from a sale to France, 8% from the UK and 12% from Germany. But arguably this practice is fundamentally flawed. By way of example, if the 'going rate' for France was in fact 10%, it would imply that a $10m film should automatically generate twice as much income from a sale to France as would a $5m film. The MG paid for the $10m film would be $1m, but for the $5m film would only be $500k. For this to make sense to the Distributor, it would itself have to generate exactly twice as much income from its territory for the $10m film. Of course in practice this rarely ever happens. The number of people who actually watch a film at the cinema, on TV or on video, is not directly determined by how much was spent on producing it. The general public rarely even know how much a film's budget is, never mind using that as a basis for whether or not they want to watch it. The amount the Distributor makes locally is a product of the quality and subject matter of the film, its cast, and the Distributor's ability to marketing it well.

Nevertheless, certain Sales Agents do in fact use these percentages to prepare Sales Estimates (although they would probably never admit to it), and certain Distributors are coerced into using the same methods in determining how much they are willing to spend for the right to exploit the film. The percentage figures do, however, change over time. During the 2001 'crash' in the German market, German sales dropped from being 'worth' an unprecedented 15% of a budget to under 10%.

The worldwide aggregate of these percentages must of course exceed 100%, otherwise the film will never go into profit, even if a sale is made to every country in the world. So, although these 'standard' percentages may be a useful tool in checking whether a Sales Agent may have got a good price for a film, they should never be used (or accepted) as the only determining factor in calculating either Sales Estimates or, alternatively, the amount actually payable as an MG on an actual distribution contract.

## The Pre-Sale

If, at the time of the sale, the film is already completed and the Distributor has seen the finished product (often during a market such as Cannes, AFM or Berlin, or at a specially arranged screening during the year), it will pay the MG in full as soon as it has checked the technical quality of the elements delivered to it. The MG goes straight into the Collection Account, and the Collection Agent pays it out according to the Recoupment Schedule (see the Recoupment and Profit section, earlier in this chapter).

However, the Producer may want to start selling the film much earlier, even before it is finished, in order to start paying back the film's financiers as soon as possible (especially if s/he has to pay them interest). When a film is sold prior to its completion, it is known as '**pre-selling**' the film. This is sometimes done by the Producer using his/her own contacts, and sometimes by the Sales Agent (if appointed by such time), who may start selling the film straight away. This way, the financiers can start to recoup their financial contributions even before the film is completed, and certainly before it hits the cinema screens.

The advantage to the Distributor of agreeing to buy the film early is that it may get a good price because it is taking a risk - that the film will ultimately be as good as it hopes. The rights to the 'finished' film (assuming it turns out well) would usually have cost more, because the Distributor would be able to actually see what it is getting, before committing to buy. However, before agreeing to pre-buy the rights to exploit the film, the Distributor, will want to see and approve a number of '**Key Elements**', including the script, lead cast, budget, shooting schedule and delivery date. Depending on how far down the line the production is at the time of the sale, the Producer may also have some 'rushes', or selected unfinished scenes, to show the Distributor, if s/he thinks these are of sufficient quality to help persuade the Distributor to make the purchase.

## Payment of the MG on a Pre-sale

On a pre-sale (unlike a 'straight' distribution deal made after the film is completed – see below), the Distributor will not normally be required to pay the entire MG at the time the deal is made. It will typically hand over only a small proportion as a deposit, usually about 20% but depending on the territory and bargaining position of the Distributor concerned. The remaining balance is only payable when the film is delivered to the Distributor, once it has actually been completed. '**Delivery**' does not just entail giving the Distributor a reel of film in a can. In fact, the negative will usually stay in a laboratory, and the Distributor will be given access to it in order to strike the prints that it needs. The Producer will, however, have to deliver (or provide access to) 'masters' for TV broadcast and video duplication, publicity materials, a trailer (if required), information to assist with foreign language dubbing, copies of relevant contracts, an explanation of restrictions that the Distributor must comply with, and a large amount of other back-up documentation (including '**Chain of Title**' – legal proof that the Producer had the contractual rights to make the film in the first place). We have set out a sample 'Delivery Schedule' in the Reference Section. The Distributor will then check that it conforms with what it was expecting (and contractually entitled) to receive, including of course the Key Elements, and only then pay the balance of the MG over to the Collection Agent. The Distributor will probably by this time have been planning its '**Release Schedule**' for the film, and so will also require the film to be delivered bang on time, otherwise it might refuse to pay for it.

## Pre-Sales as a form of Finance for the Film

As mentioned in the Introduction to this chapter, and illustrated to some extent in the 'Building' analogy, a common way to raise finance for a film is to sell off the exploitation rights to the film in certain territories before it actually goes into production. These are of course also 'pre-sales', but ones that are made before the film is even started (rather than during production). For the Producer, pre-selling is a way of getting a large proportion of the production funds together without having to give away equity (and therefore profits) in the film. It is also a good way to measure whether or not the concept for the film is attractive to the international marketplace before actually spending (other people's) money on producing it. For this reason, a gap financier (see later) may not get involved with a project until it sees that a number of key territories have already been sold by way of pre-sale.

There is one major snag, though. When making a pre-sale for the purposes of financing, the Producer will want to receive the whole MG (rather than the 20% deposit) before making the film, in order to put the entire sale price towards the cost of producing the film. It won't want to wait until it has made and delivered the film to the Distributor in order to collect the 80% or so of the MG that it required in order to make the film in the first place.

Once again, this is where the Producer has to turn to the **Bank**. The Distributor promises, in its contract, to pay the balance of the MG upon satisfactory delivery of the film. The Producer will ask the Bank if it will lend the money in the meantime, to enable the film to be made. This is known as '**discounting**' the distribution contract. The Bank lends the Producer an amount of money up front, and collects directly from the Distributor when the film is delivered to it by the Producer. Unless the Bank lends more than the price agreed for the MG, the Producer will not be able to use the whole amount for the production itself, as it will have to build in a (fairly hefty) fee for the bank, and interest during the course of the loan. For example, if the MG was $1m, the Producer may have to allocate (say) $20k as a one-off fee for the Bank (equal to about 2% of the loan). It will also need to reserve $100k or so to cover the interest (at 2% or 3% above base rate) that the loan will accumulate from the time the pre-sale was agreed (and the loan entered into) to the time that the Bank picks up the payment from the Distributor on Delivery. In this example, the Producer would therefore only be able to put $880k of the $1m sale price onto the screen itself. Alternatively, if s/he needs the entire $1m, s/he will have to borrow about $1.12m to cover the extra costs of the loan. S/he will also have to increase the overall budget of the film by $120k to cover this. Naturally, any increase in the budget will have to be subject to the approval of the other financiers. Note that these financing costs do not form part of qualifying production expenditure for tax relief purposes (see chapter 4).

As for the Bank, it will only lend against the Distributor's promise to pay the MG if it has a good relationship with the Distributor, and believes that it is likely still to be solvent (and therefore able to pay) at the time of delivery of the film. It may also require the Distributor's own bank to issue a letter of credit on behalf of the Distributor, guaranteeing that the payment can (and will) be made, as long as the Producer meets the delivery requirements. It may also agree only to discount a proportion of the pre-sale, particularly if it is uncomfortable that the Distributor will be able to pay the entire MG balance on delivery. Of course, the Bank must be sure that the film will actually be finished on time and on budget (so as to prevent the Distributor from trying to avoid payment), and so will often insist on the Producer taking out a '**Completion Bond**' to ensure that the Producer complies with its obligations to deliver. Completion bonds are discussed in more detail later in this chapter.

## Too many Pre-sales?

Although a Producer will always be optimistic that s/he will one day receive overages from the various territories, it is a more prudent approach from a financing perspective to assume that, after receipt of the full MG, the Producer is unlikely to see any further income from any territory that has been pre-sold. This clearly affects the future profitability of the film. An **Equity Investor** (see earlier in this chapter) is relying on substantial sale proceeds being paid in to the pot, in order for it to recoup its investment. If too many pre-sales are made for the purposes of financing the film, there may not be enough remaining territories around the World to be sold in order for the film's other financiers to be repaid or, if entitled, see any profits. This is because the income from these pre-sales effectively goes straight onto the screen, rather than into the pot for distribution amongst the financiers.

It is therefore not healthy to do too many pre-sales for financing purposes, and the Producer must maintain a balance between obtaining the finance s/he needs to make the film, and leaving enough territories available for future sales so that his/her other financiers will be satisfactorily paid off. It follows that the film's other financiers will have a right of approval over any deal pre-selling rights in this way.

## Straight, Flat and Outright Sales

Unfortunately, the term '**Straight Sale**' has a couple of different meanings depending on who you ask, which can make life a little confusing. One interpretation is a distribution deal that is not a pre-sale; in other words one that is made after the film is completed. It is 'straight' in the sense of 'less hassle' because the MG is paid in one go, no deposit needs to be taken, and the deal does not need to be banked ('discounted'). The other - very different and potentially conflicting - meaning attributed to the term 'straight sale' is a sale that does not have an MG at all. In these cases, the Distributor simply pays the Producer (via the Collection Account, of course) in accordance with the agreed splits from day one (although usually the Distributor is permitted to recoup its own costs and expenses from income before it has to start paying the Producer as per the splits).

If, as happens occasionally, the parties agree that the Distributor will never be required to pay the Producer any more than the original purchase amount, it is known as an '**Outright Sale**' or a '**Flat Sale**' (rather than a Minimum Guarantee). In such cases, there is no need to negotiate the splits for each format because the sales price is not a minimum guarantee against them, but a one off payment. These deals are fairly rare as the combined optimism of the parties, both hoping that the film does better than expected, usually incentivises them enough to enter into an MG-style agreement. However, sometimes certain aspects of the distribution deal are considered '**flat**', where the Producer is not allowed to share in revenues from certain formats.

For example, if the Distributor is permitted to keep all income from TV sales (ie. there is no 'split' for TV), the sale is referred to as being 'flat for TV'.

## Some Other Considerations

Sometimes a pre-sale may be made directly to a broadcaster, for television rights only, particularly if the broadcaster (eg. Channel Four or the BBC in the UK) has been in some way involved in developing the project from inception. One point to note is that a pre-sale to a TV network will have an effect on any future sale made to the theatrical (and/or video) distributor in the same territory. A TV pre-sale made without an appropriate '**hold-back**' window will affect the timing of a potential release in the cinemas (and therefore reduce the attraction of the film to a theatrical buyer). The subsequent buyer of theatrical rights will not, of course, be able to acquire the opportunity to sub-license the film for TV in its territory, so its offer price to the Producer will be lower than it would have been if it could have acquired all rights in all formats. That said, any sale is better than no sale at all, and a sale to one buyer might increase the status of the film, thereby helping to secure a sale to another buyer.

Pre-sales as a form of financing work well for established producers with a good reputation and a good project, but increasingly buyers are less keen to enter into this kind of deal (or to pay the traditional prices), due to the very real risk of not being able to achieve the estimated box office figures. Naturally, this has had a negative impact on established production companies' ability to raise finance. Today, a reputable producer with a good script, cast and production team might expect to raise maybe 10% to 50% of the film's budget this way, compared with upwards of 70% only a few years ago.

The sad but true state of affairs, however, is that a film without a distribution deal (pre-sale) in place for a major territory is likely to be a less attractive proposition for other potential financiers, especially public funding bodies and banks. This is because, as noted above, the existence of pre-sales is often considered a 'signal' that at least some Distributors in the market believe the project to be a good commercial prospect. Additionally, a less experienced Producer will benefit more from the market experience and guidance of a Distributor who is already on-board while the film is being made. It would be unfortunate if the film, once completed, was turned down by other Distributors for reasons that could easily have been addressed during production, had the Producer only known.

Whereas selling a finished film is common practice for established and non-established filmmakers, pre-selling can be much more difficult for Producers with less of a reputation. However, sometimes a Distributor can be persuaded to sign a '**letter of intent**' rather than an enforceable distribution contract. This letter acknowledges an intention to buy the film for an agreed price once it has been completed and delivered. As with a normal pre-sale, the letter will indicate certain conditions that the Producer and the finished film must meet in order for the Distributor to proceed with the acquisition. Although possessing a letter of intent would be better than approaching a potential investor without any distribution deal at all, it is by no means proof of an actual sale, and in itself would probably not be enough to persuade financiers looking for a reasonably secure investment. At the very least, a letter of intent would establish a relationship with a Distributor, and might be a useful way to demonstrate that the film is potentially of commercial interest.

# Gap Financing

Not to be confused with the fairly short-lived '**GAAP**' funds (discussed briefly in the next chapter), gap financing is a form of loan issued by a Bank to provide finance for the shortfall between other finance raised, and the total amount needed to make the film.

## Sales Estimates and Coverage

Generally, a gapping Bank will lend against the projected '**sales estimates**' relating to unsold territories, as provided by a reputable Sales Agent. Sales estimates are figures representing the amount that the Sales Agent reasonably thinks the film will sell for in the market place, once completed. In preparing them, the Sales Agent will take into account a number of factors, particularly the Key Elements (budget, cast, Director, Producer, genre, etc) and how they might be received by the general worldwide public. They are prepared on a territory-by-territory (and sometimes even format-by-format) basis, showing the likely 'best case' and 'worst case' prices attainable.

The Bank will only lend if it is satisfied by the reputation of the Sales Agent providing the estimates, and then only if the Sales Agent is actually 'attached' to (ie. committed to sell) the project. It will also usually want to see that at least one or two pre-sales have been made to major territories (being Germany, the UK, France, Italy, Spain, Scandinavia, Japan, Australia or - ideally! - the USA). This illustrates to the Bank that members of the world-wide distribution industry believe that the film has commercial potential, and also confirms that the sales estimate figures are realistic. The Bank will also want to see a clear 'margin' between the sales estimates and the amount is being asked to lend, in order to provide it with sufficient comfort that enough income will in fact be generated for the loan to be repaid. The margin required (or, as it is known, '**coverage**' – not to be confused with 'overages'!) will often be 200% or 300% of value of the loan being requested (although 150% has been known to be accepted from time to time).

In other words, if the Producer of a £10m picture has already secured £8m of finance, s/he will have a gap of £2m (ie. 20%) to plug. A gap-financing Bank will require that the 'worst case' sales estimates for all unsold territories (but excluding North America) are at least £4m to £6m, being 200% to 300% of the gap required. This will provide the Bank with some comfort that, even if the Sales agent misses its targets by some way, there will still be enough income for the Bank's loan to be re-paid (plus interest) out of those sales actually made. Coverage of 200% (or 300%) should ensure full repayment of the loan, even if the film sales ultimately only make half (or a third) of the revenue anticipated by the Sales Agent.

## The Domestic Sale

As mentioned in our 'Building' analogy earlier in this chapter, sales to the North American market (which, for some reason, is referred to as the '**Domestic**' market, even by non-Americans), although usually the most lucrative, are also often the hardest to conclude. The North American market is flooded with films from every angle and, although American filmgoers are among the most prolific in the World, there are only so many pictures a person can see. Once a Producer has secured a Domestic release, international Distributors feel that the film will automatically receive a higher profile generally (particularly as it is likely to be released, with full fanfare, in the USA before the Distributor's own territory), and they will therefore often agree to pay a higher price for it. But the fact that Domestic sales are so hard to secure, particularly prior to the film's completion, results in the Banks usually ignoring potential income from a Domestic sale (or at least limiting it to a TV / video-only sale) when looking at sales estimates and calculating necessary coverage.

## Repayment

Banks will always insist on being the first to be paid back out of income received from exploitation of the film. This suits the Producer to some extent, because the Bank usually charges higher interest than any other financier, so the sooner they are paid off, the better. Sometimes it will allow for other financiers (usually just government bodies and 'deferments') to take a small 'corridor' and recoup *pari passu* (see Recoupment and Profit section above), but this will typically be given only after strong negotiations. Even the Sales Agent (see below) may have to defer some of its commission until the loan is repaid. The Bank will also usually take security over the film until it is paid off, and this is another reason why the Producer will want the Bank to recoup as soon as possible. However, one major advantage of gap financing is that the Bank will not hold an equity share in the film so, once it has been repaid, it will receive no share in the future revenues.

## Completion Bond

Just like a Bank that discounts pre-sales (see above), a gapping Bank will also normally require a **Completion Bond** to be put in place to ensure that the film is delivered by the Producer on time, so that buyers will be obliged to pay the balance of their MGs as soon as possible, and on Budget, so that no further money needs to be borrowed from elsewhere (the basic workings of Completion Bonds are explored later in this chapter). In fact, the gapping Bank will often prefer to be the Bank that discounts the existing pre-sales in any event. That way it gets more fees and interest, and the whole operation is more streamlined, with only one bank doing all the necessary lending.

## Costs of Gapping

The costs relating to gap loans will typically include a 'gap fee', a separate arrangement fee, and/or a loan fee, together with a particularly high interest rate (due to the risk factor) payable on the loan. It is therefore an expensive form of financing. The total fees may amount to 8% or 9% of the value of the gap, interest will probably be 2% or 3% above base rate, and the Producer will also have to cover the Bank's legal fees (which can be over £50,000 for a complicated transaction).

## The rise and fall of Insurance-Backed Gap

Traditionally, gap finance was fairly easy to come by, and Banks were prepared to put up about 20% of a film's budget in this way. Later, particularly in the late 1990s, a number of insurance companies wishing to expand their exposure to high-risk markets offered to 'insure' the gap loans on individual films. The Bank would insure against the risk that the anticipated sales levels were never reached, so that it could call upon the insurance company to pay back the loan if the Producer couldn't. This additional security (ie. the risk of the film not meeting its sales expectations now being moved to some extent from the Bank to the Insurance Company) allowed the Banks to increase the size of the gap loans dramatically, sometimes up to 50% - but more usually 30% to 40% - of the budget. Naturally, many films did not meet even their 'worst case' targets, and numerous Insurance Companies were 'called in' by the Banks to cough up the difference when gap loans were left unpaid. Mass litigation ensued (much of which is still on-going) as the Insurance Companies claimed that they were misled as to the risks of the projects, either by the Banks or the Producers (or both). As a result, insurance-backed gap financing has all but disappeared (although not necessarily for TV projects), and Banks are now reluctant even to put up the 20% which was common before the Insurance Companies' heightened involvement. In addition, many of the traditional gapping banks have left the scene altogether, and others have merged and/or severely tightened up their requirements.

## Summary

A typical gap loan in the current climate will provide a Producer with between 10% and 18% of the budget of the film, assuming all the Bank's other criteria are met. It is often the only way for a Producer to meet the full budget costs of his/her film, despite not really being his/her preferred form of finance due to the high costs attached. Banks that are currently active in this field include the Royal Bank of Scotland, Bank of Ireland, Comerica and Allied Irish Bank. Their contact details can be found in *The Directory* at the back of this Handbook. Other banks that were until recently fairly prolific in this field, and who have since removed themselves from the film arena and/or been taken over by other banks, include Banque Internationale de Luxembourg, Imperial Bank, LHO, Nat West, and Barclays.

# Completion Bonds

A **Completion Bond** (also known as a 'Completion Guarantee' or more usually, using the American spelling, '**Completion Guaranty**') is not actually a form of financing at all. But as the presence of a Bond is integral to so many financing transactions, it is important to understand the basics of how they work, and they therefore a deserve a few explanatory paragraphs of their own.

## Protecting the Financiers

In essence, a Bond is a kind of insurance taken out by a Producer in order to guarantee that the film will be completed without running over budget or (equally importantly) schedule. Financiers, especially the Banks, will normally require a Producer to take out a Completion Bond to help secure their investment; the film becomes worthless if it is ends up unfinished due to running out of funding, or if delays result in losing cast or a particularly desired exploitation opportunity.

Should it be impossible to finish the film on time and on budget, the **Bond Company** (a term which is interchangeable with '**Completion Guarantor**') will, under the Completion Guaranty, be required to repay all financiers who are party to the Completion Guaranty their *entire investment* to date! This means that if the Producer runs out of money, the Bond Company has to find the sums from elsewhere (any money already contributed will of course have already been used) in order to pay back the financiers – or, alternatively, pay to finish the film itself. It will usually take out its own insurance policy with Lloyds of London (or similar institution) to protect itself against this Armageddon scenario. Naturally, no Bond Company will ever want to do this unless absolutely necessary, and so it will not get involved with any project that it feels, following careful consideration of the script, budget, shooting schedule, locations, special effects, technical requirements (etc), is likely to be a no-hoper. If it chooses to board a project, it will in any event require rights of '**take-over**' allowing it to step in to replace the production team (or part of it), including the Producer and/or Director, in order to manage the production directly, if it feels that targets are being missed.

## How the Bond works

There are two main agreements entered into in relation to a Completion Bond. The first is the Completion Guaranty itself, between the Bond Company and the financiers whose position it is protecting. This states that the Guarantor will make sure (or 'guarantee') that the film is finished (or 'completed') and delivered on time, or else the Guarantor will repay all the financiers. In practice, if it becomes inevitable that the project is going to run out of funds, the Guarantor itself will usually prefer to muster up the extra cash needed to get the film finished on time, rather than have to repay all the financiers the entire amounts spent to date (which would usually, by this stage, mean repaying most of the budget – probably a much higher amount than the '**finishing funds**' required).

The second agreement is the Completion Agreement with the Producer, which gives the Bond Company its requisite rights of take-over and to receive certain documentation throughout the production. It is in the interests of both the Bond Company and the Producer that they work hand-in-hand with each other throughout the production. A representative from the Guarantor will periodically visit the set, and the Producer will be required to send in daily and weekly reports, setting out over-costs and over-runs to-date, and so on. These give the Bond Company a clear picture on how the production is going at any given point in time. Its personnel are usually experienced producers who have a full understanding of the quirks of film production, and have an array of ideas for when things start going wrong. Where problems look imminent, the Bond Company will offer advice and, in extreme circumstances, will remove and/or replace the Director, Producer, or other Key Elements in order to get the film finished on time and delivered to the Sales Agent and Distributors. In such circumstances, the Bond Company will not necessarily be overly interested in the artistic quality of the finished film; its concern will be getting the job done, and the film delivered in accordance with the various technical delivery requirements set out in the Completion Agreement (which approximately mirror those in the Distribution Agreements and Sales Agent's Agreement – albeit not necessarily in their entirety).

This is because the Completion Bond is there to protect the rights of the various financiers (who are the '**beneficiaries**' to the Bond), and not those of the Producer. As you can imagine, the Bond Company can be a bit of a burden (albeit arguably a necessary one) for the Producer, who would in an ideal world wish to keep total control of the film s/he is producing, and not spend the substantial fees (and time) on a Completion Guaranty that s/he often thinks will never be necessary. This is the reason that on smaller budget pictures, or those where there is no Bank (or other financier requiring equivalent protection), the Producer will often avoid taking out a Bond altogether.

It should also be noted that neither the Sales Agent, to whom the Producer delivers the film, nor the Distributors (to whom the Sales Agent then delivers on), are typically beneficiaries to the Bond, unless they themselves have put up any money for the production. For example, a

Distributor whose 20% pre-sale deposit is being used directly for the financing, will only be a beneficiary to the extent that if the film collapses, it will be repaid that amount.

The Producer will initially have to provide the Bond Company with a script, schedule and budget, as approved by the financiers and (where relevant) those Distributors that have already agreed to buy the film. The Bond Company will examine these documents, and any others it requests, in order to satisfy itself that the film can realistically be completed within the proposed budget, and that the Key Elements, insurance and locations are all properly dealt with.

## Strike Price and Contingency

The financiers will have to guarantee that they will all actually pay up their contributions, to ensure that the entire budget required to make the film is made available. Otherwise the Guarantor will not being willing to guarantee that it has enough money to complete it. The amount needed to complete the film, from the Bond's perspective, is known as the '**strike price**', and is usually roughly equal to the film's total budget less certain Producer deferrals (see below). However, the Guarantor will sometimes refuse to bond certain delivery items if it feels they are unnecessary, and may also refuse to bond certain costs relating specifically to the financing of the film itself (eg. financing fees and legal expenses) as it believes these should always be borne by the financiers, even if the film ultimately collapses. The Bond Company will also require that a '**contingency**' equal to about 10% of the budget is specified as a line item and set aside to cover any unforeseen budget overruns. Likewise, the fee for the Completion Guaranty will be agreed as a line item, and is often calculated as a percentage of the budget (usually in the region of about 2% to 6%, depending mostly on the confidence the Bond Company has in the project). However, if the Guaranty is not 'called upon' (ie. the Bond Company is not required to pay up any money), there will often be a rebate equal to approximately half of the original Bond fee, especially if the original bond fee was at the higher end of the scale.

## Bond Companys' track records

As an aside, it is also important for the Producer and his/her financiers to establish whether or not the Completion Guarantor would actually be able to pay up if called upon. The Bond Company will have taken out an insurance policy to cover itself in the event of being required to pay large sums back to the investors, and the Producer and financiers have every right to enquire about this, as well as the Bond Company's track record. The more established Guarantors in the field include Film Finances, International Film Guarantors and CineFinance. Details of these and other Bond Companies are set out in *The Directory* at the back of this Handbook.

# Deferments

Many people don't think of deferments as a source of financing and, technically, perhaps they're not. But they do reduce the amount of finance required from elsewhere, and so therefore make a positive contribution to the budget. We touched on deferments briefly in our Building analogy at the beginning of this chapter and there are only a few points to add.

As mentioned, the simple concept is that certain cast and/or crew (usually starting with the Producer!) agree to their fee being paid part up-front, and part out of future sales revenue. The entire fee is included in the budget (for it is contractually payable as a cost of making the film), but the Producer does not need to find production finance to cover the whole lot. Let's say a £10m film has an A-list actor charging a £2m fee. If the actor is willing to defer £1m of this, the Producer only needs to find £9m from elsewhere to get his film on the screen. It is almost as if the actor him/herself is financing the film to the tune of £1m. The net amount required (£9m in this example) is known as the '**cash budget**', as it reflects the amount of cash actually needed to physically make the film. Actors may be willing to defer some of their fee if they really believe in the project, especially if they are taking a break from the studio system to do a 'worthy' independent picture. But they will, in return, probably require a piece of the back end.

The actor will be the first person to receive income from sales of the film, even before the gapping Bank. This is because the first sales are really just completing the financing of the film (the deferred £1m was still included in the budget), rather than subsequent income. Whether or not the Sales Agent takes any commission on these first sales is a point for negotiation (it will usually take a small proportion of its fee and defer the rest – see the section on Sales Agents' Commission, below).

There is clearly a fine line between, on the one hand, a £10m film with £1m actors fees deferred, and on the other hand, a £9m film where the actor simply has first position on the Recoupment Schedule until Net Receipts equal £1m. The financiers will generally want to claim the higher budget if they are looking to benefit from tax breaks based on budget size (as is possible in the UK at present). Accordingly, there is UK legislation limiting the inclusion of deferments in budgets of British qualifying films for tax purposes (see chapter 4 for more details).

And in practice, it is not the actors who need to be most aware of the possible need to defer fees. The first fees to go this way are usually those of the Producer, usually because the financiers demand it! To them, it is a sign that the Producer believes in the project enough to put his/her money where his/her mouth is. If s/he produces a turkey, no sales will be made and the Producer will not get paid his/her full fee. Where the Producer has sourced almost enough money to make the film, the financiers may require the budget to be squeezed a little to make it fit (rather than bring another financier on board), and the Producer's fee is the first to go.

Sometimes, particularly on very low budget films, it is the Producer him/herself who requires deferments from the rest of the cast and crew. This way s/he reduces the cash budget as much as possible, so that the amount of finance ultimately required from elsewhere is at the absolute minimum. And it is not just cast and crew who may be asked to defer in these cases. It is not unheard of for printers, laboratories, prop providers, film stock suppliers, screenwriters, (etc) to be asked to take their fees out of sales receipts (to be paid *parri passu* with each other) in order to get the film made for 'tuppence ha'penny'.

There is one other major consideration regarding deferments, and that relates to the strike price for a Completion Guaranty (see previous section). The strike price will be reduced on a bonded film by the value of any deferments because the Completion Guarantor will not need to pay back any 'financier' who has not actually put up any money and, using our £10m film example again, will acknowledge that only £9m is needed to ensure that the film gets made and delivered on time.

# Sales Agents' Commission

As has been illustrated in previous sections in this chapter, the role of the Sales Agent is fundamental to the likelihood of a film going into profit, as it is the Sales Agent whose job it is to sell the film and thereby bring in the income from which the financiers are repaid. A list of Sales Agents (with their contact details) is set out in *The Directory* at the end of this Handbook. Before we look at the Sales Agent as a potential financier (in the next section), it is important to understand the basics behind the Sales Agent's role in the whole process, its typical deal, and its commission structure.

## The cost of selling

The Sales Agent performs a function similar to any other agent in a distribution-based industry (see, for example, the comparison with an Estate Agent in the Building analogy earlier in this chapter). A good Sales Agent will strive to form business relationships with as many Distributors around the world as possible. If it has many potential buyers for a 'must have' picture, it can pitch them against each other to get the best price attainable. Unfortunately, most films are not so easy to sell, and the Sales Agent has to work hard promoting them at festivals and markets around the world. This costs money. A plush suite at Cannes can cost anything up to £50,000 for the week, and when coupled with the costs of putting on screenings (at £1,000 to £2,000 each), throwing the obligatory party (up to £50,000), and paying for A-list stars to fly over in their swanky private jets to attend market premieres (anywhere up to £100,000), expenses quickly add up. These costs (known as '**Sales Expenses**'), although laid out initially by the Sales Agent, are recoupable immediately out of the proceeds of the sales made (although after the deduction of the Sales Agent's '**commission**').

## Deferred and non-deferred Commission

The level of commission payable to the Sales Agent depends on a number of factors. Often (but not always), commission on a US ('**Domestic**') sale will be a few percentage points less than on a sale to other territories. And there is usually no commission payable on pre-sales that the Sales Agent didn't itself arrange. The commission payable will, however, usually be around the region of 10% to 25%. Where the Agent has been instrumental in helping to source other finance for the film, has been involved from the beginning, and/or has contributed creatively to the development and production of the film, it is likely to charge a higher commission (plus, usually, an executive producer's fee). Conversely, where the Agent has been appointed later in the day and has done nothing else but simply sell the picture, a typical deal might be to award it 15% on international sales, and maybe 10% on any Domestic Sale.

Any Bank providing gap finance will often try to insist that, whatever commission the Sales Agent is ultimately entitled to, it should not be permitted to actually get its hands on the money until the Bank has been paid off. The Bank will always want to paid back first, and by taking as much of each dollar of income as possible. The Sales Agent may therefore be required to '**defer**' a proportion of its commission.

For example, a Bank providing gap finance for a $20m film may require that the Sales Agent, who is contractually entitled to 15% commission on all sales, takes only two thirds of its commission (ie. 10%) until such time as the Bank has fully recouped. Ignoring any Collection Agent's fee (usually less than 1%), this will allow the Bank to be paid back 90¢, instead of

85¢, out of each dollar received from sales. If the Bank had put up 15% of the budget as gap finance (and also ignoring its interest for the purposes of this example), the loan amount that it will need to recoup is $3m (ie. 15% of $20m). If the Sales Agent's Expenses amounted to $500k, the Bank will have recouped once the Sales Agent has made sales equalling $3.888m. This is because after the Sales Agent has taken its 10% non-deferred commission ($388k) and then its $500k Expenses, there is exactly $3m left of the $3.888m sales income from which the Bank can recoup. At this point, the Bank is 'out of the picture', but the Sales Agent is still 'owed' $194k (the 5% deferred element of the $3.888m sales made to date). It will take this straight from the next sale(s) it makes (after taking its full 15% commission from such subsequent sale(s)). So if the next sale made is (say) for $500k, the Sales Agent will be entitled to 15% ($75k) as its commission on that sale, plus the deferred of $194k which accrued whilst the Bank was being paid off, totalling $269k, and leaving the remaining $231k for the pot. From then on it will just take its standard 15% commission.

Both the amount of commission that a Sales Agent takes, and the proportion that it is willing to defer, are dependent on a number of things, but mostly in relation to how much involvement the Agent has had in the project. However, one thing that is fairly standard is that it will only defer commission until the gapping Bank is 'off', and not past that point.

### Commission on pre-sales

Another point to note is that where the Sales Agent is in fact entitled to commission on pre-sales (because it arranged them), it may not be able to take it from the sale proceeds if they are being used for the financing of the film. In this case, the Sales Agent will get its commission paid out of the next sales it does. In other words, it will recoup this commission in first position, even before the Bank. All of this will, of course, be set out clearly in the Recoupment Schedule.

## Sales Advances and 'International Distribution'

Sometimes, the Sales Agent itself will actually contribute finance to the film. This is known as a '**sales advance**', and works in a similar way to gap finance. In fact it is very rare for there to be a sales advance and gap financing on the same film, as they will both want to be in first position on the Recoupment Schedule, and are both effectively advances against future sales. If there is no gap financier, the Sales Agent may agree to advance money against its first few sales, wherever they may be. By contributing finance to the production, the Sales Agent can normally negotiate for itself get a much better commission rate of up to 25% or even 30% on all future sales, depending on how much of the budget it puts forward.

Most Sales Agents do not themselves have enough cash of their own to be investing in film production. Those that are willing to put up a sales advance usually do it through an arranged facility with their own bank. That bank will provide the Sales Agent with some form of credit line, but will ask similar questions to those asked by a gapping bank.

One advantage to the Sales Agent (other than the obvious higher commission rate) is that it does not have to defer its commission behind a gapping bank. Another advantage is that, when advancing production finance, the Sales Agent can be given the role of an '**international distributor**' rather than a pure 'agent'. This means that, rather than just being appointed to sell the film on behalf of the Producer, it takes an actual licence of the distribution rights themselves, and then sublicenses them around the World. Returning to our Building analogy, this is sort of equivalent to taking a lease on all floors and then subletting them, rather than acting as an estate agent and just arranging leases directly between the landlord and the tenants. Naturally, if the agent takes the rights itself, it will have more control over them and will not be obliged to turn to seek as many approvals from the original rights owners when doing its deals. In fact, technically, a Sales Agent who takes the role of an international distributor is not really an 'agent' for anyone at all.

To recap, the amount an international distributor contributes to a budget is also similar to that provided by a gap financier; usually under 20%. It will take its full commission from the first sales it makes, and recoup its sales advance from the net amount left. Once it has recouped, it continues to take commission on future sales, and the net (remainder) is distributed according to the agreed Recoupment Schedule.

# Negative Pick-ups

As '**Negative Pick-ups**' are not really a direct form of financing, there is no need to go into much detail about them for the purposes of this Handbook, but a brief explanation may be useful.

A Negative Pick-up is an acquisition of all the rights to all territories, often by a Studio. If the Studio (or other prospective purchaser) likes the concept of a film but does not want to commit itself to financing or paying for it until after it is given the opportunity to see the finished article, it may agree to buy the whole film at a later date. After paying over the purchase price, it would effectively own the film (having 'picked up the negative' from the Producer), and can then exploit it throughout the world, by itself, and without having to pay anything back into the pot. The price it pays to the Producer for the film will hopefully exceed the cost of producing it, so that the Producer can pay back all the financiers with the proceeds of the sale, and (hopefully) keep any left-overs for him/herself and any other profit participants. The buyer will then go on to sell and/or distribute the film itself (if a Studio), or alternatively appoint a third party Sales Agent. Unless they managed to negotiate a continuing interest in the film after the acquisition, neither the Producer nor the original financiers will see any further income from it.

# Bridging Finance

One type of finance that is often confused with gap finance is bridging finance. Whereas gap finance 'closes the gap' in the budget between the amount of money needed and the amount raised (usually a maximum of 20%), bridging finance closes the gap in **time** between the film's finance being ready, and being actually needed! Bridging finance comes into play if *all* the finance is agreed in principle for 100% of the budget of the film, but due to legal technicalities, the financiers will not let go of their funds until all 'i's have been dotted and 't's crossed. The bridging financier takes a view on how far down the line the agreements are, and how soon after the commencement of '**principal photography**' (when the bulk of the money is needed) these will be tied up. If it feels that there is little chance of the entire financing falling apart, it may lend the producer the money it needs in order for in to start production, and thereby not lose any of its cast, crew, weather opportunities, locations, etc. As soon as the financing agreements are closed, the production finance will be made available for the film, and the bridging financier can be paid back whatever it has advanced to date (plus a hefty fee!).

A Producer should try to avoid using bridging finance by making sure all financing agreements are tied up before the film actually goes into production. This is because bridging finance - if available at all - is very expensive (and usually not budgeted for), and the film will not be benefit from any Completion Bond until the main financing contracts have been agreed.

# Venture Capital

Venture capitalists make high-risk investments in growth businesses with a high potential return. They may be willing to invest in projects that other lenders, such as banks, would turn down due to the high risk and the high sums required. The venture capitalist becomes a shareholder in the production company and they will often take on an executive role informing long-term business strategy. Business Angels are venture capitalists that invest in small and medium-sized enterprises (SME's) which can benefit from the Business Angel's knowledge and experience as well as their finance.

The **Enterprise Investment Scheme** ('**EIS**') and the **Venture Capital Trust** ('**VCT**') are other options, and provide tax breaks to their investors. Often, particularly under the EIS system, this type of finance will be used to pay for the entire production (especially on lower budget films), thereby reducing the need to obtain and piece together other forms of finance for the picture. These schemes are discussed in a little more detail in the next chapter, and contact details for relevant organisations can be found in *The Directory* at the end of this Handbook.

# Sponsorship and Product Placement

## Sponsorship

Sponsorship generally involves a business paying a company in cash or in kind to promote the sponsor's products or services. In the film industry, for example, a drinks company may supply free beverages throughout the production period in return for a screen credit and/or some other form of exposure. In some cases a producer may also be able to secure a cash payment from a company in return for a screen credit. For example, Adrian J MacDowall's £3000 BAFTA winning short *Who's My Favourite Girl* has a sponsor credit list at the end of the film longer than that for the cast and crew. That said, for larger budgeted pictures in particular, the amount of time spent trying to identify and secure a sponsor may not justify the amount of money received in the deal.

There is room to be creative when conceiving a sponsorship deal, which can come from the most unlikely of sources. In fact, a Producer may have a better chance of securing a sponsorship deal with a company not directly related to the film industry as the perceived glamour might be a more effective pull to a company that is not trying to make its living within it. The sponsor will want to feel like it is going to get exposure in return for its donation, and this can make it difficult for an inexperienced Producer to attract sponsorship, unless s/he is a great marketeer. Some companies have specific sponsorship budgets as part of their advertising and/or marketing allowances. *First Light*, the initiative that brings production companies and young filmmakers together, has produced short guidelines on approaching sponsorship:

> *'Businesses tend to sponsor arts activities to develop their corporate image in three ways: their relationship with their own employees, their relationship with other companies, and their relationship with their local community. Sponsorship is generally part of a wider marketing strategy and most companies won't sponsor you simply because you are deserving. You should approach potential sponsors with a sense of what you may be able to offer them, of how your film project will help their profile in the community. Sponsorship can be a time-consuming process, often for relatively small amounts of money, which are 'one-offs', so it may be best to focus your energy on getting to understand public funding, rather than pinning all your hopes on private sources. If you do find a sponsor who has never sponsored the arts before, it may be possible to get matching funds from Arts & Business'.*

## Product Placement

Product placement has become a common source of finance for big budget US productions, and is increasingly being used by UK Producers. It works in a similar way to sponsorship in that a company contributes to the production in cash or in kind. However, product placement specifically refers to the product, its brand name and/or logo, appearing on screen in the body of the film itself, rather than simply a credit for the company in the end-titles. As with sponsorship, it is more likely that an experienced producer working on a strong project will secure a product placement deal, because the advertiser will want to ensure as far as possible that the product will be seen by the general public.

Critics of this form of film finance question the involvement of advertisers in production and how much creative control they can exert over it, anxious that filmmakers do not abandon artistic integrity to get the deal. How often do you see a drink or mobile phone in a modern film where the brand is so 'in-yer-face' that you momentarily lose concentration on the film itself?

A very real problem for a director and editor is keeping the required product placement shots in the final cut if they coincide with scenes that they would otherwise choose to cut out. The brand owner will usually specify in its contract a minimum number of seconds or minutes, and sometimes even maximum intervals, for when the product must be clearly visible on screen.

Another important factor, when considering product placement, is how it might affect a television distribution deal. Most broadcasters have rules about advertising, and there is sometimes a very fine line between product placement and full-on advertising. In the UK, for example, the Independent Television Commission (now succeeded by OfCom) produced comprehensive guidelines (*The ITC Code of Programme Sponsorship*, first issued in Autumn 2000 but since updated) on product placement and advertising within television programmes and broadcast films. Although most of the guidelines concern television production, the regulations are applicable to films acquired for television broadcast, although the stipulations are a little more flexible. The full regulations can be accessed and downloaded from the OfCom web site (www.ofcom.org.uk/tv/ifi/codes). A list of companies involved in product placement and/or sponsorship, and their contact details, can be found in *The Directory* at the end of this Handbook.

# Case studies

## Owen Thomas *Elemental films*
## Completion Bonds for low budget

The great untold story of completion bonds is that bond companies don't like low budgets and generally dissuade producers who approach them. We didn't choose not to have a bond, it was more a case of the bond companies telling us they don't encourage a bond at a certain budget level. Having a bond alters the way a film gets made; the majority of our crew would never have been acceptable to a bond company, who prefer tried-and-tested talent. Our working methods would have been challenged all along the line. It would not have been the case that we needed to find the 40k to pay the bond, we would have had to find an additional one million to meet their requirements. We'd have been killed before we started.

This way we have an accomplished production which has given significant opportunities for new talent to assert itself and should provide an examplar of how to conduct film making as a fiscally sound business - profit will arrive far sooner than for comparable films made on typical budgets. What better way is there to move forward than to earn on one's own film?

From a producer's perspective, it doesn't make sense to bond a low budget picture. The cost of a bond is a big chunk of the budget, money that's better spent on the screen. We were fortunate in that our financiers accepted that 'Solid Air' would be unbonded and given that we fulfilled their requirements - that the shoot would be adequately crewed, that the schedule was achievable on the budget, they were satisfied to proceed without one.' NW

# Lee Beasley *Royal Bank of Scotland* Bank finance

*Lee Beasley heads up the Film and Television Team at the Corporate Banking Centre at the Royal Bank of Scotland plc where, during the past 11 years, he has specialised in the Film and Television sector.*

My view, in the days when we provided insurance-backed finance, was that even though we could technically rely on an insurance policy, it was always better to act as though we were actually uninsured. This set us up well for the current climate where we no longer provide insurance-backed loans, and we therefore have to take the risks ourselves, although we do now charge a higher fee to reflect this.

We are now the sixth largest bank in the world by market capitalisation and my team are currently involved in the financing of over 60 films, with an aggregate production value in excess of $400m. The projects financed by the team are not limited to British Films and in fact are predominantly UK/Canadian, UK/ Australian co-productions or involve some level of soft money from the UK or Europe. In fact, nearly all of the films financed by us involve some form of soft money. That said, since the change in the UK/Canadian spend splits from 80/20 to 60/ 40, we have seen a massive reduction in the number of Canadian/UK co-productions in the last year or so. In recent times we have been involved in a larger proportion of transactions with the Irish Film Board and Scottish Screen than with the UK Film Council'

It is quite rare for the Bank to finance a film with only one or two financing parties. More often than not the number exceeds 4 parties - patchwork finance at it's best.

Every film is different - I don't mean creatively but how they are financed. The films financed by the Bank tend to be in the budget range of between £2m and £15m. I firmly believe that films above this budget are made for a completely different market and must always have some form of US distribution attached. The opposite is true of the independent films, which we finance. We almost NEVER see US distribution attached to our projects.

I believe that there is only one basic principle for film finance from the Bank's point of view. The film has to have commercial appeal. Without this there is no foundation for Bank finance. Don't get me wrong here- this is not something that the Bank ever has any control over or indeed input in. I should point out that whenever the Bank finances a project - it has no creative control over the project whatsoever; nor do we want it! But every project must have been tested in the market. I don't mean that an equity fund has agreed to invest, or a tax partnership or even the film council, I mean that an exhibitor or broadcaster in a particular territory has agreed to pay $x on delivery and completion of the project.

I probably see over 100 projects each year; some of which have no finance attached whatsoever. I still see projects, which I originally looked at over 5 years ago. It never ceases to amaze me how many producers try to make a film wholly financed by soft money/equity and are loathe to make any pre-sales. They are adamant that the rights will be worth considerably more once the film has been made. In some cases, this will indeed be the case but in others the reverse is true.

There is a basic level of information that is required for the Bank to consider any type of film finance. I apologise for stating the obvious but we need to see, as a minimum, the script, final cast/crew list and CVs, budget, completion bond provider, finance plan, sales agents estimates and pre-sale contracts/deal memos.

All feature films funded by our Bank are required to have a Completion Bond in place. It is important to understand that the role of the Completion Bonder is not just a financial one. It has been described as both a financial tool and management tool. An important feature, which is sometimes over-looked, is that they are there to offer advice and avoid potential problems or pit-falls. I am advised that on average roughly 10% of all productions get into some form of trouble or another.

As part of the Bank's due diligence on each project we assess the credit worthiness of the Completion Bonder's insurance programme. Notwithstanding this, I am not aware of any occasions where a Completion Bonder has failed to pay its obligations. Over the past 2 years, we have had 2 instances where productions had gone severely over budget, one due to bad weather and the other due to the collapse of the post-production facility. On both occasions, overcost claims of £165k and £312k were paid in full.

Contract Discounting is our 'bread & butter' lending. We are asked to discount two types of contracts - pre-sale contracts and sales agent advance contracts.

In all cases, we need to assess the credit worthiness of the contracting party or buyer. This is done via normal channels such as published financial information or internal management accounts. Furthermore, considerable comfort is taken from the track record of the buyer with the Bank. In some instances, we have worked with a letter of credit. Buyers in Russia, Eastern Europe and some of the small Asian territories are historically slow payers. Recourse via the legal system is very expensive and often pointless. In essence, the Bank is looking to advance monies against 'watertight' contracts where the only reason for the buyer not paying is simply because they are no longer trading. The buyers are asked to enter into a notice and acceptance of assignment in favour of the Bank. This ensures that the payment due under the contract is remitted directly to the Bank or collection agent.

We also provide Gap Finance or deficit finance, as it is sometimes called. The maximum Gap must not exceed 25%, although on average the gap finance provided by the Bank is within 15% to 20% range. The producer must have secured at least 75% of the budget from other sources, some of which must come from commercial pre-sales. The Bank must recoup in first position. We provide debt finance for a fee, and do not benefit in any part of the success in terms of the Film's profits. This is reserved for the equity providers who recoup well after the Bank. We therefore insist that any future revenue from any source (theatrical, DVD, Video, Pay/free TV) flows to the Bank in recoupment of its facility subject only to the sales agents commissions. It is almost unheard of that independent films in this budget range break out theatrically in ALL territories and it is fair to say that DVD/TV provide the main sources of income.

We also require a sales agent to be on board, and sales estimates to cover the Bank gap on a 2 to 1 basis. We work with nearly all of the established sales agents, some of whom are better than others for different genres of films - It is very much assessed on a 'horses for courses' basis. I firmly believe that the sales agent should be incentivised to generate sales quickly and for this reason we allow a modest marketing budget and sales commission corridor for the sales agent during Bank recoupment. The sales agent is key to the Bank and it is sometimes worrying when you see some estimates provided for unsold territories- this is especially the case for the US. Very few films in the budget bracket that I finance go on to be released theatrically in the States. Although we don't discount this territory completely, we do tend to reduce this estimate to a PAY-TV sale rather than a theatrical sale.

For all gap finance transactions, we require two commercial pre-sales in key territories. Each project must have been tested commercially and in our opinion, the only way of doing this is by way of pre-sales. I fully appreciate that the pre-sale market is especially tough at the present time - it is very much a buyers' market and in the present climate, many can and indeed do wait to see the finished film before agreeing to buy. However, this is a key test for the Bank and also reinforces the estimates provided by the sales agent. I am often approached for gap finance where producers have raised 80 or 90% of the budget via soft sources of finance. Without evidence of commerciality I simply have to pass.

We are obviously looking to work with experienced producers/ directors in the majority of cases. However, we do work with first time directors on occasions but it is very much on the basis that the production team around them is an experienced one. If a first time director together with an inexperienced producer came to the Bank looking for gap finance it is likely that we would be unable to assist.

Gap finance goes hand in hand with contract discounting and it is very rare indeed for us to simply fund the gap portion of a film. We are also, in certain circumstances, willing to lend against the sale and leaseback benefit when we are providing gap finance. Going forward, we welcome the change to the cumbersome and expensive sale and leaseback structure, and the Bank is keen to become involved in lending against the proposed new tax credit, but there is a long way to go before the credit is entirely bankable.

Depending upon the complexity of the transaction and the number of parties involved, closing of the documentation can take anything from 3 to 6 weeks. Our security will consist of a legal charge over the rights to the film and an assignment of any contracts being discounted. All financing parties along with the producer and Completion Bonder will enter into an Inter-party Agreement which is the main financing agreement. This tends to be the hardest document to finalise primarily due to the number of parties involved. Film Production Insurance and Error & Omissions must be in place prior to drawdown with the Bank's interest noted. It is fair to say that the closing process seems to be becoming more and more protracted primarily due to the high number of financing parties involved in a film and more significantly the complex arrangements of the various tax funds. As a result, this year has seen a record number of films requiring the assistance of bridge financiers simply due to the time it takes to close the documentation.'

# Mira Nair *Vanity Fair* Working with a studio

*After winning the Golden Lion at Berlin for Monsoon Wedding, Mira Nair returned to the studio system for the first time since The Perez Family to produce a big budget adaptation of William Makepeace Thackeray's Vanity Fair with Reese Witherspoon.*

**How did you become involved in this project?**

It was an extraordinary coincidence, really, because I have loved this novel since I was 16 years old. But I had no hankering to make it into a film, and I usually originate my own films, I don't look for work. The studio had Monsoon Wedding in distribution and it was a big hit for them, and they simply offered me their best, or biggest, next thing. They didn't know that I loved this novel, and I pretty much said yes instantly.

**You had quite a bad experience with a studio when you made The Perez Family?**

It was a terrible experience.

**Did it make you leery of working within the studio system?**

It depends entirely on who you work with, you know? Vanity Fair is also a studio film and it's been a completely respectful and wonderful experience, because they came to me for my sensibility. I gave them my sensibility and they were dazzled -- that is the word they used – by it. You know, they let me be. Not so with Mr Samuel Goldwyn, who saw the piece [The Perez Family] and, you know, Four Weddings and a Funeral was out that year, and basically when they tested Perez in America, the results were so high and fantastic that he began to think that maybe it will be even better if it's just a total comedy. So the problem was that my film was this rhythm of memory and exile, which was tragic-comic, like the Cubans are, and theirs was, 'It's reading funny, let's go for the broad comedy.' That's where the fight began. It's very sad because even if you think you're winning, if you tamper with the essential rhythm of a picture, you're lost. So I lost.

**What did you learn from that?**

Just to trust myself even more and to rely on myself even more. I am an independent filmmaker and an independent producer as well, I produce my own films, so I have never looked to be on any A-list. To me the reason I do what I do is to do what I do, you know what I mean? [Laughs] That's the privilege, rather than wanting to be on an A-list.

**Were you involved in producing Vanity Fair?**

Yes. The main producer on it was Lydia Dean Pilcher, with whom I have done everything since Mississippi Masala. We work very closely. Like in this movie, Vanity Fair, I can't even believe it myself, but we shot this in 55 days. It's a huge movie, you know, and the only way we can do that is to organise the production, that is extraordinarily organised, which is how I do my own movies. You know, cutting my cloth to size, but making you believe I have all the cloth in the world. That's the trick and that's what I do with my producing partner. I have to plan it very, very carefully otherwise it doesn't look as it looks.

*Stephen Applebaum*

# Jacqueline Swanson *Checkout Girl* Product placement

*Rupert Grave's Checkout Girl, staring Pauline Quirk, is a comedy short set in a supermarket. Producer Jacqueline Swanson spent a year raising almost £25,000 in product placement fees, as well as stocking an entire supermarket with produce.*

We were first scheduled to shoot in December of 1998 on an RAF base leased to the US Airforce. The whole place was in the process of being decommissioned but the base commissary (the supermarket) was still open and they were very happy for us to use it as our set over their three-day weekends. About five weeks before we were scheduled to shoot I got a call saying that the LA press office were unable to let us continue. Films shot on US bases need to promote the US armed forces and it's recruitment. In all fairness everyone at the base felt terrible that we had gone so far down the line without being aware of the protocol but in the military I guess rules are rules and we were, unfortunately in breach of them. No amount of script doctoring was going to make us fit their criteria.

After having to call everyone to cancel the shoot I hid under my duvet for a week before resurfacing to reconsider our position. I reckoned the budget was going to go up by another £25,000 if we were going to even consider building a supermarket. To my surprise when I consulted the key cast and crew they all wanted to continue with the project and were happy to re-discuss their fees further down the line should it be necessary. It would be inappropriate for me to discuss the actual final fees but let's just say that as filmmakers Rupert and I are totally indebted to everyone who worked on the film from our runners and local extras right up to the HoDs and main cast. In a perverse way the production was so big and had so much support I did not really have the option of giving up, although we often felt that we really had bitten off too much.

Because of Pauline's schedule her next available slot was going to be December 1999 which gave me just under a year to raise the rest of the budget. We had already received production funding from Southern Arts (Rupert was from Southampton) who also then came through with post production funding. I had a very good friend at Saatchi & Saatchi who had put the script forward to a couple of account directors with some positive but ultimately non-committal feedback. Product placement was a fairly uncharted territory at that point. However, when

Sunny Delight was about to launch in the UK they had generous budgets and more scope for taking risks. It was pretty much left to me to structure the deal and suggest a fee. Although it was a significant amount for the production it really was not a big commitment for the agency so the whole process was fairly straightforward. I had suggested a four-tier payment structure; a sum on first day of photography, another on completion of shoot, a third on sale to a UK broadcaster and the final instalment on sale to a US broadcaster or Trans Atlantic in-flight entertainment programme. We also received product placement monies from HP Beans. That was also fairly straightforward. I explained to them how much the set was costing to build and asked them for a portion of the costs up front. They were happy with my proposal in the knowledge that their product was going to 'colour' the film rather than the distinctive colour of their main competitors.

*Tom Fogg*

# Kenneth D Barker *Kingdom* Angel investors

*Kenneth D Barker's debut went against the notion that the first feature should be modest and not too ambitious, but with backing from an angel investor Kingdom set out to get good returns from the family market. The film is set in the world's last dragon sanctuary and is a modern urban fairy tale with full-blown CGI dragons.*

I'd left film school and was gagging to make a feature. I figured that once I'd made it, at least I could sell copies at the local car-boot if there was no conventional interest. Most members of the public buy feature films, how many of them will buy a short? All the usual funding agencies said 'nice idea — but bugger off'. Then in a strange twist of fortune, I kept meeting all these talented people who were also looking for a break in films or television. They were model makers, make-up artists and computer graphics geeks. That's when I realised *Kingdom* was achievable on a modest budget.

A month before we were scheduled to start filming, I had £200 and a Hi8 camera to my name, which was not quite enough. It was only after a very convoluted set of circumstances that I heard about a Business Angel network and they were prepared to listen to me. I had a comprehensive business plan I had prepared. All the Angels I spoke to were initially more interested in me as a person, then me as a manager. They wanted to know if I could be trusted with their money — which is a fair way of assessing a risk. Perhaps more importantly, I was genuinely excited about making *Kingdom* and I'm sure my excitement spilt over during my presentation.

I set up a company and the angel sits on it as a non-executive director. Day to day operations are handled by myself, but we both co-own *Kingdom* and all its rights.

My advice to any other film maker looking at the Angel route is — be prepared to give up a lot of the project to get it financed, but ideally you need to retain artistic control. Then be grateful that somebody's interested in backing your wild notion.

*James MacGregor*

# Janey de Nordwall *Silver Films*
# Business angels

*Janey de Nordwall founded Silver Film in 1996, and in 2000 decided to focus the company solely on film production. She approached the North West Business Angel Network – Techinvest – and sold a percentage of her company to raise capital to part-finance two shorts – About a Girl and Jump - and a relocation to London. About A Girl was a runaway success for her and director Brian Percival, nabbing the BAFTA for Best short in 2002 and winning first prize in Turner Classic Movies short film award.*

Few people really understand business angels. Back in 2000 I did my first presentation to 70 angels in the same room. They were not investing in the films, they were investing in the company – I pitched doing a slate of three short films as a research and development process to build awareness of Silver Films in the industry and build relationships with creative talent, ahead of producing features.

I also saw making shorts as the route to learning about producing films. I already knew how to produce, production manage and build a budget and so forth from my time doing promos, but realised very quickly how different film is to commercials. I wanted to see if I could pick up on a script that I believed in and take it forward. When I sent the *About A Girl* script to people in the industry, they all said the same thing 'you don't want to make that, it'll do you no good, you want to make a comedy'. I had to sit back and think am I right, are they wrong, and after a while I decided 'this is what I believe in and want to move forward with'. What I had wanted to learn as a producer was how to trust my instinct, and the success of *About A Girl* proved to me, and the industry, that I could.

My angels are advisors as well as investors, they offer help with the business, planning, legal issues and so forth - we have monthly board meetings – they're there for the long haul, and may not get a return on investment in the next five or six years. At the end of my presentation to the business angel network I said, 'this is long term, high risk, but potentially high return' and three guys came along and said lets go for it. One in Manchester, one in London and one in Chicago. They all reinvested for more money, and I'm currently looking to a fourth investor with a bigger lump for development on the feature slate.

If you can get a slate of films together it allows the investors choice on what they want to put their money into. They may dislike foreign films for example so its nice to have a range of films on your slate, there's also slate funding out there through the Film Council and other organisations that appreciate the slate over the individual film. It adds to the longevity of production companies and of the industry. It lets people hedge their bets! Out of five films maybe one will be OK. I had three shorts slated and made just two of them: *About a Girl*, which cost £35,000 and *Jump*, which cost £55,000. My first year at Silver Films, which included moving from Manchester to London, was funded by £100,000 of investment – a mixture of money from selling equity in the company to the angels, matched by the same amount from North West Vision, my own money, sponsorship and product placement cash.

The sponsorship and product placement came from my contacts in the gaming industry. Sponsorship was from 3DO, who were making a new PR marketing campaign about how gaming crosses over so many mediums, ie that gamers are interested in sport, fashion and film. The campaign was that they are supporters of new talent in the industry, they sponsored someone in music, fashion and film and gave us £10,000 in return for a logo at the end of the Jump and use of us as marketing on the website and so forth. And they gave £2,000 for the premiere at Planet Hollywood. For product placement, we sold ad space to games that were coming out around the time of the film's premiere so we had Final Fantasy 9 on a t-shirt in a bus for £1,000.

*About A Girl* was winning awards at the same time as Yousaf Ali Khan's *Skin Deep*, which got 3rd in TCM, was a BAFTA nominee and Kodak award winner. Yousaf and myself looked at working on a feature project together, and decided to test the relationship by making a short film– *Talking With Angels*, made in Salford with much of the 80 cast and crew sourced from locals. It cost about £50,000 just to shoot and the funding on it is very different to the other two shorts: we got money from the LFVDA, from North West Vision, and some cash from Fox SearchLab which finances shorts. SearchLab is the little sister of Fox Searchlight, with whom we have a first look deal. I began discussions with them after *About A Girl* was the only British short to be accepted into Sundance. I then met up with them in LA whist I was on the Inside Pictures course. They were great and said do it in your own timescale, we want to work with you, they didn't want to read the script, they just trusted my instinct. We got funding also from B3 Projects who give money for ethnic minority work and are going to get involved in the distribution and marketing. We've also, unusually, got regional government cash, because we are making a big difference to the Salford community by using locals. There's money from Salford Council, Salford University, the Regeneration and Employment Agencies and the Cornerstone Community centre. Mike Knowles who runs the Northern Film Network, is my co-producer on this and helped set that up as he's based in Manchester still.

I'm getting my feature slate together. While it's very important to have a slate I only want to work on films that I believe in. I just go for things that turn me on – my films tend to be very social issue films, very personal, that have a message, that have social awareness – but not depressing regional drabness.

You get used to having that feeling of hitting walls. You're kind of living on the edge all the time, and there are these big highs and then these incredible lows when you don't want to have anything to do with this industry. I do get really down, in fact recently I was about to write the email saying I was about to quit the industry and go sit on a beach and plaid my hair – when you hit that sort of point you need to take some time out and think about what you're doing and what you want to achieve. The highs and lows are going to be a constant thing and you have to ask yourself, what do you want out of this? Is it kudos, is it awards, is it money? I want to achieve an emotion from an audience and that kind of makes it a lot easier than being motivated by money or fame.

*NW / Tom Fogg*

**CHAPTER FOUR**

# UK TAX-BASED MONEY

*"Sale & Leaseback is dead! Long live Sale & Leaseback!"*

Or, as Mark Twain probably would have put it: *"The reports of the death of* Sale & Leaseback *have been greatly exaggerated."*

In recent years, the most prolific use of UK tax allowances on lower budget films has been the rather complicated, composite transaction known as a '**Sale & Leaseback**', which is based around a statutory provision known colloquially as '**section 48**'. All signs were that this regime would be outlawed by the time this second edition of this Handbook went to press, but in his March 2005 Budget, the UK Chancellor of the Exchequer gave it a last minute, short-term reprieve whilst the Government (with the help of the industry) comes up with the details for its replacement – a proposed 20% tax credit, currently affectionately referred to as '**son of section 48**'. In the meantime, Sale & Leaseback transactions, and the statutory provisions on which they are based, are alive and well and living (albeit on borrowed time) in British Filmland. There's no cast-iron guarantee that section 48 won't live past its current sell-by date (31 March 2006) either, so it's important to understand how the system works, what it's based on, and how it generates funds for the Producer of a British qualifying film (a 'British Film').

This Chapter explains the entire current British tax regime (to the extent it is utilised to provide soft money for film production) on a step-by-step basis. In the first part, after a brief look at the nature of the main statutory tax allowances themselves, we illustrate how they are put to effect, examine how transactions such as Sale & Leaseback have evolved, and finish with an explanation of the proposed son of section 48 - the 20% tax credit – and what problems may arise based on the information so far released by the UK Treasury and Inland Revenue. There are also UK tax breaks relating to films financed through the Enterprise Investment Scheme ('EIS') and Venture Capital Trusts ('VCTs') and, although these tend to be more popular on lower budget films these days, it is useful for anyone considering tax-based finance to be familiar with how these schemes operate. We take a brief look at them in the second part of this Chapter. Please note that although there is also a tax allowance under section 41 of the *Finance (No2) Act 1992* for development finance (referred to in the statute as 'preliminary expenditure'), the funding of development generally is not within the scope of this book, and so we do not examine it in any detail. As this is not intended to be an exhaustive legal text, you are advised to take specialist tax advice if you wish to utilise section 41 or, for that matter, any other statutory tax allowance.

# The Current Tax Allowances

## Tax Relief for the Production or Acquisition of British Films

Unlike 'rebates', tax allowances apply specifically to the amounts 'invested' in films by financiers, rather than the amounts 'spent' by the Producers in making the films. Although perhaps a subtle distinction, an important difference is in relation to the person directly benefiting from the legislation. Obviously, at the end of the day, the idea is that both the financiers and the Producer use the tax break to everyone's advantage, so that the ultimate benefit may be shared between them. This encourages investors to put money into films, and Producers to make them. Technically, however, the person directly aided by the tax regulations currently in force in the in the UK is the investor who utilises the regime, rather than the Producer, who is really just an indirect beneficiary. The relief is available for money spent on the **production** or **acquisition** (purchase) of a qualifying British Film.

## 'British' Films

To qualify in the UK, the film must be classed by the Department of Culture, Media and Sport as a '**British Film**' under Schedule 1 of the *Films Act 1985*. Briefly, the *Films Act* provides that, in order to qualify, it must satisfy four main criteria:

1. First, the production company itself must be registered, owned and controlled in an 'Eligible State'. Generally speaking, this simply means in the EU, and by EU nationals.
2. Second, at least 70% of the cost of production must be spent in the UK. For these purposes, the cost of production does not include financing costs, overhead expenditures, underlying rights acquisition costs and certain labour costs.
3. The third criterion is a specific additional requirement relating to labour costs, in that a minimum percentage of such costs must be spent on EU, EEA or Commonwealth residents / citizens (referred to here as 'qualifying nationals'). This minimum percentage of the labour costs to be spent on qualifying nationals is the lesser of either 70% after deducting the labour cost of one non-qualifying national (such as a leading US director), or 75% after deducting the labour costs of two non-qualifying nationals, one of whom must be an actor.
4. Last, there is also a 10% cap on the use of stock footage (although for documentaries, the Secretary of State may permit a larger amount).

Any Producer wishing to make a qualifying British Film must consider all these issues before staffing cast and crew and choosing locations.

An **official UK co-production** complying with a relevant Co-production Treaty (or the *European Convention on Cinematic Co-Productions*) will also **automatically qualify** as a British Film, and therefore be entitled to utilise the UK's tax incentives. For more information on official co-productions see chapter 5 (International Financing).

## Section 42

The investors in a fund formed for the purposes of producing or acquiring UK qualifying films generally benefit from one of two tax allowances, being either section 42 of the *Finance (No2)*

*Act 1992* ('**section 42**') or section 48 of the *Finance (No2) Act 1997* ('**section 48**'). Both provisions allow income tax relief for expenditure on the production or acquisition of qualifying films. The first of these provisions, section 42, was introduced in 1992, and allows expenditure which would otherwise be considered capital expenditure, to instead be treated as revenue - or trading - expenditure, and to be set off against future income from exploitation of the film, or alternatively simply written off (at 33.3% per annum) over a three-year period. The provision applies to any size of film, so long as it qualifies as British. So if a qualifying film is 100% financed in this way, the entire budget can be written off by the Investor(s) within the three year period.

The introduction of section 42 stimulated a lot of activity by clearing banks, leasing companies, specially formed partnerships and high-net-worth individuals who access relief to mitigate their corporation or income tax liability, particularly through 'Sale & Leaseback' transactions (see below).

The introduction of section 48 in 1997 was even more appealing as it allowed for a 100% write off in the first year, rather than over a three year period. However, it only applies to films under £15m, so larger budget films still have to go the section 42 (three year write off) route. The majority of independent British Films fall within the section 48 budget parameters, and so we will concentrate more on this provision.

## Section 48

In July 1997 the UK Chancellor introduced section 48 of the *Finance (No2) Act 1997* ('**section 48**') which enhanced the incentives offered under section 42 by increasing the relief permitted on films costing under £15 million to 100% in the first year. This means that a fully-financing Investor (ie. one who pays for the entire budget) is entitled to a tax rebate during the year the film is completed of 100% of the film's production costs (or, in the case of a purchaser, to 100% of the acquisition price in the year film was bought). Investors with high earnings who belong to the high tax bracket will benefit most from this kind of tax allowance.

The idea was to provide a short-term boost to the production and distribution sectors of the UK film industry. However, the legislation was extended three times after its original implementation and, until recently, was due to expire in July 2005. It had been hoped that the new proposed tax credit regime would have been in place by then but, unfortunately, many details were still needing to be ironed out at the beginning of 2005. The continual uncertainty had been extremely unpopular with the film industry as a whole, and contributed to a 40% (!) year on year reduction in production levels from 2003 to 2004. Ultimately, it led Chancellor Gordon Brown, in his March 2005 Budget, to announce a further extension of section 48 until 31 March 2006.

This means that the current tax relief can only be used in relation to a qualifying film on which principal photography commences on or before 31 March 2006, and which is '**completed**' by 1 January 2007. The term 'completed' means that the film must be in a state where it is capable of being distributed or exhibited, even if not technically 'delivered' in accordance with relevant contracts. In other words, there needs to be a master capable of being copied and/or used for screenings, even if (say) the final music score hasn't been locked. The film will not be certified by the DCMS until it is satisfied that it is in a completed state, and the Inland Revenue will not sanction the tax allowance until it has seen the DCMS Certificate.

# Tax-Based Production Funds

A number of production funds utilising these tax breaks from the '**production**' (rather than 'acquisition') angle have been put together through which Investors can pool their money and share the risk with other Investors. These usually involve the formation of a partnership (or similar structure) between the Investors, and these partnerships will sometimes invest in more than one film in order to reduce the risk further. The legislative structure has even allowed for the Investors to 'borrow' a large amount (up to about 90%) of their investment from participating banks, and to claim tax relief on the whole lot (ie. not just their actual 'out-of-pocket' expenses). Where Investors put differing amounts into a fund, the rebate provided will be split according to their share of the investment. The percentage of the production budget provided by these funds varies wildly (from 10% to 100% on occasion) according to the objects and format of the fund itself, the size of the film, the contribution (if any) of other financiers, the right to income streams and/or Net Profit (if required), and so on. Details of companies offering section 48 production funds are set out in chapter 6 (Funding Organisations), and others are listed in the *Directory* (chapter 7). Ivan McTaggert of Baker Street Media has given us an exclusive interview, and this is set out at the end of this chapter.

The commercial sustainability of certain production funds that have a 'revolving' investment system, are very dependent on the success of the earlier investments made by them. Their ability to continue over the medium-term will become apparent in the next couple of years as the profitability (or otherwise) of the first wave of pictures financed by these funds becomes more evident.

# Sale & Leaseback

**Sale & Leaseback** has been around in the UK in various industries since at least the 1980's, and it works in conjunction with the current legislation on tax incentives. The schemes offer comparatively risk-free benefits to both the Producer and the Investor, as the benefits do not necessarily depend on the film's success in the market place. Most schemes have been based on the section 48 tax break (relating to films under £15m), applying the allowance for '**acquisition**' (rather than 'production') purposes, and so will remain an important source of finance for British qualifying films until well into 2006.

## 'Vanilla' Sale & Leasebacks

Nowadays there are companies who will offer 'Sale & Leaseback money' up front in the form of production funding. However, traditionally, the transaction took place only when the film was '**completed**', as it is only then when the tax break kicks in. We will first consider how this type of Sale & Leaseback worked, and then look at the newer 'products' available to the Producer in today's market. So, below is a (somewhat simplified) illustration of how the 'traditional' or '**vanilla**' Sale & Leaseback operates.

Say a producer has made a British Film for £10m, having received production finance in the normal way, and now wishes to enter into a Sale & Leaseback transaction. Once s/he has completed the film and obtained the relevant 'British qualifying' certificate from the DCMS, s/he will identify a Sale & Leaseback partnership to purchase the film. The partnership will be made up of various Investors, who all wish to avail themselves of the section 48 tax break (had the budget been over £15m, they would have used section 42 and a slightly different structure). The partnership will also include a 'managing partner' as part of the administrative set-up.

As the film has already been 'completed', and certified as British qualifying, the partnership (effectively being the Investors) can legitimately write off their investment (ie. the purchase price) for tax purposes, which reduces their personal income tax bill by 40% of the amount invested (assuming their income tax rate is 40%). As with the Production Funds referred to above, much of their investment may actually have been borrowed from a bank. The partnership would typically pay the Producer £10m to buy the film, as that is the amount it had cost to make, and the Inland Revenue will accept that is an appropriate price. So, under the tax break rules, the Investors are treated as if they earned £10m less in that year than they really did (because they spent £10m on a qualifying film, so it notionally comes off their income). With a reduction of £10m in their taxable income, the Investors save a total of £4m in tax liability.

However, on its own, this simple 'sale' transaction would leave the partnership of Investors owning a film they have no idea how to exploit, and the Producer with a cheque for £10m (most of which would have to go back to pay the original financiers), but no film. In practical terms, this is no good for either party. So the partnership, acknowledging that the Producer is probably better placed to exploit the film than it is, immediately 'leases' the film back to the Producer in return for periodical lease payments. This is technically a licence of all the exploitation rights whereby the Producer gets back all the rights s/he needs to exploit the film for a period of up to 15 years ('**the Term**').

Reverting to our 'Building' analogy at the beginning of chapter 3, this would be equivalent to an investor partnership buying the building from the Developer because it (the partnership) can get a tax rebate on the purchase of a completed building. However, as the investor partnership isn't really in the business of renting out apartments, it will **lease back** the building to the Developer in return for a fixed income over 15 years, and the job - and risk - of renting out (or sub-letting) the apartments also reverts to the Developer.

The lease payments will be fairly substantial, and the partnership will want to be sure that it actually gets paid throughout the entire 15 year Term. It will therefore insist that most of the £10m it paid to the Producer for the film goes straight into a separate secured bank account, from which the lease payments will be made. Using simple numbers, one could say that about £8m (including the interest earned on it) will probably be enough to pay the lease payments for the whole Term. Another £0.5m will be required for the various transaction fees (especially legal costs), and the remaining £1.5m (equal to about 15% of the budget) can go straight into the Producer's pocket (or, more likely, to start paying back the film's original financiers).

Although the partnership pays £10m for the film, only £6m of it is actually 'at risk' because the other £4m effectively comes from the taxman, having been a saving in the Investors' tax bill. It works out that £8m is an adequate sum such that, when placed in the designated bank account to generate the lease payments, the Investors get an acceptable return on their at-risk investment. It also generates some of the large fees charged by the Sale & Leaseback facilitators, something about which the Government has expressed its disquiet. In any event, it is calculated so that, by the end of the 15 year Term, there will be nothing left in the bank account, the lease comes to an end, and the exploitation rights to the film revert to the partnership (who will then own the film outright as part of its '**library**'). This means that the Producer has 15 years to make as much money out of the film as possible, before it reverts to the Sale & Leaseback partnership. That said, it is very rare for pictures to continue bringing in substantial revenue after that point and, in any event, the film is sometimes sold by the partnership back to a company connected with the Producer for a nominal fee at the end of the lease Term.

The receipts from the lease payments are themselves taxable in the hands of the partnership, so it could be said that, in reality, the Investors actually only obtain a free loan from the Government, rather than a windfall gain. That said, income received during the Term from the lease payments can be set off against other losses and/or allowances that the Investors may have in whatever year the payments are received.

Where the partnership has also taken a profit participation (which some of them do), the Investors will additionally end up with a 'share' in any Net Profits made, even after the end of the Term.

## Discounted Sale & Leasebacks

It was felt by many producers that, as much as receiving a 'gift' of 15% of the budget might be considered well-earned once they have finished the picture, in fact they would rather have some money up front in order to help finance the film in the first place, production funding being so extremely difficult to obtain. So, most Sale & Leaseback facilitators now offer to '**discount**' the amount available and, through a bank (often the one already involved in the Sale & Leaseback transaction), can provide the gift - known as the '**net benefit**' - to the Producer in time for production, albeit on certain conditions.

Naturally, the partnerships will be concerned because they will be providing money up front without the benefit of DCMS Certification (and therefore without the guarantee of being able to access the tax write-off). The concern stems from the individual Investors wanting to be sure that they will be able to write off their investment as soon as the film is 'completed'. Accordingly, the Completion Bond company (see chapter 3) will, amongst other things, be required to ensure that the Producers make the film strictly in accordance with the criteria required for it to qualify as a British Film. At first, Bond Companies were reluctant to take on this added obligation, but now most of the established Guarantors will bond the 'Britishness' of the film, and will also make sure that the film is delivered on time so that the Investors can utilise the tax-break within the anticipated financial year.

The amount of the budget (net benefit) currently available in this way is now upwards of 14%, depending on the partnership used, the Bank and its 'discount' rate, the amount that would otherwise have been available had the money been provided after completion, the profit participation taken (if any), the time of year of the transaction (it all gets very competitive each Spring as the fiscal year begins to close), and so on.

## Other Incentives

As the market for films to invest in has become much tighter, Sale & Leaseback facilitators have been offering producers more and more incentives to use their product(s). Many have offered much more than the traditional 12% or 15% contribution to the budget by coupling the Sale & Leaseback with other deals. For example, some have offered up to 20% (although more typically usually 16% to 18%) by also taking the UK (including Republic of Ireland) distribution rights by way of a pre-sale.

More popular in recent years have been transactions known as 'Super Sale & Leasebacks'. Here, the partnership will offer a large proportion of the budget in return for doing the Sale & Leaseback transaction and taking an equity stake in the film. If (say) 35% is offered, this would be seen as approximately 15% representing the Sale & Leaseback transaction itself, and 20% representing a pure equity investment. In this regard, the Producer would have to give a percentage of the '**back end**' (Net Profit) to the Investors; probably in the above example between 12% and 20% (depending how strictly the 'Six Tenths Rule' is followed – see chapter 3). Details of the more established Sale & Leaseback companies are set out in chapter 6 (Funding Organisations) under 'Private Funding Organisations'.

# Recent Changes to the Law

## Abuse of the System

Since the initial introduction of the tax-break legislation, a number of organisations have tried to milk the system so much (whilst still supposedly acting technically within the letter of the law) that the British Government has continually issued supplementary regulations to try to curb what it considers to be an 'abuse' of the system. Some argue that the Government has not been overly consistent in its approach. It is true that, in some cases, what was once considered by the DCMS and Inland Revenue to be totally acceptable and correct is now suddenly an illegal manipulation of the legislation by 'rogue' producers and financiers who, in the industry's eyes, were simply following Inland Revenue guidance. This raises the whole question of tax 'avoidance' as against tax 'evasion' which, interesting as it may be, is not really within the scope of this Handbook.

What isn't in doubt is that the effect of the recent changes has been to reduce considerably the reach and application of the tax allowances. A number of pictures have simply 'got up and left' the UK in order to avail themselves of better incentives elsewhere, the latest celebrated casualty being the threatened pull-out from Pinewood Studios of Paramount's $120m film *The Watchmen*. These continual changes in tax policy (as the industry, although not necessarily the Government, sees them) have slowly chipped away at what was originally permitted under the tax break regime. They have mostly been announced by the Chancellor in recent budgets and pre-budget reports, although a few bombshells have been dropped at other times of the year, occasionally catching much of the industry completely by surprise. Worse still, certain changes have been retroactive, throwing into disarray the plans of producers and financiers alike, and even causing certain films to collapse completely part-way through production. But, of course, no-one really doubts the good intentions of the Government who, after all, is simply trying to protect our tax money whilst at the same time encourage investment in the film industry. This year's Finance Bill (which will become the *Finance Act 2005*, subject to any amendments by Parliament) itself dedicates about 50 pages specifically to tax avoidance relating to the film industry! Anyway, below is a summary of the main changes since the primary legislation was unveiled in 1997.

## Television

In his 2002 Budget, the UK Chancellor removed **television** production from the scope of the tax reliefs. The idea was to prevent the makers of soap operas and other television programmes, which technically fell within the then loose definition of a 'film', from accessing the benefits intended for legitimate feature films. Accordingly, in order to qualify, the film must now be '**genuinely intended for theatrical release**'. This doesn't necessarily mean that at the time of applying for the DCMS Certificate, the film needs to have a theatrical distribution deal actually in place, but the Producer must be able to demonstrate that this is his/her intention. And, once issued, the Certificate will not become invalid simply because no such distribution deal is ever secured.

For a year or two following the introduction of this restriction, the amount of tax-break money raised overall did not seem to decline, and so the number of financiers looking for films (rather than television) in which to invest in fact increased. Since there was more investor capacity than content, film-financing companies started offering more attractive financing packages for the Producer. The net benefits offered to a Producer for a discounted Sale & Leaseback transaction, for example, jumped from around 9% to over 14% in a matter of months. However, the more recent policy changes and uncertainty revolving round the future of section 48 has curbed this initial flurry of excess funds to some extent, although the products offered by section 48 Investors are still more favourable than they were 3 or 4 years ago. And as investing in film is in any event considered more risky than television, Investors will still be looking for strong projects, which usually means films with names, reputation and experience attached.

## Deferments

One of the more real 'abuses' of the system was the unrealistic inflation of the budgets of qualifying films. Certain investment groups were in the business of obtaining tax relief on the whole £15m available under section 48, even though the cash budget for the films concerned (ie. the amount really needed to make them) was often under £3m or £4m. The way they structured this was by manufacturing a 'total' budget of just under £15m (excluding financing fees, remember), of which £12m or so was made up of deferments. Effectively, the Investors were claiming that certain above-the-line contributors had huge multi-million pound fees which, although forming part of the budget on paper, they were willing to defer until income came in further down the line. Of course, very few low budget British Films ever make anywhere near £12m in sales, so these fees were never really paid, but the Investors still tried to obtain the full relief (some successfully, some not). One could even argue that it was not in the interest of the schemes for the films to make any money at all, as this income would be taxable as receipts in the hands of the Investors, but not necessarily payable to them. In any event, none of these films ever had the sort of A-list stars attached who might have legitimately merited such huge fees, yet somehow certain accountancy firms were still prepared to sign off on the budgets, confirming that £15m or so was the real cost of production.

This manipulation of the rules has rightly been outlawed and, since April 2002, only deferments that are contractually - and unconditionally - payable within 4 months of completion of the film may be included as part of the 'total production expenditure' that qualifies for the tax allowance.

## Co-production minimum spends

To redress an imbalance in the proportion of money spent in the UK as opposed to in the other co-producing countries on official co-productions (which qualify for tax breaks), the Government has recently raised a number of the minimum spend thresholds. This is not technically a change to the tax regime itself, and is therefore dealt with in more detail in the next chapter (International Financing).

## GAAP Funds

As an alternative approach, a few entrants to the fund market in 2002/3 aimed to use generally accepted accounting principles (known as 'GAAPs', but not to be confused with bank 'gap' loans), rather than sections 42 and 48, in order to provide a tax-efficient scheme to their Investors. These funding schemes (with names such as 'Inside Track' from Ingenious and 'First Choice' from Grosvenor Park) were constructed following receipt of much professional advice but, as predicted in the first edition of this book, the Government soon put pay to these attempts at providing Investors with ultra-low risk tax benefits. For those who are interested, these funds were based around the idea that the film investment made in year one was effectively an automatic trading loss for the fund for that year, which could be carried forward, sideways, backward or however else the tax gurus suggested. The schemes were engineered so that somehow the tax loss generated could be utilised without the Investors ever being likely to have to pay tax on income generated from the film, due to the clever exit strategies implemented. these were effectively outlawed after two attempts in 2004 and 2005.

## Producer Fees

In September 2004, the DCMS put restrictions on the amount of fees that Producers are allowed to charge as a proportion of the budget. If the aggregate of all such fees exceeds 10% of the budget, the DCMS will need to see proof that they are really actually incurred, and that they relate directly to the production. The aim is to prevent films from qualifying as British under a Co-production Treaty (see chapter 5) when really the only money spent in the UK is on the Producer's own fees. There is a worry that, with such hefty 'producer' fees being charged by certain financiers, it will be the 'real' Producers who suffer as they are compelled to reduce their fees in order for the aggregate to stay below the limit.

## Double-Dipping

You may recall that the statutory tax relief under section 48 is available on the **production** *or* **acquisition** of a film. It was aimed at those who wanted to pay for the making of films, and at those who wanted to buy them to own as part of an exploitable library. There was a potential issue where a film that used section 48 (or 42) finance in its production, was then sold through a Sale & Leaseback scheme. Both the original financiers and the subsequent purchaser would claim relief on the amounts they spent on the film. This is known as '**double-dipping**', as two sets of investors could obtain up to 100% tax relief on the same picture. Worse still, a film could potentially be sold and resold several times with each new purchaser claiming a tax break on its acquisition price. This multiple accessing of the tax allowance was always assumed to fall foul of the regulations (although many would argue that the actual wording of the legislation did not in fact exclude it). However, simple double-dipping had been confirmed by both the Inland Revenue and Treasury to be acceptable, so long as relief was obtained only once for the production, and once for the acquisition of the film. This meant that a film financed with cash from a section 48 production fund (providing, say, 25% of the budget) could also use discounted Sale & Leaseback money (say, 15% of the budget), providing a total of 40% of a budget in soft, or soft-ish, money.

In December 2004, after giving the industry only a couple of weeks' implied notice, the Treasury announced the removal of this 'abuse', declaring that from that moment on, relief could only be obtained once on each film. As this policy took immediate effect, it meant that all the best laid plans of numerous Producers went up in smoke as they suddenly lost at least 15% of their financing. A number of these films were quickly re-financed by taking them offshore, and using alternative soft money available in other jurisdictions (which was probably not the British Government's desired effect). For those that stayed, the immediate question was then whether to drop the section 48 production fund or the Sale & Leaseback money, and different producers made different choices depending on what terms were on offer, what contractual relationships were already in place, the specific exigencies of their film, timing, etc.

## Restricting the Term to 15 years

It's mentioned above that Sale & Leaseback schemes generally run for about 15 years. This has always been the norm, although there have been some schemes where the lease runs for as little as 7 years, or - more recently - as long as 25 years. During this period, the Producer (via the designated bank account) is paying the purchaser (the Sale & Leaseback partnership) lease payments, which are taxable as income in the hands of the recipient. They can, of course, be set off against other losses in accordance with standard accounting practice. This is why the system is generally referred to as a tax **deferral** rather than a pure windfall gain. The Treasury, in its December 2004 Pre-Budget Report, effectively limited the length of time of these schemes (and thereby the dererral) to a maximum of 15 years. In principle, this restriction was not unwelcome, but the fact that it took immediate effect without considering that many longer schemes were already in operation, angered a number of the Sale & Leaseback companies who suddenly found themselves prevented from receiving lease payments after 15 years, despite having entered into longer contractual arrangements based on commercial interest calculations for the return on their investments.

## Early Exits

As with the similar GAAP structures, the Treasury had two stabs (2004 and 2005) at preventing this activity, which basically allowed Investors to 'remove' themselves from the Sale & Leaseback schemes once they had obtained their initial tax allowance. They would therefore not have to pay tax on future payments made under the lease arrangements, leaving this obligation with an unrelated vehicle set up specifically for these purposes. The new restrictions banning this activity are more of interest to the Investors than the Producer, and proper legal and tax advice should be taken before entering into any of these schemes.

## Money 'at risk', and Carrying On a Trade.

When Investors put their money into Sale & Leaseback and other tax-based partnerships, they (through the partnership) will often borrow a huge part of it, typically between 70% and 90%, from a bank. The Bank will usually be connected with the relevant Sale & Leaseback facilitator (or fund), who in turn arranges the loan for the Investor on a non-recourse or limited recourse basis (basically meaning that it will not sue the Investors if the whole scheme goes belly-up causing the loan to remain unpaid). The result is that as little as 10% of the money put up is actually the Investors' own personal hard-earned cash, yet they still get tax relief through the partnership on the whole lot.

Alternatively, some of the section 48 production funds that put up a small proportion of the budget require the film's other financiers (who are not interested in the tax breaks, such as banks, foreign investors, sales companies, etc) to give them - the fund - their budget contributions first. The production fund then pays the whole lot over to the Producer, and claims a tax break on the entire budget. In these cases, the partnership is referred to as a '**Commissioning Producer**'.

Technically, the fact that financiers may have borrowed or been given up to 90% of their contribution does not necessarily mean it doesn't become theirs to invest, so the Government has generally allowed these schemes. However, there has been more scrutiny in this regard in the last year or so. Now, in order for the partnerships to claim the tax relief in the form of trading losses (which is how the system works – the investment is treated as being revenue expenditure rather than capital expenditure, remember), the partnerships have to actually demonstrate that they are indeed carrying out a trade. They will therefore only get the tax relief on the entire budget if they can show that they spend at least **10 hours per week** in relation to their investment. Otherwise the scheme will be considered a pure capital investment, and will be subject to the rules of Capital Gains Tax rather than Income Tax or Corporation Tax.

## The end of section 42

Another announcement made in the 2005 Budget was the proposed end to section 42. This would expire at the same time as section 48 (31 March 2006), so that the new tax regime (see below) will relate to all British Films, irrespective of their budgets. This may be of more concern to the US Studios who regularly avail themselves of the higher budget relief by coming to the UK to produce major high-budget films, and accordingly form the appropriate production structures.

# The New 20% Tax Credit

## Out with the Old...

In many people's eyes, the various tweaks to the legislation outlined above have, over recent years, succeeded in stopping the 'rogue' element of hyper-academic tax-advising engineers from undeservedly stealing our hard-earned film industry tax benefits. Yet the Government was clearly not so satisfied, and has in the end 'given up' on the entire section 48 style allowance, opting instead to change the tax regime completely into a tax credit system. Some observers had hoped (and lobbied) that, after the more recent and exhaustive anti-avoidance legislation, the Government would let things settle for a while to see how they panned out, but this was not to be. Perhaps the Government's apparent obsession with preventing the 'middlemen' (see below) from getting their hands on part of the benefit earmarked for Producers and Investors has resulted in a total re-think. Whatever the reason, we are now faced with wholesale change, possibly with new opportunities for some to re-enter the market and push a brand-new system to its limits. Clearly, this is not the intention of the Treasury, and perhaps this is one of the reasons why the detailed legislation is taking so long to come out. The new tax credit was first mooted formally in the 2004 Budget, but more than a year later there are still scarce details as to how exactly it will work (if at all).

There are a number of industry and Government personnel on various committees discussing the whys and wherefores of the new system, but there still appears to be a few major problems as currently proposed, and nobody is quite sure how long it will take before we have some concrete information on how the new regulations will operate. There are also concerns that this information will be published so late that it will be difficult to put the necessary infrastructure in place in time, and there will be a time void during which there will be a vacuum of tax-based production finance. Some have even suggested that sections 48 and 42 may be extended yet further to accommodate such delays. Originally the new regime was to replace only section 48 (but raising the cap on 'low budget' films from £15m to £20m). However, following the 2005 Budget, it now seems that the tax credit will also replace the old section 42, and the £20m limit has become obsolete before it even came into force.

## ...In with the New?

It follows that anything written in this section is somewhat subject to change, although the information given below is based on the various publications and announcements given and made by the Government over the last year or so, together with input from industry insiders who have actually been sitting on the Treasury's own committee.

The Government wants to introduce a system which leaves less money in the hands of the middlemen, and more on the screen. These **middlemen** are the various tax advisors, fund 'managers', Sale & Leaseback facilitators, lawyers, accountants, discounting banks, etc, who all take fees for putting together the structures for the assortment of funds available. The Treasury is aware that although the Investors are effectively getting a tax break equal to 40% of the amount invested, only about 15% actually ends up in the hands of the Producer as a net benefit. So the Government has come up with a solution that, on the face of it, provides a 20% benefit (ie. more than the current net benefit) directly to the Producer.

## Eligibility and Timing

So under the proposed system, as with section 48, films eligible for the new tax relief must be British qualifying (as certified by the DCMS), and intended for theatrical release in the commercial cinema. In the unlikely event that the tax credit comes into force before sections 42 and 48 expire, producers will not, of course, be able to use both regimes on the same film. However, the new system will work in conjunction with reliefs claimed under EIS or VCT schemes (see below). The 'person' eligible to claim the credit will be the person '*responsible for the activities undertaken worldwide to make the master version of the film, and which owns that master version on completion*'. In other words, the Producer. Or more literally, the single purpose vehicle set up by the Producer to make the film. The relevant year during which the relief can be claimed is the year in which the film is completed (defined as before). Unlike section 48, which was always intended to provide a short-term boost to the film economy, the new tax credit has no expiry date as yet. It seems, therefore, that the Government wishes to introduce it as a long-term financing tool that will hopefully bring a little stability to this end of the financial market.

## Production Expenditure

The relief will apply to the whole production expenditure, which will be defined in the same way as it is under the current regime. It will include all pre-production, production and post-production expenditure, but not financing fees, stock footage, general overheads or (unless unconditionally payable within four months of completion) deferments. It will also not be limited only to expenditure in the UK, so long as the film itself qualifies as British.

## How it is supposed to work!

As mentioned above, there are very few details available as to how the system will actually operate. Based on what is currently published, the following is a very simplified explanation, incorporating the rules that we know so far....

The first element is that the Producer will be entitled to a **150% deduction** of total production expenditure from its income when calculating its profit. In other words, if the film costs £10m to make, revenue of at least £15m will have to be received before the production company is obliged to pay tax. So far so good. However, one of the main stumbling blocks is in relation to what is considered income for the company. Generally, a production company receives its production funds from the various financiers, and then spends it on the film. The next lot of revenue it receives goes to pay back the financiers, and then (hopefully) the film finds itself breaking even, and therefore 'in profit'.

## The problem with income

The problem is that the receipt of the production funds are themselves considered income in the hands of the production company. If we assume that the production company puts, say, 15% of the budget in as its own money (or by using the tax credit – see below), it will need to receive 85% from the other financiers. The issue is that this production finance will be treated as 'income', meaning that the production company can only receive further *non-taxable* revenues equal to 65% of its budget. Using our £10m film as an example, the production company can make a £15m (150% of £10m) deduction from income before the production company has to start paying tax. Having already received £8.5m in production funds, it will therefore have to start paying tax after it has received a further £6.5m. But (assuming in this example that there is no soft money) it still has £8.5m of financiers who need to be paid back their money. This means that the production company will have to start paying corporation tax (at 30%) before its own financiers have recouped in full, and therefore before(!) the film is in profit. This is one of the main points to which the industry is currently objecting, and is waiting to hear the Treasury's response.

## The 20% tax credit

So where does the headline '**20% Tax Credit**' come in? Well, rather than deduct the whole 150% of the value of the budget from income, the production company can choose to 'surrender' 100% of it straight away in order to obtain a 20% tax credit. In other words, taking our £10m film, once it is in a completed state, the production company can apply for a credit of £2m, but will then only be able to offset an amount equal to 50% (instead of 150%) of the budget against future income. The Inland Revenue would effectively give a cheque for £2m to the Producer, who could then receive a further £5m (equal to 50% of the budget, having 'surrendered' 100% in return for the tax credit) in sales revenues before having to start paying tax. However, as mentioned above, if the £8.5m finance received for the production is then recouped from future revenues, it will swallow up the £5m enhanced part of the deduction (known as the '**uplift**'), and the production company will have to pay tax on the residual £3.5m (ie. £1.05m at a 30% tax rate) until the film breaks even, and on every penny received from that moment on.

Another point to note at this stage is that the 'enhanced' part of the deduction (ie. the 50% uplift) can only be offset against income from exploitation of the film, whereas the basic 100%, if *not* surrendered for the tax credit, could have been used as a 'trading loss' against other areas of trading income within the production company's group.

## Discounting the tax credit

Receipt of the 20% tax credit itself will not, of course, be deemed taxable income in the hands of the production company. As with Sale & Leaseback under the current regime, this tax credit will probably be discountable by a bank (or other 'middlemen'?!), in order to be used as part of the production funding. Naturally, the bank will have to take similar precautions as those taken today, in particular in relation to the appointment of a Completion Guarantor to ensure that the picture satisfies the requirements of a British Film.

Once discounted, the credit itself will probably be worth closer to 15% than the headline 20% amount, as interest and fees will need to be deducted. But it will, on the face of it, provide the Producer with about 15% of his/her budget (hence the suggestion above that the Producer will need to find 85% from elsewhere).

## Minimal net benefit to the Producer

However, that's not necessarily the end of the story! Returning to our example above, the Producer will have accrued a £1.05m tax bill by the time the film breaks even, equivalent to 10.5% of the budget. If the credit is only really worth £1.5m (15%), and £1.05m of this has to be paid to the Inland Revenue, the net benefit to the Producer could actually be as little as 4.5% of the budget.

This does seem ludicrous, and the industry is looking forward to receiving clarification on the rules as soon as possible, particularly as the Government has consistently stated that the net benefit to the Producer will 'typically' be 20%, being more then the 15% currently offered by Sale & Leaseback transactions.

## Moving Forward

There are a number of things that might happen before the rules are finally crystallised. If the 'uplift' is changed to 85% instead of 50% (ie. a total deduction of 185%), then using the figures above, the Producer will not have to pay tax until after the film has broken even, as is the case under the current regime. This is close to what the Government's advisory panel originally suggested (see the interview with Libby Savillle at the end of this chapter). A tax deduction of 185% would allow the Producer to use up 100% in return for the tax credit, and the remaining 85% to offset against the external production finance received for the film. This would give the Producer a net benefit of about 15% (the real value of the discounted tax credit).

Alternatively, it is possible (albeit highly unlikely) that the credit will be raised from 20% to, say, 33% (equal to, perhaps, 27% once interest and fees for discounting are deducted). This would mean that the Producer need only find 73% (ie. 100% less 27%) of the production finance from elsewhere. With the currently suggested 50% uplift, only revenues worth 23% (ie. 73% less 50%) will be taxable by the time the film breaks even. At 30% corporation tax, this will generate a tax bill equal to about 6.9% (ie. 30% of 23%) of the budget, leaving the Producer with a real net benefit of 20.1% (being 27% less the tax bill), much closer to the Government's headline rate of 20%. The Government has said all along that it wants the Producer to be better off under the new Regime than the old.

To summarise, the treatment of the receipt of production finance in the hands of the production company needs to be considered in more detail. If this is ultimately treated as 'income', then either the 150% threshold, or the 20% tax credit (or both!), will need to be increased in order to achieve the Governments objectives.

As mentioned earlier, it is possible that section 48 will be extended further if the details on the new system are not released in time. Of course, at the time of going to press, we have a General Election due, and by the time this book hits the shelves, there is a possibility that we will all be dealing with a totally different Government with completely different objectives, resulting in a wholly different regime of film tax incentives, or even none at all! For example, based on its election manifesto, a future conservative Government would continue with section 48 but introduce a distribution-led incentive for larger budget films.

In the meantime, there are articles on the websites of the Treasury and the Inland Revenue which attempt to explain the tax credit in more detail, in addition to those on various law firms. Libby Saville, a partner at Olswang solicitors and a member of the Government's advisory panel, has provided the *UK Film Finance Handbook* with an **exclusive interview** on the subject, and this is set out in full at the end of this chapter.

In any event, we would suggest that until the main issues are addressed by the Government and new guidelines issued, no Producer makes any irrevocable decision based on the proposed tax implications of financing of any film due to commence after 31 March 2006 and/or complete after 31 December 2006.

# Enterprise Investment Schemes and VCTs

With the number of UK tax-based financing options decreasing rapidly, it may be that Producers will return to looking at the **Enterprise Investment Scheme** ('**EIS**') as an alternative way to finance their films. EIS has been around since 1994, having replaced the old Business Expansion Scheme. The objective of the EIS is to help certain types of small higher-risk unquoted trading companies, including those producing films, to raise capital. It does so by providing a range of tax reliefs for Investors in qualifying shares in these companies. However, in the film industry, the schemes have been somewhat neglected over the years, partly because of their early reputation for rarely spawning a profitable film.

But EIS might just be on the rebound. Particularly in relation to lower budget pictures where the entire production finance often comes from private sources. The Government would certainly like to see them used more often (despite the need for middlemen!), and this may why much of the literature released to date mentions that the new proposed tax credit can be used in conjunction with an EIS company.

EIS schemes work by setting up a special purpose production company, in which individual Investors subscribe for shares. Each Investor must put up a minimum of £500 in return for shares in the company (but may not own more than 30% of the company if s/he want to qualify for the Income Tax relief). There is a limit of £200,000 in the amount an individual may invest in EIS schemes per year. The investment in shares itself qualifies for Income Tax relief (up to 20% of the value of the investment), while any gains in the value of the shares on a sale are free from Capital Gains Tax after three years. Any losses made as a result of the investment can be set against the Investor's personal capital gains or income in the year in which his/her shares are sold. If the Investor sells other assets at the time s/he buys the EIS shares, s/he can also get Capital Gains tax relief on those disposals.

The schemes are set up by teams of specialist financial advisers and open and close on a regular basis, depending on demand. A current list, including copies of open prospectuses, can usually be found on the website www.taxshelterreport.co.uk (and then clicking the enterprise investment schemes link), run by Allenbridge Group plc. The Enterprise Investment Scheme Association (www.eisa.org.uk) also provides impartial advice. Details of companies offering Enterprise Investment Schemes for film production are also listed in the *private funds* section of chapter 6 (Funding Organisations) and in the *Directory*. Anyone considering this scheme should definitely seek advice from a professional organisation and read the Inland Revenue guidelines (available on their website).

A related investment scheme is the **Venture Capital Trust** ('**VCT**') vehicle. VCTs are effectively trust funds set up and approved by the Inland Revenue to invest money in a range of companies (whereas EIS schemes relates to a single company). VCTs are run by a Fund Manager who invests in a range of eligible small high risk unquoted companies. They offer their investors similar tax breaks to those available in EIS schemes. Sometimes, but not often, VCTs are prepared to invest in film companies or in individual projects. Again, www.taxshelterreport.co.uk is the place to find which VCTs are currently open to Investors, and to identify the type of company in which they are willing to invest. VCTs tend to offer less risk for their Investors because their investments are spread over a larger number of companies. The trusts themselves must be listed on the London Stock Exchange, which provides higher security for the Investor, but also higher costs to pay the middlemen.

Details of companies offering Venture Capital advice are listed in *The Directory* at the back of this Handbook.

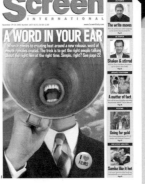

# Libby Savill *Olswang*
# The Proposed 20% Tax Credit

*Libby Savill is a partner at law firm Olswang, which specialises in all aspects of commercial law, particularly in the media sector. She is on the official panel advising the Government on the new tax credit legislation*

**Under the proposed new system, when I make money on my film, I will be able to choose to deduct income equalling 150% of the cost of my film from my group profits, or take my 20% tax credit and still have a 50% deduction left over, right?**

That's almost correct, except that the 50% uplift can't be surrendered to your other group companies. It can only be set off against income from the exploitation of your film. Anyway, in practice, you are unlikely to go for the 150% deduction option (as opposed to the 20% credit).

**Why is that?**

Partly because to do so, you [the production company] would have to have adequate current profits to shelter within your group, which will very rarely be the case.

If you do choose to deduct 150% of the cost of the film in order to generate losses to be set against current or future income, 100% of the cost can be surrendered to other group companies (and therefore set against current or future income unrelated to the film), but the additional 50% cannot, because it must be set against profits from the film.

**So the 100% deduction can go outside, to the group companies?**

Yes, but I suppose for most people, whether you're an inward investing studio coming to make a movie here, or an independent UK producer, you're not planning on using the group relief provisions, because in the short term you have probably not got sufficient UK taxable profits against which to off-set the 150% deduction. And besides, you're not funding the film. In fact this is the key point – you're generally not funding the film from your own resources.

If you were a company that was financing the film from your own working capital, then the idea of having the 150% deduction to set off against income from the film would be fine, and you could just stretch it over a period of time. Or if you had available group profits, you might set some or all of the 100% against those profits (so as to utilise the tax deduction sooner). But the fact of the matter is that 99% of companies that fund films in the UK are funding them from different sources which will be treated as income in the hands of the production company. This is the case whether you adopt a commissioning producer structure or combine a set of pre-buys, UK Film council investment, or other methods of funding. All such sources of funding are income receipts which will be taxed in the hands of the production company.

So, 100% of costs of making the film will be on your production company's books. But if, for argument's sake, the benchmark for the financing of the film is to fund 30% from your own working capital, and before you green-light the film to have the remaining 70% of the costs of your film 'laid off' elsewhere, that third party funding of 70% will be income in the hands of the production company. So you immediately need to use at least 70% of your 150% deduction to set off against the cost of making the film. Otherwise, you are going to have to pay tax on those sources when they come into your hands. So, whether the film is funded through a pre-buy, Film Council money, or an advance against estimates or pre-sales that then materialise - all such financing methods are income. And I think from an accounting perspective, when you anticipate that these will turn into actual income, you actually have to put them in your books there and then.

So, I think it's a bit naive to assume that people will use the 150% deduction. I mean very few people go into financing a film without having some idea that the film will get out there and be distributed, and have someone else sharing the risk on that, whether it be a pre-buy, Film Council or whatever else. And, as I have said, this option is not attractive because all of those methods of financing are income in the hands of the production company, and as such the benefit of the 150% deduction is immediately reduced.

**So most people will choose the 20% tax credit optoin?**

In terms of the straight tax credit, from my experience sitting on the experts panel and before that various committees, and also discussing the issues with lots of other industry experts, I don't think anyone disagreed that 99% of the time, if the new tax credit was going to be implemented, the film makers would choose to access the 20% tax rebate.

**How do you access the 20% tax rebate?**

Well, the production company completes the film and will have 100% of the production costs on its books. Instead of using the 150% deduction option, it can surrender 100% of the production costs directly to the Revenue in order to get a 20% tax credit cash payment. The problem with the tax credit is that it only then leaves another 50% additional deduction against income from the film, and yet the production company has 80% of the film costs which still need be to covered before it would wish to pay tax on them.

**So, if the Government said the actual 'income' that the producer receives as production finance isn't treated as income for tax purposes, we'd be fine?**

We'd be more than happy, as we'd then have an extremely generous system because you'd have 50% of your real profits still not being taxable.

**But when the new concept was released, didn't a lot of people think that that is what was originally intended?**

No, I don't think this was what they were originally intending, or what most people thought was being proposed by the Inland Revenue. That would be to fly in the face of Inland Revenue basic principles. You don't turn taxable income into non-taxable income. That would be such an exception for the film industry that it's never, ever going to happen.

Our original 'suggestion' detailing a proposed new tax credit system was put forward to the Inland Revenue knowing that they had set certain parameters within which the tax credit had to operate. For example, that the tax credit had to be claimed through the Inland Revenue system and thereby had to be claimed by a company caught within the UK tax net. Also, it couldn't be a straight production grant, because that would be 'state aid' which would raise EU problems. But working within the parameters, our 'suggestion' was pretty much what we got except that, instead of the deduction being 150%, we had proposed a 180% deduction. And I think you can see from the maths, that an 180% deduction would have made a lot more sense. If you surrendered the first 100% of the deduction to get back 20%, you would still have an 80% uplift left to set against your other sources of finance. In other words the 80% would be effectively give you a deduction to match your other usual sources of finance. As such, you would only be paying tax on the real profits from the film.

**And the remaining 20% would be the tax credit?**

That's correct, although you'd have to borrow against it. The 20% is in any event tax free, when you get it back from the Revenue. So the real costs of your film suddenly become 80%. If you had a deduction equal to 180% of your costs of production, you would have given up your initial 100% deduction, and would still have an 80% uplift. This would mean the cost of making your film would be tax deductible in your hands. The general principle of film financing is very much that if you spend 100 making the film, you are able to receive 100 of income before you have to start paying a penny in tax.

**So has anyone worked out what the real benefit to the film industry would be, using a 150% deduction instead of 180%?**

Well this can be calculated quite simply. Talking in percentages, if you have received 20 from the Revenue (having surrendered 100), and only have another 50 left over to off-set against taxable income, your total relief then equals 70. So the remaining costs of the movie, ie. the 30, is taxable income in the hands of the production company – just for making the movie! So the production company would have to pay tax at 30% - being the UK corporation tax rate - on that 30, equalling 9% of the movie costs. So although you have a tax credit which on the face of it is worth 20, it really is only worth 11 because you have to pay 9 back to the Revenue immediately.

So that's the problem with the structure as currently proposed. The Government's statements have always said that the new system would 'typically' deliver 20%. We can't see, whether you use the 150% deduction method I mentioned before, or access for the 20% tax credit, how this could ever be delivered.

**And that's not taking into account the cost of discounting the tax credit.**

Exactly.

# Ivan McTaggert *Baker Street*

# Taxing Questions

The UK's film tax financing industry has, over the last few years, resembled a Roadrunner cartoon. The government up on a cliff top, repeatedly dropping anvils to try and crush naughty tax financiers, only to see them pop up somewhere entirely different.

In particular, February 10th 2004, 'Black Tuesday' as it has come to be known, when a broadside from the Treasury brought down schemes like Ingenious' 'Inside Track' and Grosvenor Park's 'First Choice', and December 2nd 2004 ('Brown Thursday?') when 'double dipping' was outlawed, brought grave pronouncements about the inevitable death of the British film industry.

At the time of writing (four months after the latter announcement) Ingenious are reported to have raised in excess of £100m for Ingenious Film Partners, their latest feature film production partnership, Baker Street have just closed financing on three new feature films and Grosvenor Park are rumoured to be re-entering the market with a new scheme so beautiful in form that investors will be powerless to resist. From the perspective of the British film producer, the anvil seems to have missed again.

However, what we don't see at ground level are a whole host of schemes that have now been put to bed permanently; schemes that were previously costing the treasury an enormous amount of money. For example, the sale and leaseback transactions on British qualifying Hollywood movies like the 'Harry Potter' series which were carried out at levels that were many multiples of their production budget, on the (perfectly reasonable some would say) basis that their value was far greater than their cost.

Reasonable or not, these transactions were costing the British taxpayer a lot of money; exactly how much is unclear. The majority of the schemes in operation raise money from private individuals, and hence the figures showing how much tax relief has been obtained via film schemes are hidden in thousands of individual tax returns at tax offices all over the country and there is no accurate reckoning of the extent to which the treasury has been subsidising the film industry.

Martin Churchill of 'Tax Efficient Review' estimated that in the tax year to April 2004 film tax schemes sheltered over £2bn of taxable income, losing (or to be precise deferring) tax payable of over £800m. When you consider that this was around half of the total amount the government raised in capital gains tax in the year to April 2003, you can see why they have been taking things so seriously. Less money available for schools in order that a US studio can save money on production of its latest blockbuster is a difficult argument to sustain.

It's clear that the government's intention is to reduce the amount of money lost to the treasury from film schemes, abusive or otherwise, and the reforms that have recently been introduced will have a big effect. There will still be film tax schemes, but fewer and smaller. The biggest roadrunners have been crushed, and it's my belief that from here on any scheme over a certain size acting irresponsibly will be closed down.

The new tax credit under development (and it has a fair way to go before it will be ready) seeks to replace the complicated, fee heavy structures that have been used previously with a simple 'luncheon voucher' scheme where your British film certificate entitles you to a cash payment of 20% of its qualifying cost from the government. The March 2005 budget revealed, as suspected, that a tax credit scheme will operate for all British films, large and small, replacing both S48 and S42. This way the Treasury can push a button on their computer, and it can immediately tell them how much the tax credit has cost them to date.

Private investors wanting tax relief for investing in films will be pointed towards schemes using the Enterprise Investment Scheme and Venture Capital Trusts, neither of which give the large upfront tax deferrals previously on offer.

It is almost certain that the result of all this will be less money available to the film industry, though perhaps a little extra for hospitals. However, I am personally optimistic that forcing British film producers to work harder to secure funding from the marketplace is in the long-term interest of the industry.

The influence of the British broadcasters on the British film industry is sometimes criticised on the basis that their motivation is to make films to show on TV and they therefore encourage less cinematic film making. By contrast to a broadcaster, consider a financier whose only motivation is to make a film, any film, by tax year end in order to shelter tax and to earn a fee. It has been said that there are two types of film tax fund – those that are in the film business (and anyone who has worked with Baker Street would include them in this category) and those that are just in the money business. What is the effect on the industry of funders who have little or no interest in the quality of the project they are backing?

The number of British films made every year has increased significantly since the introduction of the Section 48 tax break in the late 1990s. However, the number of those films not finding distribution is woefully high.

If the changes in legislation reverse this, it has to be a good thing. We may have less British films made, but if more of them are distributed, and more of them have real commercial value, the British film business will no longer exist solely to create losses to shelter rich individuals' tax liabilities, but can move to generating some taxable profits of its own.

*Ivan Mactaggart is a producer with Meteor Pictures, and also the Head of Business Affairs at Baker Street Media Finance. The views expressed are personal and not those of Meteor Pictures or Baker Street.*

*Meteor Pictures Ltd, 96-98 Baker Street, London W1U 6TJ.*
*Tel +44 (0)870 246 1900 Fax. +44 (0)870 246 1901 | Email. ivan@meteorpictures.com*

## CHAPTER FIVE

# INTERNATIONAL FINANCING

As mentioned in the previous Chapter, in order to be able to access UK tax benefits, a picture has to qualify as a "**British Film**". There are two ways to do this; either by meeting the four criteria set out in Schedule 1 to the *Films Act 1985* (outlined at the beginning of Chapter 4), or by fulfilling various conditions to become an **official co-production**.

| UK CO-PRODUCTIONS | | |
|---|---|---|
| **Main country** | **2003** | **2004** |
| UK | 18 | 18 |
| France | 22 | 12 |
| Canada | 16 | 8 |
| Denmark | 4 | 5 |
| Ireland | 6 | 5 |
| Spain | 1 | 5 |
| Italy | 7 | 4 |
| Australia | 2 | 3 |
| New Zealand | 3 | 3 |
| Romania | 1 | 3 |
| Germany | 7 | 2 |
| Luxembourg | 1 | 2 |
| Netherlands | 5 | 1 |
| Czech Republic | 2 | 0 |
| South Africa | 2 | 1 |
| Other | 2 | 4 |
| Not available | - | 9 |
| **Total** | **99** | **85** |
| *Source: UK Film Council International* | | |

But as with the UK, many other countries' governments are eager to promote their own local film industry, and have themselves introduced various incentives for producers to make films that qualify as "**National**" films within their jurisdictions. In a way, the provision of national subsidies could be seen as governments unfairly promoting their own economies and citizens at the expense of other countries, skewing cross-border competition and conflicting with general EU principles. But the European Commission has expressly permitted the regimes to continue for the film industry, at least until June 2007, by which time there should be a pervasive review and possibly, therefore, a change of policy. In the meantime, the various incentives available are proving very popular with British and European producers, as well as with those from Hollywood (2005 Oscar® winners *The Aviator* and *Million Dollar Baby*, for example, were both substantially funded by European money).

Depending on the country concerned, the range of benefits available to a National film includes simple "cash-back" from the relevant government on completion of the picture, tax incentives for investors, exemptions from paying certain taxes when engaging local crew or using local facilities, access to local public-money production funds, and so on. As with British Films, in order to qualify as a National film in another country, a picture will usually need to have a large proportion of its budget spent there, and/or have a predominantly local cast and crew.

For a Producer, the beauty of the **official co-production** route is that s/he can also avail him/herself of whatever soft money options there are in *all* the applicable co-production country(ies). This is because if a film qualifies as an official co-production (see below), it will automatically qualify as a "National" film in each of the relevant countries. In other words, a National British Film would be eligible for British benefits, a National Canadian Film would be eligible for Canadian benefits, but a film made under the *UK-Canada Co-production Treaty*, would qualify for both. So the rationale for making an official co-production, at least from a financial perspective, is to enable producers to become entitled to the financial benefits available in more than one country. Some of these benefits are not insubstantial, and it is not unheard of for a carefully structured picture to have 30% or more of its budget covered by this so-called "**soft money**".

Some countries do not offer official co-production status with the UK (see below), but nevertheless offer specific incentives to entice Producers to come and make National Films within their borders. Although these benefits cannot be combined with the UK tax allowances, they are often sufficiently appealing to attract inward investment in film production from other countries anyway, including from the UK. Other states (in places such as South America, East Asia, Africa and – although recently becoming more expensive – Eastern Europe) have such low production costs that, despite having no particular formal arrangements to entice Producers, the simple budget cost-savings are enough to compel Producers to consider them seriously when deciding on locations, studios and post-production facilities.

In this Chapter, we explain **how to qualify** as an official co-production (the Treaties and the Convention), and what **international benefits** await those films that do. We also provide a brief description of the film-related benefits available to National films of other countries which might be of interest, even though they don't offer the co-production option. These soft money incentives comprise tax allowances, rebates, credits, etc, and we note each of these in turn (if applicable). Where there are major direct funding opportunities (as opposed to tax incentives) available to qualifying National films of various countries, we detail these in the International section of **Chapter 6** (Funding Organisations). We do not, however, cover in this Handbook those countries which are attractive solely for non-film related reasons, such as exchange rates and low cost of living.

## Co-Productions

The Producer of a film clearly needs to carry out several tasks in order to get his/her picture made. These include raising the finance, securing talent, engaging the crew, preparing budgets, sourcing locations, arranging post-production, and so on. There are times when it makes sense to pool resources with another producer, splitting these responsibilities in accordance with their respective expertise and resources. Where more than one producer makes a film as a collective effort in this way, it is known as a "**co-production**", and the producers are referred to as "**co-producers**". The co-producers (who may or may not be from the same country) will enter into a **co-production agreement** that will set out their respective rights and obligations, together with their financial interest in the film.

However, in the industry, the term "co-production" is generally used specifically to refer to a film that is made under the umbrella of a particular governmental co-production treaty (a "**Treaty**"), or the *European Convention on Cinematic Co-Production* (the "**European Convention**"). It is this type of co-production, better referred to as an "**official co-production**", that is of most interest, as it is through this vehicle that Producers can obtain the financial benefits set out in this and the previous Chapter.

# "Official" Co-productions

There are two main types of official co-production; those made under the European Convention, imaginatively known as "**Convention Co-productions**", and those made under the bilateral Treaties, or "**Treaty Co-productions**".

The UK currently has bilateral treaties with seven other countries: **Germany** (since 1975), **Canada** (since 1975), **Norway** (since 1983, although the DCMS has proposed that it be terminated at its next renewal date), **Australia** (since 1990), **New Zealand** (since 1993), **France** (since 1995), and **Italy** (since 1998).

In February 2005, the British Government announced that it was working towards entering into Co-Production Treaties with five other "emerging" countries, being **South Africa, India** (both of which have been expected for some time)**, China, Morocco** and **Jamaica.** At the time of going to print, however, no details had been released relating to their prospective salient terms, or likely date of implementation (although rumours suggest Summer or Autumn 2006). That said, the rules of the existing Co-Production Treaties are fairly standard, although there are some important differences between them, and we don't expect the new Treaties to vary too much from the norm.

## Competent Authorities

Each country has a "competent authority" appointed by its government, which has the role of granting official co-production status to films that comply with the relevant regulations. In the UK, the relevant authority is the Department of Culture, Media and Sport ("**DCMS**"), and it is to this body that an application for co-production status must be made. Details of the relevant "competent authorities" in the seven other countries with which the UK has a Treaty are set out later in this chapter under the country concerned, as are the website URLs for the full text of the Treaties themselves.

# Qualification Criteria for the Bilateral Treaties

Whereas the benefits available in each country range quite considerably, the qualification criteria under the various Treaties - although not identical - do follow certain themes. The following is a summary of the typical requirements, imposed by the UK's co-production Treaties, which a film must satisfy in order to be granted official co-production status. However, there are exceptions in nearly every case and, before applying for official co-production status, a producer should check carefully the terms of the relevant Treaty under which s/he wishes the film to qualify. The Table in the Reference Section of this Handbook sets out the relative requirements in more detail.

## Common Management and Control

The co-producers must be independent from each other, and may not be linked by common management (except to the extent that it is inherent in the making of the film itself).

## General Contractual Terms

The Treaties require certain provisions to be included in the co-production agreement between the co-producers. These terms include an explanation of the financial commitment (including dates) and recoupment position(s) of the respective co-producing companies, and must set out the contingency arrangement (ie. what happens to the film and any money invested in it) in the event that the picture is not ultimately - or even provisionally - granted official co-production status. Generally, the income of each co-producer received from the exploitation of the film should be roughly proportional to that co-producer's financial contribution. Ownership of the negative (or, in the case of the Canadian Treaty, the copyright) must also be clearly specified, together with an acknowledgement that each co-producer has the right to access and copy the finished product. Producers should take proper advice when drafting the co-production contract, particularly in ensuring that these provisions are correctly worded.

## Minimum Financial Contribution

Until recently, each country's co-producer had to provide a minimum of **20%** of the financial contribution to the film (except under the Treaties with Germany and Australia, where the minimum stated is 30%). However, because the soft money benefits in some Treaty countries relate solely to the amount of money spent there (as opposed to the UK tax allowances, which apply to the entire budget no matter where it is spent), many UK co-productions have been structured so as to spend as little money as possible in the UK, and as much as possible abroad. This has annoyed the British Government because the purpose behind entering into the Treaties was, on aggregate over time, to share the benefits and burdens equally with the partner countries. Instead, the bulk of UK-Canadian co-productions (for example) were "majority-Canadian", with 80% of the budget being spent in Canada and the minimum 20% being spent in the UK.

This caused the British Government, in 2003/4, to unilaterally raise some of the minimum requirements relating to UK spend, with a view to increasing reciprocity. The Treaties are only supposed to be amended by agreement between both governments, but the DCMS in its inimitable wisdom has decided to go it alone and refuse to certify as British any Treaty Co-production with **France**, **Italy** or **Canada** (or Convention Co-productions with **Denmark** or **Iceland** – see below) unless at least **40%** of the budget is spent in the United Kingdom. The big fear is that, instead of increasing the amount of production in the UK from 20% or 30% to 40% of a budget, producers will simply go elsewhere altogether. Canada and France have more Co-production Treaties than any other country, and most of these allow 80% to be spent in Canada or France (as the case may be). With the United Kingdom already a relatively expensive country to produce in, there is a good chance that many producers will continue to choose to make Canadian or French co-productions, but with countries other than the UK.

## Creative Contribution

The general rule is that the "creative" contribution must be approximately proportional to the "financial" contribution. Occasionally (as with the UK Treaties with Italy and France), a substantial "finance only" contribution is permitted, where one co-producer may provide only finance (ie. no creative elements), without disqualifying the picture from official co-production status.

## Location

The film must be made (including post-production) in the countries of the co-producers' origin. Generally, the majority of production must take place in the country from where the majority of the finance is provided. Location shooting in another country is usually permitted, subject to the competent authorities' approval. Personnel involved in making the film who are nationals or residents of one co-producing country are granted easy access to the other co-producing country(ies), without the need to obtain work permits.

## Qualifying Nationals

This is often the trickiest area, particularly when the project and/or lead cast originate from the United States. The basic rule is that all individuals taking part in the making of the film must be nationals or residents of one of the co-producer's countries (including a third co-producer's country, if any) or a Member State of the European Union. However, "exceptional circumstances" (sometimes only if dictated by the script) will permit the competent authorities to approve certain talent (often only the leading roles) from another state, depending on which Treaty is being utilised. This is incredibly important where an American director or lead artist is attached to the project. Also, where the authorities have approved location filming in another country, "necessary" local crew and/or crowd artists may be hired.

## Musical Score

Generally, the music must be composed (and sometimes "directed" and performed) by nationals or residents of one of the co-producer's countries (including that of a third co-producer) or an EU Member State. The rules sometimes vary slightly for music that is not specifically commissioned for the picture.

## Third Country Participation

A three-way co-production, with a producer from a third country, will usually be able to access the benefits of all three countries, but only if the third country has also entered into a co-production treaty with one of the other two. For example, as Canada has a co-production treaty with Algeria, a UK-Canada-Algeria co-production will be permitted under the UK-Canada Treaty, even though the UK has no treaty with Algeria. Of course, the film will only actually qualify if all the other criteria in the treaty are also satisfied.

# The European Convention

The aim of the European Convention is to allow qualifying co-produced films the benefits that are available to National films in each convention country. Almost all countries in the EU (and many more in the European geographical area) have signed up to the Treaty, so it applies to nearly every co-production made anywhere on the continent. As is the case for Treaty co-productions, each co-producer can utilise whatever benefits are available in his/her own country. Again, the creative and financial contributions to the film must be relatively proportional, and must generally exceed 20% (potentially 10% for multilateral co-productions) of the total budget. The recent change of DCMS policy (see above) now requires a minimum

UK spend of 40% on any co-productions with **France, Italy, Denmark** or **Iceland**. A financial-only contribution of between 10% and 25% is also permitted under certain conditions. Co-producers from one or more non-member states may be brought into a co-production agreement under the Convention, provided that (i) it/they bring(s) no more than 30% to the table, (ii) at least three other Convention country co-producers are party to the co-production agreement, and (iii) the points system (below) is still satisfied.

Note that the Convention is not currently in force in **Bosnia, Norway, Ukraine** and, until 1 July 2005, **Turkey** (plus some of the smaller jurisdictions). The Council of Europe website has the Convention in full, and also a list of the signatories (including dates when the Convention came into force in each country). The English language URL is: http://conventions.coe.int/Treaty/Commun/QueVoulezVous.asp?NT=147&CM=8&DF=4/9/05&CL=ENG, or if that's a bit of a mouthful, try http://conventions.coe.int/, and then click full list (on the left) and look for Treaty No. 147.

## The points system

Unlike the Treaties, where individuals' nationality and/or residence are relevant for qualification purposes, the Convention is generally only concerned with nationality. However, for Convention Co-productions involving the UK, the DCMS has recently stated that nationals *and/or* residents will qualify. There is a "**points system**" ascribing values to various contributors (artists, creative department heads etc), and to qualify as a Convention co-production, the film must have 15 of the 19 points. As the director, writer and first lead artist are each "worth" three points, clearly only one of these may be from a non-convention country. The second lead artist is worth two points, and all the other contributors (third lead artist, composer, cameraman, sound recordist, editor, art director, studio or shooting location, and post-production location) are all worth a point each. If the film has a strong "European identity", but only has 13 or 14 points, it may still be possible to make it under the Convention, as the 15/19 points rule can potentially be waived slightly by the relevant competent authority(ies).

# Convention or Treaty?

## Bilateral co-productions

The general rule is that where there is a bilateral Treaty between two Convention countries, the film should be made under that Treaty rather than under the Convention, and the Treaty rules will generally be applied. So, for example, the 30% minimum contribution under the UK-Germany Treaty would still apply to a German-UK co-production, despite the Convention allowing 20%. However, in the DCMS press release of 28 February 2005, the UK Government *"proposes that we should continue to co-produce films with Germany and Italy using the European Convention rather than the individuall bilateral agreements"*, but at the time of going to press, there was no confirmation that this rule had yet been implemented. Where there is no relevant Treaty between two Convention countries, the film should, of course, be produced under the Convention. In these cases, the Convention effectively serves as a bilateral co-production treaty, where there is no actual bilateral agreement in force between the two countries. In such circumstances, and subject to DCMS policy, the minimum contribution from the minority co-producer must be at least 20%.

### Multilateral co-productions

Where there is a Treaty that would cover the film, it may be used (and the DCMS would prefer that it is) so long as it does not contravene the specific provisions of the Convention. Effectively, the film will be made, and the documentation needs to specify that it will be made, "under the terms of the Treaty". As mentioned above, the various UK Treaties require a minimum 20% or 30% financial commitment, but the Convention allows for as little as 10% (reflecting the Eurimage position). As there is a direct conflict on this point, the Convention rule will override the Treaties, allowing a 10% minimum contribution. In other words, the 30% requirement in the UK-Germany Treaty would be overridden by the Convention in a UK-Germany-Spain "three-way" Treaty co-production, and a 10% minimum would apply. Where there is no Treaty covering the co-production, the Convention will of course apply, assuming the relevant countries are signatories.

# The Application Process

Achieving **official co-production** status depends on meeting two main requirements: keeping to the terms indicated in the provisional agreement, and ensuring each co-producer meets the conditions of the relevant Treaty (or Convention).

Applying for official co-production status is a lengthy and stringent three-step process:

1. "Provisional" co-production status is granted by the competent authorities on the strength of an approved agreement between the co-producers
2. Each co-producer, being eligible to benefit from National Film status in their country, then raises finance and makes the film
3. Once the film is completed, a successful audit allows the competent authorities to grant the film official co-production status

### The Provisional Application

The detailed procedure to be followed whilst preparing the provisional application form can be extremely daunting and unnerving, unless the Producer is careful to pay close mind to the various guidelines set out, and is completely appraised of what is required of him/her(as well as of current treaty regulations).

The first crucial point to be aware of is that the UK co-producer must submit its preliminary application to the Department of Culture, Media and Sport (DCMS) at least 6-8 weeks before production (ie. principal photography) commences. Any application that arrives later than this will be rejected automatically.

There are several other factors that can cause the application to be immediately rejected by the DCMS, such as listing costs that may be deemed inflated, showing intent to employ personnel who are not covered by the respective treaty or simply leaving a box on the application form blank. It may prove beneficial to either enlist the experience of an executive producer, or to hire a law firm that specialises in facilitating and advising on the process. The DCMS can also provide valuable guidance, so it is useful to try to take advantage of their expertise at as early a stage as possible.

Along with the application, copies of documents such as the shooting script, full budget, chain of title and the co-production agreement will also need to be submitted.

Full details and application forms can be found at the Department of Culture, Media and Sport website - www.culture.gov.uk/creative_industries/film/Co-productionagreements.htm

Any questions regarding certification or co-production should be e-mailed to filmcertification @culture.gov.uk

## The Final Audit and Adjustments of Contributions

Upon completion of the film, the competent authority will contact the co-producer(s) to request an audit, to confirm whether the film merits official co-production status. This must be carried out by either an independent accountancy firm that is recognised under Section 25 of the *Companies Act 1989*, or an accountant recognised under Section 34 of that Act. Note that a film is classed as completed when it is ready to be shown to the general public, not simply when shooting has been finished and/or it is still in post-production.

Each co-producer is required to arrange an audit of their own accounts, and these audits are then brought together to be presented to all relevant competent authorities for examination. Rather than pay two firms to liaise with each other over respective receipts, payments and finance, it is acceptable, and may be preferable, to employ one accountancy firm to carry out the full production audit for both co-prooduction parties.

The accountants will assess how much money was sourced from the respective countries, and where this money was spent. Although the guidelines for a provisional agreement are extremely strict with regards to the co-producers' proportionate amounts, the competent authority does allow for some flexibility in accepting changes that may occur with the final shares in the production. However, it is advisable to keep the authority apprised of any potential or certain changes throughout the production period.

As obtaining official co-production status depends on the co-producers making certain financial and creative contributions, the budgets for each co-producer should be kept separately. Financial contributions are defined as the finance each co-producer raises for the budget. Creative filmmaking contributions represent the costs spent on labour, locations, facilities and resources in each territory. These contributions are weighed against the total budget, to establish whether they meet the required percentages. Any contributions or costs relating to parties of/from countries not covered by the relevant Treaty must also be budgeted separately, so that the proportion of those figures - as part of the total budget - can be clearly examined.

If, in the final analysis of the budget/contributions(s), the shares between co-producers work out to be different to those specified in the provisional agreement, the relevant Competent Authorities may still approve the film as an official co-production, provided the minimum requirements are still met. If this were to occur, the share of revenues and rights between co-producers must be amended to reflect the changes. The Competent Authorities may also approve a co-production where a co-producer's financial contribution has not been equal to its creative filmmaking contribution; the respective interests in the success of the film would be re-aligned, and entitlement to any distribution advances re-apportioned.

# Examples of Available Benefits

Governmental incentives do not last forever. Tax breaks come and go (perhaps the most poignant examples being the sudden exclusions of television product and double-dipping from the UK tax allowance regime). However, below are summaries of some of the fiscal benefits available around the world at the time of publication. For countries that have a Co-production Treaty with the UK, the relevant "competent authority" details are also noted. Naturally, producers should check their eligibility at any given time, and make sure that, where necessary, their films are completed in time in order to access the relevant benefit before it disappears (assuming its phasing out is actually announced in advance!). In each case, there are numerous eligibility criteria that will apply, often relating to such elements as the size of the budget, the nationality of cast/crew/producer/investor, ownership of copyright, extent of the investment, etc, and there is no substitute for taking proper advice before embarking on your production.

The UK is arguably the world-leader in engineering funds that utilise available tax breaks. With our own tax-breaks being whittled down, a number of English private funds have branched out abroad and are now offering "German money" or "Australian money" (etc). Where information about such funds is known or published, we have noted it with the other details pertaining specifically to these companies in the previous Chapter, rather than in this section.

## AUSTRALIA

### Competent Authority Details

#### THE AUSTRALIAN FILM COMMISSION

*Level 4, 150 William Street, Woolloomooloo, NSW 2011, GPO Box 3984, Sydney 2001, Australia | tel: +61 2 9321 6444 | fax: +61 2 9357 3737 | web: www.afc.gov.au*

*Catherine Waters, manager, Legal Affairs*

Download the Treaty from www.culture.gov.uk/PDF/uk-australia1990.PDF, or order a copy by phoning The Stationary Office Photocopying Department on 020 7873 8455 and quoting Cmd No 1758 Treaty Series No. 90 (1991) ISBN 0101175825

### What's Available?

There are a number of tax breaks available in Australia.

The so-called **10B** and **10BA 100% tax allowance** schemes provide Australian resident taxpayers with a 100% reduction in taxable income (equal to the amount they invest in local films) on the acquisition of copyright in an Australian film. 10BA (the more popular scheme) is available in relation to culturally relevant pictures with high Australian content that are certified by the DCITA (Department of Communications, Information Technology and the Arts) as qualifying Australian films. They must be made substantially in Australia (or, of course, as an official co-production). Money is usually raised through brokers, and the films need to be completed within 2 years of the investment.

The "FLIC" (**Film Licence Investment Company**) scheme provided a **100% tax concession** to investors in companies that are licensed to invest in a slate of television and film product. This was a pilot scheme, and there were initially only two such FLICs. They were permitted to raise and invest up to about A$40m (approx. £15.5m) over two years in projects that satisfy certain criteria. The scheme closed in June 2003, but the Australian Government is reviewing the situation, and there is much lobbying to repeat it.

There is also a newer "**Refundable Tax Offset**" scheme for larger films where more than A$15m (approx. £6.1m) is spent in Australia. It is effectively a **12.5% tax rebate** applicable to all qualifying Australian production expenditure ("**QAPE**"). QAPE must also exceed either 70% of the budget or A$50m (£20m).

More information on all the above schemes is available at www.afc.gov.au/gtp/mptax.html.

**South Australia Film Corporation** is shortly bringing out an additional **10% rebate** on the cost of local cast and crew, on a trial basis (it already has a tax exemption on production wages).

# BELGIUM

The long-awaited **150% corporation tax allowance** scheme in Belgium has finally got off the ground, although the numbers involved aren't exactly huge. Basically, the scheme (known as the **Belgian Cinema Tax Shelter**) allows a corporation tax set-off of up to E750,000 (approx. £515,000). Tax relief is calculated at 150% of the investment (which must not exceed 50% of the film's budget or 50% of the investing company's pre-tax profits), so an investment of E500,000 (approx. £345,000) would trigger the maximum relief. Note that some publications currently state – wrongly in our view - that the amount of investment, rather than the amount of the tax relief, is capped at E750,000, giving a total tax allowance of E1.125m. In any event, up to 40% of the investment can be borrowed in the form of a loan. Films for television will only be included from 2006, and more than one company can obtain the tax benefit by investing in the same film.

# BRAZIL

There are two options available to a Brazilian qualifying film. A law known locally as **Article 1** provides an **income tax rebate** (max 3% of total income tax owed) to a Brazilian individual or company (or Brazilian Branch) for investment in an audiovisual work. Alternatively, **Article 3** allows a certificated film to attract finance from foreign producers, distributors or intermediaries, who get a **70% tax deduction**, applicable to income or royalties from (Brazilian or foreign) film exploitation in Brazil. Apparently only one studio has actually used this incentive on a regular basis.

# CANADA

## Competent Authority and Telefilm Details

### TÉLÉFILM CANADA

*360 St. James Street, Suite 700, Montreal, Quebec, H2Y 4A9, Canada | tel: +1 514 283 6363 | fax: +1 514 283 8212 | web: www.telefilm.gc.ca*

*contact: Brigitte Monneau - Manager, Co-productions, Services des relations internationals, Director, International Relations*

CANADIAN AUDIO-VISUAL CERTIFICATION OFFICE

*Department of Canadian Heritage, 100 Sparks Street, 4th Floor, Ottawa, Ontario, K1A 0M5 Canada | tel: +1 888 433 2200 Toll-free or +1 613 946 7600 | fax: +1 613 946 7602 | cavco_bcpac@pch.gc.ca | www.canadianheritage.gc.ca/cavco/*

Download the treaty from www.culture.gov.uk/PDF/uk-canada1991.PDF, or order a copy by phoning The Stationary Office Photocopying Department on 020 7873 8455 and quoting Cmd No 1807 Treaty Series No 9 (1992) ISBN 0101180721

## What's Available?

Canada has been a very popular destination for those looking for co-production related benefits, as a substantial proportion of local expenditure (particularly labour tax costs) can be claimed back in the form of **subsidies** or **tax credits**. There are benefits available at both the federal and provincial level.

## Federal Funding

The **Federal Production Tax Credit** ("**CPTC**") is currently available to Canadian content productions, at the rate of 25% of qualified labour expenditure. The maximum permissible qualifying expenditure is now **60%** of the total budget, so this tax credit can potentially yield up to 15% of the budget. The films must be produced and owned by an established Canadian tax-paying company. There is also an alternative **production services tax credit** ("**PSTC**"), which applies to Canadian and non-Canadian films whereby up to **16% of salaries** paid to Canadians can be reclaimed.

## Regional Funding

Specific **provinces** also have labour-based tax credit programmes which apply to official co-productions and locally qualifying films tax credit, with rates varying from 20% to 40% (there have been a number of welcome recent increases). These schemes usually require the individuals concerned to have been resident in the relevant province at the end of the financial year prior to start of principal photography. Some are aimed specifically at Canadian qualifying productions, and some are not. Generally, the PSTCs can be used on *any* Film shooting in the province, whereas other tax credit schemes can only be used for Canadian *qualifying* productions (including co-productions). Also, what "qualifies" as eligible expenditure differs slightly from scheme to scheme and from province to province, and the ability to use more than one scheme for any one film is usually restricted (although the provincial schemes can all be combined the federal CPTC). Take local professional advice before committing! Below are the basic details, but all the provinces have websites providing clear information on the respective systems.

**British Columbia** offers a number of interlinked schemes. Under the **BC Film Incentive**, Canadian companies can get a 30% tax credit on qualifying BC labour expenditure, and even more if the picture is filmed outside of Vancouver, it involves a training programme, and/or it uses a large amount of visual / digital effects. BC also has its own PSTC of 18% (or more if outside Vancouver, and/or with high levels of visual / digital effects) for any films over C$1m, but the applicant itself must be a BC company owning the copyright.

**Manitoba** has a Manitoba labour tax credit of 45% (more for "regulars", rural shoots and/or training).

Both **New Brunswick** and **Newfoundland & Labrador** have something similar, equal to 40% of eligible labour expenditure (but for New Brunswick, capped at 50% of total production costs). 25% of all wages must go to local residents.

**Nova Scotia**'s credit is 35% of eligible labour expenditure (more for "regulars", or if shooting outside Halifax), capped at 15% of the budget.

**Ontario** has two alternative systems, a Film and TV Tax Credit ("OFTTC") and a PSTC. The OFTTC gives a 30% tax credit on eligible Ontario labour expenditure, with bonuses for shooting outside the Toronto area and for first time producers. The producer needs a TV deal in place for the film to be broadcast in Ontario within 2 years of completion. The PSTC is calculated at 18% of eligible Ontario labour expenditure, and the Film (minimum budget C$1m) does not need to be a qualifying Canadian production.

**Quebec** also has two systems. Its Film & TV Production Tax Credit offers Canadian Productions 30% on eligible labour expenditure (not exceeding 50% of the budget). The PSTC, available on any production, offers a 20% credit.

**Prince Edward Island**'s Rebate Programme allows 30% of eligible labour expenditure, or 15% of total eligible production costs.

**Saskatchewan**'s Film Employment Tax Credit offers 35% (with rural bonuses) on eligible wages, not exceeding 50% of the budget, and the qualification criteria tend to be less restrictive.

**Yukon** has a Film Incentive programme which provides a 35% rebate (with bonuses for rural and training) on eligible Yukon labour expenditure, capped at 50% of total expenditure. A minimum 25% of the Yukon labour expenditure must be on Yukon residents.

Official co-productions will also be eligible for **Telefilm Canada** assistance, such as the Feature Film Fund and the Broadcast Program Development Fund.

# FRANCE

## Competent Authority Details

### CENTRE NATIONAL DE LA CINEMATOGRAPHIE

*12 rue de Lubeck, 75784 Paris Cedex 16, France | tel: 0033 1 44 34 36 26 | fax: 0033 1 44 34 36 97 | www.cnc.fr | Francois Hurard, Le Directeur de la production cinematographique*

Download the treaty from www.culture.gov.uk/PDF/uk-france1994.PDF, or order a copy by phoning The Stationary Office Photocopying Department on 020 7873 8455 and quoting Cmd No 2992 Treaty Series No .82 (1995) ISBN 0101299222

## What's available?

Like Canada, France seems to have co-production treaties with almost every country that has a semblance of a film industry. However, traditionally, its benefit regime has not been nearly as attractive, the main tax-break scheme for production finance being the "**SOFICA**" system. Certain entities, known as SOFICA companies, are tax efficient vehicles for their investors, and will part-finance qualifying films by taking shares in the relevant production company (thereby always participating in the profits from the film). They have a limited amount of money, and usually hit their maximums.

Now, however, there is a new tax credit system in place for local producers, known as a **credit d'impot**, which can be used as a corporation tax set-off, or received as a cash payment. It is limited to E1m (£680k) per film, and provides between 10% and 20% of the below-the-line budget for films shot in France with French personnel, and is therefore difficult to combine with soft money from other countries; this may have influenced the 50% decline in UK-France co-productions in 2004.

The CNC also offers various regional funding schemes, sometimes putting up to 33% of the budget. It also provides grants based on producers' previous success at the box office (and on TV / video). These grants, administered through "accounts" at the CNC, are no longer limited to French or European producers.

# GERMANY

## Competent Authority Details

### BUNDESAMT FÜR WIRTSCHAFT UND AUSFUHRKONTROLLE (BAFA)

*Post fach 5171, 65726 Eschborn, Germany | tel: 0049 6196 404 401 | fax: 0049 6196 404 422 | www.bawi.de | Herr Peter Reuß*

Download the treaty from www.culture.gov.uk/PDF/uk-germany1975.PDF, or order a copy by phoning The Stationary Office Photocopying Department on 020 7873 8455 and quoting Cmd No 6155 Treaty Series No. 103 (1975) ISBN0101615507

## What's Available?

The days when exuberant German media companies ran around offering upwards of 30% of a film's budget, in return for what seemed like little more than German-speaking rights, are long gone. Those companies that have managed to remain in business are now much more prudent about their investment strategies. There are still a number of active tax-based German "funds" around, based on a federal income and corporation **tax allowance** system (available on investment in films) pursuant to the **Income Tax Code (Media Decree)**. They continue to make equity investments in qualifying pictures; some only in German or local films, and some not. They do tend to require certain creative control and impose a number of conditions relating to the size of the investment and/or overall budget, the location of production (and post-production), copyright ownership, decision-making, etc. The private funds come and go in cycles as money is raised from the German taxpayer and spent on production funding. One thing that can sometimes cause difficulty is that these funds (backed by private equity investors) usually have to take the role of producer or co-producer, and must own the copyright and physical materials. That makes them incompatible with several types of soft money from other jurisdictions. They will normally also require a profit share. The investors get to write off 100% of their investment.

In addition to these private funds, the **Filmforderungsanstalt** (German film promotion agency) will in certain circumstances provide finance in the form of a grant, and there are also many regional funds willing to put up public money in return for using their locations, studios and/or production facilities

The German Government is currently considering implementing a **tax allowance** model more similar to the UK's current system, allowing sale & leaseback type transactions, but nothing yet has been published. Expect details by summer 2005.

## HUNGARY

Hungary has a new-ish two-pronged **tax rebate** system for investment in films by companies paying tax in Hungary, imaginatively called the **Hungary Film Law**. The rebate is equal to 20% of the Hungarian spend, on any film. For official co-productions, the rebate is available on the entire budget, but a Hungarian distributor must also be attached. Note that details published in the English language are not always entirely consistent!

## ICELAND

There is a simple **12% rebate** on production costs spent in Iceland. If more than 80% of the budget is spent in Iceland, the producer can receive a refund equal to 12% of the entire budget (provided that the remainder of the budget is spent in an EEA country). The main caveat is that the production must be "suited to the promotion of Icelandic culture and the nature of Iceland".

## IRELAND

Known affectionately throughout the industry as "**section 481** finance (s481)" (replacing the old "section 35 finance"), the main Irish incentive is an **80% tax allowance**. The scheme has been extended for another 5 years from April 2005, and allows investors to cover up to 55% of larger films' budgets (over E6.35m, approx. £4.35m) or 66% for smaller pictures (under E5.08m, approx. £3.5m), with a sliding scale in between, so long as it is spent on Irish elements. The investors usually require that at least 80% of the amount invested is already covered by pre-sales and placed in escrow pending delivery. This comforts the banks, which actually lend the investors the bulk of their "investment". There are limits on the amounts that can be invested per film, and by any particular person or company. The personal limit is currently E33k (approx. £22.7k), making it quite difficult to raise s481 money for higher budget films. The film itself must "make a significant contribution to the national economy of Ireland and/or act as an effective stimulus to the creation of an indigenous film industry". Further, a certain amount of production work must be carried out in Ireland. The net benefit of the production is generally in the range of 12%, and the write-off available for the investors is 80% of the amount invested. From 1 January 2005, a pre-certification system from the Irish Revenue has been introduced, making the whole thing more costly and timely.

## ISLE OF MAN

The government of the Isle of Man can provide up to **25%** of the local spend in the form of **direct equity**, so long as at least 50% of principal photography takes place, and 20% below-the-line budget is spent on the island. This has been a popular scheme, and is often combined with the UK Sale & Leaseback.

# ITALY

## Competent Authority Details

### DIREZIONE GENERALE PER IL CINEMA

*Dirigente Servizio III Produzione, e Distribuzone Cinematografgiaca, Via della Ferraratella in Laterano, 51 – 00184, Roma, Italy | tel: 00 39 06 773 2484 | fax: 00 39 06 773 2430 | www.c inema.beniculturali.it*

*Dr Francesco Ventura, Ministero per i Beni e le Attivita' Culturali*

Download the treaty from www.culture.gov.uk/PDF/uk-italy1998.PDF, or order a copy by phoning The Stationary Office on 0870 600 5522 and quoting Cmd No 4840 Treaty Series No. 105 (2000)

## What's available?

Still nothing in place as yet, but the latest word from the government is that we should expect a tax shelter of some description to be in place by the end of 2006. Don't hold your breath.

The government has, however, set up a **private equity fund** called "**Cinefund**" through state-owned Cinecitta and financed with public money, which can be tapped for official co-productions. It intends to spend an average of £1m (approx. E1.4m) per film on up to 40 films over 5 years. Also, **Banca Nazionale del Lavoro** do special production loans, but these are inconsistent with Sale & Leasebacks, and a nightmare to organise.

# JAPAN AND SOUTH KOREA

For a couple of years, governments of both countries have been mooting the introduction of specific legislation to encourage local production, but nothing substantial is yet in place.

# LUXEMBOURG

The **Audiovisual Investment Certificate** is a **transferable tax credit** accessible by Luxembourg production companies. Up to **30%** of local spend (capped at E6m) can be refunded in the form of a transferable (ie. sellable) corporation tax credit.

# MALTA

The **Business Promotion Act 2005** (which will be ratified in June 2005 but should be backdated to January) will allow the government to provide a **cash rebate** equal to up to **20%** of the Maltese spend. This is in addition to specific tax incentives available for producing in Malta, such as a low 12.5% corporation tax rate and a **50% tax credit** for investing in Maltese productions.

# THE NETHERLANDS

The "**Film CV**" system, is based on a scheme originally intended for the shipbuilding industry. The "new improved" version came into force in July 2002, following amendments resulting from alleged serious abuse of the original system. It only really relates to films with budgets under E15m, and allows a Dutch investor an **income tax allowance** against his/her investment. The benefit to the film's budget can be as high as 30%, but the film must have at least one

Dutch producer, and at least half of its budget must be spent in The Netherlands. In addition, the producer has to show the existence of a large number of pre-sales and equity, covering the majority of the budget, and that the film is intended for theatrical release.

There was initially some negative press and industry vibe about the ability to raise cash under the scheme, and the fairly cumbersome and expensive procedure involved in accessing it. A number of banks left the market in 2002, although the quasi-quango **FINE** (amongst others) is still fairly active. The scheme was temporarily suspended in 2004, and the even newer and more improved 2005 version is - at time of going to print - still to be formally implemented. There is very little accurately written English-language documentation available, and so local advice must be sought.

# NEW ZEALAND

## Competent Authority Details

### NEW ZEALAND FILM COMMISSION

*PO Box 11-546, Wellington. New Zealand, | tel: 00 64 4 382 7680 | fax: 00 64 4 384 9719| www.nzfilm.co.nz | Mladen Ivancic, deputy Chief Executive*

Download the treaty from www.culture.gov.uk/PDF/uk-newzealand1993.PDF, or order a copy by phoning The Stationary Office Photocopying Department on 020 7873 8455 and quoting Cmd No 2638 Treaty Series No 39 (1994) ISBN 0101263821

## What's available?

Under the **Large Budget Screen Production Grant Scheme**, similar to the Australian refundable tax offset, a production company (which must be New Zealand tax-paying) can obtain a **12.5% rebate** on the New Zealand spend, providing it exceeds NZ$15m (£5.7m). Where the value of the qualifying New Zealand production expenditure ("**QNZPE**") is between NZ$15 million and NZ$50 million, it must also be at least 70 per cent of the films total production expenditure. Where the value of the QNZPE is NZ$50 million or more it will qualify for the grant regardless of the percentage ratio of QNZPE to the screen productions total production expenditure.

# NORWAY

## Competent Authority Details

### NORWEGIAN FILM FUND

*Filmens Hus, Dronningensgate 16, P.O Box 752, Sentrum, NO-0106 Oslo, Norway | tel: 0047 22 47 80 40 | fax: 0047 22 47 80 41 | www.filmfondet.no/ | Stein Slyngstad, Director General*

Download the treaty from www.culture.gov.uk/PDF/uk-norway1982.PDF, or order a copy by phoning The Stationary Office Photocopying Department on 020 7873 8455 and quoting Cmd No 9007 Treaty Series No 46 (1983) ISBN 0101900708

## SOUTH AFRICA

The tax authorities here offer a kind of "gap" finance in the form of a **25% tax rebate** (if it qualifies as a South African film; otherwise 15%) on qualifying South African spend by a South Africa tax-paying company. This spend must be at least R25m (£2.15m), and represent 50% of the time spent on principal photography (with a minimum of 4 weeks). The maximum rebate on any one project will be R10m (£860k). A two year **tax deferral** is also available in order to allow producers to receive greater exploitation income from which to pay tax bills, as well as various **investment incentives** for local individuals investing in film production. The **Industrial Development Corporation** also provides loans of at least R1m (£85k), which can be used by qualifying producers for up to 50% of the production budget. It is fairly difficult, but not impossible, to discount the rebate at the present time.

## SPAIN

There are certain limited recourse loans available from the **Instituto De La Cinematografia**, and apparently an **income tax credit** of up to 20% of the cost of production (less and finance-only contribution from a co-producer). Nothing seems to be written in English, so you need to take local advice.

## UNITED STATES OF AMERICA

Although the USA is not renowned for providing financial assistance to the film industry, there are actually 40 states offering incentives of one sort or another, together with the new **Federal tax allowance**, available since October 2004 (implemented by the new **section 181** of the Internal Revenue Code 1986).

This tax allowance is available for films under US$15m (£7.9m), or US$20m (£10.6m) if produced in a "distressed area", which have no sexually explicit content. The entire production spend can be written off, so long as at least 75% of it relates to services provided in the USA.

A few of the state incentives are also worth mentioning. **Louisiana** offers a **transferable tax credit** equal to 10% or 15% of a film's budget. The 10% figure applies to films with budgets between US$300k (£160k) and US$8m (£4.5m), and the 15% figure for higher budgets. The credits are then sold on by local brokers. A 15% rebate is available on production in **New Mexico**, 10% for expenditure in approved **New York** production facilities and 20% for qualifying expenditure in **Pennsylvania** (if 60% of the budget is spent there). **Florida**, **Oklahoma** and **Illinois** also have credits and rebates. **Hawaii** also has a particularly lucrative, but highly convoluted, system and local advice should definitely be sought if producers with to utilise it.

# Carlo Dusi

# *The importance of international co-productions*

## FOR THE UK FILM INDUSTRY

There has been a lot of controversy over the past few years in relation to the number of co-productions that have "abused" the British funding system by accessing the local tax reliefs, either in the form of sale and leaseback or section 48 equity, and about the disproportionally small amount of production activity in the United Kingdom that these features have been able to carry out while still receiving funding from the UK which was calculated on their entire production budget.

The Department of Culture, Media and Sport ("DCMS") has, understandably, taken action over time in order to curb the most prominent instances of such imbalance, for instance by raising the thresholds of minimum expenditure on UK elements first for all official co-productions with Canada, and subsequently for all official co-productions with France, Italy, Denmark and Iceland.

Needless to say, as a UK tax payer I too share the concerns of the Inland Revenue and the DCMS that the tax reliefs which we all effectively fund through our contributions to the UK fiscal system are applied fairly, effectively, in accordance with the objectives that they are meant to achieve, and in a way that ensure a proportionate benefit to this country and its people. I do, however, also feel that, in the context of the ongoing witch-hunt against UK minority co-productions, one sometimes forgets quite how valuable these are and, for that matter, all co-productions with producers from outside the UK can be above and beyond the mere calculation of what percentage of the budget is ultimately spent on UK elements.

Firstly, I do not think that one can underestimate how any UK co-production with some production or post-production activity in the country contributes to some continuity in the activity of our crew, actors and facilities. At a time when the US Dollar is increasingly weak against the Pound and it is becoming more and more expensive for US independent producers and studios to justify carrying out any part of their production activities in the UK, the stability and continuity which are the essential backbones to any healthy integrated industry are increasingly under threat.

Inevitably, the benefit of work being available to our industry members in the context of foreign productions may ultimately make the crucial difference between them being able to continue to operate within the UK film industry or having to shut down shop and find themselves something else to do within a stabler and more reliable business. The latter situation would in turn lead to a gradual haemorrhaging of the talent that the local industry has been working so hard to develop over the past few years through the training and education on which the Government has focused so strongly, in particular through the activities of the UK Film Council.

Secondly, one should never forget how, in particular within a creative industry like film, any experience is ultimately good experience. Minority co-productions, like all co-productions which involve members of the UK industry to any extent, have already enabled a generation of new producers to cut their teeth on projects requiring only a contained amount of production activity in the country under their supervisions, therefore bridging that all-essential gap between the industry-specific training and education that they may have had, and the (often so different) realities of actually making a feature with all of the practical and logistical difficulties that the process entails. Similarly, with many of our heads of department and other technical positions, there is nothing quite like learning on the job to develop one's abilities, and it is inevitably the case that the more opportunities available to them to practise and hone their skills (whether majority funded out of the UK or not) the more marketable a commodity each of them may become at an international level.

Thirdly, and equally importantly, the principle of reciprocity on which we have so often relied when complaining about other countries taking unfair advantage of the UK system inevitably also works the other way. Within the UK industry, we currently find ourselves in an extremely competitive climate when it comes to raising production finance for our own projects. The latest Government changes to the legislation regulating our section 48 and section 42 reliefs, coupled with ongoing market caution at international level and the lack of acquisition activity from broadcasters in a number of key European countries (to name but a few important factors), are all contributing to a very difficult landscape for the independent producer in Britain, where increasingly less funding is now available from their own country and more reliance therefore needs to be placed on access to foreign sources of finance.

As the international presale market remains difficult for most independent projects, foreign finance can only be accessed in the forms of subsidies and incentives available under the terms of a qualifying co-production structure. However, one could understand how the relevant authorities of the countries in question may not be too enthusiastic about allowing their local producers to share the benefit of their local support systems with UK producers. That is unless they could be confident that the same level of support could be obtained from the UK, should the roles be inverted and their own local producer be trying to access the final piece of their funding puzzle from a country other than its own. As our reliance on our ability to work with other foreign producers under the auspices of our Treaty system and the European Convention therefore increases, we must remember that in order to be in a position to ask other countries for their collaboration we must also retain a system at home which is open enough to support their projects, and make them feel that there is genuine reciprocity at play. In the same way that we know how this principle was often applied in an unbalanced way by certain foreign producers, in particular within the countries for which the DCMS has now raised the minimum level of UK spend, we must also take care not to go too far the other way and start expecting more from our foreign counterparts than what we can actually offer to them ourselves.

All this being said, I always remain a strong advocate of the principle that co-productions must make creative and practical sense first and foremost, and should not be relied upon for all projects in all cases without an in-depth analysis of what each film actually needs. Furthermore, one should never underestimate the difficulties of structuring a co-production in a sensible and efficient manner for the specific project at hand, consistent with both the provisions of the applicable legislation and guidelines and the realities of the current market place.

Expert advice through the structuring process from an early stage is therefore thoroughly recommended and often essential to the success of the production itself, and the time, effort and costs involved should be weighed in carefully from the beginning. That being said, we should not forget the wider and sometimes less obvious ways in which all foreign co-productions can benefit the UK film industry and its many different players, and should all continue to work together to ensure that, within a fair and balanced international system of co-operation and collaboration, our industry can continue to reap these benefits.

*Carlo Dusi, Aria Films Limited - www.ariafilms.co.uk*

## CHAPTER SIX

# FUNDING ORGANISATIONS

This chapter details every fund in the UK for which information was available to us at the time of going to press. We also provide details for some of the larger foreign funds. All of these organisations provide finance for film production, but under a variety of different circumstances, and subject to all sorts of different criteria. The amount of money available, and the percentage contributions towards the budget also vary wildly.

We have tried to provide as much information as succinctly as possible on the type of finance and organisation, how to qualify for funding, and what you might expect to receive. Of course this is somewhat of a moveable feast as funds open and close at regular intervals. But most of these organisations have been around for some time so, if the information given on a particular fund falls out of date, the likelihood is that the entity providing it has moved on to offer something else in its place. In any event, you should check directly with the organisation concerned as to what they currently have on offer.

The funds in this Chapter are split into a number of different categories. We start with the UK's largest funding body, the UK FIlm Council, with an annual budget of around £55m. The UK private funds are those offering pure equity, or finance based around the tax beaks referred to in Chapter 4 (eg. *section 48 production funds, sale & leasebacks*, etc). Other sections include UK financing producers which pulls out a small selection of notable UK producers with external finance arrangements in place (ie BBC Films, Film Four, Working Title and the slate funded production companies). Further UK sections covering national and regional screen agencies, national public funds, regional funds and competitions. The international funds section gives similar information on some of the main public funds available for film financing outside the United Kingdom.

# UK Film Council

**www.ukfilmcouncil.org.uk**
*10 Little Portland Street, London, W1W 7JG, UK | tel: 020 7861 7861 | fax: 020 7861 7862 | info@ukfilmcouncil.org.uk*

As the lead agency for film, the UK Film Council aims to stimulate a competitive, successful and vibrant UK film industry and culture. It uses National Lottery support to develop new filmmakers, fund new British films such as *Touching the Void* and *Vera Drake* and give audiences the opportunity to see a wider choice of films such as *The Motorcycle Diaries* and *The House of Flying Daggers*. The UK Film Council also helps to promote Britain as a filmmaking location and to raise the profile of British films abroad.

A strategic national film organisation was one of the recommendations of the Stewart Till-steered Film Policy Review Group, set-up shortly after Labour came to power in 1997.

Heralding the start of a new close relationship between the UK government and the film industry, the UK Film Council launched in April 2000 as the interface between the public and private sector. It both distributes public money and acts as a research and lobbying body on behalf of the industry.

## THE BOARD

UK Film Council's Board of Directors includes Chair Stewart Till; Mark Devereux, Senior Partner of the law firm Olswang; Nigel Green, joint Managing Director of Entertainment Film Distributors; Stephen Knibbs, Chief Operating Officer at Vue Entertainment; Anthony Minghella, director and chair of the BFI; John Woodward, Chief Executive of the UK Film Council; Andrew Eaton, company director of Revolution Films; David Sproxton, co-founder and Director of Aardman Animations Ltd; Marc Samuelson, Deputy Chair of the British Screen Advisory Council and a Governor of the National Film & Television School; Alison Owen, co-director of Ruby Films; Colin Brown, Chairman of Cinesite Worldwide; and Gurinder Chadha, film director (Bend it Like Beckham, Bride & Prejudice).

## STRATEGIC PRIORITIES

**Advocacy and leadership** - to lead on issues where a single powerful voice reflecting properly considered views is most effective.

**Partnership** - to work in partnership with government, industry and the private, public and voluntary sectors in the UK and overseas.

**Economy** - to work with the grain of the market to stimulate competitiveness and enterprise, and to deliver sustainable development and best value.

**Diversity and inclusion** - to promote social inclusion and celebrate diversity so that every citizen in the nations and regions of the UK has access to film culture and so barriers to working in the industry are reduced.

**Excellence and innovation** - to encourage excellence and innovation particularly through the use of new digital technologies.

**Openness, transparency and accessibility** - to be open, transparent and accessible to stakeholders, industry and public alike.

## OVERVIEW OF FUNDING

Funding is divided into the following strands: Training; Production & Development; Distribution & Exhibition; and Publications.

The **Training Fund** is now delivered through Skillset, the Sector Skills Council for broadcast, film, video interactive media and photo imaging, which receives the Film Council's £6.5m lottery grant for training.

The Film Council also administers the **Regional Investment Fund for England** (RIFE) to each of the 9 Regional Screen Agencies, each of whom deliver funding through schemes developed to meet their regional priorities. Production & Development funding supports feature film and short film production through three departments.

The **Development Fund** (headed by Jenny Borgars) supports script development through its initiative 25 Words or Less, seed funding and pre- pre-production funding for single projects and slate development for established production companies. It has an annual budget of £4m.

The **New Cinema Fund** (headed by Paul Trijbits) supports production of original and cutting edge features, shorts and pilots and post production of features, by new and emerging talent. Shorts funding from the NCF is delivered through the short film production schemes, such as Cinema Extreme, the Completion Fund and Digital Shorts (Digital Shorts is delivered through the Regional Screen Agencies). The New Cinema's Fund's annual budget is £5m.

The **Premier Fund** (headed by Sally Caplan) is a high investment fund supporting feature production of commercial projects with an international market. The annual budget for the Premier Fund is £8m.

The **Distribution & Exhibition fund** was set up in 2002 to support film exhibition and distribution in the UK, particularly for films which traditionally find it difficult to achieve wide exhibition and distribution. Funding is delivered in four main areas.

The **Print & Advertising Fund** aims to bolster the P&A budgets of specialised films. The UK Film Distribution Programme is designed to minimise the risks associated with releasing British Films theatrically in the UK.

The **Publications** Fund (headed by Chris Chandler as head of New Projects) supports print and on line publications with the intention of educating public audiences or more targeted film audiences and that encourage debate about film culture, education and production.

### TYPICAL TERMS AND CONDITIONS

The terms and conditions of each fund will be different and should be checked with the relevant fund before applying. However, there are general similarities between all the funds administered by the UK Film Council.

**Investment.** Most of the funding from the UKFC is made as an investment to be recouped.

**Applicant Eligibility.** Most applications will need to be from an organisation or company, rather than an individual, that can display an ability to perform the project requirements. Much of the time, evidence of a track record and industry contacts within the area of the funding application will need to be demonstrated.

**Assessment.** All projects will need to meet objectives set out by the UKFC and will be assessed against these. These objectives will be fairly general to allow for creative and business innovation.

**Requirements of the UKFC.** These will often relate to the credit the UKFC should receive for its investment and the systems of control in place for the project, such as accounting requirements and ongoing project assessment.

## Development fund

The Development Fund, headed by Jenny Borgars, distributes £4m of lottery money annually across single projects and company slates to cover script development through to early pre-production. There is an interview with Jenny Borgars at the end of the chapter.

**DEVELOPMENT FUND - 25 WORDS OR LESS** This scheme is targeted towards writers with high concept script ideas with commercial appeal and an eye on an international audience.

**For:** Script Development | **Size of fund:** £4m per year for Development Fund | **Award range:** £10,000 | **Number of awards:** Up to 4 per round | **Platform:** Cinema | **Deadline:** 3 times per year

**Further details:** Each round invites screenwriters to submit script ideas for three different genres. The scheme has had three rounds so far and the genres have ranged from horror to love stories. The scheme will assist the successful applicants to write the first draft of their script idea with a script editor assigned to support the process. Although the UKFC state that the scheme is designed for new and established writers alike, one of the conditions of applying is that the writer either has an agent or is a full member of the Writers Guild. It is very difficult for a beginner with no track record to achieve either of these requirements.

**DEVELOPMENT FUND - SINGLE PROJECTS - PARTNERED DEVELOPMENT** As above

**For:** Production Development | **Size of fund:** £4m per year for Development Fund | **Award range:** Up to 75% of 'hard' costs of development | **Platform:** Cinema | **Deadline:** Applications may be made at any time.

**Further details:** Funding in this category is aimed at producers who have a financial partner on board. It will cover full development costs. Partnered Development will cover: writer's fees, research fees, overhead costs of producer, option rights, producer fees, producer's legal costs, script editor's fees, script readings with cast, special effects/storyboarding, executive producer/mentor, financial/presentation 'package', preparation of production budget, preparation of production schedule, director's development fee/script work, casting, and training courses.

**DEVELOPMENT FUND - SINGLE PROJECTS - PRE PRE PRODUCTION** As above

**For:** Production Development | **Size of fund:** £4m per year for Development Fund | **Award range:** Up to 50% of pre pre production costs | **Platform:** Cinema | **Deadline:** Applications may be made at any time.

**Further details:** Funding for projects at a more advance stage of development will be considered as long as interest from investors is established. Pre-pre production funding will cover: writer's fees for polish only, location survey/recce, casting, preparation of production budget, preparation of production schedule.

**DEVELOPMENT FUND - SINGLE PROJECTS - SEED FUNDING** The aim of the Development Fund is to develop high quality scripts and to support new talent and established companies alike in the development process.

**For:** Production Development | **Size of fund:** £4m per year for Development Fund | **Award range:** Not stated | **Platform:** Cinema | **Deadline:** Applications may be made at any time.

**Further details:** Seed funding is for projects at an early stage of development. Seed funding will cover: writer's fees, research fees, overhead costs of producer, option rights, producer fees, producer's legal costs, script editor's fees, executive producer/mentor, financial/presentation 'package', and training courses.

**DEVELOPMENT FUND - SLATE PROJECTS** The Slate Funding scheme from the Development Fund is aimed at supporting business growth for the successful applicant and partners through developing a slate of films and developing business relationships.

**For:** Production Development | **Size of fund:** £4m per year for Development Fund | **Award range:** Between £250,000 and £500,000 per year up to three years | **Number of awards:** 7 | **Platform:** Cinema | **Deadline:** Every three years (the previous call closed in September 2004, so the next call will be in 2007). | **Notable investments:** The seven new development slate companies announced in December 2004 are listed later in the chapter under Financing Producers.

**Further details:** The fund has three facets to it. The first, called Working Capital Facility, is an optional element of slate funding. It allows for up to 20% of the annual slate fund (the total amount including the UKFC's investment and the partnership investment) to be channelled towards the company's overhead costs. The second obligatory element is termed, Third Party Umbrella Deals, which insists on 30% of the annual slate fund going towards producing relationships with other UK production companies. The third obligatory element is the Slate Development Projects, for which the company must spend the remaining slate funding on developing individual projects.

Applicants must be able to match at least 100% of the slate funding applied for. This inherently means that more established companies will form the main applicant base for this scheme. As the scheme is intended to boost growth and production for the company and within the UK, a performance review will be carried out at the end of each year of the three year term. The renewal of the UKFC's investment will depend on the outcome of this review.

## Distribution & Exhibition fund

Headed by Peter Buckingham, formerly head of distribution for FilmFour, the fund supports distribution and exhibition in the UK. This ranges from provision of small grants to regional film groups right through to the Digital Screen Network, a £13.5m programme to create Europe's largest collection of digitally equipped cinemas with up to 250 screens on some 150 sites, that it is hoped will create a more flexible distribution platform for independent cinema releases.

**CINEMA ACCESS PROGRAMME - RESEARCH & DEVELOPMENT** Based on findings from the Cinema Access Technology Report, current closed captioning systems are inadequate for audience needs. This fund aims to support research that can improve current systems.

**For:** Audience | **Platform:** Cinema

**Further details:** Funding will cover research into developing new systems and market research into audience preferences and demands.

**DIGITAL FUND FOR NON THEATRICAL DISTRIBUTION** This initiative supports the acquisition of screening equipment by non-theatrical exhibitors such as mobile cinemas, film clubs and societies.

**For:** Audience | **Size of fund:** £500,000 per year | **Award range:** Up to 80% of the costs with a ceiling of £5,000 | **Platform:** Cinema | **Deadline:** One annual deadline

**Further details:** Funding will support acquisition of digital equipment to screen films, such as digital players, digital projectors, digital sound systems and screens that support digital exhibition.

The equipment acquired must be used for the benefit of public audiences.

**DIGITAL SCREEN NETWORK** The Digital Screen Network is an initiative aimed at all screening venues across the UK to install a digital screening alternative to the expensive 35mm format. The intention is to encourage the release of more specialised films by offering the less expensive digital screening format.

**For:** Audience | **Size of fund:** £13.5m over four years | **Platform:** Cinema

**Further details:** Each screening venue is eligible to apply to the UKFC for a contribution towards the latest digital technology and equipment. Participating venues will be required to apportion a certain amount of screening time to more specialised films. In return for the UK Film Council's investment, cinemas must agree to screen a proportion of 'specialty content' such as *Howl's Moving Castle* or *Tarnation*, and a certain amount of cinema time to films that will be centrally booked by the UK Film Council for content such as shorts, archive material or educational programing.

**EDUCATION FUND** This award is aimed at broadening audience understanding and appreciation of film. The award is a new initiative at time of going to press with further details so far unannounced.

**For:** Audience | **Size of fund:** £1m per year | **Platform:** Cinema | **Deadline:** Not yet announced

**UK FILM DISTRIBUTION PROGRAMME** This fund supports distributors with the release of UK films with a commercial sensibility. It is designed to reduce the risk involved in releasing a UK film theatrically by offering distributors a 'plug' for the shortfalls once a film is released.

**For:** Distribution | **Size of fund:** £1m per year | **Award range:** Up to £300,000 | **Platform:** Cinema | **Deadline:** Applications may be made at any time. | Notable investments: So far, two investments have been made under this scheme: £300,000 to Icon Film Distribution for *'Bright Young Things'* in September 2003; and £300,000 to Warner Bros Distribution for '*Trauma*' in August 2004.

**Further details:** Once the applicant film has reached £750,000 in gross UK box office receipts, the distributor will be entitled to receive the amount equivalent to the shortfall between these box office receipts and the P & A costs. If there is no shortfall and the film is in profit, the distributor will not be eligible to receive an award. To be eligible to receive this award, the applicant must have been accepted on to the programme before the film has been released.

**PRINT & ADVERTISING FUND** The aim of the P & A Fund is to support and encourage distributors in the theatrical release of specialised films within the UK, by contributing to the film's P & A budget and boosting it to a higher level than might otherwise have been achieved. The intention is to increase the access and availability for audiences to see such films.

**For:** Distribution | **Size of fund:** £1m per year | **Award range:** Between £50,000 to £100,000 | **Number of awards:** 20 | **Platform:** Cinema | **Deadline:** Applications may be made at any time. | **Recent investments:** Pathé Pictures received £100,000 for '*Bad Education*' in May 2004. Tartan Films received £66,764 for '*Capturing the Friedman's* in February 2004. UGC Films UK Ltd received £85,000 in June 2004 for '*Story of the Weeping Camel*'.

**Further details:** Funding will cover various elements of a film's P & A budget, which includes, for example, production and design of marketing campaigns, prints and distribution, media costs, publicity, promotions and research.

A film must be classified as specialised by the UKFC to be a successful application. Although this will be determined on a case-by-case basis, in a general sense, such films tend to be seen as less obviously commercial than a US studio release and may address cultural, social and political issues. Foreign language films and releases of classic and archived films can also be considered by this fund.

## New Cinema Fund

The New Cinema Fund is headed by Paul Trijbits, and with a £5m annual budget, funds between 7 and 10 features a year. These range in budgets from £300,000 up to about £3m with an investment of on average 15-20% of the budget.

Short films make up around 20% of the department's spending with around 130 short films made each year across a number of different programmes. An interview with Paul Trijbits is at the end of this chapter.

NEW CINEMA FUND - FEATURE FILMS The New Cinema Fund's key areas of commitment lie in supporting exciting new talent, work from the regions and minority communities, and encouraging the use of digital technology.

**For:** Production | **Size of fund:** £5m per year for New Cinema Fund | **Award range:** Between 15% and 50% of the feature film's budget | **Platform:** Cinema | **Deadline:** Applications may be made at any time.

**Further details:** The New Cinema Fund invests in feature films particularly from new and diverse talent. Projects should be in advanced stage of development.

NEW CINEMA FUND - PILOTS As above

**For:** Production | **Size of fund:** £5m per year for New Cinema Fund | **Award range:** Up to £10,000 | **Platform:** Cinema | **Deadline:** Applications may be made at any time.

**Further details:** The New Cinema Fund will invest in pilot projects to establish the potential of a project.

CINEMA EXTREME This is a scheme aimed at experienced filmmakers with an original and evocative short film idea. The idea is for the applicant to use this project as a springboard to getting the first feature off the ground.

**For:** Short film | **Award range:** Up to £50,000 | **Number of awards:** Up to 4 films commissioned per year | **Platform:** Cinema | **Deadline:** Three deadlines per year.

**Further details:** Cinema Extreme has been developed from previous year's schemes to include a development process for shortlisted applicants, leading to the possible commissioning of the developed project by the UKFC and Film Four. Applicants should have a track record with short films shown in international festivals or single dramas broadcast.

**COMPLETION FUND** The fund supports the completion of short films that show originality and cinematic flair.

**For:** Short film | **Size of fund:** £50,000 per year | **Platform:** Cinema | **Deadline:** Annually in October

**Further details:** Funding supports the post production process for films which have reached the rough cut stage.

Funding does not simply cover the transfer of finished films from one format to another.

DIGITAL SHORTS

**For:** Short film | **Award range:** £10,000 | **Number of awards:** 8 | **Platform:** Cinema, DVD, online

**Further details:** See details on each regional Digital Shorts scheme

## Premiere fund

The Premiere Fund is the UK's biggest public fund. It is designed to make large investments in films which are commercially viable. That is to say, films which can support high budgets through the promise of reaching a wide, international audience. Sally Caplan, former president of Icon Film Distributors, takes over as fund head in mid 2005.

**For:** Production | **Size of fund:** £8m per year | **Award range:** Up to 35% of a feature film's budget. | **Platform:** Cinema | **Deadline:** Applications may be made at any time. | **Recent investments:** £2m to Potboiler Productions for '*The Constant Gardener*'. £700,000 to Young Pirate Films for '*The Festival*' (which also received £2943 from the Development Fund). £1,505,000 to Autonomous for '*The Proposition*' (which also received £31,334 from the Development Fund at around the same time and £200,000 from the Premiere Fund two years previously). | Notable investments: £2m in January 2001 for '*Gosford Park*'. '*Mike Bassett: England Manager*' received in total £2,103,000 made up of four instalments (£1,200,000 in November 2000, £33,000 and £620,000 in August 2001, £250,000 in September 2001). '*Sylvia*' received £37,643 in August 2003.

**Further details:** The fund supports the development, production and distribution of feature films intended for theatrical release.

The combination of the right project and the right company delivering the project is particularly important for this scheme. Strong emphasis is placed on ensuring projects have solid commercial potential as high investments tend to be made. This is normally a more viable prospect for established companies to fulfil, who have a track record and industry relationships in place to secure the deals which will allow a return of investment.

## Publication Fund

This fund is designed to support both current and new publications/periodicals. The aim is to encourage education and understanding of film and the industry to the general public and more targeted audiences, as well as providing a forum for debate. Publications in areas that are generally underrepresented are particular encouraged.

**For:** Market development | **Size of fund:** £100,000 per year | **Award range:** Between £1000 and £20,000 | **Platform:** Print, online | **Deadline:** Annually in May | Notable investments: ScriptWriter Magazine received £17,000 in June 2003. Shooting People productions received £14,000 in June 2003 for the Wideshot scheme. First Film Foundation received £16,000 for First Facts also in June 2003.

**Further details:** Funding can cover: printing and publishing costs, software/technical expertise, distribution costs, marketing costs, and staff costs. Details about the next launch of the fund will be published in September 2005.

# Private Funding Organisations

*Other funds for which no 2005 details were available at the time of going to press are listed in the Directory.*

## Baker Street Media Finance

*96 Baker Street , London, W1U 6TJ | tel: 020 7487 3677 | fax: 020 7487 5667 | enquiries@bakerstreetfinance.tv | www.bakerstreetfinance.tv*

Baker Street was founded in 1997 and has since invested in 27 films ranging from the animated feature *Valiant* to the BAFTA Award winning *My Summer of Love*, and from *Ladies in Lavendar* starring Judi Dench and Maggie Smith to the much-awaited *Hooligans* starring Elijah Wood. Typically, funds managed by Baker Street will provide up to 25% of a budget as an **equity investment** in British qualifying feature films. It is a private company specialising in the production financing and structuring of British feature films, and British qualifying co-productions. As a leading company in the area of **tax efficient film partnerships**, Baker Street arranges and manages a series of private investor vehicles designed for individuals and corporations interested in the field of film productions.

## Future Films Group

*Future Films Ltd, 25 Noel Street, London, W1F 8GX | tel: 020 7434 6600 fax: 020 7434 6633 | www.futurefilmgroup.com*

Future Film is a UK **Sale and Leaseback** facilitator. It offers competitive rates with forward funding if the budgets are £3m and up. It is launching a **German Fund** which works with Sale & Leaseback, again with competitive rates and recoupment positions. It is also launching an **Australian Fund** in April 2005, which will focus on Australian films including UK-Australian Co-productions. It has a production base in Russia which will offer cheaper production costs, and the possibility of equity investment in the projects. As **Russia** is a signatory to the European Convention, this can be combined with finance from the UK, Germany and other signatory countries.

## Grosvenor Park Media Limited

*53-54 Grosvenor Street, London, W1K 3HU | tel: 020 7529 2500 | fax: 020 7529 2511 | funding@grosvenorpark.com | www.grosvenorpark.com*

Grosvenor Park provides **Sale & Leaseback**, Special Opportunity **GAP financing**, and **Production Services**. It is a specialist in monetising tax benefits in jurisdictions around the world. Grosvenor Park has the ability to cash-flow the Sale & Leaseback benefit in the U.K. as well as government tax credits in numerous jurisdictions including **Canada, Luxembourg, Hungary, New Zealand, Serbia, New York State, New Mexico, Louisiana** and other state level tax credits in the United States. Grosvenor Park also has the ability to provide flexible **gap financing** and credit enhancement to commercial motion pictures shooting anywhere in the world irrespective of tax benefits.

## Ingenious Film & Television Limited

*100 Pall Mall, London, SW1Y 5NQ | tel: 020 7024 3600 | fax: 020 7024 3601 | enquiries@ingeniousmedia.co.uk | www.ingeniousmedia.co.uk*

Ingenious provides both **Sale & Leaseback** and **equity investment**. At the time of going to print, it had not finalised its 2005/6 offering. Ingenious claims to be the UK's leading provider of project finance to the UK film and television industry. Since 1998, it has completed over £2.7 billion in Sale & Leaseback transactions, supported over £370 million of British film production with equity investments, and launched an independent television production fund.

An experienced team of media specialists and investment professionals can offer both investment opportunities and operational and strategic advice.

## Invicta Capital

*33 St James's Square, London, SW1Y 4JS | tel: 020 7661 9376 | fax: 020 7661 9892 | info@invictacapital.co.uk | www.invictacapital.co.uk*

Invicta Capital provides **Sale & Leasebacks** under both **section 48** and **section 42**. Through the provision of **debt**, **equity** and structured finance, Invicta has developed an influential position in the UK and US film industries. Invicta advises private clients and corporations on equity and **tax efficient investments** in film production and distribution. It enjoys strong relationships with decision makers in the major UK and US film production and distribution companies and has a proven track record for successfully completing complex cross border financing of film productions and international distribution arrangements.

## Matrix Film Finance LLP

*Gossard House, 7-8 Savile Road, London, W1S 3PE | tel: 020 7292 0800 | fax: 020 7292 0801 | enquiries@matrix-film-finance.co.uk | www.matrix-film-finance.co.uk*

Matrix currently only offers **Sale & Leaseback** finance. Its "Producer Net Benefit" rates are competitive, varying between 11% and 15% depending on the budget of the film in question. Matrix is keen to make offers to film producers on any films with budgets of more than £4m. Since 1997 Matrix Film Finance has been involved with the financing of over one hundred feature films, including the £130 million Oliver Stone epic *Alexander*.

## Prescience Film Finance

*45 Wycombe End , Beaconsfield, Buckinghamshire, HP9 1LZ | tel: 020 8354 7331 | fax: 014 9467 0740 | www.presciencefilmfinance.co.uk*

A funder of British, European and international feature films and television programming, working with leading producers through the Foresight limited liability partnerships and studio productions with **EIS offering**.

## Random Harvest Limited

*Pinewood Studios, Iver Heath, Buckinghamshire, SL0 0NH | tel: 017 5378 3900 | fax: 017 5363 0651 | films@randomharvest.co.uk* | www.randomharvestpictures.co.uk

Random Harvest offers services in production, executive production and production fund raising. It has a number of different funds and schemes including **Enterprise Investment Scheme** production funds (Harvest Pictures I, II and III), section 48 **Sale & Leaseback** partnerships (Soho Film Partnership), and **section 48 film production partnerships** (Random Harvest Film Partnerships I, II, III).

## Scion Films

*18 Soho Square, London, W1D 3QL | tel: 020 7025 8003 | fax: 020 7025 8133 | info@scionfilms.com | www.scionfilms.com*

Scion run a Guernsey based **Sale & Leaseback** partnership (the General Guernsey Partnership (including gearing), and a standard UK based Sale & Leaseback (Scion Sale & Leaseback LLP), each, with a minimum gross investment of £100k. They also have two super Sale & Leaseback schemes through general Guernsey partnerships, being Scion Creation Partnership (producing *Three Bad Men*, *Vacuum*, *The Duelist* and *Good*) and Scion Platinum Partnership (producing *Pride and Prejudice*), also with a minimum gross investment of £100k (including gearing)

## Scotts Atlantic

*3 De Walden Court, 85 New Cavendish Street, London, W1W 6XD | tel: 020 7307 9300 | fax: 020 7307 9292 | info@scottsatlantic.com | www.scottsatlantic.com*

Scotts Atlantic provides **Sale & Leaseback** funding for British Films. In addition it may provide mezzanine or **equity finance** dependent on strict investment criteria.

## Visionview Ltd

*3 Fitzhardinge Street, London, W1H 6EF | tel: 020 7224 0234 | fax: 020 7486 7200 | info@visionview.co.uk | www.visionview.co.uk*

Visionview has for some years been offering executive production and co-production services, together with tax-based **equity funding**. 2005/6 products had not been finalised at publication, although they are likely to be providing some sort of taxed-based funding, possibly through the Enterprise Investment Scheme.

# Financing producers

## BBC / BBC FILMS

www.bbc.co.uk
*BBC Television Centre, Wood Lane, London, W12 7RJ | tel: 020 8743 8000*

*BBC Films, 1 Mortimer Street, London, W1T 3JA | tel: 020 7765 0091 | fax: 020 7765 0194*

*www.bbc.co.uk/newtalent | www.bbc.co.uk/bbcfilms | www.bbc.co.uk/commissioning | www.bbc.co.uk/writersroom*

The BBC began as an independent radio broadcaster in the 1920's, financed from the outset by the license fee, a means to keep the organisation independent of commercial and political involvement and pressure. In the 1930's television was introduced to the BBC service.

Film producers can approach the BBC with finished features, or they can approach BBC Films with a project in development. There are also various ways that emerging talent can work with the BBC through the production and writing initiatives promoted online in the Writers Room and the Talent site.

### BBC ACQUISITIONS

**Who do they work with?**

The department deals with independent producers, distributors and sales agents, and inevitably they are offered a lot of product, a large proportion from the US. Approximately £10m of the department's £70m budget was spent on British films in 2004.

**How do they work with independent producers?**

Generally, the acquisitions department will look at finished product, rather than dealing in pre-sales on unfinished films. Unfinished and new projects would usually be deferred to BBC Films.

**How should producers approach them?**

They do accept unsolicited material and producers should send in a finished film on tape.

**What are they looking for?**

Steve Jenkins, senior editor of films in feature film acquisitions says, "we would assess their usefulness to us, i.e. would they easily find a slot in our schedules, and if appropriate, make an offer of a certain amount, based on length of license, number of runs, rights granted, etc."

### BBC FILMS

Headed by David Thompson, BBC Films has been a major producer of UK films, expanding investment since the successes of *Billy Elliot* and Last Resort in 2000. As part of the BBC's charter renewal, Director General Mark Thompson committed to extending the BBC's investment in film production. BBC backed films released in 2005 include Saul Dibb's *Bullet Boy*, Danny Boyle's *Millions*, Woody Allen's first British feature *Match Point* and Stephen Frears *Mrs Henderson Presents*.

**Who do they work with?**

They work with new and established producers as co-producers.

**How do they work with independent producers?**

BBC Films suggest that a new producer work with an experienced producer, depending on the scale of the project.

**How should producers approach them?**

They do accept unsolicited material from writers and producers, and will read everything sent to them, though newer writers should apply to the New Writing Initiative (see below). A new producer should submit the source material (if the project is based on a pre-existing work), a treatment or outline, a sample of the writer's work, or suggestions for writers and directors. BBC films says, "We are very accessible; our address is not a secret and we often answer our phones; we have a reputation for responding swiftly; it's best to have something to send us to read - cold verbal pitching is often the trickiest way of trying to get an idea across. People often feel that pitching is obligatory because that's what they do in LA, but it's not really a part of the culture here."

**What are they looking for?**

"If you look at our past range, from comedies to drama, strong drama like *Iris*, to uplifting films like *Billy Elliot*, to more gritty social films reflecting the many aspects of our culture like *Bullet Boy*, through to musical comedy, like *Mrs Henderson*, there's all kinds of films we are doing. We're particularly looking for comedy, and particularly lighter, more uplifting films." David Thompson, head of BBC Films (see full interview at the end of this chapter)

## THE NEW WRITING INITIATIVE

The New Writing Initiative is a scheme that welcomes and identifies new writing talent for all fields of BBC activity, including television, radio, and film. New writers are sought out through agents, readings, and contacts with theatres and films schools. They ask writers to inform them about any forthcoming readings, productions or screenings of their work, and they also accept unsolicited scripts (but only by post to the New Writer's Initiative at the BBC Writer's Room, contact details as above). Scripts will be assessed for their quality and suitability and recommended to the relevant BBC department.

The Writers Room receives over 10,000 submissions a year across features, TV and radio drama and comedy. They guarantee to read the first ten pages of anything sent to them, and more if the project attracts the interest of the reader.

A particular scheme, Northern Exposure, running in the North of England funds writers-in-residence schemes, workshops, master classes, and so on, by working with theatres, film groups and arts organisations.

## BBC NEW TALENT NEW FILMMAKER AWARD

BBC Talent regularly holds initiatives to find new talent in writing, directing, presenting, acting and so forth to encourage and nurture new British creative talent. The New Filmmaker Award is an annual competition with BBC3 for new filmmakers, featuring a first prize of £5,000 and two runner-up prizes of £2,500 as well as a broadcast on BBC3 and screening at the Brief Encounters Film Festival in Bristol. The deadline is the end of June each year with further details at www.bbc.co.uk/newtalent/newfilmmaker/.

# CHANNEL 4 / FILMFOUR

*124 Horseferry Road, London, SW1P 2TX | Tel: 020 7396 4444*

*www.channel4.com | www.channel4.com/4producers | www.channel4.com/film | www.ideasfactory.com*

Channel 4 was launched in 1982 and is funded by commercial revenue. Film producers work primarily with FilmFour and FilmFour Lab, and may approach Channel 4 Acquisitions department with a finished feature. There are many opportunities for filmmakers to work with the broadcaster through FilmFour and Channel 4 production initiatives.

## Channel 4 Acquisitions

### Who do they work with?

They will accept material from producers, sales agents and distributors.

### How do they work with independent producers?

Channel 4 says, "we acquire feature films which have had UK theatrical release, and these can range from studio pictures to independent films."

### How should producers approach them?

Producers should send in a cover letter and VHS screening copy of the film in the first instance. However, producers should note that Channel 4 deals "with the person or organisation who holds the UK TV rights; this generally tends to be a sales agent/distributor rather than the producer directly. If a producer has a distributor, then that organisation should contact us rather than the producer."

### What are they looking for?

They deal with acquiring feature films and live action and narrative fiction short films as long as they are under 25 minutes. On average, 900 films will be acquired and scheduled each year. In particular they "are looking for strong titles which have made an impact at the UK box office and/or are editorially appropriate for the various film slots on Channel 4."

## Channel 4 Production Schemes

### A I R - WWW.A-I-R.INFO

The Animator in Residence scheme is an annual joint initiative between Channel 4 and the BFI which has been running for twelve years. The scheme invites animators resident in the UK to submit a proposal comprising a story outline and storyboard drawings for a three minute animated film as well as a VHS showreel to be judged by a panel of professional animators, writers and producers.

Four animators will be selected to work on their proposal for a three month residency in the new animation booth at the National Museum of Film, Photography and Television with £1600 for materials and £3000 grant. At the end of the residency the animators are asked to present their idea to Channel 4 with a full storyboard, a completed script, an explanation of the soundtrack, and how the film will be produced, around one minute of animation, film or video which has been produced during the residency and an animatic of the film. Channel 4 will consider each proposal for further development and broadcast.

### ANIMATE! - WWW.ANIMATEONLINE.ORG

This animation funding scheme has been running since 1990, a joint initiative between Channel 4 and the Arts Council of England, managed by Finetake. There is an annual call for entries with a deadline in March inviting applications from artists, animators, emerging talent, and collaborations between artists of different media. Four to six entries will be chosen to produce an animation film on a budget between £5000 and £20,000 over a period of no longer than 14 months. Animation in this case is given a broad definition encompassing a range of techniques and technologies excluding live-action.

The films must be made in the UK, be no more than six minutes long, with a 16:9 widescreen aspect ratio. Applicants must be resident in the UK and students may not apply. Entries should be made in the form of a treatment of an animation idea and include a schedule, a budget, a full or sample storyboard, a script, additional artwork, application form and examples of past work. Proposals will be judged for creativity, originality, suitability for a television audience, and the likelihood of achieving the idea within budget and schedule. The applicant's previous work will be assessed for artistic and technical quality.

The completed films will be broadcast up to three times on Channel 4, streamed on the Animate! Web site, may be internationally distributed on DVD and copies deposited to the National Film & Television Archive.

### MESH - WWW.CHANNEL4.COM/MESH

This is an annual joint initiative between Channel 4 and NESTA to produce computer generated animation and interactive fiction by emerging talent. Each September digital animators resident in the UK are invited to submit a proposal for a three minute digital film by sending in a synopsis, a storyboard of the first few scenes, an idea of the technique to be used, a VHS showreel, a CV an SAE and submission form.

Six proposals will be selected for further development with mentors and masterclasses over four months. At the end of this time four projects will be commissioned to be completed and broadcast in autumn on TV and online.

## FilmFour

FilmFour was closed as an independent company in 2002 and brought in house as an internal Channel 4 department headed up by Tessa Ross, ex-head of C4 drama and producer of Billy Elliot. She has a budget of £10 million a year to invest in films, typically as a co-financier with third party distribution. In 2004 budgets ranged from £500,000 to £7m with a total 6 – 8 films produced a year and a particular interest in 'sharp comedies, clever contemporary horror and feature documentaries'.

Films in 2004 included the Oscar nominated global box office success *The Motorcycles Diaries,* Penny Woolcock's *The Principles of Lust*, Robert Michell's *Enduring Love*, and Shane Medaow's thriller *Dead Man Shoes*.

Releases slated for release in 2005 include James Marsh's *The King*, *The League of Gentleman's Apocalypse*, Annie Griffin's *Festival*, Miranda July's *You, Me and Everyone We Know* and Billy O'Brien's *Isolation*.

**Who do they work with?**

Primarily with independent producers who will have their own relationships with writers and directors which we can support. They welcome fresh ideas from both established and newer producers.

**How do they work with independent producers?**

'We have a very proactive development approach, and sometimes ideas will come to us at a very early stage and we will work closely with the producer on the development of a project, including the choice of writer/director/on-screen talent. It is also possible for producers to approach us at a much later stage looking for additional co-production funding.'

**How should producers approach them?**

Production companies can submit projects by registering via www.channel4.co.uk/4producers after which they can submit an online proposal. FilmFour does not accept unsolicited materials other than through new talent schemes such as the Cinema Extreme programme run with the UK Film Council and a National Film & TV School graduate programme which offers a development bursary to two graduating teams from the NFTS to develop a feature film project.

**What are they looking for?**

Primarily British based, contemporary stories which if not these things, must resonate with a modern British audience. All ideas should be bold and distinctive with a strong sense of identity. They aim to work with both established and emerging filmmakers across a broad range of material which should feel fresh and original, but also have a commercial edge.

## DEVELOPMENT SLATE COMPANIES

Receiving between £250,000 and £400,000 a year over three years from the Film Council Development Fund, the development slate companies replace the three lottery franchises as publicly-financed, joint-venture powerhouses intended to stimulate UK production with an extensive investment in scripts and new projects.

### CAPITOL FILMS PRODUCTIONS LIMITED

*23 Queensdale Place, London, W11 4SQ | tel: 020 7471 6000 | fax: 020 7471 6012*

Receiving £400,000 from the Development Fund per year over three years, Capitol Films Productions operates umbrella deals with Tiger Aspect Pictures, Samuelson Productions, Feel Films, Element Films (Ireland) and Cuba Pictures and a key partnership with Ascendent Pictures (US).

### DARLOW SMITHSON PRODUCTIONS

*Highgate Business Centre, 33 Greenwood Place, London, NW5 1LB*

Gets £250,000 of Lottery money per year over three years to develop a range of contemporary documentaries and drama-docs for the cinema. The company reteams the partners on the British hit film *Touching the Void*, Pathé Pictures Limited, FilmFour and Channel 4. With further links with IFC Entertainment (US) and the Tricycle Theatre.

## EALING FRAGILE ICON

*95-97 Dean Street, London, W1N 3XX | tel: 020 7287 6200 | fax: 020 7287 0069 | fragile@fragilefilms.com | www.fragilefilms.com*

A joint venture between Ealing Studios Enterprises Limited, Fragile Films Limited and UK Icon Group. The joint venture will bring development, production, UK distribution and international sales under one roof with £400,000 a year. The venture has an umbrella deal with Riverchild Films and operates an open door policy for independent producers.

## JUPITER

*c/o Littlebird, 9 Grafton Mews, London, W1T 5HZ | tel: 020 7380 3980 | fax: 020 7380 3981*

A joint venture between Little Bird and Recorded Picture Company will receive £400,000 of Lottery money per year over three years. The venture positions international sales input at the core of its activities with core partners HanWay Films and FilmFour. The joint venture will also operate umbrella deals with John Battsek at Passion Pictures Limited, Robyn Slovo at Company Pictures Limited and Chris Collins at Home Movies Limited and offers offer an open door policy for independent producers.

## NUMBER 9 FILMS

*First floor, Linton House, 24 Wells Street, London, W1T 3PH*

Number 9 Films, Elizabeth Karlsen and Stephen Woolley's production company, is to receive £400,000 over three years and will work with key partners FilmFour, sales company Intandem, the Irish Film Board (via Parallel Films) and Tartan Films to house a wide range of projects and source potentially large sums of funding to move projects on from development into production. Number 9 Films will also be working with producers Alan Moloney in Ireland, Christine Vachon and Pam Koffler's Killer Films in the US, and upcoming UK producer Nick Brown.

## PATHE PICTURES

*Kent House, 14-17 Market Place, London, W1W 8AR | tel: 020 7462 4406 | fax: 020 7436 1693 | www.pathe.co.uk*

Pathé Pictures Limited will receive £350,000 of Lottery money per year over three years. Drawing on in-house expertise of international sales and distribution, Pathé Pictures will boost their in-house development slate as well as operating key umbrella relationships with Blueprint Pictures, Forward Films Limited and Glasshouse Films Limited.

## SCARLET FILMS

A new venture bringing together producers Alison Owen (Sylvia, Elizabeth), Aimee Peyronnet (Upcoming Lovely Bones, Vernon God Little) and Paul Lister, formerly a Senior Executive at Dreamworks, will receive £300,000 per year over three years. They will partner with Momentum Pictures and BBC Films with equity investment from Ingenious Media, and have an additional umbrella deal with Octagon Films. The partnership will also offer an open door policy for independent producers.

# DNA FILMS

*15 Greek Street, London, W1D 4DP | tel: 020 7292 8700 | fax: 020 7292 8701 | www.dnafilms.com*

DNA was one of three 'Lottery Franchises' backed with £29m funding from the UK Film Council. In September 2003 a new joint venture was created between DNA and Fox Searchlight to finance, produce and distribute British films worldwide and build a company with long term viability.

Previous credits include *28 Days Later*, *Heartlands*, *The Parole Officer*, *Strictly Sinatra*, *The Final Curtain* and *Beautiful Creatures*. The first film out of the joint venture is Separate Lives, which was produced with Celedor and will be released in 2005.

**Who do they work with?**

They work with first time and established writers, producers and directors from film television and theatre.

**How do they work with independent producers?**

DNA provides finance and Producers Andrew Macdonald and Allon Reich act as executive producers on the films made with independent producers. DNA has around 10 projects in development at any time, taking two-to-three a year through into production with budgets generally under $15m.

**How should producers approach them?**

They will not accept unsolicited material and should be contacted through a literary agent or production company. Production companies should make an initial contact with the project idea, rather than sending in a script.

**What are they looking for?**

They are looking for British films of any genre. Priority is for high quality writing, contemporary stories with commercial appeal.

# WORKING TITLE

*Working Title, Oxford House, 76 Oxford Street, London, W1B 1BS | tel: 020 7307 3000 | www.workingtitlefilms.com*

Working Title is one of Europe's most successful film producers. Co-chaired by Tim Bevan and Eric Fellner, the duo have produced a host of successful British comedies including Notting Hill, *Bridget Jones Diary*, *High Fidelity*, *Four Weddings and a Funeral* and *Bean*; as well as Oscar winners *Elizabeth*, *Dead Man Walking* and *Fargo*. In 1999 the outfit closed a five-year $600m output deal with Universal Studios, after it bought up PolyGram whom Working Title had formerly worked with. At the time of the deal Working Title productions had grossed almost $1bn worldwide from less than $200m investment, making the duo one the world's most bankable producer teams.

Releases in 2004 included *The Thunderbirds*, *Wimbledon* and *Bridget Jones: Edge of Reason*. Releases for 2005 are *The Interpreter, Pride And Prejudice* and *Nanny McPhee.*

The company is also committed to producing lower budget films through their division, WT2, which came to attention with *Billy Elliot* in 2000. Releases in 2004 included *The Calcium Kid*, *Shaun of the Dead* and *Inside I'm Dancing*. 2005 sees the release of Irish Drama *Mickybo & Me*.

**Who do they work with?**

They work with both new and experienced producers.

**How do they work with independent producers?**

They will be creatively involved in any project they co-produce, but the level of involvement depends on the circumstances of the individual production.

**How should producers approach them?**

They will deal with producers directly or through a writer's or director's agent. The project can be at any stage of development: at outline, screenplay stage, or close to production. Producers should approach Working Title with an outline, a pitch or a screenplay, depending on the stage of the project. They say that "it's dependent on the nature of the material and the talent involved whether it's something we would get involved in very early on, or whether we would prefer to see a draft first."

**What are they looking for?**

Working Title films say they are looking for "original material, or a fresh angle. Sometimes the attachment of an exciting new director or a key piece of cast can make a difference". They give this advice for new producers: "focus on UK or European based films. Take time to unearth the exciting emerging writers and directors that bigger production companies may not have come across. Think laterally in terms of sourcing projects. Don't rush development, and don't abandon the script the moment it looks like your funding has fallen into place. It can always be made better."

## Screeen agency map

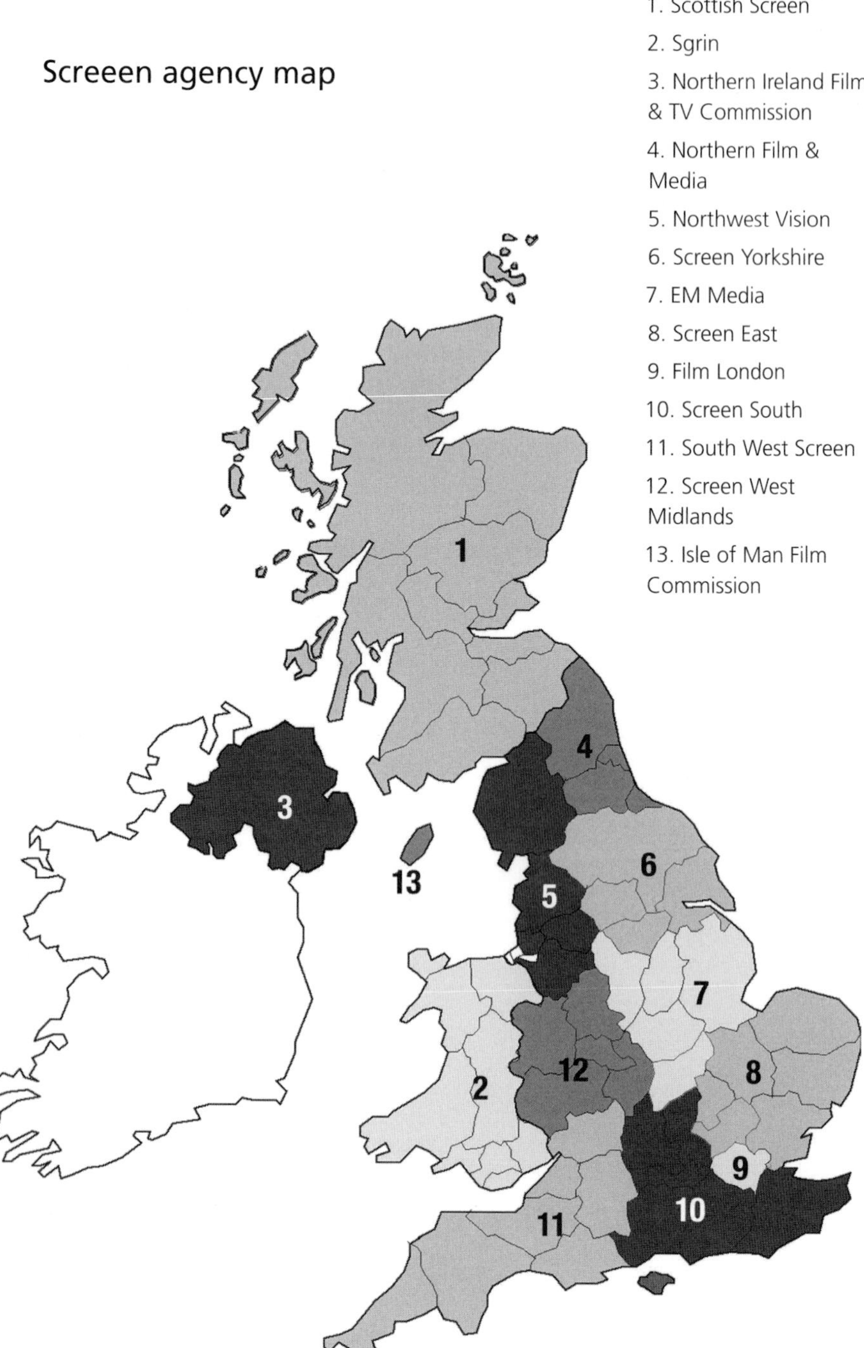


1. Scottish Screen
2. Sgrin
3. Northern Ireland Film & TV Commission
4. Northern Film & Media
5. Northwest Vision
6. Screen Yorkshire
7. EM Media
8. Screen East
9. Film London
10. Screen South
11. South West Screen
12. Screen West Midlands
13. Isle of Man Film Commission

# UK Screen Agencies

## SCOTTISH SCREEN

www.scottishscreen.com
*249 West George Street, 2nd Floor, Glasgow , Scotland, G2 4QE, UK | tel: 014 1302 1700 | fax: 014 1302 1778 | info@scottishscreen.com*

*Covers Scotland*

Scottish Screen develops, encourages and promotes every aspect of film, television and new media in Scotland, promoting Scotland as an international centre of excellence in the creative industries. Support is available hrough script and company development, short film production, distribution of National Lottery film production finance, training, education, exhibition funding, film commission locations support and the Scottish Screen Archive. There is an interview with Becky Lloyd, Short Film Executive at the end of this chapter.

### Strategic priorities

To develop a world class production business in Scotland; to attract major productions to Scotland; to champion a culture of investment in the screen industries; to nurture and develop talent and audiences; to preserve and present Scottish Screen production; to encourage and support international outlook; to drive screen policy from school to statute.

### Funding

Lottery funding is divided into the following areas: feature film production; short film production; script development; project development and short film schemes. Scottish screen also runs the following production schemes: New Found Land & New Found Films; Tartan Shorts; Tartan Smalls; This Scotland; First Writes; Archive Live.

**ARCHIVE LIVE** To promote the creative use of materials held in the Scottish Screen Archive

**Open to:** Individuals & Organisations | **For:** Audience | **Award range:** Development funds of £5000 leading to potential of £25,000 to realise. | **Number of awards:** 5 initial investments leading to 2 final awards. | **Format:** Archive footage | **Platform:** web, cinema | **Deadline:** One annual deadline

**FEATURE FILM PRODUCTION FUNDING** Feature film production

**Open to:** Organisations | **For:** Production | **Award range:** Up to £500,000 or 25% of the total production budget | **Genre:** feature length animation, fiction or documentary | **Deadline:** Eight deadlines per year

**Further details:** All productions should be intended for theatrical release

**FIRST WRITES** Script development for short films no longer than 10 minutes by young people between 11 and 16.

**Open to:** Individuals | **For:** Script development | **Number of awards:** 3 | **Deadline:** One annual deadline

**Further details:** Supported by BBC Scotland and Learning and Teaching Scotland

**NEW FOUND LAND** Commissions six digital 24-minute dramas for TV broadcast and theatrical, running every two years

**For:** TV Production | **Award range:** £50,000 | **Number of awards:** 6 | **Format:** DV | **Platform:** TV, cinema | **Genre:** TV drama | **Deadline:** Once every two years

**Further details:** Scottish Television and Grampian Television support the scheme.

**NEW FOUND FILMS** Two digital feature length documentaries are commissioned every two years (alternating annually with New Found Land scheme)

**For:** TV Production | **Award range:** Development funds potentially leading to a maximum £300,000 investment. | **Number of awards:** 10/12 initial investments leading to two final awards. | **Format:** DV | **Genre:** Features

**Further details:** Scottish Television and Grampian Television support the scheme.

**PROJECT DEVELOPMENT FUNDING** Advanced stages of development

**Open to:** Production Companies | **For:** Script development | **Award range:** Up to £25,000 or 75% of total development budget | **Genre:** feature film, live action, drama, theatrical documentary or animation projects | **Deadline:** Eight deadlines per year

**Further details:** All productions should be intended for theatrical release

**SCRIPT DEVELOPMENT FUNDING** Early stages of development

**Open to:** Production Companies | **For:** Script development | **Award range:** Up to £25,000 or a maximum of 90% of total development budget | **Genre:** feature film, live action, drama, theatrical documentary or animation projects | **Deadline:** Eight deadlines per year

**Further details:** All productions should be intended for theatrical release

**SHORT FILM PRODUCTION FUNDING** Short film production

**Open to:** Production Companies | **For:** Short Film production | **Award range:** Up to £75,000 or 50% of the total production budget | **Genre:** drama, documentary, animation | **Deadline:** Eight deadlines per year

**Further details:** All productions should be intended for theatrical or festival release

**TARTAN SHORTS** Short film production for films of no more than 9 minutes.

**For:** Short Film | **Award range:** Up to £65,000. | **Number of awards:** 3 | **Format:** DV or s16mm for 35mm blowup | **Deadline:** One annual deadline

**Further details:** Applicants are yet to make a feature. Projects must be intended for theatrical release. BBC Scotland supports the scheme.

**TARTAN SMALLS** Short film production of films no longer than 9 minutes intended for a child audience between 6 and 13 years old.

**Open to:** Individuals & Organisations | **For:** Short Film | **Award range:** Up to £40,000 | **Number of awards:** 3 | **Format:** DV, delivered on Digibeta | **Genre:** Drama for a 6-13 year old audience | **Deadline:** One annual deadline

**Further details:** Applicants must be filmmakers new to the youth audience. CBBC Scotland supports the scheme.

**THIS SCOTLAND** Production of documentaries 24 minutes long

**For:** Production | **Number of awards:** 6 | **Format:** DV | **Genre:** documentary | **Deadline:** One annual deadline

**Further details:** Productions must be intended for broadcast or theatrical release. Scottish Television and Grampian Television support the scheme.

# SGRÎN CYMRU WALES

**www.sgrin.co.uk**

*The Bank, 10 Mount Square, Cardiff Bay, Cardiff, Wales, CF10 5EE, UK | tel: 02920 333 300 | fax: 029 20 333320 | sgrin@sgrin.co.uk*

*Covers Wales*

SGRIN was established in 1997 as the national body for film, television and new media in Wales. It is responsible for developing strategic film policy in Wales, and administers the film lottery fund on behalf of the Arts Council for Wales to support film production in the region.

## Strategic priorities

Sgrin Cymru Wales is responsible for the formulation of a strategic vision for the development of the economic and cultural aspects of film, television and new media. We undertake activity under 5 headings: New Talent, Content Development, Access and Education, Marketing and Information and Business Support.

## Funding

Lottery funding is divided into the following areas: script development; short film production; feature film production. Sgrin also runs the following productions schemes: Animated Gems, Digital Visions, Screen Gems.

**ANIMATED GEMS** Production for short animated films of 3-minutes in length.

**Open to:** Organisations | **For:** Short Film | **Award range:** Up to £25,000 | **Number of awards:** 3 | **Platform:** cinema | **Genre:** Animation | **Deadline:** One annual deadline

**Further details:** In partnership with S4C

**DIGITAL VISIONS** Production finance for short digital films of no more than 10 minutes.

**Open to:** Individuals & Organisations | **For:** Short Film | **Award range:** Up to £10,000 | **Number of awards:** 8 | **Format:** DV | **Platform:** cinema | **Genre:** Fiction, documentary | **Deadline:** One annual deadline

**Further details:** Two independent production companies can apply to produce a slate of four films each.

In partnership with the UK Film Council's Digital Shorts scheme and BBC Cymru Wales.

**LOTTERY FEATURE FILM PRODUCTION** Production of fully-developed features

**Open to:** Organisations | **For:** Production | **Award range:** Up to £250,000 or 50% of project costs | **Platform:** cinema | **Genre:** Fiction, animation, documentary | **Deadline:** Applications can be made at any time.

**Further details:** All productions should be intended for theatrical release.

**SCREEN GEMS** Production scheme that brings writers and directors with a project together with new producers to produce 3-minute films.

**Open to:** Individuals & Organisations | **For:** Short Film | **Number of awards:** 10 | **Format:** 35mm, DV, hi-def | **Platform:** cinema | **Genre:** Fiction | **Deadline:** One annual deadline

**Further details:** 2 independent production companies can apply to produce a slate of five films each.

The scheme is supported by the Arts Council of Wales and ITV1 Wales.

**LOTTERY FEATURE FILM DEVELOPMENT** Development for feature productions.

**Open to:** Organisations | **For:** Script Development | **Award range:** Up to £20,000 or 75% of project costs | **Genre:** Fiction, animation, documentary | **Deadline:** Applications can be made at any time

**Further details:** All productions should be intended for theatrical release.

**SHORT FILM PRODUCTION** Short film production of films not longer than 10 minutes.

**Open to:** Organisations | **For:** Short Film | **Award range:** Between 50% and 90% of project costs with a ceiling of £36,000 | **Genre:** Fiction, animation, documentary | **Deadline:** Annually in April

**Further details:** All productions should be intended for theatrical release.

# NORTHERN IRELAND FILM TELEVISION COMMISSION

**www.niftc.co.uk**

*3rd Floor, Alfred House, Alfred Street, Belfast, Northern Ireland, BT2 8ED, UK | tel: 028 9023 2444 | fax: 028 9023 9918 | info@niftc.co.uk*

*Covers Northern Ireland*

The NIFTC was established in 1997 as a Film and Television Commission for Northern Ireland, with the objective of attracting film production to the region. In 2002, the Arts Council of Northern Ireland designated NIFTC with the responsibility of distributing the annual lottery film funds.

## Strategic priorities

To encourage and facilitate development and production; to develop access to moving image heritage; to support company development and training; to provide information services; to develop an education policy.

## Funding

Lottery funding is divided into the following areas: feature films and television drama production; script development; local cultural production and distribution. The NIFTC also runs the short film production scheme, Deviate, which is part of the national scheme, Digital Shorts.

**DEVIATE (I.E. DIGITAL SHORTS)** Production scheme for digital short films

**Open to:** Individuals | **For:** Short Film | **Award range:** Up to £8000 | **Format:** DV | **Deadline:** One annual deadline

**Further details:** Writers, directors and producers with a script may apply.

**FEATURE FILMS & TV DRAMA PRODUCTION** Production of feature films, short films, documentary, animation and television drama

**Open to:** Organisations | **For:** Production | **Award range:** Up to 50% of project costs with a ceiling of £150,000 (Lottery Funding). The Film Production Fund can provide between £150,000 and £600,000 of project costs. | **Platform:** Cinema, TV | **Genre:** Fiction, animation, documentary

**Further details:** Applications for under £50,000 can be made at any time of year. Applications for more than £50,000 have four deadlines per year.

**LOW BUDGET FEATURE FILM FUND** Annual production of a low budget feature with a budget of no more than £200,000, towards which the NIFTC provides 75% funding.

**Open to:** Organisations | **For:** Production | **Award range:** Up to 75% of project costs with a ceiling of £150,000. | **Platform:** Cinema, TV | **Format:** digital

**Further details**: The film should be entirely set and shot in Northern Ireland. Priority will be given to projects having a very strong cultural resonance for Northern Ireland; that offer important developmental opportunities to key Northern Ireland talent; that use a digital format appropriate to the budget; and projects with sales agents or distributors already attached

**MINI - MADE IN NORTHERN IRELAND PRODUCTION FUNDING** Support for the local industry in production and distribution.

**Open to:** Individuals & Organisations | **For:** Production | **Award range:** The funding is available in four streams. Individuals can receive up to 90% of costs for a Project with costs of no more than £2,500. Projects with costs of no more than £5000 can receive up to 90% of project costs. Projects with costs of no more than £30,000 can receive up to 75% of project costs. All other projects will receive up to 50% of project costs with a ceiling of £50,000. Distribution and promotion of a single film will receive up to 10% of project costs with a ceiling of £5000. | **Platform:** Cinema, TV, online | **Genre:** Feature films, short films, TV drama series and singles, documentaries, animation, digital media content.

**Further details:** Production companies rather than distribution companies are eligible. Applications for under £50,000 can be made at any time of year. Applications for more than £50,000 have four deadlines per year.

**SCRIPT DEVELOPMENT** Development of feature films and television drama, cultural and arts documentaries.

**Open to:** Organisations | **For:** Script Development | **Award range:** Up to 50% of project costs with a ceiling of £20,000.

**Further details:** Applications for under £50,000 can be made at any time of year. Applications for more than £50,000 have four deadlines per year.

# EM MEDIA

**www.em-media.org.uk**

*35-37 St Mary's Gate, Nottingham, Nottinghamshire, NG1 1PU, UK | tel: 0115 934 9090 | fax: 0115 950 0988 | info@em-media.org.uk*

*Covers Derbyshire, Leicestershire, Lincolnshire, Northamptonshire, Nottinghamshire, Rutland*

EM Media is the gateway for everything to do with film and media in the East Midlands, from funding, training and production through to locations, support services and business development.

## Strategic priorities

To develop viable film and media businesses; to develop and promote regional talent; to develop access and opportunities for the end user.

## Funding

Lottery funding is divided into audience and market development, business development, and production and market support. EM-Media also runs EMMI - East Midlands Media Investments, which invests in development, production and short film production. Em Media runs the production scheme, Digital Shorts.

AUDIENCE AND MARKET DEVELOPMENT Aims to develop audiences, participation, understanding and enjoyment of all forms of media, through encouraging greater access to media experiences and opportunities

**Award range:** Maximum £20,000 in any given project or activity, up to a maximum of 75% of total project cost.

**Further details:** To assist with the development of audiences, knowledge, understanding and marketing of film and media product. Examples include projects supporting access to cinema in rural areas, film education and media literacy activities, trade development initiatives and film festivals

BUSINESS DEVELOPMENT Aims to develop and sustain an innovative and distinctive media sector, through supporting the increase in business activity, competitiveness and employment.

**Award range:** Maximum investment of £1,000 towards the costs of consultancy support for new business; Investment up to £5,000 as a start-up or business re-engineering loan

**Further details:** To support business development through investment in specialist consultancies and start-up or business re-engineering loans.

PRODUCT DEVELOPMENT AND PRODUCTION To develop and promote regional talent, supporting product and slate development, individual production awards, and production co-finance.

**Award range:** Investment levels vary according to type of project; examples include: short films could range from £500 to £5,000 to £10,000; investment larger scale projects (feature films, projects for television, games development, etc) could

range from a very small initial investment up to a maximum of £95,000; production co-finance for features and large scale projects will to a maximum of £250,000

**SKILLS DEVELOPMENT** To support the development of skilled and experienced practitioners and workforce, providing individual skills development awards and company skills development awards

**Award range:** Investments up to 50% of the total costs, up to a maximum of £1,000 for individuals, or £1,000 per employee per company (up to a maximum of £10,000)

**Further details:** Projects that have partners on board that cross regional and national borders will be welcomed.

# FILM LONDON

**www.filmlondon.org.uk**

*20 Euston Centre, Regents Place, London, NW1 3JH, UK | tel: 020 7387 8787 | fax: 020 7387 8788*

*Covers London - All*

Film London is the strategic agency for film and media in the UK's capital, working to sustain, promote and develop London as a major international film-making and film culture capital. Film London commissions and funds both creative and industrial initiatives, and works to develop the city as a world-class film location. Film London is funded by the UK Film Council and the London Development Agency through Creative London.

**FILM LONDON EAST** Film London East is a £1.8 million initiative to develop and support film and media businesses and freelancers in the East London and Thames Gateway area to increase their likelihood of survival and growth.

**Open to:** Individuals & Organisations | **For:** Business Development

**Further details:** Building on the success of the East London Moving Image Initiative which enables small and medium sized enterprises to strengthen and build sustainable futures in the screen industry. Offers seminars and advice sessions on marketing, distribution and sales strategies; short film production; online information; networking.

Info at www.filmlondon.org.uk/east

**AUDIENCE DEVELOPMENT FUND** Open to London based organisations who wish to apply for project funding to support education and audience development in film and media.

**Open to:** Organisations | **For:** Support for Exhibition and Education projects

**Further details:** This is the only Film London scheme to fund film related exhibition (e.g. film festivals), participatory video and education projects.

**LONDON ARTISTS FILM & VIDEO AWARD** LAFVA, now in its fifth year, is managed by Film London in partnership with Arts Council England. Full details for the next round of LAFVA will be available in Autumn 2005.

**For:** Artists video work | **Award range:** £2,000 to £20,000

**Further details:** Awards are available to artists working in the context of contemporary moving image practice and producing work intended for exhibition in galleries, festivals, specialist venues and as site specific installations. Awards are intended for fully developed projects with a realisable exhibition and distribution plan.

**PULSE** Launched in 2002 in partnership with the UK Film Council's New Cinema Fund. The ambition is to produce a new generation of film-makers who use digital technology creatively to tell stories in groundbreaking ways.

**For:** Digital Shorts | **Award range:** no more than £10,000 | **Format:** DV

**Further details:** The New Cinema Fund invests £5million each year in films that illustrate unique ideas and innovative approaches. £500,000 per year from the Fund is invested into digital short films across the UK. New scheme to begin Spring 2005 – further details not available at publication.

**LOW BUDGET DIGITAL FEATURE FILM SCHEME** England's first micro budget feature film production scheme to set to be launched in late 2005 with details unconfirmed at time of publication but posibilities including 100% financing on films with budgets under £400,000 and the provision of services support (post production, equipment, etc) for projects on the scheme. The London Artists Film and Video Awards will be opening up for submissions in Autumn.

# NORTH WEST VISION

**www.northwestvision.co.uk**

*233 Tea Factory, 82 Wood Street, Liverpool, L1 4DQ, UK | tel: 015 1708 2967 | fax: 015 1708 2984 | info@northwestvision.co.uk*

*Covers Cheshire, Cumbria, Lancashire, Liverpool, Manchester*

North West Vision is the television, film and moving image development agency for England's North West. North West Vision is at the pulse of the Northwest's film and TV industry and committed to shaping a sustainable and dynamic film and television industry in England's Northwest.

## Strategic priorities

Organisational & Individual Development; Production & Development; Audience Development

## Funding

Lottery funding is divided into the following areas: training; sector specific support for companies or organisations; professional development of individuals; development; film production; audience development. North West Vision also run the production scheme, Virgin Shorts.

**AUDIENCE DEVELOPMENT** To ensure audiences have access to a wide and diverse range of cinema and learning opportunities.

**Open to:** Organisations | **For:** Film Festival Funding | **Size of fund:** £80,000 per annum | **Award range:** Between £5000 and £20,000 | **Number of awards:** Usually support 6-8 film festivals each year | **Deadline:** 2006/2007 funding deadline will be end of 2005 | **Recent investments:** Kendal Mountain Film Festival; Commonwealth Film Festival; Liverpool Gay & Lesbian Film Festival

**Further details:** Priority is to support festivals (or similar activities) that celebrate diversity and actively involve culturally diverse communities. Match funding of at least 30% must be secured.

**FEATURE FILM DEVELOPMENT** Feature film development including script development and development of documentary features

**Open to:** Individual writers or production companies with writers & rights secured | **For:** Script Development | **Award range:** Up to £5000 per draft | **Number of awards:** Usually support 15 projects each year | **Genre:** Any genre | **Deadline:** Twice a year in April and October | **Recent investments:** Leigh Campbell's "*Big Stella Little Stella*" - Winner of Cannes pitching competition

**Further details:** North West Vision has a high quality threshold for this funding programme as we run several writers development schemes to support less developed projects. Well developed step outlines or first drafts must be submitted with application.

**FEATURE FILM ADVANCED DEVELOPMENT** Feature film seed funding to secure production finance on well developed projects with rights secured.

**Open to:** Regional Production companies | **For:** Feature Film Seed Funding | **Award range:** Up to £5000 | **Number of awards:** 2 projects supported in 2004/05 | **Genre:** Any genre | **Deadline:** Can apply any time (except over Dec/Jan) | **Recent investments:** Binary Films for feature film "*A Grand Crossing*"

**Further details:** North West Vision has a high quality threshold for this funding programme. Projects should be sufficiently developed to be promoted in the market place. Final drafts of the feature film scripts must be submitted with application.

**FILM PRODUCTION** Completion funding for short films

**Open to:** Regional Production companies | **For:** Production | **Award range:** Up to £5000 for short films | **Number of awards:** 2 projects supported in 2004/05 | **Genre:** Wide range of genres, platforms and media | **Deadline:** Can apply any time (except over Dec/Jan) | **Recent investments:** Paradocs Films documentary short set in Cuba "*Los Quinsos*"

**Further details:** Priority is to support high quality films that show great promise but need vital funding to complete. Story, content and visual style should be clear from rough cut.

Rough cuts of the completed film must be submitted with application.

**PROFESSIONAL DEVELOPMENT OF INDIVIDUALS** Professional development for individuals to improve their skills

**Open to:** Individuals | **For:** Individual Development/ Training | **Award range:** Between £500 and £5000 | **Number of awards:** 10 projects supported in 2004/05 | **Deadline:** Can apply any time (except over Dec/Jan).

**Further details:** To support attendance at conferences and festivals, training and skills development for producers, directors and writers.

**SECTOR SPECIFIC SUPPORT FOR COMPANIES OR ORGANISATIONS** Business development for media companies.

**Open to:** Organisations | **For:** Business Development | **Award range:** Between £500 and £5000 | **Number of awards:** 12 projects supported in 2004/05 | **Deadline:** Can apply any time (except over Dec/Jan).

**Further details:** To support skills development, market research, collective marketing initiatives, attending trade shows, markets and festivals.

**TRAINING** Projects delivered by training providers that address the skills shortages in the region.

**Open to:** Organisations | **For:** Education/ Training | **Award range:** Between £500 and £5000 | **Number of awards:** 9 projects supported in 2004/05 | **Deadline:** Can apply any time (except over Dec/Jan).

**Further details:** Priority is to support training programmes that develop new talent (particularly producers, directors and writes; in particular training for under-represented groups

**DIGITAL SHORTS** This scheme is delivered in association with the UK Film Council and is part of their UK Digital Shorts Scheme.

**Open to:** Individuals & Organisations | **For:** Short Film | **Size of fund:** Approx £80,000 per annum | **Award range:** Up to £10,000 | **Number of awards:** Usually 12 awards | **Format:** Digital | **Genre:** Wide range of genres | **Deadline:** Once a year usually in the summer | **Recent investments:** Springheeled Jack; Flight; Unhinged, Punch; Tiz and Connecting | Notable investments: Unhinged; Punch.

**Further details:** Purpose of this scheme is to develop filmmakers skills by producing short films that will be promoted professionally. Short film scripts and showreels must be submitted with application.

**VIRGIN SHORTS** Production bursaries for short narrative films made by filmmakers new to North West Vision.

**Open to:** Individuals | **For:** Short Film | **Size of fund:** Approx £12,000 per annum | **Award range:** Up to £1000 | **Number of awards:** Usually 12 awards | **Format:** Any | **Genre:** Wide range of genres, platforms and media | **Deadline:** Once every two years.

**Further details:** Purpose of this scheme is to allow filmmakers new to North West Vision to make a short film and showcase their skills. Short film scripts and showreels must be submitted with application.

## NORTHERN FILM & MEDIA

**www.northernmedia.org**

*Central Square, Forth Street, Newcastle, NE1 3PJ, UK | tel: 019 1269 9200 | fax: 019 1269 9213 | info@northernmedia.org*

*Covers Durham, Newcastle, Northumberland, Tees Valley, Tyne & Wear*

Northern Film & Media is the Regional Screen Agency covering the North-East of England. Their core aim is to encourage more people to make, watch and work in film, television and interactive media. They also have a free Locations Service that helps filmmakers pin-point and use some of the region's world-class locations.

## Strategic priorities

Economic sustainability and creative quality in media businesses; encouraging investment; innovation in the use of digital technologies; improving international relationships; increasing opportunities for audiences.

## Funding

Lottery funding is divided into the following areas: development of people; development of content; development of audiences; development of networks. North Film & Media also runs the production scheme, Digital Shorts.

DEVELOPMENT OF AUDIENCES Development of size and diversity of audiences for specialist film and moving image media. Also development of education opportunities.

**Open to:** Individuals & Organisations | **For:** Audience development | **Award range:** Up to £5000 for individuals and up to £20,000 for organisations. | **Genre:** All genres, screen platforms and screen media

**Further details:** Examples of projects likely to receive funding are festivals, venues, technology, access and inclusion, participation, education, and archives.

DEVELOPMENT OF COMPANIES Growth and development for media businesses.

**Open to:** Organisations | **For:** Business Development | **Award range:** In conjunction with Business Link Tyne & Wear. Awards to be determined.

**Further details:** This scheme is for organisations which have been established for at least 36 months. Examples of projects likely to receive funding are business development, mentoring, marketing, training support, and skills and talent attachment.

DEVELOPMENT OF CONTENT Developing, producing and delivering creative content with a commercial market in mind.

**Open to:** Individuals & Organisations | **For:** Production | **Award range:** Up to £10,000 for individuals and up to £40,000 for organisations. | **Genre:** All genres, platforms and media

**Further details:** Examples of projects likely to receive funding are script development, production of moving image, post production, and marketing.

DEVELOPMENT OF NETWORKS Encourage the sharing of resources, skills and information on a regional, national and international scale.

**Open to:** Individuals & Organisations | **For:** Market Development | **Award range:** Up to £1500.

**Further details:** Examples of projects likely to receive funding are regional networks, partnerships, attendance of events, regional conferences, trade visits, and screenings.

DEVELOPMENT OF PEOPLE Developing training, education and vocational schemes.

**Open to:** Individuals & Organisations | **For:** Education/Training | **Award range:** Up to £5000 for individuals and up to £10,000 for organisations.

**Further details:** The fund will support both the scheme providers and the users. Examples of projects likely to receive funding are industry standard training courses, industry placements, and mentoring schemes

DIGITAL SHORTS Training, development and production for short films.

**Open to:** Individuals | **For:** Short Film | **Format:** DV | **Award range:** Up to £8,000

**Further details:** Writers, directors and producers with a script may apply.

# SCREEN EAST

**www.screeneast.co.uk**

*2 Millennium Plain, Norwich, Norfolk, NR2 1TF, UK | tel: 016 0377 6920 | fax: 016 0376 7191 | funding@screeneast.co.uk*

*Covers Bedfordshire, Cambridgeshire, Essex, Hertfordshire, Norfolk, Suffolk*

Screen East is the regional screen agency dedicated to developing, supporting and promoting film and media industry and culture in the East of England (Bedfordshire, Cambridgeshire, Essex, Hertfordshire, Norfolk and Suffolk). Screen East is funded by the UK Film Council and allocates Lottery funding through the Regional Investment Fund for England (RIFE).

## Strategic priorities

To promote the East of England as an ideal location for film and television production and attract inward investment by marketing the locations, facilities, skills and expertise available in the region.

To develop the talent, skills and innovation of the region's new and existing workforce.

To invest in the development of film, television and digital media businesses based in the East of England.

To create opportunities for audiences to enjoy and experience moving image culture and heritage.

To celebrate the diversity of the people who live and work in the region in order to break down barriers to working in the media industries

## Funding

Lottery funding through RIFE. Funding is divided into the following areas: development finance; production finance; company development investment; small scale capital awards; investment to support access for audiences; educational projects and initiatives; archive services and access for audiences. Screen East also runs the production scheme; Digital Shorts. Regional eligibility criteria apply for all funds.

**COMPANY DEVELOPMENT INVESTMENT** Development of a slate of projects for promising regional production companies

**Open to:** Organisation | **For:** Business Development | **Award range:** Up to £20,000 | **Deadline:** Rolling Deadline, subject to available funds

**Further details:** Applicants must have more than one project in their slate and demonstrate financial support from broadcasters, film financiers or distributors.

**DEVELOPMENT FINANCE** Script and project development prior to pre-production

**Open to:** Individuals & Organisations | **For:** Production Development | **Genre:** Features - Fiction, documentary, digital media, animation | **Deadline:** Rolling Deadline, subject to available funds

**Further details:** For low budget feature films intended for theatrical release

**DIGITAL SHORTS** Training, development and production for short films.

**Open to:** Individuals | **For:** Short Film | **Award range:** Up to £8000 | **Format:** DV | **Deadline:** Rolling Deadline, subject to available funds

**Further details:** Writers, directors and producers with a script may apply.

**PRODUCTION FINANCE** Indigenous and independent film production, post production and distribution

**Open to:** Organisations | **For:** low budget feature film | **Award range:** Up to £50,000 | **Genre:** Fiction, documentary, digital media, animation | **Deadline:** Rolling Deadline, subject to available funds

**Further details:** Films must be intended for theatrical release.

Collaborations between traditional, new media organisations and broadcast companies are welcomed.

**FESTIVAL FUND** Festival fund for new and established Festivals in East England.

**Open to:** festivals in the region | **For:** Festival fund | **Award range:** Up to £20,000 per annum | **Deadline:** March/April (annually) | **Recent investments:** Cambridge Film Festival; Great Yarmouth Film Festival

**Further details:** Festivals apply to one deadline in March for the entire year covered by the fund, and must have combined creative and commercial focus in the business plan.

**SMALL-SCALE LOTTERY AWARDS** Short course funding, travel and training costs for freelance filmmakers

**Open to:** Individuals & Organisations | **For:** Business Development; training; travel bursaries | **Award range:** Up to £500 | **Deadline:** Rolling Deadline, subject to available funds

**Further details:** Match funding required at a minimum level of 30% of total project costs. Applicants must include a CV and full course, festival or training plan details.

## SCREEN SOUTH

**www.screensouth.org**

*Folkestone Enterprise Centre, Shearway Road, Folkestone, CT19 4RH, UK | tel: 013 0329 8222 | fax: 013 0329 8227 | info@screensouth.org*

*Covers Kent, Buckinghamshire, Hampshire, Oxfordshire, Surrey, Berkshire, East Sussex, West Sussex, Isle of Wight*

Despite receiving one of the smallest investments from the UK Film Council Regional Investment fund out of any of the regional screen agences, Screen South is active across archive, exhibion, education, production & development, vocational training, and film commision / inward investment.

## Strategic priorities

Screen South has set its regional priorities as the need for a sustainable media industry to increase opportunities for audiences and to develop talent. Its lottery programme is structured in three priority streams.

## Funding

Lottery funding is channelled into each of the strategic priority areas: to develop viable film and media businesses; to develop audiences and cultural partnerships; to develop and discover regional talent.

DEVELOPING AND DISCOVERING REGIONAL TALENT Developing projects and scripts, and production and distribution of screen projects.

**Open to:** Individuals & Organisations | **For:** Production & Development | **Award range:** Up to £5000 for individuals and up to £10,000 for organisations. | **Genre:** Wide range of genres, platforms and media

DEVELOPING AUDIENCES AND CULTURAL PARTNERSHIPS Development of accessibility to film and moving image media and audience education and participation.

**Open to:** Individuals & Organisations | **For:** Audience Development | **Award range:** Up to £5000 for individuals and up to £10,000 for organisations. | **Genre:** Wide range of genres, platforms and media

**Further details:** Projects bringing diverse audiences and cinema together are welcomed.

DEVELOPING VIABLE FILM AND MEDIA BUSINESSES Development of a sustainable media industry.

**Open to:** Individuals & Organisations | **For:** Business Development | **Award range:** Up to £5000 for individuals and up to £10,000 for organisations.

**Further details:** Welcomed projects include business partnerships, organisational and capacity building, networking events.

SCRIPT DEVELOPMENT SCHEMES Script development for screenwriters

**Open to:** Individuals & Organisations | **For:** Script Development | **Award range:** Various

**Further details:** See website for details of current schemes

DIGITAL SHORTS Short Scheme in partnership with the UK Film Council

**Open to:** Individuals & Organisations | **For:** Short Film | **Award range:** £1,500 to £10,000 | **Number of awards:** 8 - 12 | **Format:** DV | **Platform:** Cinema, web, TV | **Genre:** Wide range of genres & styles

**Further details:** Drama, documentaries & animation

GOOD FOUNDATIONS Producer & market led creative team development & training.

**Open to:** Individuals & Organisations | **For:** Feature Film Development | **Award range:** £1,600 to £5,000 | **Number of awards:** 8 - 12 | **Format:** All | **Platform:** Cinema | **Genre:** Wide range of genres & styles

ONE-TO-ONE European co-production mentoring scheme for producers with a short film project

**Open to:** Individuals | **For:** Short Film | **Format:** All | **Platform:** All | **Genre:** All

# SCREEN WEST MIDLANDS

**www.screenwm.co.uk**

*31/41 Bromley Street, Birmingham, B9 4AN, UK | tel: 0121 766 1470 | fax: 0121 766 1480 | info@screenwm.co.uk*

*Covers Birmingham, Herefordshire, Shropshire, Staffordshire, Warwickshire, West Midlands, Worcestershire*

Screen West Midlands' mission is to create a thriving screen media industry in the region.

They aim to support, promote and develop the screen media industry through areas such as production, education, exhibition, archive and skills development. They receive core funding through the UK FILM COUNCIL, Advantage West Midlands and The Learning and Skills Council.

## Strategic priorities

To promote and reflect the diversity of the region; to encourage social inclusion into film and screen media industry and culture; and to offer high quality ideas with good standards of design and planning, which can be practically achieved with the resources available

## Funding

Screen West Midlands covers several operational areas, including feature film investment, short film initiatives, freelancer and company training schemes, and RIFE Lottery investment to support, promote and develop the screen media industries in the West Midlands.

**PRODUCTION INVESTMENT FUND** Production investment for feature films with co-financing and distribution already in place, that can demonstrate a strong regional spend in return for the investment.

**For:** Feature Film Finance | **Award range:** Up to £300k or 25% of project budget (whichever is the lesser). | **Format:** Any | **Platform:** Feature film. | **Genre:** Feature film drama or documentary. | **Deadline:** Rolling

**Further details:** Funded through the European Regional Development Fund.

**LOTTERY SCRIPT GRANTS** Development fund to support writers looking to develop first or second drafts from treatment or early draft stage.

**Open to:** Individuals | **For:** Feature film development. | **Award range:** Up to £5,000 per project. Additional £2,000 available for script editor costs to successful applicants. | **Number of awards:** Average 4-5 per round. | **Format:** n/a | **Platform:** Feature film. | **Genre:** Drama. | **Deadline:** 22nd April 2005; 28th October 2005.

**Further details:** Funded by RIFE Lottery through the UK Film Council.

**ADVANTAGE BROADCAST FUND** Stimulation of broadcast commissions

**For:** TV Production & Development | **Size of fund:** £500k over 2 years | **Award range:** Between £5k-£30k, average award £10-15k

**Further details:** For more information please email in the first instance production@screenwm.co.uk

**MOVING UP** Skills development scheme for new entrants to the industry (0-2 years experience), with workshops on freelancer skills and support for training course costs.

**Open to:** Individuals | **For:** Training (new entrants) | **Award range:** Up to £1,000 towards course costs (up to 100%), plus small subsistence contribution. | **Number of awards:** 16 places per programme.

**Further details:** Funded in partnership with Learning & Skills Council. Includes an NVQ module in Health & Safety.

**SCREEN, PLAN & SELECT** Flexible skills development scheme with option to have a training needs analysis surgery, before drawing up an action plan and accessing funds to attend training courses. Alternatively, just apply for the funding support if you already know your needs.

**Open to:** Individuals | **For:** Training (freelancers) | **Award range:** Up to £1,000 towards course costs (up to 100%), plus small subsistence contribution

**Further details:** Funded in partnership with Learning & Skills Council.

**RESEARCHER TRAINING PROGRAMME** Placements for researchers from ethnic minority backgrounds with television production companies. In partnership with Channel 4 Researcher Centre.

**Open to:** Individuals | **For:** Training (freelancers) | **Number of awards:** 2

**WRITER'S PASSAGE** Intensive 9-month development programme for writers to take a project through 3 complete drafts, supported by industry mentors.

**Open to:** Individuals | **For:** Training/development | **Number of awards:** 8

**Further details:** In partnership with The Script Factory.

**MANAGEMENT ACTION PROGRAMME (MAP)** A company-wide practical active programme containing six modules to provide understanding and to introduce resources to be applied to each business.

**Open to:** Individuals & Organisations | **For:** Training (freelancers) | **Number of awards:** 14

**Further details:** In partnership with Birmingham City Council.

**BUSINESS FOUNDATION** Streamlined version of the MAP programme aimed at new businesses/sole traders, covering the basics of business start-up and market awareness.

**Open to:** Individuals & Organisations | **For:** Training (freelancers)

**Further details:** In partnership with Birmingham City Council.

**ENHANCE & ADVANCE** Flexible skills development scheme with option to have a company training needs analysis surgery, before drawing up an action plan and accessing funds to attend training courses. Alternatively, just apply for the funding support if you already know your needs.

**Open to:** Organisations | **For:** Training (companies) | **Award range:** Up to £5,000 towards employee training costs (max. £1,000 per employee).

**Further details:** Funded in partnership with Learning & Skills Council.

**RIFE LOTTERY** Regional investment fund to projects developing the screen media industries in area including archives, exhibition, education and new talent.

**Open to:** Organisations | **For:** Regional development | **Size of fund:** £300k per annum | **Award range:** Up to £10,000 for a local project. Higher ceilings for regional high impact projects. | **Number of awards:** Approx 20 per year

**Further details:** Funded by RIFE Lottery through the UK Film Council.

DIGITAL SHORTS Training, development and production for short films.

**Open to:** Individuals | **For:** Short Film | **Award range:** Average £8-9k per film, minimum of 8 films produced | **Number of awards:** 8 | **Format:** Any digital format | **Platform:** Primarily cinema, but films are also showcased through DVD and the web | **Genre:** Drama or documentary. Live action or animation.

**Further details:** Writers, directors and producers with a script may apply.

# SCREEN YORKSHIRE

**www.screenyorkshire.co.uk**

*Studio 22, 46 The Calls, Leeds, Yorkshire, LS2 7EY, UK | tel: 011 3294 4410 | fax: 011 3294 4989 | info@screenyorkshire.co.uk*

*Covers Humberside, North Yorkshire, South Yorkshire, West Yorkshire*

Screen Yorkshire is 'the gateway to the best in film, broadcast and digital media in the Yorkshire and Humber region'. They are responsible for inspiring, promoting and supporting a successful long-term film and media sector for the region. Screen Yorkshire's vision for the future is to help grow and develop strong film, broadcast and digital media industries in Yorkshire and Humber, with a highly skilled workforce.

## Strategic priorities

To invest in development and promotion of regional talent; to increase the size and competitiveness of the film and moving image sector; to build audiences, participation, knowledge and culture.

## Funding

Lottery funding is divided into the following areas: script development and screenwriting talent; short film development, production and distribution; development and distribution of low budget films; research, feasibility and company development studies; events and schemes which encourage collaboration and partnerships; organisational development and capacity building; building audiences, participation, knowledge and culture.

BUILDING AUDIENCES, PARTICIPATION, KNOWLEDGE AND CULTURE Improving audience access to and understanding of the moving image.

**For:** Audience | **Award range:** Up to £5000 for individuals and up to 80% of project costs. | **Platform:** feature films (drama and documentary), short films, television, animation, interactive media (games, online)

DEVELOPMENT AND DISTRIBUTION OF LOW BUDGET FILMS Development of small and mid scale feature films along with assistance in securing further finance.

**Open to:** Individuals & Organisations | **For:** Production Development | **Award range:** Up to £5000 for individuals and up to £10,000 for organisations. | **Platform:** feature films (drama and documentary), short films, television, animation, interactive media (games, online)

**DIGITAL SHORTS** Training, development and production for short films.

**Open to:** Individuals | **For:** Short Film | **Format:** DV | **Platform:** feature films (drama and documentary), short films, television, animation, interactive media (games, online) | **Award range:** Up to £8000

**Further details:** Writers, directors and producers with a script may apply.

**EVENTS AND SCHEMES WHICH ENCOURAGE COLLABORATION AND PARTNERSHIPS** Development of partnerships and networks for the screen industries

**For:** Market Development | **Award range:** Up to £5000 for individuals and up to 80% of project costs. | **Platform:** feature films (drama and documentary), short films, television, animation, interactive media (games, online)

**ORGANISATIONAL DEVELOPMENT AND CAPACITY BUILDING** Developing market intelligence, business development for companies and developing slates of projects.

**For:** Business Development | **Award range:** Up to £5000 for individuals and up to 80% of project costs. | **Platform:** feature films (drama and documentary), short films, television, animation, interactive media (games, online)

**RESEARCH, FEASIBILITY AND COMPANY DEVELOPMENT STUDIES** Business and Sector development

**For:** Market Development | **Award range:** Up to £5000 for individuals and up to 80% of project costs. | **Platform:** feature films (drama and documentary), short films, television, animation, interactive media (games, online)

**Further details:** This will include testing of ideas, market research company development plans.

**SCRIPT DEVELOPMENT AND SCREENWRITING TALENT** Development of scripts, storyboards and ideas.

**Open to:** Individuals & Organisations | **For:** Script Development | **Award range:** Up to £5000 for individuals and up to £10,000 for organisations. | **Platform:** feature films (drama and documentary), short films, television, animation, interactive media (games, online)

**SHORT FILM DEVELOPMENT, PRODUCTION AND DISTRIBUTION** Development, production and distribution of short films and skills development of personnel involved.

**Open to:** Individuals & Organisations | **For:** Short Film | **Award range:** Up to £5000 for individuals and up to £10,000 for organisations. | **Platform:** feature films (drama and documentary), short films, television, animation, interactive media (games, online)

**SHORT FILM DEVELOPMENT, PRODUCTION AND DISTRIBUTION** Development and Production fund

**Open to:** Individuals & Organisations | **For:** Short Film | **Award range:** Up to £5000 for individuals and up to £10,000 for organisations. | **Platform:** feature films (drama and documentary), short films, television, animation, interactive media (games, online)

**Further details:** Supported by regional development agency, Yorkshire Forward.

# SOUTH WEST SCREEN

**www.swscreen.co.uk**

*St Bartholomews Court, Lewins Mead, Bristol, BS1 5BT, UK | tel: 0117 952 9977 | fax: 0117 952 9988 | info@swscreen.co.uk*

*Covers Gloucestershire, Wiltshire, Bristol, Somerset, Dorset, Devon, Cornwall*

South West Screen works to develop and sustain all areas of film, television and digital media activity in the South West.

## Strategic priorities

To develop a strong and sustainable infrastructure in the media industry; to develop talent; to increase opportunities for audiences

## Funding

Projects that are funded need to meet the following criteria: cultural quality and industrial benefit offered by the project, including plans for marketing and envisaged regional and wider industry impact; public benefit; meeting regional priorities and fitting with regional and local authority cultural and economic development plans; financial and economic viability of the project and strength of partnership funding, including impact on the organisation/personnel involved and overall value for money; ability of personnel/organisation to manage the project; mix of expertise and strength of delivery partnerships.

REGIONAL DEVELOPMENT South West Screen invites proposals from organisations that fulfil one or more of the following objectives: leadership in developing regional and sub-regional sector partnerships; promotion of the South West's profile as a centre of excellence for film, television and digital content; advocacy for the region at national and international level.

PRODUCTION DEVELOPMENT Supports: script development initiatives run by nationally recognised organisations to be run in the South West; development initiatives which address the creative development of writers and or directors; development initiatives which include both production and distribution elements; innovative ways of developing creative talent

**Open to:** Organisations | **Size of fund:** £20,000 | **Award range:** Between £1,000 and £8,000 | **Deadline:** 12-Jul-05

PRODUCTION Details were not available for the feature film and long length TV production scheme at publication but will be available later in 2005 from the SW Screen website

**Open to:** Organisations | **Deadline:** Dec-05

AUDIENCE DEVELOPMENT Considers applications from organisations such as cinemas, arts centres, touring and mobile schemes, village hall operators - to support developing elements of their programmes.

**Open to:** Organisations | Size of fund: £28,000 | **Award range:** Between £1,000 and £5,000

AUDIENCE DEVELOPMENT Supports projects which bring the moving image to new audiences such as schools, community groups or mentoring programmes.

**Open to:** Organisations | Size of fund: £10,000 | **Award range:** £500 to £2,000 | **Deadline:** 12-Jul-05

**FESTIVALS** Supports strategic film festivals: film festivals based in the South West which have a national and/or international impact; embryonic and emergent film festivals: festivals which have strong audience development potential which are in the early stages of development.

**Open to:** Organisations | **Size of fund:** £54,000 | **Award range:** Between £2,000 and £5,000 for the emergent strand and between £8,000 and £15,000 for the strategic strand | **Deadline:** 12-Jul-05

**DIGITAL SHORTS** Training, development and production for short films.

**Open to:** Individuals | **Format:** DV

# UK-wide funds

## AWARDS FOR ALL

**www.awardsforall.org.uk**

*Ground Floor, St Nicholas Court, 25-27 Castle Gate, Nottingham, NG1 7AR, UK | tel: 011 5934 9350 | fax: 011 5934 9355, enquiries.england@awardsforall.org.uk*

Awards for All is a National Lottery grants scheme from the Heritage Lottery Fund for local community projects which fulfil three aims: to extend access and participation; to increase skill and creativity; to improve quality of life.

### Funding

The scheme can fund projects that enable people to take part in art, sport, heritage and community activities, as well as projects promoting education, the environment and health in the local community.

AWARDS FOR ALL ENGLAND, NORTHERN IRELAND, SCOTLAND & WALES
This scheme funds a wide range of projects based in the arts, sport, heritage, education, environment and health which involve and benefit the local community.

**For:** Community projects | **Award range:** Between £500 and £5000 | **Number of awards:** Unlimited | **Deadline:** Rolling scheme (no deadline)

**Further details:** Applicant organisations must be not-for-profit.

## BIG LOTTERY FUND

**www.biglotteryfund.org.uk**

*1 Plough Place, London, EC4A 1DE, UK | tel: 020 7211 1800 | fax: 020 7211 1750 | enquirie@biglotteryfund.org.uk*

The Big Lottery Fund was set up by the Department of Culture, Media & Sport in June 2004 to absorb two lottery funds into one entity: the New Opportunities Fund, and the Community Fund.

## Funding

Funding from this body is concerned with aiding local communities, particularly those which face hardship and disadvantage. This is delivered through two main funds: the Young People's Fund and the Community Fund.

**YOUNG PEOPLE'S FUND - GRANTS TO INDIVIDUALS** Young people with an idea for a project that can make a difference in their community are encouraged to apply for this award.

**For:** Community Projects | **Award range:** Between £250 and £5000

**Further details:** This award is designed for 11 - 25 year olds applying individually or in small groups.

**YOUNG PEOPLE'S FUND - GRANTS TO NATIONAL ORGANISATIONS** This fund aims to support large-scale, nationwide programmes and initiatives that will work with young people in a way that will impact positively on their communities, lives and futures.

**For:** Community projects | **Award range:** Around £1m over a three year period.

**Further details:** Groups and organisations that work with 11-25 year olds. Priority themes for this award are: being healthy, staying safe, enjoying and achieving, making a positive contribution, and economic well being. Applications should aim to cover one or more of these themes. Those which deal with being healthy and staying safe are particularly encouraged.

**YOUNG PEOPLE'S FUND - GRANTS TO ORGANISATIONS** Awards are designed to go to projects which help disadvantaged young people, to bring them together and involve them in activities.

**For:** Community projects | **Award range:** Between £5000 and £150,000 over a three year period

**Further details:** Voluntary and community groups working with 11-25 year olds are eligible to apply for this award. Priority themes for this award are: being healthy, staying safe, enjoying and achieving, making a positive contribution, and economic well being. Applications should aim to cover two or more of these themes.

# FIRST FILM FOUNDATION

**www.firstfilm.co.uk**

*9 Bourlet Close, London, W1P 7PJ, UK | tel: 020 7580 2111 | info@firstfilm.co.uk*

The First Film Foundation was established in 1987 to springboard filmmakers, new writers, producers and directors to make their first feature film. It aims to provide new filmmakers with high quality development support; a link to the established film industry; impartial, practical advice and information on how to develop a career in the film industry.

## Funding

The First Film Foundation offers mainly 'in kind' support through workshops, professional coaching, events, showcasing and screenings to promote and encourage new talent.

**FIRST DEVELOPMENT** Feature script development over 6 months with workshops run by industry professionals.

**For:** Script Development | **Award range:** In kind | **Number of awards:** 9 | **Deadline:** Annual

**Further details:** This is delivered with funding from The Jerwood Charitable Trust.

**JERWOOD SHORTS PROGRAMME** Short script development over 4 months with workshops run by industry professionals

**For:** Short Film | **Award range:** In kind | **Deadline:** Annual

**Further details:** This is delivered with funding from The Jerwood Charitable Trust.

# FIRST LIGHT

**www.firstlightmovies.com**

*Progress Works, Heath Mill Lane, Birmingham, B9 4AL, UK | tel: 012 1693 2091 | fax: 012 1693 2096 | info@firstlightmovies.com*

First Light receives funding from the UK Film Council to support short filmmaking by young people. Funding and resources are offered to organisations across the country who work with people between the age of 5 and 18, and who would like to make short films with them.

## Funding

Funding falls into two schemes. The Pilot Award is designed for groups which are used to working with young people but who are first time filmmakers. The Studio Award is for groups who are familiar with working with young people and with filmmaking.

**PILOT AWARD** The Pilot Award supports organisations that allow the production of one short film of no more than 5 minutes long by young people.

**For:** Short Film | **Award range:** Up to 80% of project costs with a ceiling of £4000 | **Genre:** Any genre | **Deadline:** 26 April 2005, 27 September 2005, 24 January 2006

**Further details:** This award is aimed towards groups who are new to filmmaking but experienced at working with young people between the ages of 5 and 18. All funded projects must involve young people in key roles of the project ensuring it is authored filmed and produced by young people.

Films must be no more than 5 minutes long.

**STUDIO AWARD** The Studio Award supports organisations that allow the production of 2-4 short films of no more than 10 minutes long by young people.

**For:** Short Film | **Award range:** Up to 60% of project costs with a ceiling of £20,000 | **Genre:** Any genre | **Deadline:** 26 April 2005, 27 September 2005, 24 January 2006

**Further details:** This award is aimed towards groups who have experience of making films in collaboration with young people between the ages of 5 and 18. All funded projects must involve young people in key roles of the project ensuring it is authored filmed and produced by young people.

Films must be no more than 10 minutes long.

# HERITAGE LOTTERY FUND

**www.hlf.org.uk**

*7 Holbein Place, London, SW1W 8NR, UK | tel: 020 7591 6000 | fax: 020 7591 6001 | enquire@hlf.org.uk*

The Heritage Lottery Fund is a public body, assigned by the Department of Culture, Media & Sport to distribute lottery money to local, regional and national heritage projects and schemes. It offers a range of grant-giving programmes, and has been active since 1995.

## Funding

The fund administers various grants aimed at supporting local heritage. Those schemes that might be of interest to readers of this Handbook are: Your Heritage, Heritage Grants, and Young Roots. The Heritage Lottery Fund offers a range of grant-giving programmes.

**HERITAGE GRANTS** To qualify for a grant, projects should conserve and enhance the UK's diverse heritage or encourage communities to identify, look after and celebrate their heritage, or both. Project should also ensure that everyone can learn about, have access to, and enjoy their heritage.

**For:** Heritage | **Award range:** £50,000 or more

**Further details:** You can apply for a grant if your project is concerned with heritage and you are a not-for-project organisation.

**YOUNG ROOTS** This scheme is designed for organisations that work with people aged between 13 and 20 (up to 25 for those with special needs) to help promote the involvement of young people with the heritage of the UK.

**For:** Heritage | **Award range:** Between £5000 and £25,000

**Further details:** The project must increase opportunities for young people to learn about heritage.

**YOUR HERITAGE** To qualify for a grant, projects should conserve and enhance the UK's diverse heritage or encourage communities to identify, look after and celebrate their heritage, or both. Projects should also ensure that everyone can learn about, have access to, and enjoy their heritage.

**For:** Heritage | **Award range:** Between £5000 and £50,000

**Further details:** Can support activities that will increase people's understanding and enjoyment of their heritage or to help people to experience it.

# THE JERWOOD CHARITABLE TRUST

**www.jerwood.org.uk**

*22 Fitzroy Square, London, W1T 6EN, UK | tel: 020 73886287 | info@jerwood.org*

The Jerwood Charity was established by the Jerwood Foundation in 1999. It changed its name in 2004 to distinguish its activities from the Jerwood Foundation more clearly. In 1999 the Jerwood Charity took over the administration of a number of initiatives of the Jerwood Foundation, including the Jerwood Painting Prize, Jerwood Applied Arts Prize and Jerwood

Choreography Award. It currently receives an annual grant from the Foundation, and in 2003 the Jerwood Foundation made a capital endowment to the Charity in the first step towards independence.

The Jerwood Charity continues to develop projects and make grants within the terms of its Funding Guidelines, continuing the vision of its founding Chairman, Alan Grieve.

## Funding

Arts funding from the charity tends to go towards projects that support production, education and career development for practitioners, rather than directly supporting production. Schemes currently funded by the Jerwood Charitable Trust include two script development schemes run by First Light (First Development and Jerwood Shorts Programme) and the First Cuts Documentary Award run by the Sheffield International Documentary Festival. Jerwood will offer seed funding for the early stages of a project or initiative.

**JERWOOD CHARITABLE TRUST FUND** The charity will fund arts initiatives that support and educate practioners in their field.

**Open to:** Organisations | **For:** Arts | **Award range:** for the lower range up to £10,000 and more substantial grants in excess of £10,000 and up to £50,000 | **Deadline:** Rolling scheme (no deadline).

**Further details:** Applications should be by letter, outlining the aims and objectives of the organisation, and the aims and objectives of the specific project or scheme for which assistance is sought.

# NESTA

**www.nesta.org.uk**

*Fishmongers' Chambers, 110 Upper Thames Street, London, EC4R 3TW, UK | tel: 020 7645 9500 | nesta@nesta.org.uk*

NESTA is the National Endowment for Science, Technology and the Arts. It was set up by an Act of Parliament in 1998 to invest in individuals and projects that suggest innovation, creativity, dynamism and longevity. At the time of going to press, it had made 675 awards. Its purpose is to invest in ideas before they are fully developed and researched, so they can reach the point at which other investors may come on board.

## Funding

NESTA offers 6 programmes of investment, which cover: Invention & Innovation, Learning, Fellowship, Creative Piooneer, Ignite!, and NESTA Futurelab, in addition to various other partnerships and schemes. One of these other schemes is Pocket Shorts, delivered through Short Circuit (see competitions in this chapter).

**CREATIVE PIONEER PROGRAMME** This scheme offers career and business support for graduates in the creative industries. Successful applicants follow training at the NESTA Academy to develop their business ideas with the chance of winning a cash award at the end of their training to business cover start-up costs.

**For:** Career Development | **Award range:** Up to £35,000 | **Deadline:** 6 September 2005

**DREAM TIME FELLOWSHIP** These are tailor-made awards for talented individuals, which allow them the opportunity to focus on their work and research. Support can cover training, research, travel, facilities and displaying work. Applications for 2005 were closed at time of publication with new awards to be launched in 2006

**For:** Career Development | **Award range:** Up to £75,000

**INVENTION & INNOVATION** This scheme invests in ideas that can be turned into cutting edge products, services and techniques, with an identifiable commercial outlet. Successful applicants will receive mentoring and business development support and guidance alongside the funding.

**For:** Development | **Award range:** Between £30,000 and £85,000

# THE PRINCE'S TRUST

**www.princes-trust.co.uk**

*18 Park Square East, London, NW1 4LH, UK | tel: 020 7543 1234 | fax: 020 7543 1200 | webinfops@princes-trust.org.uk*

The Prince's Trust offers a range of activities, schemes and grants that encourage young people who have undergone hardship in one way or another and are particularly in need of support.

## Funding

Funding from the Prince's Trust can support individuals to meet training and education costs through the Grants for Education, Training Or Work, and groups of young people to support their communities through the Group Awards

**DEVELOPMENT AWARDS** Grants under this scheme will fund training, education and the costs of finding employment.

**For:** Grants for Education, Training or Work | **Range of award:** £50-£500

**Further details:** Applicants must be aged between 14 and 25.

**GROUP AWARDS** Funding under this stream is awarded to projects by young people aimed at supporting young people within their community.

**Further details:** Applicants must be groups of between 3 and 12 people between 14 and 25. Not all the regions offer these awards.

**BUSINESS START-UP AWARDS** Funding under this stream is awarded to projects for unemployed people between 18 and 30 looking to raise cash to start a business with a low interest loan and in some instances a grant.

**For:** Grants for Education, Training or Work | **Range of award:** a loan of up to £4,000 for a sole trader or up to £5,000 for a partnership. A grant of up to £1,500 is sometimes available and a further £250 for test marketing.

**Further details:** Also includes ongoing business support and specialist advice. Applicants need to be working less than 16 hours a week.

# SKILLSET

**www.skillset.org**

*Prospect House, 80-110 New Oxford Street, London, WC1A 1HB, UK | tel: 020 7520 5757 | fax: 020 7520 5758 | info@skillset.org*

Skillset is the Sector Skills Council for the Audiovisual Industries. Its role is to research and fill skills gaps to ensure the sustainability of the UK screen industries.

## Funding

Various funding initiatives are on offer from Skillset. These include the Freelance Training Fund and the Film Skills Fund - both of which support training providers and encourage them to deliver training in key priority areas - and the Film Futures, Grants for Individuals, which offer training bursaries to professionals.

**SKILLSET FILM FUTURES - GRANTS FOR INDIVIDUALS** Skillset offers bursaries to individuals in the film industry to cover the costs of training courses within the priority areas of business skills, impact, and use of new technologies.

**For:** Training | **Award range:** Freelancers can apply for up to 80% of course fees, accommodation and travelling costs with a ceiling of £800. Employees can apply for up to 50% of course fees, accommodation and travel costs with a ceiling of £500.

**Further details:** Professionals with a minimum of 2 years experience are eligible to apply.

**SKILLSET FILM SKILLS FUND - GRANTS FOR ORGANISATIONS** Funding for organisations to develop, deliver or facilitate film specific training within priority areas agreed by industry. See Programme Areas on Skillset's website.

**For:** Training | **Award range:** No minimum or maximum grant size. All projects must have partnership funding. Percentage varies for different programmes.

**SKILLSET FREELANCE TRAINING FUND** Organisations are encouraged with this fund to offer vocational training for freelancers within the priority areas of animation, construction, and production including technical and craft grades.

**For:** Training | **Award range:** Normally between 60-80% of costs. | **Number of awards:** Four per year

# UNLTD

**www.unltd.org.uk**

*123 Whitecross Street, London, EC1Y 8JJ, UK | tel: 020 7566 1100 | fax: 020 7566 1101 | info@unltd.org.uk*

UnLtd was formed in 2000 as the foundation for Social Entrepreneurs. It took over the management of the Millennium Awards from the Millennium Commision in 2002 with an endowment of £100m of lottery money.

UnLtd's Millennium Awards provide practical and financial support to social entrepreneurs in the UK – people who have both the ideas and the commitment to develop projects which will benefit their community.

## Funding

The Millennium Awards are designed for projects which benefit the community and educate the person or group carrying out the project. They are delivered at two levels: under £5000 and over £5000.

**MILLENNIUM AWARDS** Potential applicants in the Greater London area will need to attend a surgery before submitting an application form.

**Open to:** Individuals | **For:** Community | **Award range:** Level 1: between £500 and £5000. Level 2: between £5000 and £15,000. | **Number of awards:** Approx 1000 per year | **Recent investments:** rolling scheme (no deadline)

# THE WELLCOME TRUST

**www.wellcome.ac.uk**

*The Wellcome Building, 183 Euston Road, London, NW1 2BE, UK | tel: 020 7611 8888 | contact@wellcome.ac.uk*

*Covers UK*

The Wellcome Trust is an independent charity set up by Sir Henry Wellcome in 1936. It has an endowment of about £10m to fund biomedical research aimed at improving human and animal health.

## Funding

**SCIART PRODUCTION AWARDS** The Sciart project is aimed at supporting innovative projects which explore new modes of enquiry and stimulate thinking and debate between arts and science. This fund is targeted at projects which encourage public engagement with science. Funding can cover major activities run by arts, science and broadcast organisations, such as exhibitions, film, programmes, arts projects and so on.

**For:** Science | **Award range:** Above £50,000

**Further details:** Individuals can apply so long as they are attached to a recognised organisation.

**SCIART RESEARCH & DEVELOPMENT AWARDS** The Sciart project is aimed at supporting innovative projects at the cross between arts and science. This fund supports ideas and initiatives at their early stages. Funding can cover research, small-scale productions, performances, broadcast proposals or digital media.

**For:** Science | **Award range:** Up to £15,000

**Further details:** Arts and science practitioners, mediators, academics and health professionals are expected to apply for this fund.

# UK Regional Funds

## ALT-W

**www.alt-w.com**

*Leisure and Arts Department, Floor 13, Tayside House, Dundee, DD1 3RA, UK | tel: 013 8243 3042 | info@alt-w.com*

*Covers Scotland*

This award supports the production of digital, experimental and interactive productions intended for delivery via the web. Scottish Screen, Dundee Council, Scottish Enterprise, Dundee College, University of Abertay, and the School of Television and Imaging at the University of Dundee support the scheme.

### Funding

Up to ten people will be awarded up to £2,500 each as a contribution to production costs. They will also have the opportunity to receive training and mentoring to enable them to make the most of their idea.

**ALT-W** Production of digital experimental and interactive productions to be delivered through the web.

**Open to:** Individuals & Organisations | **For:** Short Film | **Award range:** Up to £2500 | **Number of awards:** 10 | **Format:** DV | **Platform:** Interactive | **Genre:** Experimental | **Deadline:** Annually in December

**Further details:** Supported projects will also receive training and mentoring.

## ARTS COUNCIL OF ENGLAND

**www.artscouncil.org.uk**

*14 Great Peter Street, London, SW1P 3NQ, UK | tel: 020 7333 0100 | fax: 020 7973 6590 | enquiries@artscouncil.org.uk*

*Covers England*

The Arts Council is the national development agency for the Arts in England and is responsible for distributing lottery money to the Arts. Alongside making funding available, the Arts Council carries out research that will assist the ongoing development of Arts practice and cultural life in England.

### Strategic priorities

To support the artist; to enable organisations to thrive, not just survive; to champion cultural diversity; to offer opportunities for young people; to encourage growth; and to live up to the Arts Council's values.

## Funding

Funding from the Arts Council is aimed towards all the arts, including the moving image. However, film finance is not available from the Arts Council. The main Arts Council fund is the Grants for the Arts scheme. This falls into three categories: Individuals, Organisations and National Touring; Stabilisation & Recovery; and Capital. There are also other schemes such as Arts & Science Research Fellowships, Capture 4 (which combines dance with the moving image), and Fellowships in Impact Evaluation. Funding is available through the Regional Arts Boards.

Applications involving the moving image must be works of art, rather than the kind of screen and broadcast productions that would be funded by a Screen Agency.

ARTS & SCIENCE RESEARCH FELLOWSHIPS This award is delivered in conjunction with the Arts & Humanities Research Board and the Scottish Arts Council. The scheme is aimed at individuals allowing them to undertake collaborative cross-platform research across at academic institutions. Each fellowship lasts for 6-8 months.

**Further details:** Applicants should hold a postgraduate qualification relevant to the application.

CAPTURE 4 Capture funds production of work combining dance with film, video, new media and installation.

**Award range:** Between £5,000 and £20,000 | **Number of awards:** 9

FELLOWSHIPS IN IMPACT EVALUATION This award is delivered in partnership with the Arts & Humanities Research Board. Fellowships should be carried out at a higher education institution with the aim of developing the concept, research and practice of impact evaluation within the arts.

**Award range:** Between £40,000-£45,000 | **Number of awards:** 3 per year over three years | **Deadline:** Annually in February

**Further details:** Applicants should hold a postgraduate qualification relevant to the application.

GRANTS FOR THE ARTS - CAPITAL Capital funding covers the cost of new buildings, improvements on existing buildings, new technology, staff training, acquiring of skills, and company restructuring for arts based organisations.

GRANTS FOR THE ARTS - INDIVIDUALS, ORGANISATIONS AND NATIONAL TOURING This fund supports arts-based activities, organisations and practitioners in England.

GRANTS FOR THE ARTS - STABILISATION AND RECOVERY This scheme is designed to support arts organisations with development of their project to allow longevity and sustainability.

**Further details:** Organisations whose turnover exceeds £250,000 per year or whose audience numbers are over 25,000 per year are eligible for this scheme.

# ARTS COUNCIL OF NORTHERN IRELAND

**www.artscouncil-ni.org**

*MacNiece House, 77 Malone Road, Belfast, BT9 6AQ, UK | tel: 028 9038 5200 | fax: 028 9066 1715 | reception@artscouncil-ni.org*

*Covers Northern Ireland*

The Arts Council of Northern Ireland will support film and video artists in their development and to produce artwork for gallery installation. Production companies and filmmakers seeking to produce and distribute film projects are not eligible for funding.

## Funding

The General Art Awards Scheme and the Major Individual Award Scheme can be accessed by individual filmmakers from the area for video art, though production companies and filmmakers seeking to produce and distribute film projects would not be eligible for funding.

**GENERAL ART AWARDS SCHEME** This award is for artists resident in Northern Ireland seeking support for specific projects, specialised research, artistic development and payment for professional services, materials and equipment. The emphasis is on challenge and innovation, particularly with new technology.

**Open to:** Individuals | **For:** Arts | **Award range:** Awards of up to £5,000 in total inclusive of any materials/equipment/professional services are offered in this scheme. | **Genre:** Crafts, Dance, Drama, Literature, Music, Visual Arts | **Deadline:** Two annual deadlines in March and September

**Further details:** Individuals working in any art form or discipline, resident in Northern Ireland for at least one year, and with an artistic track record in Northern Ireland. Exceptions may be made for Northern Irish applicants living elsewhere. Projects that involve collaborations of cross-disciplines are also eligible. Production companies and filmmakers seeking to produce and distribute film projects are not eligible for funding.

Collaborative applications from individual artists working together in cross-discipline projects/activities are encouraged. One application form should be used for the complete collaborative project. Collaborative projects are not eligible for more than the standard £5,000 limit.

Full details can be found at www.artscouncil-ni.org/award/siap_general_arts.htm

**MAJOR INDIVIDUAL AWARD SCHEME** This fund supports established artists of any discipline in Northern Ireland to enable them to work on extended or ambitious work.

Three major awards are offered to create the circumstances in which established artists can develop individually with a view to attempting extended or ambitious work. One of these awards each year will be discipline-specific. In 2005/06 the discipline will be Poetry.

**Open to:** Individuals | **For:** Arts | **Award range:** Up to £15,000 | **Number of awards:** 3 | **Genre:** Crafts, Dance, Drama, Literature, Music, Visual Arts | **Deadline:** Annually in June

**Further details:** Established artists working in any art form or discipline resident in Northern Ireland for at least one year, and with an artistic track record in Northern Ireland. Exceptions may be made for Northern Irish applicants living elsewhere.

Production companies and filmmakers seeking to produce and distribute film projects are not eligible for funding.

The following criteria should be proven: evidence of the artist's achievement in terms of the artistic quality, innovation, challenging nature and extent of the artist's work; evidence of the artist's contribution to the arts in Northern Ireland; evidence of the artist's continuing professional practice.

Full details can be found at www.artscouncil-ni.org/award/siap_major_individual.htm

# ARTS COUNCIL OF WALES

**www.artswales.org.uk**

*9 Museum Place, Cardiff, Wales, CF10 3NX, UK | tel: 029 2037 6500 | fax: 029 2022 1447 | info@artswales.org.uk*

*Covers Wales*

The Arts Council of Wales is responsible for the development and funding of the arts in Wales. It distributes the National Assembly for Wales funding to the arts, and is also the distributor of National Lottery funding to the arts in Wales.

## Funding

Several funds from the arts Council of Wales can be accessed by filmmakers (not production companies). These include Professional Development; Creative Wales Awards; Capacity Building and Development; and the Individual Screenwriters Awards.

CAPACITY BUILDING AND DEVELOPMENT FUND This award supports the development of artists and arts organisations to encourage growth and sustainability. The awards are intended to be able to meet individual applicants' needs, including grants for start-up organisations and company development, support for arts bodies and forums, research grants, improving professional standards and practice, encouraging community development, and support for sector representatives. Funding will cover operational, development, research and travel costs for individual projects within a time limit.

**Open to:** Individuals & Organisations | **For:** Business Development | **Award range:** Individuals can apply for between £25 and £5,000. Organisations can apply for between £250 and £50,000 | **Genre:** Crafts, Dance, Drama, Literature, Music, Visual Arts | **Deadline:** Applications under £5000 can be made at any time. Applications over £5000 have two deadlines per year in May and December

**Further details:** Individuals and organisations based in Wales.

PROFESSIONAL DEVELOPMENT: CREATIVE WALES AWARDS This fund supports new and established artists working in any discipline by offering bursaries to develop skills and produce new and experimental work without needing to consider audience development concerns. Funding will cover salaries, travel, training, networking, research and other costs relating to the project being undertaken.

**Open to:** Individuals | **For:** Education/Training | **Award range:** Between £500 and £25,000, with an average award of £10,000 | **Genre:** Crafts, Dance, Drama, Literature, Music, Visual Arts, | **Deadline:** Applications under £10,000 have an annual deadline in May. Applications over £10,000 have an annual deadline in November

**Further details:** Individual artists resident in Wales who plan to undertake their project in Wales are eligible to apply. The applicant may collaborate with other artists.

# CINEWORKS

**www.cineworks.co.uk**

*Glasgow Media Access Centre, Third Floor, 34 Albion Street, Glasgow, G11 1LH, UK | tel: 0141 553 2620 | fax: 0141 553 2660, info@cineworks.co.uk*

*Covers Scotland*

Cineworks commissions five short films a year in the genres of drama, documentary and animation by new filmmakers. The scheme was initiated by Glasgow Media Access Centre and Edinburgh Media Base and supported by Scottish Screen, The Film Council's New Cinema Fund and BBC Scotland.

## Funding

Each film is eligible to receive between £10,000 and £15,000 for production, as well as receiving support from industry professionals who will act as mentors throughout development. Producers and Directors are teamed up with projects and selections are made to allow production of five of the ideas. Training may be provided for the applicants before production which is supported by GMAC and Edinburgh Mediabase.

**CINEWORKS COMMISSIONS** Short film production scheme matching producers, writers and directors.

**Open to:** Individuals & Organisations | **For:** Short Film | **Award range:** Between £8,000 and £15,000 | **Number of awards:** 5 | **Format:** Mainly digital | **Platform:** Primarily a festival release | **Genre:** Fiction, documentary, animation | **Deadline:** Annually in Autumn | **Recent investments:** Golden Bear at Berlinale 2005 for Milk by Director Peter Mackie Burns

**Further details:** Applicants must not have a previous broadcast credit.

# CORNWALL FILM

**www.cornwallfilm.com**

*Pydar House, Pydar Street, Truro, Cornwall, TR1 1EA, UK | tel: 018 7232 2886 | fax: 018 7232 2887 | office@cornwallfilm.com*

*Covers Cornwall and the Isles of Scilly*

Cornwall Film - developing Cornwall's media industry. We offer a Production Fund, Development Fund, and Company and Individual Development Fund.

## Strategic priorities

To work towards the development of a sustainable media industry in Cornwall via product development, sector development and inward investment.

## Funding

Production Fund, Development Fund, Company and Individual Development Fund. Cornwall Film is supported by the European Union, and a partnership of South West Screen, Cornwall County Council and Penwith District Council.

**PRODUCTION FUND** A production fund for projects that invest in Cornwall and the Isles of Scilly, using Cornish crew and facilities

**Open to:** Organisations | **For:** Production investment

**DEVELOPMENT FUND** Investment in the development stages of projects, products and joint ventures in new media, television and film for companies based in Cornwall and the Isles of Scilly

**Open to:** Organisations | **For:** Investment fund for film TV and new media project and product development

**COMPANY AND INDIVIDUAL DEVELOPMENT FUND** Specialist mentoring and investment for company and individual growth and to help media businesses in Cornwall and the Isles of Scilly to reach new markets

**Open to:** Individuals & Organisations | **For:** Development support for film TV and new media practitioners and companies

# LONDON BOROUGH OF CROYDON

**www.croydon.gov.uk/clocktower**

*Croydon Media Awards, Croydon Clocktower, Katharine Street, Croydon, CR9 1ET, UK | tel: 020 8686 4433 | fax: 020 8253 1032*

*Covers London - Croydon*

## Funding

This award supports up to 8 short films of dramatic, documentary or an experimental nature, of no more than 8 minutes long. Applications may be made by directors or director-producer teams resident within a seven mile radius of the Croydon Clocktower. Successful applicants will also be given the use of MiniDV camera kits and postproduction facilities, along with consultancy sessions from a professional producer and script advisor.

**ARTS PROJECT GRANT** For community arts projects which benefit Croydon residents

**Open to:** Organisations, collectives or individuals collaborating | **For:** Community/participatory arts projects | **Award range:** Scheme 1 - up to £1000 Scheme 2 - up to £3000 | **Deadline:** Annually in February

# LONDON BOROUGH OF ENFIELD FILM FUND

**www.enfield.gov.uk**

*London Borough of Enfield, Arts Unit, Forty Hall, Forty Hill, Enfield, EN2 9HA, UK | tel: 020 8363 8196 | fax: 020 8367 9098 | forty.hall@enfield.gov.uk*

*Covers London - Enfield*

The Enfield Film Fund is run by Enfield Council and Film London

### LONDON BOROUGH OF ENFIELD PRODUCTION FUND

**Award range:** Grants usually range from £1,000 to £5,000 | **Deadline:** Normally open for applications in March with a deadline in April.

**Further details:** Applicants must live, work (and in some areas study) in the borough.

# FOUR MINUTE WONDERS (SCOTLAND)

**www.4minutewonders.com**

*Studio 120, 96 Rose Street, Edinburgh, Scotland, EH2 4AT, UK*

*Covers Scotland*

# FOUR MINUTE WONDERS (WALES)

*Greenmeadow Springs, Tongwynlais, Cardiff, Wales, CF15 7NE, UK | tel: 029 2069 4900 | fax: 029 2069 4999*

*Covers Wales*

4 Minute Wonders was created to enable filmmakers to take the first stop in feature film production by making high quality music videos. This can then be used as part of a showreel, a calling card, a piece of work for festivals and also as an important curve for managing people and budgets and taking a production from concept right through to distribution.

## Funding

There is up to £5,000 available to produce each music video in one month, with access to production facilities and support as part of the budget. The track to be used is available for download via the website. The video will be streamed through the web site for feedback from visitors to the site. At the end of the year, all the videos will be screened and judged at a presentation evening for industry professionals. The winner will be awarded a prize.

**4 MINUTE WONDERS** Music video production for new music tracks featured on the web site

**Open to:** Individuals | **For:** Short Film | **Award range:** Up to £5000 | **Number of awards:** 1 | **Genre:** Music videos | **Deadline:** monthly

**Further details:** Details for 2005 were not released at time of publication.

# GLASGOW FILM OFFICE

**www.glasgowfilm.org.uk**
*City Chambers, Glasgow, G2 1DU, UK | tel: 014 1287 0424 | fax: 014 1287 0311 | film.office @drs.glasgow.gov.uk*

*Covers Glasgow*

Since 1997 Glasgow Film Office has supported in excess of 40 high value productions spending over £36m. The aim now is to build on that success by supporting both local companies and mobile high value television and film producers. Grants will now focus on expanding the City's production capacity, boosting the creative content capacity of identified local growth companies, and enhancing their location liaison service.

## Strategic priorities

With production companies, the intention is to move high-impact productions and, for TV, high value content into production. High-impact productions are those having a budget in excess of £200k or directly contributing in excess of £100k into the local economy - these could be feature films, feature documentaries, commercials etc. High value TV content is that having a commissioned value of at least £50k. GFO does not offer production funding for feature length drama. Additionally, all grants offered by GFO will require the beneficiaries to raise at least 50% of the cost from their own resources or by introducing private sector funds (GFO cannot 'double-fund' alongside other public agencies). The grants are drawn from a limited financial resource, therefore not all applications will be successful.

## Funding

GFO offers various awards and support, all designed to bring new talent together with established companies.

TECHNICAL SKILLS DEVELOPMENT This small fund is intended to support a diverse range of activities, e.g. approved courses/seminars, designed to improve the knowledge and skills base of freelance personnel working in the industry.

**Award range:** Normal grant will be 50% of cost of course (this does not cover travel and accommodation) up to £1,000, to be paid in arrears on production of receipts.

**Further details:** Experienced freelance personnel wishing to develop their industry skills.

INFRASTRUCTURE SUPPORT GRANTS These grants are offered to mobile productions as a cash incentive to buy in approved local facilities and services rather than import these facilities and services from outside.

**Award range:** 50% of actual approved facilities and services costs up to £50,000.

**Further details:** High-impact productions considering locating in Glasgow.

PRODUCT COMMERCIALISM Applicants should be growth companies working to a business plan.

**Open to:** Organisations | **For:** Business Development | **Award range:** Much of the assistance offered in this scheme will be in the form of advice and guidance. Additional assistance may take the form of access to specialist advisers in, for example, intellectual property. Direct grants under this measure will depend on proposed activity and presentation of detailed budget.

**NEW WRITER INTEGRATION** GFO will share the risk of working with unproven writing talent by contributing to the initial development costs of selected projects presented by local independent production companies committed to innovation in high value content creation. The aim is to nudge established companies to look beyond tried and tested writers and for GFO to share the gamble in developing fresh ideas.

**Open to:** Organisations | **For:** Script Development | **Award range:** Grant Levels of £5,000, £3,000 and £1,000 can be awarded, depending on the unit value of the commissioned product (minimum of £50k per hour).

**Further details:** Applications should be made by production companies intending to work with new writing talent.

**GROWING THE SERVICE BASE** This programme aims to help facilities and services companies penetrate the market generated by international film production, network TV commissions and new platforms for digital output.

**Open to:** Organisations | **Award range:** The majority of the support in this scheme is earmarked for specialist consultancy services, with the remainder offered in support for the pursuance of new market opportunities. The maximum level of support to one company will be £10k for staged development of the company's business plan.

**Further details:** Applicants should be local facilities and service companies.

## GREENWICH FILM FUND

**www.greenwichfilms.co.uk**

*Studio 2B1, The Old Seager Distillery, Brookmill R, Greenwich, London, SE8 4JT, UK | tel: 020 8694 2211 | fax: 020 8694 2971 | fund@greenwichfilms.demon.co.uk*

*Covers London - Greenwich*

Greenwich Film Fund is co-ordinated by Greenwich Films in partnership with Film London and is normally open for applications in October with a deadline in December.

### GREENWICH FILM FUND

**Award range:** Grants usually range from £1,000 to £5,000

**Further details:** Applicants must live, work (and in some areas study) in the borough.

## ISLE OF MAN FILM COMMISSION

**www.filmmann.com**

*Hamilton House, Peel Road, Douglas, Isle of Man, IM1 5EP, UK | tel: 016 2468 7173 | fax: 016 2468 7171 | iofilm@dti.gov.im*

*Covers Isle of Man*

The Isle of Man Film and Television Fund offers equity investment for films and television productions that are shot at least in part on the island.

## Funding

The Isle of Man is self-governing with its own laws. The government has made available equity funding for films shot on the island, to encourage film production and to boost the local economy.

**ISLE OF MAN FILM & TV FUND** Investment to attract film production to the island

**Open to:** Organisations | **For:** Film Fund | **Award range:** Up to 25% of budgets with no upper or lower limits | **Genre:** Any genre | **Deadline:** Applications may be made at any time.

**Further details:** All productions must be for theatrical release or broadcast with at least 50% of principal photography taking place on the island and at least 20% of below-the-line costs spent on local services. Applicants must also have a sales agent or distributor on board.

# LONDON BOROUGH OF NEWHAM FILM FUND

**www.newham.gov.uk/filmfund**

*London Borough of Newham, Regeneration & Partnerships Division, 330 Barking Road, East Ham, London, E6 2RP, UK | tel: 020 8430 2793 | Carole.Thomas@newham.gov.uk*

*Covers London - Newham*

The Newham Film Fund is run by Newham council and Film London for the production of a 10 minute film, animation or 25-minute documentary.

### LONDON BOROUGH OF NEWHAM PRODUCTION FUND

**Award range:** Grants usually range from £1,000 to £5,000 | **Deadline:** Normally open February with deadline in April.

# SCOTTISH ARTS COUNCIL

**www.scottisharts.org.uk**

*12 Manor Place, Edinburgh, EH3 7DD, UK | tel: 013 1226 6051 | fax: 013 1225 9833 | help.desk@scottisharts.org.uk*

*Covers Scotland*

The Scottish Arts Council distributes lottery funding across the Arts through streams covering Crafts, Dance, Drama, Literature, Music, Visual Arts, and Capital funds. Within each stream the two priorities are for individual artists and non profit-making arts organisations. Film and video artists are eligible to apply for the Individual Awards under the Visual Arts stream, which supports Creative and Professional Development project funding and bursaries

## Funding

Filmmakers in Scotland can also access the Creative Development Fund and the Amsterdam Studio Residency offered by the Arts Council.

**ARTIST FILM AND VIDEO** Run in association with Scottish Screen, awards are available to support innovative and experimental work by visual artists using film and video.

**Award range:** £5,000 - £15,000 | **Fund size:** a total budget of £50,000 is available | **Deadline: 10 October 2005**

# THE TOWER HAMLETS AND HACKNEY FILM FUND

*Brady Centre, 192 Hanbury Street, London, E1 5HU, UK | tel: 020 7364 7920 | fax: 020 7364 7901 | filmsoffice@towerhamlets.gov.uk*

*Covers London - Tower Hamlets & Hackney*

The Tower Hamlets and Hackney Film Fund is run by the Tower Hamlets Film Office and is part of the Film London East initiative.

## Funding

Supports a new generation of filmmakers with awards of up to £4,000 to make short dramas, animations or documentaries.

**TOWER HAMLETS & HACKNEY FILM PRODUCTION FUND** Short film production for new and emerging filmmakers

**Open to:** Individuals | **For:** Short Film | **Award range:** Up to £4000 | **Number of awards:** 7 | **Format:** Any Format | **Platform:** Cinema | **Genre:** Any genre | **Deadline:** Please contact the Films Office to find out deadlines.

**Further details:** Filmmakers must live, work or study in Tower Hamlets or Hackney.

# WANDSWORTH FILM FUND

**www.wandsworth.gov.uk/arts**

*London Borough of Wandsworth, Arts Office, Room 224A, The Town Hall, Wandsworth High Street, London, SW18 2PU, UK | tel: 020 8871 8711 | arts@wandsworth.gov.uk*

*Covers London - Wandsworth*

The Wandsworth Film & Video Awards are run by Wandsworth Council and Film London.

**WANDSWORTH FILM & VIDEO AWARDS** Short film production fund.

**Open to:** Individuals & Organisations | **For:** Short Film | **Award range:** Up to £5000 | **Genre:** Any genre | **Deadline:** Annually in September

**Further details:** Open to filmmakers who live, work or study full time in the Borough of Wandsworth.

# WEST LONDON FILM FUND AWARDS (FOCUS WEST)

**www.focuswest.co.uk**

*Business Enterprise Centre, TEK House, 11-13 Uxbridge Road, London, W12 8TB, UK | tel: 020 8746 0355 | fax: 020 8740 0493*

*Covers London - West*

Supporting media businesses in the London Boroughs of Hammersmith and Fulham, Brent and Ealing, in conjunction with Film London and funded by the London Development Agency and BBC.

## Strategic priorities

Focus West's aim is to support the development of Inner West London's existing media cluster, to provide the environment for long term growth of existing media SMEs and of the West London media sector as a whole. Focus West aims to ensure a coherent provision of business support for the sector in West London in line with LDA activity and complementary to the LDA's forthcoming hubs strategy for the creative sector.

## Funding

The main aim of the fund is to encourage sustainable creative filmmaking activity across the boroughs of Ealing, Brent and Hammersmith & Fulham.

**FOCUS WEST** Provides an annual fund of over £15,000 to assist in the production or completion of film projects. The maximum award per company is £3,000. The fund only contributes towards a maximum of 50% of the total cost of the film project, the rest must be matched from any private sector source.

**Open to:** Organisations | **Genre:** The scheme seeks to support a diverse range of films - including documentary, drama and fiction, and projects that cut across these categories. All genres and subject matter are welcomed. | **Deadline:** June, August, October, December.

**Further details:** The selection of awards will be made on the basis of written proposals, a business plan and consideration of applicants' previous creative work. An awards panel made up of experienced business people and industry practitioners shall assess applications to the fund.

The scheme is open to businesses local to Hammersmith & Fulham, Brent and Ealing, and open to all businesses that fulfil these criteria, but is targeted particularly at under-represented groups: businesses managed or owned by women, people from black and minority ethnic groups (BME) and people with disabilities.

# CITY OF WESTMINSTER ARTS COUNCIL

**www.cwac.org.uk**

*Room 70, Marylebone Library, Marylebone Road, London, NW1 5PS, UK | tel: 020 7641 1017 | fax: 020 7641 1018 | paula@cwac.org.uk*

*Covers London - City of Westminster*

The City of Westminster Arts Council is funded by the Westminster City Council and the film award is run in association with Film London.

### FILM, VIDEO AND MOVING IMAGE BURSARY

**For:** Short film | **Award** range: Grants usually range from £1,000 to £5,000 | **Deadline**: applications can be made at any time.

**Further details:** Applicants must live, work (and in some areas study) in the borough. Free editing time is also donated by Paddington Arts, and Westminster Arts Council will organize a screening.

# Competitions

## DEPICT!

**www.depict.org**

*Brief Encounters Short Film Festival, Watershed Media Centre, 1 Canon's Road, Bristol, BS1 5TX, UK | tel: 011 7927 5102 | fax: 011 7930 9967 | lucy.jefferies@brief-encounters.org.uk*

**DEPICT!** Asks new filmmakers to make a micro-movie of under 90 seconds, which can win a cash prize of £3,000, have the film promoted online, published on a DVD and see it screened at Brief Encounters Bristol International Short Film Festival. The winner is picked by a panel of distinguished industry professionals, whose brief is to uncover distinctive voices - originality, style, clarity of idea & impact are key.

## DM DAVIES AWARD

**www.iffw.co.uk**

*Cardiff Screen Festival, 10 Mount Stuart Square, Cardiff, Wales, CF10 5EE, UK | tel: 029 2033 3324 | fax: 029 2033 3320*

*Covers Wales*

In collaboration with the Cardiff Screen Festival, the DM Davies Award is one of the largest short film prizes in Europe, and the competition has high calibre entries every year. All eligible films entered for the award will be screened to the public at the festival. A shortlist of 6 films will be determined by a jury of award sponsors with the winner being selected by an invited jury of film makers, actors and media professionals.

The director must be of Welsh origin, been a resident of Wales for two or more years, or a graduate from a Welsh college or university for the best short film submitted to the competition.

All work must have been completed in the last 2 years, not have been screened publicly (theatrical to a paying audience or tv transmission, but excepting festival screenings) prior to the opening of the festival, and should not have been previously submitted. The duration of the work submitted must be no more than 25 minutes.

The winner of the award will receive a comprehensive package of funding, facilities and assistance to enable the production of a new 10 minute short film to be made in Wales.

## EUROSCRIPT

**www.euroscript.co.uk**

*Suffolk House, 1-8 Whitfield Place, London, W1T 5JU, UK | tel: 020 7387 5880 | info@euroscript.co.uk*

EUROSCRIPT The company supports screenwriters by offering consultancy, development programmes, workshops and promoting scripts. It is run on an international level, funded initially by the Media II European funding programme. Euroscripts also runs a biannual international scriptwriting competition for features, single TV drama and TV series in any genre. The selected scripts go on to benefit from script development to reach first draft stage. There are two deadlines per year.

The competition is open to international applicants but the screenplays must be in English. Adaptations of pre-existing works are accepted as long as an option has been acquired. Selected submissions are short-listed for further development over the following nine months with an experienced script consultant, encouraging each project to reach first draft stage. There is an entry fee of £35. In addition to the application form, applicants must submit an outline of an idea, a CV, and sample pages from a screenplay. Shortlisted writers may be asked to submit a full-length script. Each project developed by Euroscripts must be credited on the first page and on screen if the screenplay is produced. The full copyright will stay with the writer.

## KODAK

**www.kodak.com/UK/en/motion/news/short**

*Kodak House, Station Road, Hemel Hempstead, HP1 1JU, UK | tel: 014 4284 5945 | fax: 014 4284 4458 | daniel.clark1@kodak.com*

*Covers UK*

KODAK SHORT FILM SHOWCASE Kodak invites completed short films to be submitted to the Kodak Short Film Showcase that is held at BAFTA London annually in September. Producers whose films are short-listed will be invited to attend the event and screen their film. Winning producers and directors will be invited to join Kodak on an expenses paid trip to the Dinard British Festival, and the winning short will also be screened at the festival in front of the closing night feature film.

Films must be originated on Kodak film stock, have a running time of 15 minutes or less, have been completed in the last 18 months, and be available to screen on 16mm or 35mm prints.

## NICHOLL FELLOWSHIPS

**www.oscars.org**

*Academy of Motion Picture Arts and Sciences, 1313 North Vine Street, Los Angeles, California, 90028, USA | tel: + 1 310 247 3059 | nicholl@oscars.org*

**NICHOLL FELLOWSHIPS** The Nicholl Fellowships in Screenwriting program is an international competition open to screenwriters who have not earned more than $5,000 writing for film or television. Entry scripts must be the original work of a sole author or of exactly two collaborative authors. Entries must have been written originally in English. Adaptations and translated scripts are not eligible. Up to five $30,000 fellowships are awarded each year.

The screenplays must not be based on pre-existing works. Students may apply, but should they win, the fellowship year will be deferred until their course is finished. There is an entry fee of US$30, which is reduced for early applications. In addition to the application form, applicants must submit a full screenplay. Applications will be accepted by post or courier only. Short listed applicants will be asked to write to the fellowship explaining their interests in receiving the award. The fellowship will give a copy of the screenplays submitted to the Academy during the fellowship year, but the Academy will not hold any rights. The competition awards up to five fellowships a year at $30,000 each and the successful writers must produce a feature screenplay during the following year.

## OSCAR MOORE FOUNDATION

**www.screendaily.com/omf.asp**

*Screen International, 33-39 Bowling Green Lane, London, EC1R 0DA, UK | tel: 020 7505 8080*

**THE OSCAR MOORE FOUNDATION** The Oscar Moore Foundation was established in 1997 as a charitable foundation administered by film trade Screen International, in memory of its former editor-in-chief Oscar Moore (also Guardian columnist and novelist) who died of an AIDS-related illness in 1996.

The aim of the Foundation, whose patron is the Oscar-winning screen-writer Emma Thompson, is to foster new European screen-writing talent by awarding an annual prize of £10,000 to the best first draft screenplay in a specified genre which changes each year. In addition to the £10,000 development funding (co-funded by The Film Council), the winner also receives a place on a residential writers workshop run by Arista, and a professional reading of their script by The Script Factory.

## POCKET SHORTS

**www.pocketshorts.com**

*The Old Caretakers House, Turnbridge Mills Quay Street , Huddersfield, West Yorkshire , HD1 6QT , UK | tel: 014 8430 1805 | info@pocketshorts.co.uk*

Pocket Shorts gives new filmmakers opportunities to experiment with mobile technologies.

**POCKET SHORTS, C/O SHORTCIRCUITS** Supported by Nesta and operated by Shortcircuits, Pocket Shorts ran in November 2004 and is expected to run again in November 2005, although no details were available at time of publication. The scheme offered commissions for 8 films intended for distribution across mobile phones - either a 1 minute short for download from a wap site, or four 15 second shorts that can be downloaded or forwarded as an MMS from one website to another. The commissioned filmmakers received up to £2,000, plus training and support. If the scheme is continued, details should be available from Short Circuits from August 2005 or later.

## SHELL LIVEWIRE

**www.shell-livewire.org**

*Hawthorn House, Forth Banks, Newcastle upon Tyne, NE1 3SG, UK | tel: 019 1261 5584 | fax: 019 1261 1910 | shell-livewire@pne.org*

*Covers UK*

**SHELL LIVE WIRE** The Shell Live Wire scheme began in 1982, to support 16-30 year old residents of the UK to start up and develop businesses. The programme offers factual advice and support programmes, in addition to an annual competition, the Young Entrepreneur of the Year Awards, to reward business start-ups.

The awards, with prizes of £10,000 out of a £200,000 pot, are open to business start-ups run by individuals aged between 16 and 30, who are living and running a company in the UK, and that have been trading between 3 and 18 months. Applicants must register for the awards, after which a local co-ordinator will help the applicant prepare for entry into the awards. Entrants must submit a business plan, as well as an application form, before the end of January each year.

## STRAIGHT 8

**www.straight8.net**

*Godman, 10a Belmont Street, London, W1 8HH, UK | ed.ben@straight8.net*

**STRAIGHT 8** Organised by the production company Godman, this event asks filmmakers to shoot a 3 minute film on one cartridge of Kodak Super 8mm film. The filmmakers must edit in-camera and hand over the unprocessed film, along with an original soundtrack burned onto CD, to the competition organisers who arrange for it to be processed. All the received films are screened in public on the prize-giving night without the filmmakers having seen the results of their work. The audience votes for their favourite film. Several events of this nature are run throughout the year and filmmakers should subscribe online to receive email updates.

## TURNER CLASSIC MOVIES SHORT FILM COMPETITION

**www.tcmonline.co.uk/classicshorts**

*Turner House, 16 Great Marlborough Street, London, W1F 7HS, UK | nick.hart@turner.com*

*Covers UK*

**TURNER CLASSIC MOVIES CLASSIC SHORTS** TCM, together with the Times BFI London Film Festival, provides a showcase for the directors of the future. Classic Shorts was launched in 2000 and has already discovered and encouraged some of the best new talent in the country. The competition has gained in stature and exposure in the five years it has been running. 2005 is expected to attract even more attention than before as TCM celebrates its fifth anniversary broadcasting on cable and satellite in the UK. Judges have included Lord David Puttnam, Sir Alan Parker, Stephen Woolley and Jonny Lee Miller.

The competition is open to British/UK and Republic of Ireland productions only. To qualify films must have substantial British contributions in all areas of production, principal cast and crew. The subject should be fictional although a dramatisation of real events may be accepted at the sole discretion of the judges. Documentary films are not eligible for entry.

Submitted films should preferably be no more than 20 minutes long, must be suitable for screening on UK television, shot on film or a professional video format and must be made in the UK and be in English. Applicants must send in a completed application form with the film on VHS, and be sure that they have a screen quality copy available.

# International funds

## AUSTRALIA - AUSTRALIAN FILM COMMISSION

**www.afc.gov.au**

*Level 4, 150 William Street, Woolloomooloo, NSW 2011, Sydney, Australia | tel: +61 2 9321 6444 | fax: +61 2 9357 3672 | marketing@afc.gov.au*

The Australian Film Commission (AFC) is an Australian Government agency established by the Australian Film Commission Act in 1975. It operates under the Commonwealth Film Program (Department of Communications, Information Technology and the Arts) to ensure the creation, availability and preservation of Australian screen content. The National Film and Sound Archive has been part of the AFC since 1 July 2003.

The goal of the AFC is to enrich Australia's national identity by:

- fostering an internationally competitive audiovisual production industry
- making Australia's audiovisual content and culture available to all
- developing and preserving a national collection of sound and moving image.

The AFC maintains offices in Brisbane, Canberra, Melbourne and Sydney.

## AUSTRALIA - FILM FINANCE CORPORATION AUSTRALIA LTD (FFC)

**www.fff.gov.au**

*130 Elizabeth Street, Level 12, Sydney, NSW 2000, Australia | tel: +61 2 9268 2555 | fax: +61 2 9264 8551 | ffc@ffc.gov.au*

Principal agency of the Australian government for funding the production of films and television programmes. The government supports film and television production to ensure that Australians have the opportunity to make and watch their own screen stories. The FFC will only fund projects with high levels of creative and technical contribution by Australians, or projects certified under Australia's Official Co-Production Program.

Since its establishment, the FFC has invested in 875 projects with a total production value of $1.96 billion.

## AUSTRALIA - FILM VICTORIA

**www.film.vic.gov.au**

*7th Floor, 189 Flinders Lane, Melbourne, Victoria, 3000, Australia | tel: +61 3 9660 3200 | fax: +61 3 9660 3201*

Film Victoria is a cultural organisation that encourages and assists the development, production, exhibition and knowledge of film, television and new media.

Funding is available for a variety of schemes, including development and production of feature films, short films and digital animation.

## AUSTRALIA - SOUTH AUSTRALIAN FILM CORPORATION

**www.safilm.com.au**

*3 Butler Drive, Hendon Common, Hendon, 5014, Australia | tel: +61 8 8348 9300 | fax: +61 8 8347 0385 | safilm@safilm.com.au*

Starting life as a production company in 1972, the SAFC is a statutory body established under the South Australian Film Corporation Act, and has helped to foster an internationally recognised industry that has produced hundreds of feature films, television dramas and documentaries.

## BELGIUM - FLEMISH AUDIOVISUAL FUND

**www.vaf.be**

*Handelskaai 18/3, B-1000 Brussels, Belgium | tel: +32 2 226 06 30 | fax: +32 2 219 19 36 | info@vaf.be*

The Flemish Audiovisual Fund annually receives a E12.5 (approx. £9) million grant from the Flemish government. A minimum of 78% of the annual budget goes to production support. Filmmakers can apply for support to fiction, documentary, animation and experimental media production. VAF makes a distinction between four types of support; scriptwriting support, development support, production support and support towards promotion.

## CANADA - BRITISH COLUMBIA FILM

**www.bcfilm.bc.ca**

*2225 West Broadway, Vancouver, British Columbia, V6K 2E4, Canada | tel: +604 736 7997 | fax: +604 736 7290 | bcf@bcfilm.bc.ca*

Offers development and production financing to British Columbia filmmakers through a variety of funding programs and professional development to producers, writers and directors through marketing and skills assistance programs. It is a private, non-profit society that also administers the provincial tax credit program on behalf of the provincial government.

## CANADA - NATIONAL FILM BOARD OF CANADA

**www.nfb.ca/e**

*Postal Box 6100, Centre-ville Station, Montreal, Quebec, H3C 3H5, Canada | tel: +514 283 9000 | fax: +514 283 7564*

A public agency that produces and distributes films and other audiovisual works which reflect Canada to Canadians and the rest of the world. Since its very beginnings it has played an important role in Canadian and international filmmaking.

## CANADA - NEW BRUNSWICK FILM

**www.nbfilm.com**

*16th Floor, Assumption Place, 770 Main Street, Moncton, New Brunswick, E1C 8R3, Canada | tel: +1 506 869 6868 | fax: +1 506 869 6840*

Film Commission and film development agency for province of New Brunswick, Canada. Provides information and advice on tax credits, finding investors and development loans.

## CANADA - NEWFOUNDLAND & LABRADOR FILM DEVELOPMENT CORPORATION

**www.newfilm.nf.net**

*189 Water Street, 2nd Floor, St John's, Newfoundland, A1C 1B4, Canada | tel: +709 738 3456 | fax: +709 739 1680 | info@newfilm.nf.net*

Aims to foster and promote the development and growth of the film and video industry in Newfoundland and Labrador, and to increase the national and international visibility of Newfoundland and Labrador as a location.

NLFDC also provides production assistance in the form of an Equity Investment Program (EIP) and a Development Program, as well as information and advice on tax credits.

## CANADA - NOVA SCOTIA FILM DEVELOPMENT CORP

**www.film.ns.ca**

*1724 Granville Street, 2nd Floor, Halifax, Nova Scotia, B3J 1X5, Canada | tel: +1 902 424 7177 | fax: +1 902 424 0617 | noviascotia.film@ns.sympatico.ca*

Nova Scotia Film Development Corporation attempts to grow Nova Scotia's film, television and new media industries with partners by stimulating investment and employment and by promoting Nova Scotia's producers, productions, locations, skills and creativity in global markets. Provides information and advice on tax credits, finding investors and development loans.

## CANADA - ONTARIO MEDIA DEVELOPMENT CORP

**www.omdc.on.ca**

*175 Bloor Street East, South Tower, No. 501, Toronto, Ontario, M4W 3R8, Canada | tel: +1 416 314 6858 | fax: +1 416 314 2495*

The OMDC is an agency of the Ontario Government that provides a range of services and programmes to stimulate the growth of Ontario's film, television, book and magazine publishing, sound recording and digital media industries.

OMDC has a series of funding programs available for business development, as well as information and advice on investment and tax credits.

## CANADA - TELEFILM CANADA

**www.telefilm.gc.ca**

*360 rue Saint-Jacques, Suite 700, Montreal, Quebec, H2Y 4AD, Canada | tel: +1 514 283 6363 | fax: +1 514 283 3317 | info@telefilm.gc.ca*

A Federal cultural agency dedicated to the development and promotion of the Canadian film, television, new media and music industries. Telefilm offers a range of film funding schemes, for screenwriting, development, production and marketing, and low budget film assistance.

## DENMARK - DANISH FILM INSTITUTE

**www.dfi.dk**

*Gothersgade 55, Copenhagen, 1123, Denmark | tel: +45 33 74 3400 | fax: +45 33 74 34 35 | dfi@dfi.dk*

The Danish Film Institute is the national agency responsible for supporting and encouraging film and cinema culture, and for conserving these in the national interest. The Institute's operations extend from participation in the development and production of feature films, shorts and documentaries, over distribution and marketing, to managing the national film archive and the cinematheque.

## FRANCE - CENTRE NATIONAL DE LA CINEMATOGRAPHIE (CNC)

**www.cnc.fr**

*12 rue de Lubeck, 75784 Paris, Cedex 16, France | tel: +33 1 44 34 37 80 | fax: +33 1 44 34 36 59*

A government institution, under the auspices of the Ministry of Culture. Its areas of concern are the economics of cinema and the audio-visual industries; film regulation; the promotion of the cinema industries and the production of cinema heritage. CNC offers financial assistance in all aspects of French cinema (production, exhibition, distribution, business infrastructure).

## FRANCE - RHONE-ALPES FILM COMMISSION

**www.rhone-alpes-cinema.fr**

*24 Rue Emile Decorps, 69100 Villeurbanne, France | tel: +33 4 72 98 07 98 | fax: +33 4 72 07 99 | sergetachon@comfilm-rhones-aples.fr*

In addition to the national funds, some of the departments and regions of France offer film funding which international co-productions may be eligible to benefit from, if the film is shot in their region.

## GERMANY - BAVARIAN FILM & TELEVISION FUND

**www.fff-bayern.de**

*Sonnenstraße 21, 80331 Munich, Germany | tel: +49 89 544602 0 | fax: +49 89 544602 21 | filmfoerderung@fff-bayern.de*

Annually the Bavarian Film and Television Fund (FFF) made available a total of approx. E32m (approx. £22m) for screenplay, production, distribution and sales, as well as theatre funding. Financial support can be requested at each stage of the production process starting with script funding to packaging, production of theatrical and TV-movies as well as exhibition of same. At least 150% of the production support must be spent in Bavaria, and feature films can be supported with up to E1.6m (approx. £1.1m), as long as the producer or co-producer is based in Germany. Foreign producers can only access FFF funding by submitting an application through a local partner.

The distribution of the funds is based on the criteria set out in the Guidelines (accessible via the website). Applications for Film funding must be submitted by 1st of July.

# GERMANY - FILM & ENTERTAINMENT VIP MEDIENFONDS GMBH

**www.vip-muenchen.de**

*Bavariafilmstrasse 2, 82031, Grunwald, Munich, Germany | tel: +49 89 74 73 43 43 | fax: +49 89 74 73 43 44*

A successfully operating media fund, having placed funds with a volume of E100m and co-produced international TV and feature films.

# GERMANY - FOCUS GERMANY

**www.focusgermany.de**

*Germany | tel: +49 211 930 500 | fax: +49 211 93050 85 | info@focusgermany.de*

FOCUS Germany is a coordinating service for film professionals seeking information and professional guidance regarding Germany's broad range of funding and production possibilities. Established in 1990 as an umbrella organisation for the major German film funding institutions, it was launched at a time when regional funding in Germany was becoming increasingly important on the national an international production scene. FOCUS Germany supplies the necessary contacts for an efficient co-production with Germany including every aspect of production from location research to post production.

# GERMANY - GERMAN FEDERAL FILM BOARD

**www.ffa.de**

*Große Präsidentenstraße 9, 10178 Berlin, Germany | tel: +49 30 27577 0 | fax: +49 30 27577 111 | presse@ffa.de*

For foreign producers to access the national funding available from the German Federal Film Board, they must be part of a German co-production, though the production need not take place in the country. The FFA has an annual budget of around E70m (approx. £48) million at its disposal.

Funding is available for the production and distribution of feature films and short films, and project funding can amount as a rule to E250,000 (approx. £171k), and up to E1m (approx. £680k) in individual cases.

## GERMANY - HAMBURG FILM FUND

**www.ffhh.de**

*Friedensallee 14-16, D - 22765 Hamburg , Germany | tel: +49 40 398 37 0 | fax: +49 40 398 37 10*

FilmFörderung Hamburg, who part financed *Bend It Like Beckham*, is a company that supports film and TV production in Hamburg through funding, film commission, services and events. Their previous annual budgets has been up to E9.5m (approx. £6.5m), details of which can be found on their website.

## GERMANY - MEDIENBOARD BERLIN-BRANDENBURG GMBH

**www.filmboard.de**

*August-Bebel-Str. 26-53 , Potsdam-Babelsberg , 14482, Germany | tel: +49 331 743 870 | fax: +49 331 743 87 99 | info@medienboard.de*

Medienboard Berlin-Brandenburg GmbH is the central access point for all players in the region's media industry. The board is a joint venture of the two states in the area of film promotion and location development. Medienboard's film promotion supports films and film-related projects in the categories of script development, project development, package promotion, production, distribution and sales, and other activities.

## ICELAND - ICELANDIC FILM CENTRE

**www.icelandicfilmcentre.is**

*Túngata 14, 101 Reykjavik, Iceland | tel: +354 562 3580 | fax: +354 562 7171 | info@icelandicfilmcentre.is*

Public organisation allocating funds for the development and production of features, shorts, TV live action, and documentaries. Involved in promotion of Icelandic films abroad and promoting the general development of film culture in Iceland.

## IRELAND - IRISH FILM BOARD

**www.filmboard.ie**

*Rockfort House, St Augustine Street, Galway, Ireland | tel: +353 91 561398 | fax: +353 91 561405 | info@filmboard.ie*

Ireland's National screen agency funding feature films, documentaries, short films, and animation. The Film Board provides both development and production funding for feature length projects, and also runs a wide range of short film schemes.

## LUXEMBOURG - FILM FUND LUXEMBOURG

**www.filmfund.lu**

*5, rue Large, 1917, Luxembourg | tel: +352 47 82 165 | fax: +352 22 09 63 | info@filmfund.etat.lu*

The Film Fund of the Grand-Duchy of Luxembourg exists to promote and to encourage the development of the country's audiovisual production sector, and to administer film-making incentive and assistance schemes.

## THE NETHERLANDS - FILM INVESTORS NETHERLANDS (FINE BV)

**www.fine.nl**

*Sarphatikade 12, Amsterdam, 1017 WV, Netherlands, The | tel: +31 20 530 4700 | fax: +31 20 530 4701 | info@fine.nl*

FINE BV acts as an intermediary between producers and potential investors, seeking venture capital for film projects through a network of financial institutions such as banks.

## NEW ZEALAND - FILM NEW ZEALAND

**www.filmnz.com**

*PO Box 24142, Wellington, New Zealand | tel: +64 4 385 0766 | fax: +64 4 384 5840 | info@filmnz.org.nz*

Film New Zealand's role is to provide information, introductions and support to filmmakers both internationally and locally, including help with production environment, regional film offices, diverse locations, state-of-the-art facilities, experienced crews, and guidelines about shooting and who can help make projects happen.

The New Zealand Government has introduced a Large Budget Screen Production Grant (LBSPG) scheme whereby an eligible applicant will be granted a sum totalling 12.5% of the Qualifying New Zealand Production Expenditure on films of budgets greater than $15m (see chapter 5, International Financing).

## NEW ZEALAND - NEW ZEALAND FILM

**www.nzfilm.co.nz**

*PO Box 11 546, 0 Wellington, New Zealand | tel: +64 4 382 7680 | fax: +64 4 384 9719 | mail@nzfilm.co.nz*

New Zealand Film provides financial assistance for New Zealand feature film projects and New Zealand filmmakers, by way of loan or equity financing. It commits up to 8% of its annual budget to feature film development financing, and up to 60% to feature film production financing. Development decisions are made by either the senior staff group (up to $15,000 per project) or the Development Committee (up to $75,000 cumulative per projects). The Film Commission Board makes decisions involving financing beyond $75,000 for either advanced project development or for production financing.

## NORWAY - NORWEGIAN FILM COMMISSION

**www.norwegianfilm.com**

*Georgernes Verft 12, Bergen, N-5011, Norway | tel: +47 55 56 43 43 | fax: +47 55 56 43 48 | post@norwegianfilm.com*

An autonomous, national foundation whose purpose is to attract production of international films to Norway.

Schemes are in place to sustain development of ideas, talent and competence, and to support the production of feature-length films, short films, television series and development for film production companies.

## NORWAY - NORWEGIAN FILM FUND

**www.filmfondet.no**

*Postbox 752, Sentrum, Oslo, NO-0106, Norway | tel: +47 22 47 80 40 | fax: +47 22 47 80 41 | post@filmfondet.no*

A civil executive body under the auspices of the Royal Ministry for Cultural Affairs, it administers all financial support for film production in Norway.

## SOUTH AFRICA - SOUTH AFRICAN FILM FINANCE CORPORATION

**www.theimaginarium.com**

*Glenmain Bldg, 1st Floor, 359 A Main Road, Sea Point, Cape Town, 8005, South Africa | tel: +27 21 434 2851 | fax: +27 21 434 1229 | info@theimaginarium.com*

The Imaginarium provides financing of feature films in Southern Africa and executive production services. Funding is secured through the South African Film Finance Corporation (SAFFCO). SAFFCO is South Africa's leading film finance company, with expertise in the structuring of complex financial, legal and multi-country co-productions. SAFFCO secures financing in a variety of forms, including equity, gap, tax incentives and facilities deals.

## SWEDEN - SWEDISH FILM INSTITUTE

**www.sfi.se**

*Box 27 126, Stockholm, 102 52, Sweden | tel: +46 8 665 11 00 | fax: +46 86 663 698 | uof@sfi.se*

The Swedish Film Institute aims to promote, support and develop Swedish cinema in its cultural and broader contexts; and allocates grants for the production, support and promotion of films at an international level. The Film Institute's funds are used for production support for Swedish films, support for the distribution and public screening of films throughout Sweden and support for cultural activities relating to cinema.

# Pan European Funds

## CULTURE 2000

*Cultural Contact Point UK, EUCLID, 85-89 Duke Street, Liverpool, L1 5AP, tel: 0151 709 25 64 | fax: 0151 709 86 47 | info@euclid.co.uk | www.euclid-uk.info | www.culture2000.info*

The aim behind the Culture 2000 programme is to promote the culture, heritage and diversity of Europe, and to encourage integration between European countries and support practice and participation in arts and culture. EUCLID is the official EC Cultural Contact Point in the UK for Culture 2000, providing support and assistance for potential applicants to this programme and guidance on other EU funding opportunities for the cultural sector.

In summary, eligible projects:

- Can be focused on any of: performing arts, visual arts, cultural heritage or books/ reading (mainly translation)
- Must have something uniquely European about them (ie. not just a tour of a UK performance or exhibition)
- Must be developed and implemented by at least 3 partner organisations from 3 different European countries
- Must last either for 1 year or, in exceptional cases, for 2-3 years
- Will have a total budget of between E100,000 to E300,000 (1 year projects) or E500,000 per year (2-3 year projects)
- Can receive, from Culture 2000, a maximum of 50% (1 year projects) or 60% (2-3 year projects) of the budget
- Will not include expenditure on buildings or buying new equipment - Culture 2000 can only fund the projects themselves.
- Applications will be invited across all four sectors: performing arts, visual arts, cultural heritage, and books, reading & translation.

Further details, guidance notes, sample budgets and application forms can be downloaded at the Culture 2000 website.

## EURIMAGES

*Eurimages, Avenue de l'Europe, 67075 Strasbourg, Cedex, France | tel: +33 3 88 41 20 00 | fax: +33 3 88 41 27 60 | eurimages@coe.int | www.coe.int/eurimages*

Eurimages is the Council of Europe fund for the co-production, distribution and exhibition of European cinematographic works. Set up in 1988, it currently has 32 Member States. Eurimages aims to promote the European film industry by encouraging the production and distribution of films and fostering co-operation between professionals. Since being set up, Eurimages has supported the co-production of more than one thousand full-length feature films and documentaries.

Eurimages has three support programmes:

- Support for co-production
- Support for distribution
- Support for cinemas

The Fund's resources are mainly derived from the member States' contributions and from the reimbursement of advances of which almost 90% goes to supporting co-production. The UK is **not** a member of Eurimages, so is only eligible to benefit from the fund if invited to join a co-production project by a member of Eurimages, and the contribution is limited.

## How Eurimage support for co-production works

Eurimages supports full-length feature films and animation, as well as documentaries of a minimum length of 70 minutes. Because the support is for co-production, all projects submitted must have at least two co-producers from different member States of the Fund. The participation of any majority co-producer must not exceed 80% of the total co-production budget, and the participation of the minority co-producer must not be lower than 10%. For bilateral co-productions with a budget above E5m (approx. £3.4m), the participation of the majority co-producer may go up to 90% of the total budget of the co-production. The conditions concerning the European origin of projects are fundamental. They are evaluated according to the provisions in the European Convention on Cinematographic Co-Production and the sources of financing.

## The nature and amount of support

The support is awarded in the form of an interest free loan, repayable from the first Euro. The amount of support is subject to a ceiling and fixed with reference to the project's actual funding needs and effective budget. Applicants should request an amount that reflects the film's actual funding requirements. The Secretariat will assess the amount requested, in consultation with the film's producers, and then report to the Board of Management. Support is paid in three instalments.

## Selection criteria

The Executive Secretary will provide the Board of Management with a systematic and detailed analysis of each project. In selecting the project, the Board of Management will take into consideration the Fund's cultural and economic objectives. In doing so, it will carry out a comparative analysis of the applications submitted, upon the basis of the following selection criteria:

- Artistic merits of the project
- Experience of the director, producers, talent (authors, scriptwriters, casting, etc.) and technical teams
- Circulation potential of the project
- Commercial potential of the project
- Artistic and/or technical co-operation between the co-producers
- Level of confirmed financing for the project

# England's Regional Screen Agencies

Through the Regional Investment Fund for England, the UK Film Council invests £7.5 million a year in nine regional screen agencies covering England - collectively known as Screen England. Each agency also receives funding from other sources. The Regional Screen Agencies support a range of activity intended to strengthen their local film industries and to develop education about and public access to film and moving image.

Film activity in the regions include:

- Production funding
- Cinema audience development
- Archive development
- Training and Education
- Business and Skills Development
- Assistance to filmmakers working in the region - location finding, crewing, etc.

Please contact the individual agency directly for details.

Contact details for the agencies and further information on the work of the UK Film Council are also available at www.ukfilmcouncil.org.uk or tel +44 (0)20 7861 7861.

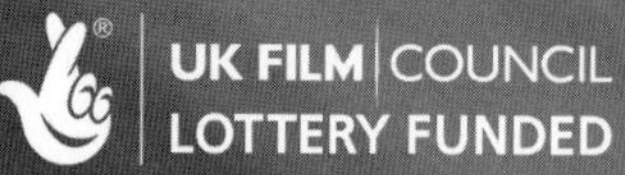


**Regional Screen Agency contacts**

**EM-Media**
35 - 37 St Mary's Gate
Nottingham NG1 1PU
Tel + 44 (0) 115 934 9090
Fax + 44 (0) 115 950 0988
Email info@em-media.org.uk
www.em-media.org.uk

**Film London**
20 Euston Centre
Regent's Place
London NW1 3JH
Tel + 44 (0) 20 7387 8787
Fax + 44 (0) 20 7387 8788
Email info@filmlondon.org.uk
www.filmlondon.org.uk

**Northern Film & Media**
Central Square
Forth Street
Newcastle-upon-Tyne NE1 3PJ
Tel + 44 (0) 191 269 9200
Fax + 44 (0) 191 269 9213
Email info@northernmedia.org
www.northernmedia.org

**North West Vision**
233 The Tea Factory
Liverpool L1 4DQ
Tel + 44 (0) 151 708 2967
Fax + 44 (0) 151 708 2984
Email info@northwestvision.co.uk
www.northwestvision.co.uk

**Screen East**
1st Floor
2 Millennium Plain
Norwich NR2 1TF
Tel + 44 (0) 1603 776 920
Fax + 44 (0) 1603 767 191
Email info@screeneast.co.uk
www.screeneast.co.uk

**Screen South**
Shearway Business Park
Shearway Road, Folkestone
Kent CT19 4RH
Tel + 44 (0) 1303 298 222
Fax + 44 (0) 1303 298 227
Email info@screensouth.org
www.screensouth.org

**Screen West Midlands**
31/41 Bromley Street
Birmingham B9 4AN
Tel + 44 (0) 121 766 1470
Fax + 44 (0) 121 766 1480
Email info@screenwm.co.uk
www.screenwm.co.uk

**Screen Yorkshire**
Studio 22
46 The Calls
Leeds LS2 7EY
Tel + 44 (0) 113 294 4410
Fax + 44 (0) 113 294 4989
Email info@screenyorkshire.co.uk
www.screenyorkshire.co.uk

**South West Screen**
St Bartholomew's Court
Lewins Mead
Bristol BS1 5BT
Tel + 44 (0) 117 952 9977
Fax + 44 (0) 117 952 9988
Email info@swscreen.co.uk
www.swscreen.co.uk

# MEDIA FUNDING

*UK MEDIA Desk, Agnieszka Moody, Fourth Floor, 66-68 Margaret Street, London, W1W 8SR | tel: 020 7323 9733 | fax: 020 7323 9747 | england@mediadesk.co.uk | www.mediadesk.co.uk/england*

*MEDIA Antenna Scotland, Emma Valentine, 249 West George Street, Glasgow, G2 4QE | tel: 0141 302 1776/7 | fax: 0141 302 1778 | scotland@mediadesk.co.uk | www.mediadesk.co.uk/scotland*

*MEDIA Services Northern Ireland, Cian Smyth, c/o Northern Ireland Film Commission, Third Floor, Alfred House, 21 Alfred Street, Belfast , BT2 8ED | tel: 02890 232 444 | fax: 02890 239 918 | media@niftc.co.uk | www.mediadesk.co.uk/northernireland*

*MEDIA Antenna Wales, Gwion Owain, c/o SGRIN, 10 Mount Stuart Square, Cardiff Bay, Cardiff, CF10 5EE | tel: 02920 333 304 | fax: 02920 333 320 | email: wales@mediadesk.co.uk | www.mediadesk.co.uk/wales*

The objectives of the MEDIA Plus programme are to promote the development of projects, submitted by independent European production companies, aimed at European and international markets by providing financial support.

## DEVELOPMENT SINGLE PROJECTS

Support for the development of film, television or multimedia projects. Funding is available for up to 50% of the eligible development costs of the following categories of projects:

- Drama projects with a minimum duration of 50 minutes (one-off or series)
- Creative documentary with a minimum duration of 25 minutes (for a series, 25 minutes is the required length per episode)
- Animation projects with a minimum duration of 24 minutes (one-off or series)
- Multimedia concepts

**Award range:** Different fixed amounts can be applied for in each case for drama, documentary, animation and multimedia. Up to E50,000 (approx. £34k) for drama projects, up to E30,000 (approx. £21k) for creative documentaries, up to E50,000 for animation projects, up to E80,000 (approx. £55k) for feature animation projects for theatrical release, up to E50,000 for multimedia projects. MEDIA's contribution is a maximum of 50% but may be raised to 60% for projects that exploit or reflect European cultural diversity. The company must secure the matched funding | **Deadline** - In February and May annually. Further details: On reaching production, the company must reinvest the same amount of financial support into the development of a new project(s) within 6 months of the delivery of the project. In the event of default, the full amount must be repaid to the Commission. In the event of a project being abandoned, provided the contractual obligations of the company have been met, no reimbursement will be owed.

## DEVELOPMENT SLATE OF PROJECTS

Development funding for independent European production companies for slates of projects. Two different levels of slate funding are available: Slate 1 and Slate 2. Fifty per cent of the eligible development costs are available. If the company abandons a project, as long as it has met its obligations to the commission, there will be no repayment. At the end of the agreement period, any portion of the MEDIA contribution which has not been invested or reinvested in the development of projects has to be repaid to the Commission. Award range: Slate 1 for 3 to 6 projects: E60,000, E70,000, E80,000, E90,000 (approx. £41k-62k), Slate 2 for 3 to 10 projects: E100,000, E110,000, E125,000, E150,000 (approx. £69k-103k). MEDIA contribution is a maximum of 50% but may be raised to 60% for projects that enhance or reflect cultural diversity. The applicant must secure the matching funding | **Deadline:** in February and May annually.

**Further details:** For Slate 1: Applicants must, within a 3 year period prior to application, have produced ONE audiovisual work which has been distributed/broadcast in at least one country other than its country of origin. For Slate 2: Applicants must, within a 3 year period (or 5 year period for fiction/animation slates) prior to the date of application, have produced TWO audiovisual works which have been broadcast/distributed in at least one country other than their country of origin. MEDIA funding granted to any approved project is repayable on the first day of principal photography of that project to a Dedicated Bank Account. Within six months of the first day of principal photography, successful applicants must re-invest sums paid to the Dedicated Bank Account into the development of those projects listed in the Development Plan.

## SINGLE ANIMATION PROJECTS

This grant will fund animation projects that run no less than 25 minutes, and which are intended for theatrical release or television broadcast. Specific items this scheme will cover are graphics research and pilot production.

**Award range:** amounts of E10,000, (£6,900 approx.) E20,000 (£13,700 approx.), E30,000 (£20,500 approx.), E40,000 (£27,500 approx.) and E50,000 (£34,200 approx.) can be applied for. Feature length animation intended for theatrical release may apply for E80,000 (£55,000 approx.) | **Deadline:** dates for 2005 and 2006 were not available at publication.

**Further details:** In addition to the application form, applicants must submit items such as a producer's/director's statement of intent, a treatment, sample dialogue, a script, illustrations, production costs, CVs, details of crew and key personnel. The production company must have produced at least one twenty-five minute animation production or two animated shorts prior to their application. This must have received national distribution for first time applicants, and international distribution for previous applicants.

## SINGLE DOCUMENTARY PROJECTS

The grant will fund creative documentaries that run for no less than twenty-five minutes and which are intended for theatrical release or television broadcast. Specific items this scheme will cover include realisation of a video treatment.

**Award range:** Amounts of E10,000 (£6,900 approx.), E15,000 (£10,300 approx.), E20,000 (£13,700 approx.), and E30,000 (£20,500 approx.) can be applied for | **Deadline:** Dates for 2005 and 2006 were not available at publication

**Further details:** In addition to the application form, applicants must submit items such as a statement of intent, a treatment, CVs and details of crew and key personnel. The production company must have produced at least one twenty-five minute creative documentary or fifty minute fiction production previous to their application. This must have received national distribution for first time applicants, and international distribution for previous applicants.

### SINGLE FICTION PROJECTS

The grant will fund fiction projects that run no less than 50 minutes which are intended for theatrical release or television broadcast.

**Award range:** Amounts of E10,000 (approx. £6,900), E20,000 (approx £13,700), E30,000 (approx. £20,500), E40,000 (approx. £27,500) and E50,000 (approx. £34,200) can be applied for. | **Deadline:** Dates for 2005 and 2006 were not available at publication.

**Further details:** In addition to the application form, applicants must submit items such as: a statement of intent, a treatment, sample dialogue, a script, CVs and details of crew and key personnel. The production company must have produced at least one fifty minute fiction or twenty-five minute creative documentary production previous to their application. This must have received national distribution for first time applicants, and international distribution for previous applicants.

# Other international funds

## JAPAN FOUNDATION

*The Japan Foundation London Office, 17 Old Park Lane, London, W1K 1QT | tel: 020 7499 4726 | fax: 020 7495 1133 | info@japanfoundation.org.uk | www.jpf.go.jp*

The Japan Foundation was established by the Japanese Government to promote Japanese culture abroad, and to build on Japan's international relations. It has offices worldwide and primarily supports schemes that encourage cultural exchange between nations.

### FILM-PRODUCTION SUPPORT PROGRAM

This scheme aims to encourage original film, TV and audio-visual productions which help to increase understanding of Japanese culture abroad and have a good chance of achieving broadcast or public release.

**For:** feature films, TV programmes, video works, CD Roms and other audio-visual works may be funded in any language and the content must relate to Japan | **Award range:** the maximum grant available is 50% of the production costs with a ceiling of ¥5m (approx. £26,250). The grant will only be paid once the production is completed and will not go towards research and development costs | **Deadline:** there is an annual deadline in December

**Further details:** Applicants should contact their national Japan Foundation Office to discuss the project. In addition to the application form, applicants must submit a summary of the project and detailed synopsis, previous work, background information, budget and finance plans, partnership funding, schedule, script, letter of recommendation from a distributor, and other items. Applications must be sent by post or courier.

Applications will be assessed against the following criteria: the ability of the applicant to deliver the project; applicant's track record; the need for the grant; realistic planning; potential for success; potential for public screening; no religious or political connotations; originality; the stage of the project (those in production or post-production are favoured). The applicant will not receive the grant until the project is completed and a copy given to the Foundation. The Foundation must receive a screen credit and may publicise their involvement in the project. They do not require the grant to be repaid at any time.

## ROY W. DEAN GRANTS

*Carole Dean, The Wye Cottage, Rd 1 Highway 63 # 4613, Blenheim, New Zealand 007321 | www.fromtheheartproductions.com*

The Roy W. Dean Grant Foundation was established in 1992 primarily to support documentary filmmakers. The foundation encourages the film community to give resources and services to each award winner, enabling them to produce their film ideas.

### LOS ANGELES FILM GRANT & LOS ANGELES VIDEO GRANT

Winning filmmakers of each of these awards have the opportunity to benefit from a range of free products and services to allow them to film their proposal in Los Angeles. The prizes are worth in excess of $40,000 (around £25,000) and include musical score, camera rental, editing, titles and opticals, production management, production and technical advice, film processing, marketing strategy, equipment, screenwriting software, and various discounts. The deadline is in July.

### NEW YORK CITY FILM GRANT

A range of products and services are made available to the winner of this award, enabling them to film their proposal in New York. The award is worth in excess of $65,000 (over £41,000) and includes editing time, musical score, film stock, titles, equipment, tap transfers, sound and mixing sessions, animation, storyboarding and digital compositing, internet promotion, fundraising consultation and screenwriting software. Four runners up will also receive prizes worth $750 (around £470) in film stock and access to production facilities.

### EDITING GRANT

The recipient of this award is given the opportunity to do an off-line edit of completed film footage. The prize includes a return ticket to New Zealand, four weeks residency in a furnished cottage on the South Island, $120NZ (around £40) a week to live on and access to a car and phone card. The recipient must have a dub of the footage with original time-code on mini-DV and will work with a local filmmaker and local facilities. The deadline is in September.

### WRITING/RESEARCH GRANT

The recipient of this award is given the opportunity in March or September to work on their writing and research for features, short films and documentaries for four to six weeks in a cottage on the South Island of New Zealand. The prize also includes return ticket, access to a computer, money for expenses, a phone card, access to a car, and screenwriting software.

### FILM GRANT FOR NEW ZEALAND

Documentary filmmakers chosen to receive this award are given access to goods and services that enable them to film a documentary in New Zealand. The prize includes film stock, film processing, camera hire, equipment, editing, music, tape transfers, a web site and legal advice. The deadline is in February

**Further details for all awards:** Finished films will be screened on Discovery, Starz, PBS, History and other networks. The application is open to filmmakers, students, independent producers and independent production companies. There is no restriction on where applicants are based, but the awards are given in the relevant location (New York, Los Angeles or New Zealand). Applicants for each award must submit a completed application form, a fee of $38 or $28 for students, plus a proposal for the project and examples of past work.

The awards are given to new film and video documentary projects that are unique and benefit society, and works in progress. There is no restriction on length.

## SUNDANCE DOCUMENTARY FUND

*8530 Wilshire Boulevard, 3rd Floor, Beverly Hills, California 90211, USA | tel: +1 310 360 1981 | sdf@sundance.org | www.sundance.org*

The Sundance Documentary Fund is dedicated to supporting worldwide documentary films and videos focused on current and significant issues and movements in contemporary human rights, freedom of expression, social justice, and civil liberties. In supporting independent vision and creative, compelling stories, the Sundance Documentary Fund hopes to give voice to the diverse exchange of ideas crucial to developing an open society, raise public consciousness about human rights abuses and restrictions of civil liberties, and engage citizens in a lively, ongoing debate about these issues. Two distinct project categories will be considered for funding:

### DEVELOPMENT FUNDS

Development funds are available for projects in the research or preproduction phase. Grants in this category range up to US$15,000 (approx. £8,000). Grantees receiving development funds may reapply for additional support upon completion of at least a rough cut of their documentary. New applications must be accompanied by a work in progress VHS tape and a comprehensive project update.

### WORK IN PROGRESS FUNDS (PRODUCTION OR POST-PRODUCTION)

Work in progress projects must be in production or postproduction. These submissions are eligible for the maximum grant award of US$75,000 (approx. £40,000), but generally, awards in this category will range from $20,000 to $50,000 (approx. £11k to 26k). Applicants are required to submit a rough cut or fine cut of their work in progress.

**Further details:** The Fund only accepts projects dealing with contemporary issues, and does not accept historical projects, biographies, or series. Individuals from around the world may apply with documentary film or video projects that range in length from full broadcast hour to long format feature. Applicants must have creative and budgetary control over the proposed documentary. The Sundance Documentary Fund is extremely competitive and only a fraction of submitted proposals will be funded. Quality of work samples, strength of proposal, potential for broad international distribution, and the issue's significance are elements heavily weighed during the review process.

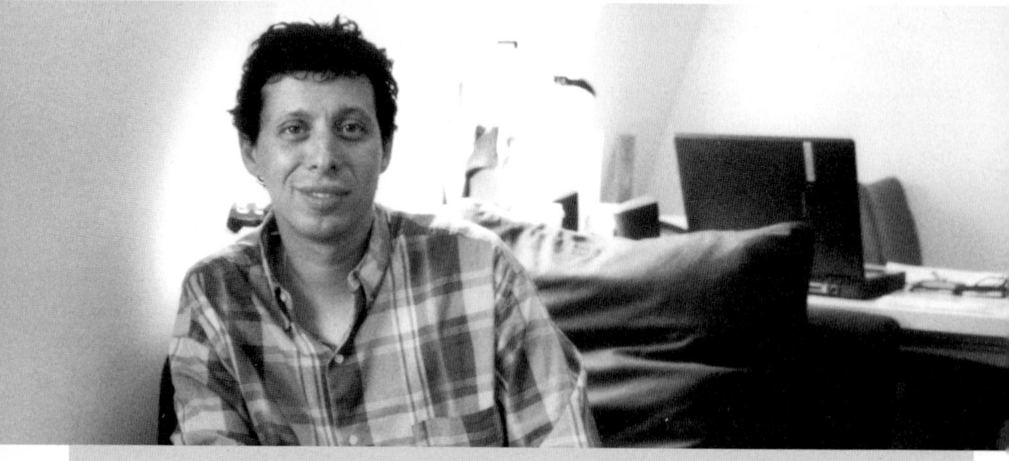

# Paul Trijbits
# *New Cinema Fund*

*As head of the UK Film Council's New Cinmema Fund, Paul Trijbits manages a £5m annual budget, of which 20% is spent on short films.*

**How does the New Cinema fund approach short films?**

Shorts films for us and the amount of money that we invest in it is very much seen as R&D. And I am personally, and the fund as a whole is, of the opinion that short films aren't particularly worth much money, if any. And making money's not probably the right reason for making shorts because the number of traditional outlets for them, both at the cinema or on television has virtually dried up. So what we are doing is very much using the amount of money that we invest as R&D. The fact that they get seen and we've come up with, I think, some interesting ideas as to how they can be seen, is a bonus for us. And the way that we do it is by trying to be more specific and more targeted. We put a bunch of our films from the Cinema Extreme programme on the front cover of Dazed and Confused. We recently created USB memory sticks that we used at the Talent Campus. So that's another way of promoting the films as opposed to distributing them, promoting them; to an audience that is likely to enjoy watching those kinds of films.

**What is the fund looking for?**

Someone was criticising me and the fund by saying it was impossible to gauge what kind of films we might go for. I know it wasn't meant as a compliment, but I have to say I have quietly and privately taken it as a compliment, as I see it as exactly the role of the New Cinema fund and the fund head to support and back as broad a range of films as is humanely possible to support. So whether on the one hand you do digital creative film like *This is Not a Love song*, or a more mainstream like *Anita and Me,* or you do Paul Greengrass' *Bloody Sunday,* or you a documentary like *Touching the Void*, or Alex Cox's *Revengers Tragedy*. I could go on but it's a very broad range of films. I think that's what I see us wanting to continue to do. I think that what will be interesting is looking at films we've done - we've been involved in about 38 or 39

- and to try to look at the ambition of the films and filmmakers and our hopes and ambitions for those films and see what's happened to them.

**Have many of your projects paid back their investment?**

When you do *Touching the Void* or *Magdalene Sisters* for very little money, they do extremely well. There's at least two films that are in net profit, which is pretty healthy. It's quite hard because - with money on films it may be very successful and work. But some films take a very long time and it trickles and trickles and trickles and you have to project income over 5, 6,7 ,8 years and possibly even longer than that, before you might know what it does. Some films are more perennial, to take some garden analogy - the crocuses in the spring season.

And it is a very distinct feature of the New Cinema Fund that the prime measure is not money or recoupment, because that would stop films getting made. It's about 'Are they going to say something other films haven't said? Are they going to represent Britain at major film festivals and show a different part of British culture.' That is as important, if not more important, as the recoupment on a single film.

You've got to remember that it's got tougher. The market for independent films is a volatile and ever-changing world. At the moment, for instance, the studios, through all their specialty divisions, are competing very aggressively in making independent films with budgets of 15, 18, 20 million dollars. And that's competing for the same audience as some of our much smaller budget independent films. So it's tough out there at the moment.

**How should producers present themselves and their projects to the New Cinema fund?**

I think the words packaging and New Cinema fund don't go particularly well together.

The very first thing that we're interested in is the material, in the script, and in the vision of the filmmaker. That is what we make our first assessment on. I really do say that everything else will come later. Of course if you have other financing partners, or you have talent attached, then that can be very helpful. But the New Cinema fund has become the first port of call for filmmakerr and producers to come to, and we tend to come in first rather than last.

I think what is helpful for producers is to look at the kind of films we've done, look at the range of films we've done, look at the range of budgets and the sums of money that we've invested. I do sometimes worry that people don't do quite enough homework or look at the things we've done and at the things that are realistic.

And I think other than the fund's remit itself, for instance, The Relph Report is a very important tool about why might a film cost what it cost. What could it cost, what should it cost. It's something that I think British producers have not been particularly good at trying to cast their budget to the market. And the market in this case is not purely the commercial market, but part of the support mechanism such as the Film Council and the BBC and FilmFour

Many films have been made for too much money that will never work. Either commercially or semi-commercially. And that is something I think people should pay more attention to.

**What sort of projects do you receive too much of?**

For a little while we did some monitoring on the different types of films that exist. We've been monitoring the different types of films that exist. It is interesting and sometimes worrying that 90% of the material we receive is drama. And I mean serious drama. If you go and speak to a distributor they will say, no, not another unrelenting drama. I think it's fair to say that Britain is itself focussed on drama, but looking at the number of applications we get, there isn't an appetite for only doing that. Now I'm not suggesting we only make science fiction films or horror films, because probably that will take years to develop the skill or ingenuity to pull that off. But maybe drama with a twist, or drama with an infusion of comedy, instead of very tough drama which is the majority of what we receive.

**Could the New Cinema fund follow some of the other regional funds into microbudget funding?**

Well, we are in the process at the moment with Film Four to see if we can stimulate a particular kind of low budget filmmaking. Maybe not dissimilar to a scheme we run with the BBC, but more holistically organised and funded through a low budget film scheme. And we're hoping we will be able, and we're in the process of trying to ascertain whether there is the appetite of other funders and appropriate companies to manage such a programme. The idea is that we would be able to create an opportunity for maybe 8 or 10 films over a period of time to be fully funded and to be made in a more protected environment, if you like. I don't think those budgets will be as low as what Film London is proposing but they will be between I think half a million and a million pounds.

# Jenny Borgars
## *Development Fund*

*Just over 60% of Jenny Borgar's £4m annual budget is spent on the development slate companies; the remainder is open to individual project financing. By mid-2005, 23 films that received development fund investment have gone into production, out of the 100 to 120 that have been in development at any time since the fund began in 2001.*

**How do the application and funds' development processes work?**

I'll give you an idiot's guide to the application process, and then I'll give you a guide to what happens if you go into development.

When someone applies, whether a writer on their own, or a producer, it arrives in with us at the Film Council and we get a reader to look at it. We have a pool of ten readers who work for us. They're all freelance readers, but they are very closely involved with the fund. So they take the first look at the material. We all then have a meeting with the three execs who work with me on the fund.

If we're rejecting the project, we offer the rejected applicant the chance to get a feedback service report done so they can get some constructive criticism on their material. But if it's is something that is deemed good by the reader; if it is interesting, controversial sometimes - or I just don't know what it is, but there's something there that needs following up on - then we'll do a second reading on the project either with another reader or, in most cases, with an executive here. And then if the executive deems there is something interesting, they'll go through the process of sitting down and meeting with the writer or whoever sent the application in. And often they'll go through a series of meetings with them. They're trying to assess the team and the individual as well, and how a process might work going forward in development. And when they are going through those meetings they'll be looking at what might be a plan for taking the project forward; what that may cost, what are the main issues. And if they want to take it into development then they come to me, at which point I'll probably look at the project briefly, and I'll be talking to the execs here. If they speak passionately about it, in most cases they can get it into development here.

So if you get into development, the next stage is to work out with the writer or the production team not only financially what is needed, but the tools and resources that the team needs to develop the project effectively. They'd definitely end up working with an executive here to move the project forward. We might look to see if it's useful to employ a script editor on the project; to match-make them with a producer or a mentor; to enable them to get some training for the project and charge it off to the development budget. Whatever it is we think they need. We'll talk to the team to see what they need. All those things can be paid for through the development budget they applied for here. And then on a day-to-day basis they'll be engaging with the executives when they are delivering scripts, and always trying to discus a strategy for what the next step will be in advance of us hitting that next step.

**At what stage do you want projects to come to you?**

We kind of deal with everything here. Other than a specific scheme, like "25 Words or Less", it is a completely open application process. So we're not only getting projects that have no attachments to them other than the writer themselves, we're also getting projects at a very early stage, including treatment, right up to projects that are applying for pre- pre-production funding, which is the last stage of development funding. This is more about bringing a casting director on board, or doing a "recce", or getting a location manager. Whatever that requires. So that's determined by what comes through the door.

We do get an awfully large number of submissions from writers simply working on their own. What we try and do when looking at their projects is really try and assess and talk to them and see if the best next step is to be investing in the writers directly and giving them the funds to work on another draft of the script. Or if they should work hand in hand with another producer or financier who might work jointly on the process of trying to move that project forward.

**What sort of projects is the fund looking for?**

It's really quite difficult to answer that question. We have a very broad remit. It stretches from the ultra low budget to the very experimental, to the mainstream, to the ultra commercial, to the hugely ambitious very high budget, and everything in between. Ultimately you're always looking for a great story brilliantly told. You're always looking for something that's got cinematic potential.

If you're asking me personally, it would be great to see more ambitious but commercially focussed material coming out of the UK. In terms of what is coming to us we certainly don't see enough of that. Another of the things that the fund does is look for the gaps in what is being developed.

So we're putting more time into genre writing - it's not as dirty a word as it was in the past. We had last year a science fiction thriller: we had a pair of fantastic writers who came in with an incredible pitch, wrote a fantastic first draft and Working Title picked it up.

**Do you receive too much of anything?**

Whenever we do our SWAT analysis of the different genres, drama is always the biggest. There's always a reason for that, it tends to come out of the UK.

Whether or not drama occupies over 90% of cinema audiences, drama is what we get a lot of. Period drama we get a lot. Social drama we get a lot. But I never want to say don't bring it to us. But, for instance, we don't get enough comedy scripts as we would like. Certainly not enough great comedy scripts as we would like.

**Do you have any general advice for people applying?**

What we are asking is for people to set their own standards as high as absolutely possible before they even approach us. We would like people to have done their homework, not only really knowing their project and knowing and having an instinct for the next step - in a film world, in a financing world - but really thinking of how to make a link to an audience. And really having that uppermost in their minds when they're thinking of an idea right from its inception.

And presentation, of course. We need people who are going to present their material professionally. But fundamentally it's 'Do your homework and be prepared'. Be over prepared when you're submitting to us; if it's a script, a treatment, or you're coming in for a meeting.

The level of preparation is something we all need to focus on in the UK.

**What do you think of script reading schemes run by, say, Rocliffe?**

I think anything you can do to make screenwriting come alive to the people who are involved in it is a really useful tool. Let's not forget, the script is only a part in the process of making a film, which is an incredibly collaborative and vital process. Everything is interlinked and it is important to make everyone involved aware of this fact, and that no one part of the process sits in isolation.

I was talking to a theatre writer recently who is moving across to film and she said 'When I work in the theatre, I know everyone who works in production, and I know everything they do, and I know that if the set designer is having a problem with something I can write something that will be a solution to that problem'. But in the screenwriting process she said she felt incredibly isolated and ignorant about how the other parts of the jigsaw fitted together. And she felt if she had a bit more knowledge she would be better informed in how to construct her screenplay to make the most of those skills and other disciplines.

I think that if you go back to the notion of training, anything we can do that also introduces everybody to the other needs and parts of the filmmaking process is really useful. You know, have an editor read your screenplay and get their views on the story and you get an incredible amount of feedback on how the storytelling fits together and how fluid it can be.

# David Thompson
# *BBC Films*

*From Oscar winning Iris to the $100m grossing Billy Elliot, David Thompson has steered BBC Films through a string of critical and commercial successes. With a £10m annual budget for mainly co-productions, including Woody Allen's first British feature, BBC Films has become one of the UK's most active and inspiring producers.*

**What sort of skills are you looking for in the new producers you work with?**

We're looking for a combination of skills which is hard to find because producers don't get many chances to make films. Sadly, producers get a chance to make one film and then not another one for a long time.

You need a combination of creative ability, ability to work with scripts, and an understanding of casting. You also need to be able to put deals together and run productions, so it's a very complex list of skills that are required which is not easy to achieve, except on the job. And that's the paradox and the challenge for the British film industry really.

Unless you've been working, say, in television, where you're acquiring many of the same skills, or up to a point, in commercials, it is very hard to learn on the job.

But you do need a big range of skills. You need tact, diplomacy, creativity, some vision, and a kind of mad, manic drive really. A manic belief in turning the impossible into the possible.

**And generally the first time feature producers you've worked with, have they all come from a particular background?**

No they come from all kinds of backgrounds; documentary, commercials, theatre, all kinds of worlds. I wouldn't say there was a particular way in, but I would say TV and commercials are really good as a way in. But also coming up through the production line - a lot of big first ADs or big script editors become producers. There's all different ways. Through the script editing route; through the production route; up from runner. No one way is better than the other. You also need to have also an understanding of how the creative process works. Both the nuts and bolts and the creative process are really important.

**At what stage should an indie producer approach BBC Films? How developed are you looking for projects to be?**

You can come with an initial idea. We often get treatments, scripts; a mixture of things. There's no right or wrong. You can come early or late. Come early with a treatment if it's a really hot idea. If it's just 'lets do an adaptation of a classic book' and you've got no take on it then it's kind of pointless. But if you've got the rights, or nearly got the rights on a really interesting book, then that's worth coming to us. Or a really unusual idea - albeit in a short treatment form - then its still worth coming to us.

**What kind of films is BBC Films looking to develop?**

Well we do all kinds of film. If you look at our past range, from comedies to drama, strong drama like *Iris,* to uplifting films like *Billy Elliot*, to more gritty social films reflecting the many aspects of our culture like *Bullet Boy*, through to musical comedy, like *Mrs Henderson*, there's all kinds of films we are doing.

We're particularly looking for comedy, and particularly lighter, more uplifting films. They're the harder ones to find. Films that can play on BBC1. Ones that can really cross over and be hits. We have more drama, and so does the industry in general.

We're not looking to do horror. We would do spoof horror maybe, if it was the right kind of thing. Comedy, entertainment uplift, and some strong dramas but we're quite well stocked with strong dramas.

So the emphasis is on films that can cheer people up and make them feel better about themselves and the world. Which are harder to find. Which is not to say we're not only going to do those films. Of course not. The bulk of the films we do will be more on the edge, that's the truth of it.

But we've got a big range in the films that are up and coming. From Michael Winterbottoms new film *Cock and Ball Story,* to Danny Boyle's new film *Millions,* which is more of an uplifiting family film. And we're still doing period films from time to time, but not so many.

I should rephrase that slightly, we are particularly looking for comedy.

**How much is your commissioning strategy defined by programming for BBC channels?**

We're trying to find more that will play on BBC1. In the past the bulk has been on BBC2, but we're trying to shift it a bit more so more of it will fit on BBC1. The bulk of it will probably still go on BBC2.

**There was talk of your budget, which is £10m being, raised.**

I'm hoping it's going to happen, but it's not happened yet. We're awaiting an announcement. We very much hope we will get funding. Obviously we feel we need it and we want it and we can use it very wisely, and we think that the British film industry will benefit if we have more to spend.

**It is remarkable how much you achieve with that budget**

I must admit there is a kind of slight of hand and magic, a bit like the feeding of the five thousand with not many fishes and loaves. The truth is we do make our money go a long way because we gear up more money. In other words we co-produce so much. Everything we do, almost, is co-produced. A little seed money can go a long way. It's a big strain to get a film going on those terms. And it's harder and harder to do it. Us trying to put in a tiny bit of money into films where we still want to retain very strong editorial involvement. Which is always what we want to do. Even if we get more money we'll still have to make the money go a very long way, it's not suddenly going to be bread and jam tomorrow. It's still going to be a strain, because some of the money we get will only go to replace the tax funding that has dropped away. So it's not going to suddenly be all easy, but I hope it will be a little bit easier because right now it's very tough. Certainly we've got a very strong co-production team. And co-production, co-financing and partnership is at the heart of what we do. Almost every project we do is partnered. But that of course that has its problems, because sometimes partners don't see eye to eye and the film suffers in that mix, because people take different views and the film ends up in a hole down the middle.

Much more straight forward if you're fully funding your own thing.

**Do you fully fund anything?**

Hardly ever. We sometimes regret we haven't. We very much regretted not fully funding *My Summer of Love*. But we couldn't do it, and very rarely can we do it. Can't remember the last film we fully funded, actually. It was a long time ago.

**Last Resort was done on a £400,000 budget.**

We did fully fund that. Often we are in the invidious position of where we have so little cash we end up selling off rights not necessarily in the way we want to just to get the film financed. So we weaken our own position in films, but because we only have £10m for the whole operation we have to do that. It doesn't involve us adopting the soundest commercial principles.

*Billy Elliot* was a classic example of that, if we had lots of money we could have fully financed the film and we'd be very rich by now. But there we are.

**Do you come in at a certain stage as a co-producer. Are you usually first in?**

We're often first in, we're usually first in, but we sometimes come in right at the end, We look for opportunities when things are fully developed, we're not adverse to that, particularly where people are looking for smaller sums. The bulk of things we do we developed ourselves, but we're not exclusive about that or precious about that. We'll take a good script from wherever it comes, even if we haven't developed it; more than happy to.

**Do you retain the option, if a project hasn't come out as you expected, to move it away from a theatrical release to a TV broadcast?**

Only by consent - of the producer involved. It rarely happens, but if it needs to happen we would rather that than it not happen at all.

**How many projects have you got in development at any one time?**

We've got about 30 projects in active development, maybe a little more.

**And how many will go into production?**

Well in Hollywood it's one in a hundred. We'd like one in four to get off the ground at one stage or another. One in four, one in three, somewhere in between the two. That's quite a difficult thing to pull off. Because in the film industry it's not good enough just to have a good script, like it is in television where it will get made properly. You need a good script that will attract finance at that particular time, that will attract actors at that particular time. So what you need is many more good scripts that are ready to go.

It's not always the best script that tickles someone's fancy at a particular time. You need to have a lot of scripts ready. We'd be happy to get to a ratio of three to one, compared with Hollywood which is hundreds to one I think we do pretty well.

**The success ratio on the films seems pretty high.**

I think we'd like to have more 'commercial hits', obviously making more money, but that's not what we're there to do. The primary reason we're here is to reflect the BBC's public service remit, which is to make films that explore British society in all kinds of different ways, which deal with all kinds of different issues and reflect the world we live in all its manifold aspects. To back new talent, express ideas in forms that might otherwise not be expressed and be doing something a bit from the general market place, that is our brief, thank goodness. As well as having some mainstream films as well.

I must say one other thing about development of scripts, which is a really important thing. Just because a script doesn't get made at a particular time doesn't make it's a waste of money. It's all part of a process of training and people learning and all that. Obviously they learn more if it does get made, but for a first time writer it often won't get made the first time. It's all part of the process of building an industry. It's something that's not readily available in the industry, always to work with script teams and editors and build an idea.

It's part of R&D development and it's not necessarily a waste of money because you don't make a film at a particular time out of the script. There's all sorts of things that may come out of it; a relationship with the writer. The writer may have learned other things.

It's all part of the process.

**And do you see BBC Films moving into microbudget as some screen agencies are exploring?**

We want to be in all the sectors. We want to do lower budget films and bigger budget film. I do think that many British films are far too expensive for what they are; unnecessarily expensive. And made in old fashioned ways. And we've been trying very much to pioneer new ways to make films. And the films that we've done with Dominic Savage, Francesca Josepf and Pawel Pawlikowski have been good examples of that. Working with different technology in different ways. But British indie films are far more expensive than American indie films, and that's not really sustainable in the long term.

**And what do you think will be the key thing that changes that?**

There won't be the money around any more. There won't be these tax breaks, it won't be so easy to do it. So we'll have to find ways to make films more cheaply.

Multi crewing, multi-tasking, all this stuff. Using different equipment; the equipment is getting cheaper all the time so the process should get easier. Michael Winterbottom has pioneered this, with *In this World* which was done with very small crews and new technology. There needs to be more of that going on.

**With a new Director General, the culture seems more positive towards BBC Films**

For years film at the BBC was quite an equivocal process. People weren't sure if they did or they didn't want it. Because it wasn't top of the agenda. But now the BBC has got right behind it and stated its commitment to backing British Films, and that's really good news. It makes it a much more positive environment to work in. We're very much part of the proposition for the charter renewal and that's obviously a good position to be in. We can offer something valuable to the British film industry and indeed the BBC.

Let me just say one more thing, which I think is really important, there will have to be more speculative script writing. I think that's the way to get started, I'm afraid. It happens much more in America. People can't hang around waiting to get a commission. Having said that, there is money for commissioning with all the money from the Film Council for development. But people will have to be more prepared to write spec scripts and do more work on spec, because that's how the industry works in the rest of the world.

*Dirty Pretty Things* was kind of a spec script. We didn't commission it in the first place; we got the script and then commissioned further drafts of it. We got that from Steve Knight who created *Who Wants to be a Millionaire*, but he hadn't been a writer before that, or not much. We got one before called the *Theory of Flight* that literally came through the post, for Ken Brannagh and Helena Bonham Carter.

To summarise, you just have to be slightly insane, totally driven, never give up and be prepared to suspend all disbelief to make a film, and push through and make your vision happen.

# Pawel Pawlikowski
## *The Last Reosrt*

*Pawel Pawlikowski's feature debut, Last Resort, is that rare combination – a critically acclaimed BAFTA winner that made a good profit for its producers. The average British feature film takes around £350,000 at the box office. Pawel managed to shoot his first feature for less than that with a surprising amount of freedom from the BBC.*

We went to the drama department of the BBC and told them that if they gave us a certain amount of money then we'd come back with an interesting film. I'd done a lot of documentaries that had won a lot of awards before, so I had kudos. Anyway, we went away and came back with a dram. But if you want to be successful you need to have an executive who believes in the thing and will push it - whose career depends on it. The guy who commissioned the thing left the Beeb just afterwards, and then the guy who replaced him didn't really know what to do with it because it wasn't his baby.

It was a documentary budget of around £320,000 - a lot more has been spent since, but shooting that low meant that I had complete freedom. It meant we were very sparing with extras and because we didn't have any sort of production design budget. We just stripped the locations down and shot in a particular way. That's why it feels like such a weird place. We rented this house for the cast and crew to stay in to save money and so we could be together. Dina Korzun (Tanya) would come to me in the middle of the night saying 'I don't understand this scene, can we just imagine it again'? Her and Paddy Considine (Alfie) became partners and a lot of the scenes were invented the day before or on the day.

One of the things about this film, taught by bitter experience in the past, was that I only worked with close friends and people that I liked. It wasn't necessary to have a great track record; I needed very generous people because it was a pretty risky project. We didn't have much of a script so we would re-jig certain scenes while we were shooting. If I'd been with normal British professionals it would have been a nightmare. They would have wanted a perfect script and just executed the plan, whereas I had a tiny documentary group who all lived in one house and they were all very, very supportive.

I tried to short-circuit the system. When you make a film here or in any western country it's all about rewrites and script editors. It becomes a collective effort, but the more people get involved the more formulaic it becomes. So we just tried to get a small amount of money and make the film without getting other people involved. The funny thing is the way the media works, it's more important to have a media image than to make a good film.

England - it's a funny country where you are conned into believing that everything is booming, London is moving and the youth culture is fantastic. And yet everyone carries a misery and total despondency with them. It's a society where all the belief systems have disappeared, where families have collapsed and where joie de vivre has vanished. The simple pleasures just aren't there unless it's drugs or music and it's a very abstract environment. You wouldn't believe that if you were in Soho but that is all just window dressing. It's a very grizzly, empty country and I find that interesting. The question is how to tell a story in an environment like this - I think I've found the key to it. The problem with English films, I don't enjoy watching them actually, is that they just deal with sociology. They translate this [indicating the environment] into social problems, people are miserable, because they are unemployed and they all embody some particular social type. Very few English directors look at what's underneath the surface of society.

*Tom Fogg*

# Becky Lloyd - Scottish Screen

## *Short Film Applications*

*In charge of shorts for Scottish Screen, Becky Lloyd overseas more short film schemes per head than anyone else in the UK, and has been tirelessly inventive in creating and managing new schemes to cover documentary, new media, experimental, children's films and, of course, shorts.*

**What are the most common mistakes people make when they apply for funding?**

I think it is important to distinguish between the short film schemes and the Lottery Short Film Production Fund that we operate:

With the film schemes in general, the most common mistake is probably to try and second guess what the commissioners are looking for in terms of themes, genres and stories, as the resulting applications can appear stale and derivative. I think this is a particular problem with schemes that are part-funded by broadcasters, as there is a tendency to make assumptions about what is appropriate for TV.

To be more specific about certain schemes: Tartan Smalls suffers from people writing scripts that *feature* children, but which don't really work as films *for* children. Proposals for the documentary scheme This Scotland are sometimes underdeveloped with no real sense of characters or storyline.

The most common mistake made when applying to the Short Film Production Fund is not reading the guidelines and application form properly. The films have to be ready to go into pre-production which means that they should be well developed at the point of application, so we require a great deal more detail than we would with the Schemes.

**What could people do to make the job of processing applications easier?**

I'm repeating myself, but read the guidelines and application forms carefully and provide the information and documentation that you've been asked to provide. It may sound old-fashioned, but presentation and deadlines are also important. A badly presented application using unconventional formats for scripts, budgets and schedules, and that misses the deadline, does not inspire confidence in the professionalism of that particular applicant, particularly if they are the producer.

**Do you get too many applications around certain subjects or genres or is it always changing?**

I am very wary of being prescriptive about the subjects or genres, so I would not want to suggest that there are too many of any particular type of film as people would then go too far the other way. I want people to write/make the films they want to make. Our main drive is to nurture new talent, so we would not dismiss a fantastic proposal just because it is "yet another film viewed through the eyes of a child". However we have to make sure that we continue to encourage a range of subjects or genres by being extremely open-minded about the way we commission, by taking risks, by not letting our own "tastes" get in the way and by acknowledging that there are audiences for all types of films from slick, commercial comedy to poetic, character driven drama.

**What are you looking for in applicants?**

This obviously depends on the scheme, but very generally we are of course looking for that spark of real talent, whether it is an ability to construct intelligent, complex screenplays, a real feeling for comedy, or a uniquely sensitive or surreal vision. A tangible passion for the project can also make an applicant stand out, particularly at the interview stage.

# Irvine Allen - Daddy's Girl
# *Palme D'Or winning Tartan Short*

*It must have given Irvine Allen considerable satisfaction to have the £45,000 Scottish Screen backed short he shot, from the script that so many had rejected, accepted at Cannes and put into competition. And even more when he got a call from Cannes to say his film had landed the Palme D'Or.*

It's a universal story about a neglected child waiting outside a pub for her daddy. It follows her subsequent misadventures as she is left prey to the whims and fancies of passing strangers. The themes are neglect and loss of innocence and she learns the cunning needed to survive the street, among some other unsavoury ideas, before being rescued by a local shopkeeper. Her rescue is only temporary though as her father soon appears. It's set over 8 1/2 minutes real time, in the rain. The style is spare and simple, nothing fancy; no cranes, dolly or track. Just a lot of rain machines.

It was shot for £45,000. BBC2 Bristol 10x10 series 12 gave me £18,000, Scottish Screen provided £20,000, the BFI £2000, and the Glasgow film Office another £5000; all acquired in that order. When it was finished, Scottish Screen were on the case quick, and really supportive. They struck a new print which was subtitled into French by a friend of mine. They also gave me a "Go-and-See" grant for a flight to Cannes. They also produced posters and handled publicity. The British Council had been supportive of the film before Cannes and during it.

The pressure I did feel concerned whether I should go or not. My partner Annie was expecting our first child that week so I decided to stay but it wasn't an easy decision. At first I kidded myself that it was too important for my future not to go, but I soon realised that I was fooling myself for the sake of an ego massage. To do a film about a neglected child, and not be there for my own family at such an important time would have been an absolute hypocrisy.

I have spent a lot of time at short film festivals over the last 2 years. I must have seen over five hundred short films and I feel qualified to comment on the biggest mistakes short filmmakers make, so here goes: forgetting you need a good script; not reigning in the actors trying for the Oscar; miscasting; trying to be Quentin Tarantino with a budget of 5 bob. Also, relying on style rather than substance.

To short filmmakers I'd say apply to every short film scheme going. Bust a gut or the budget to stay on film, or at least print to 35mm at the back end. That way you can get into the best festivals; that's where you're going to make your name. Also, don't give up, I spent two years trying to get Daddy's Girl made. Find a good crew who you can get on with, and a DoP who'll give you your place. If all else fails, get a handcam and just do it. Taking pictures is easier than getting good sound so don't skimp on the sound requirements.

*Tom Fogg*

# Gina Fegan - Screen South

*As Chief Executive of Screen South, Gina Fegan has one of the smallest budgets to work with out of any of the English regional agencies and so places a special focus on skills development.*

Our ethos goes against the subsidy culture – we're not hand-out, but hand-up.

Usually people will come to us wanting to make a short film - 80% of applications are for short films, but we actually try not to fund them - we prefer to offer support and skills training. The application process is one where the filmmakers learn to professionalise. Through the funding round, they will pitch to a panel of people from different sides of the industry and those people will give their own advice, as well as our staff, so you're getting quite high level feedback just by the process of applying. We've worked with Scott Meek of Indigo Productions, Alex Marshall of Spice Factory, Dawn Sharpless at Dazzle Films, Linda James at Alibi.

We also run a workshop for everyone wanting to apply to us. We go through the process of funding – does the project have legs; how should you view your own project; the various budgeting info you need to know. So by the time the filmmaker gets to the panel, they should have a budget, a treatment and an outline that could convince any investor in the validity of the project. They've been encouraged to prepare a written statement and have had an experience of making an oral presentation – so they've had proper industry experience.

The open funds are where we have a much more open view. Sometimes people will propose a project which is about how to move them on in the industry. Such as 'I want to present my feature film proposal to the industry'. And this is where we fund the lunch and they do the work in getting the industry to come along, So we allocate a sum of money to their project – they in turn include perhaps another three projects attempting to do the same from the Region who will also join in, and get their industry contacts along, so each is bringing something in. We've used their time and energy and given the money to present the screening – and they've gained the skills in presentation. Of course, to do this they would need to have a viable and developed project - we wouldn't pick someone who hadn't applied to us in the past.

We don't give development money, we give the tools to develop the project – if there are a number of filmmakers then we will back something appropriate, such as help with international sales estimates, preparing to present to financiers, or packaging or pitching, as we can see there's a list of things you need in your toolbox as a filmmaker. It's very much about the skills based needs of the filmmaker, and we try to respond with appropriate projects. We recently sent a group of filmmakers with features to sell out to LA for 10 days – we covered flights and accommodation, helped them prepare their pitch and they did the legwork. The most common failure is people not treating themselves as professionals. We expect everybody to be a professional.

## CHAPTER SEVEN

# DIRECTORY

## Banks

### Barclays Bank Media Banking Centre

27 Soho Square
London
W1A 4WA
Tel: 020 7445 5717
Fax: 020 7445 5802

### Citibank

15233 Ventura Boulevard
Sherman Oaks, California, 91403
USA
Tel: +1 818 528 7593
Fax: +1 818 528 7590
www.citicorp.com
Institutional asset manager investing in the media industry.

### Comerica / Benfield Imperial Entertainment Finance

Comerica Bank, 55 Bishopsgate
London, EC2N 3BD
Tel: 020 7578 7037
www.comerica.com
Comerica is a leading specialty entertainment finance corporation assisting domestic and international clients in all areas of co-production, including accessing territorial tax subsidies and investments for film and television projects abroad. Affiliated office in the UK is Benfield Imperial Entertainment Finance Limited.

### ICB Entertainment Finance (ICBEF)

1840 Century Park East
Los Angeles, California, 90067
USA
Tel: +1 310 712 8678
www.icbef.com
Providing banking, advisory and collection services to the entertainment industry for over 20 years.

### LHO Group

175 Post Road
West Westport, Connecticut, 06880
USA
Tel: +1 203 571 1088
Fax: +1 203 571 1096
www.lhogroup.com
LHO is an investment advisory and fund management firm, providing financial planning advice and designing customised solutions that address the clients specific financial needs.

### Royal Bank of Scotland PLC

Mayfair Media Centre, 65 Piccadilly
London, W1A 2PP
Tel: 020 7290 4649
Fax: 020 7290 4692
www.rbs.co.uk
Specialising in the financing of independent feature films.

### Salem Partners LLC

11111 Santa Monica Boulevard, Suite 1070
Los Angeles, California, 90025
USA
Tel: +1 310 806 4208
Fax: +1 310 806 4201
www.salempartners.com
A full service investment bank, providing services to the media and entertainment industries.

### Union Bank of California

445 South Figueroa Street, 16th Floor
Los Angeles, California, 90071
USA
Tel: +1 213 236 5827
Fax: +1 213 236 5852
Communications, Media and Entertainment division of a boutique bank that can help obtain financing for films, working capital, cash services or capital market products for independent producers and distributors.

## Business Support

### British Venture Capital Association (BVCA)

3 Clements Inn
London
WC2A 2AZ
Fax: 020 7025 2951
bvca@bvca.co.uk
www.bvca.co.uk

The BVCA is a representative body for the UK equity industry. It seeks to assist growth in the industry and to provide information, guides and guidelines to encourage high standards among its members. It also produces guides to investment and private equity that can be downloaded from the web site, including information about the Venture Capital trust and the Enterprise Investment Scheme. The British Venture Capital Association has around 165 members, which represents the vast majority of UK based private equity and venture capital firms.

### Government Office for London

Riverwalk House, 157-161 Millbank
London
SW1P 4RR
Tel: 020 7217 3328
Fax: 020 7217 3450
enquiries.gol@go-regions.gov.uk
www.go-london.gov.uk

### National Business Angels Network (NBAN)

40-42 Cannon Street
London, EC4N 6JJ
Tel: 020 7329 2929
Fax: 020 7329 2626
info@bestmatch.co.uk
www.bestmatch.co.uk

The NBAN aims to assist the equity market by promoting the growth of venture capital in small to medium sized enterprises. It is a non-profit-making organisation, supported by the Small Business Service at the Department of Trade and Industry and is sponsored by high street banks. The network provides a point of contact between businesses and investors and helps each to find a good match. It does this through various services including local programmes, issuing monthly bulletins, and a matching programme between business and investor.

### European Private Equity & Venture Capital Association

*(see EVCA under Belgium)*

### The Enterprise Investment Scheme Association (EISA)

Tylers Croft, Hitchen Hatch Lane
Sevenoaks, Kent
TN13 3AY
www.eisa.org.uk

The EIS Association is an association of member companies and firms which are involved in the promotion of the Enterprise Investment Scheme ('EIS') for the benefit of small to medium sized companies. It has an established history of dealing with tax effective investments in small to medium sized companies for over 14 years. Members who currently provide financial services to the film industry include Baker Tilly, Ingenious Media and Davenport Lyons.

## Competitions

### DM Davies Award

Cardiff Screen Festival, 10 Mount Stuart Square
Cardiff, Wales, CF10 5EE
Tel: 029 2033 3324
Fax: 029 2033 3320
www.iffw.co.uk

### DepicT!

Brief Encounters Short Film Festival Watershed Media Centre
1 Canon's Road, Bristol
BS1 5TX
Tel: 011 7927 5102
Fax: 011 7930 9967
lucy.jefferies@brief-encounters.org.uk
www.depict.org

### Euroscript

Suffolk House, 1-8 Whitfield Place
London
W1T 5JU
Tel: 020 7387 5880
info@euroscript.co.uk
www.euroscript.co.uk

**Kodak**
Kodak House, Station Road
Hemel Hempstead
HP1 1JU
Tel: 014 42 84 5945
Fax: 014 4284 4458
daniel.clark1@kodak.com
www.kodak.com/UK/en/motion/news/short

**Oscar Moore Foundation**
Screen International, 33-39 Bowling Green Lane
London
EC1R 0DA
Tel: 020 7505 8080
www.screendaily.com/omf.asp

**Pocket Shorts**
The Old Caretakers House, Turnbridge Mills
Quay Street
Huddersfield, West Yorkshire
HD1 6QT
Tel: 014 8430 1805
info@pocketshorts.co.uk
www.pocketshorts.com

**Shell LiveWIRE**
Hawthorn House, Forth Banks
Newcastle upon Tyne
NE1 3SG
Tel: 019 1261 5584
Fax: 019 1261 1910
shell-livewire@pne.org
www.shell-livewire.org

**Straight 8**
Godman, 10a Belmont Street
London
W1 8HH
ed.ben@straight8.net
www.straight8.net

**Turner Classic Movies Short Film Competition**
Turner House, 16 Great Marlborough Street
London , W1F 7HS
nick.hart@turner.com
www.tcmonline.co.uk/classicshorts

## Completion Guarantors

**cineFinance**
1875 Century Park East, Suite 1345
Los Angeles, California, 90067
USA
Tel: +1 310 226 6800
Fax: +1 310 226 6810
www.cinefinance.net

cineFinance is a premier international completion guarantor providing the highest level of professionalism, security and client service. Adept at servicing large-scale pictures, films that involve complex financing and/or distribution arrangements, as well as more modest conventional co-productions, the partners, together with a distinguished roster of international production consultants, use their background, expertise and ability to offer value-added service focused on a specific client's particular needs.

**Film Finances Ltd**
14-15 Conduit Street
London
W1S 2XJ
Tel: 020 7629 6557
Fax: 020 7491 7530
filmfinances@ff.co.uk
www.ffi.com

Provider of completion bonds for film productions.

**International Film Guarantors UK (IFG Ltd)**
19 Margaret Street
London
W1W 8RR
Tel: 020 7636 8855
Fax: 020 7323 9356
ukinfo@ifgbonds.co.uk
www.ifgbonds.com

**International Film Guarantors (IFG LP)**
10940 Wilshire Boulevard, Suite 2010
Los Angeles, California, 90024
USA
Tel: +1 310 208 4500
Fax: +1 310 443 8998
usinfo@ifgbonds.com
www.ifgbonds.com

IFG is aleading filmed entertainment completion guarantor, supporting productions with skill, exceptional service and the financial strength of an internationally licensed insurance carrier. They provide filmmakers with high calibre production support while protecting the interests of banks and other financiers of motion picture production.

IFG is the leading filmed entertainment completion guarantor, supporting productions with skill, exceptional service and the financial strength of an internationally licensed insurance carrier. They provides filmmakers with the highest calibre production support while protecting the interests of banks and other financiers of motion picture production. Offices in London and Los Angeles.

## Development Agencies

### Advantage West Midlands (AWM)

3 Priestly Wharf, Holt Street
Aston Science, Birmingham
B7 4BN
Tel: 012 1380 5480
www.advantagewm.co.uk

### Cultural Industries Development Agency (CIDA)

Business Development Centre, 7-15 Greatorex Street
London
E1 5NF
Tel: 020 7247 4720
Fax: 020 7247 7852
info@cida.co.uk
www.cida.co.uk

This agency supports the cultural industries in Tower Hamlets, Hackney and Newham across East London. Once registered, a company can benefit from business, marketing and development support services, information services, creative industry networks, education, training and skills development, advertising opportunities, and small grants. In addition the organisation focuses on social inclusion, capacity building, inward investment, and fundraising activities.

### England Regional Development Agencies (RDA)

Broadway House, Tothill Street
London
SW1H 9NQ
Tel: 020 7222 8180
Fax: 020 7222 8182
www.englandsrdas.com

Regional Development Agencies (RDAs) were set up by Government to promote sustainable economic development in England. Their main tasks are to help the English regions improve their relative economic performance and reduce social and economic disparities within and between regions.

### East Midlands Development Agency (EMDA)

Apex Court, Citylink
Nottingham, NG2 4LA
Tel: 011 5988 8300
Fax: 011 5853 3666
www.emda.org.uk

### East of England Development Agency (EEDA)

The Business Centre, Station Road
Histon, Cambridge , CB4 9LQ
Tel: 012 2348 4519
www.eeda.org.uk

### London Development Agency (LDA)

Devon House, 58-60 St. Katherines Way
London
E1W 1JX
Tel: 020 7954 4688
www.lda.gov.uk

### Northwest Regional Development Agency

PO Box 37, Renaissance House, Centre Park
Warrington, Cheshire
WA1 1XB
Tel: 019 2540 0100
Fax: 019 2540 0400
www.nwda.co.uk

### One North East (ONE)

Stella House, Goldcrest Way
Newburn Riverside, Newcastle Upon Tyne
NE15 8NY
Tel: 019 1229 6200
Fax: 019 1229 6201
www.onenortheast.co.uk

### South East of England Development Agency (SEEDA)

Cross Lanes
Guildford, Surrey
GU1 1YA
Tel: 014 8348 4200
Fax: 014 8348 4247
seeda@seeda.co.uk
www.seeda.co.uk

**South West of England Regional Development Agency (SWRDA)**
Sterling House, Dix's Field
Exeter, Devon
EX1 1QA
Tel: 013 9221 4747
Fax: 013 9221 4848
enquiries@southwestrda.org.uk
www.southwestrda.org.uk

**Yorkshire Forward**
Victoria House, Victoria Place
Leeds, Yorkshire
LS11 5AE
Tel: 011 3394 9600
Fax: 011 3243 1088
www.yorkshire-forward.com

## Distribution - Theatrical

**Amber Films**
5 & 9 Side
Newcastle-upon-Tyne
NE1 3JE
Tel: 019 9232 2000
Fax: 019 230 3217
amberside@btinternet.com
www.amber-online.com

**Arrow Film Distributors**
18 Watford Road
Radlett, Hertfordshire
WD7 8LE
Tel: 019 2385 8306
Fax: 019 2385 9673
info@arrowfilms.co.uk
www.arrowfilms.co.uk

**Artificial Eye Film Company**
14 King Street
London
WC2E 8HR
Tel: 020 7240 5353
Fax: 020 72405242
www.artificial-eye.com

**Axiom Films**
12 D'Arblay Street
London
W1V 3FP
Tel: 020 7243 3111
Fax: 020 7243 3152
mail@axiomfilms.co.uk
www.axiomfilms.co.uk

**bfi Distribution**
21 Stephen Street
London
W1T 1LN
www.bfi.org.uk

**Blue Dolphin Films**
40 Langham Street
London
W1W 7AS
Tel: 020 7255 2494
Fax: 020 7580 7670
info@bluedolphinfilms.com
www.bluedolphinfilms.com

**Blue Light**
231 Portobello Road
London
W11 1LT

**Bollywood Films**
384 D Northolt Road
South Harrow, Middlesex
HA2 8EX

**Buena Vista International**
3 Queen Caroline Street, Hammersmith
London
W6 9PE
Tel: 020 8222 1000
Fax: 020 8222 2795
www.disney.co.uk

**Cinéfile Ltd**
12 Sunbury Place
Edinburgh, Scotland
EH4 3BY
Tel: 013 1224 6191
Fax: 013 1225 6971
info@cinefile.co.uk
www.cinefrance.co.uk

**City Screen**
Hardy House, 16-18 Beak Street,
London
W1F 9RD

**Columbia TriStar Films (UK) / Sony Pictures**
Europe House, 25 Golden Square
London
W1F 9LU
Tel: 020 7533 1111
Fax: 020 7533 1105
wwww.sonypictures.co.uk

**Contemporary Films**
24 Southwood Lawn Road
London, N6 5SF

**Content International Film and Television Ltd**
19 Heddon Street
London
W1B 4BG
Tel: 020 78516500
www.contentinternational.com
Sales, finance, and production of feature films.

**Dogwoof Pictures**
Unit 2 Central Square, 27 St Mark Street
London
E1 8EF
Tel: 020 7488 0605
Fax: 020 7900 3270
info@dogwoofpictures.com
www.dogwoofpictures.com
A film distribution company, specialising in foreign language independent films.

**Entertainment Film Distributors Ltd**
Eagle House, First Floor, 108-110 Jermyn Street
London
SW1Y 6HB
Tel: 020 7930 7744
Fax: 020 7930 9399
Leading independent UK distributor.

**Eros International**
Unit 23, Sovereign Park
Coronation Road
London
NW10 7QP
Tel: 020 8963 8700
Fax: 020 8963 0154
www.erosentertainment.com

**Feature Film Company**
19-21 Heddon Street
London
W1B 4BG

**Gala**
26 Danbury Street
London
N1 8JU

**Guerilla Films**
35 Thornbury Road
Isleworth
TW7 4LQ
Tel: 020 8758 1716
Fax: 020 8758 9364
www.guerilla-films.com

**Ian Rattray**
10 Wiltshire Gardens, Twickenham
Middlesex
TW2 6ND
Tel: 020 8296 0555
Fax: 020 8296 0556
ianrattray@blueyonder.co.uk

**ICA Projects**
12 Carlton House Terrace, The Mall
London
SW1Y 5AH
Tel: 020 7766 1416
www.ica.org.uk
ICA Projects is the Institute of Contemporary Art's film distribution company, theatrically releasing world cinema films in the UK.

**Icon Entertainment**
The Quadrangle, Fourth Floor
180 Wardour Street
London
W1F 8FX
Tel: 020 7494 8100
Fax: 020 7494 8151
www.icon-entertainment.co.uk
A film sales, finance and production company which has established itself as a leading supplier of theatrical feature films to the independent film market.

**Kino Kino!**
24c Alexandra Road
London
N8 0PP
www.dothtm.boltblue.com

**Maiden Voyage Pictures**
The Basement, 18 Cleveland Street
London
W1T 4HZ
enquiries@maidenvoyagepictures.com
www.maidenvoyagepictures.com

**MatCine**
63 Dean Street
London
W1D 4QC
Tel: 020 7287 2332
Fax: 020 7287 2664
capers@btinternet.com
www.matcine.com
A film distribution company, specialising in films for a grown-up audience; the over 40's.

**Metrodome Distribution Ltd**
Fifth Floor, 33 Charlotte Street
London
W1T 1RR
Tel: 020 7153 4424
Fax: 020 7153 4446
www.metrodomegroup.com

An independent distributor acquiring film rights for theatrical and video exploitation in the UK.

**Millivres Multimedia**
Unit M, 32-34 Spectrum House
London
NW5 1LP
Tel: 020 7424 7400
info@millivresmultimedia.co.uk
www.millivresmultimedia.co.uk

**Miracle Communications Limited**
38 Broadhurst Avenue
Edgware, Middlesex
HA8 8TS
Tel: 020 8958 8512
Fax: 020 8958 5112

**Momentum Pictures Limited**
Second Floor, 184-192 Drummond Street
London
NW1 3HP
Tel: 020 7388 1100
Fax: 020 73830404
info@momentumpictures.co.uk
www.momentumpictures.co.uk

An aggressively expanding distribution company, investing considerably in British production.

**Optimum Releasing**
22 Newman Street
London
W1T 1PH
Tel: 020 7637 5403
Fax: 020 7637 5408
info@optimumreleasing.com
www.optimumreleasing.com

A rights distribution company, servicing the release of a diverse range of feature films across theatrical, video, television and online media.

**Pathé Entertainment**
Kent House, 14-17 Market Place
London
W1W 8AR
Tel: 020 7462 4406
Fax: 020 7436 1693
www.pathe.co.uk

**Redbus Film Distribution**
Ariel House, 74A Charlotte Street
London
W1T 4QJ
Tel: 020 7299 8800
Fax: 020 7299 8801
pa@redbus.com
www.redbus.com

One of the leading independent film distributors and producers in the UK.

**Tartan Films Distribution**
Atlantic House, 5 Wardour Street
London, W1D 6PB
Tel: 020 7494 1400
Fax: 020 7439 1922
info@tartanfilms.com
www.tartanfilms.com

**Twentieth Century Fox**
20th Century House,
31-32 Soho Square
London, W1V 6AP
Tel: 020 7437 7766
Fax: 020 7434 2170
www.fox.co.uk

**UGC Films UK**
34 Bloomsbury Street
London
WC1B 3QJ
Tel: 020 7631 4683
Fax: 020 7323 9817
info@ugcfilms.co.uk

UK film distribution arm of the UGC Group.

**United International Pictures (UIP)**
12 Golden Square
London
W1A 2JL
Tel: 020 7534 5200
Fax: 020 7534 5201
www.uip.co.uk

**Universal Pictures Ltd**
Oxford House, 76 Oxford Street
Fourth Floor, London
W1D 1BS
Tel: 020 7079 6058
Fax: 020 7079 6486

**Vertigo Films**
The Big Room Studios, 77 Fortress Road
London
NW5 1AG
Tel: 020 7428 7555
Fax: 020 7485 9713
reception@vertigofilms.com
www.vertigofilms.com

**Warner Brothers**
98 Theobolds Road
London
WC1X 8WB
Tel: 020 7984 5000
Fax: 020 7984 5211
www.warnerbros.co.uk

## Distribution - Video

**2 Entertain Video Ltd**
33 Foley Street
London
W1W 7TL
Tel: 020 7612 3000
www.2entertain.co.uk

**Abbey Home Media**
435-437 Edgware Road
London
W2 1TH
Tel: 020 7563 3910
www.abbeyhomemedia.com

**ADV Films**
18 Soho Square
London
W1D 3QL
Tel: 020 7025 8034
www.advfilms.co.uk

**Anchor Bay Entertainment UK Ltd**
6 Heddon Street
London
W1B 4BT

**BBC Worldwide Ltd**
Woodlands, 80 Wood Lane
London
W12 0TT
Tel: 020 8433 2000
www.bbc.co.uk

**BMG Entertainment UK & Ireland**
Bedford House, 69/79 Fulham High Street
London
SW6 3JW
Tel: 020 7384 7500
www.bmg.com

**Buena Vista Home Entertainment**
3 Queen Caroline Street, Hammersmith
London
W6 9PE
Tel: 020 8222 1000
www.disney.co.uk

**Channel Four DVD**
124 Horseferry Road
London
SW1P 2TX
Tel: 020 7396 4444
www.channel4.com

**Columbia Tristar Home Entertainment**
Sony Pictures Europe House
25 Golden Square
London
W1F 9LU
Tel: 020 7533 1200
www.cthe.co.uk

**DD Home Entertainment**
11 Churchill Court, 58 Station Road
North Harrow, Middlesex
HA2 7SA
Tel: 020 8863 8819
www.ddhe.co.uk

**Eagle Rock Entertainment Ltd**
Eagle House, 22 Armoury Way
London
SW18 1EZ
Tel: 020 8870 5670
www.eagle-rock.com

**EMI Music UK**
EMI House, Brook Green
London
W6 7EF
Tel: 020 7605 5000
www.emirecords.co.uk

**Entertainment UK**
243 Blyth Road
Hayes, Middlesex
UB3 1DN
Tel: 020 8848 7511
www.entuk.com

**Eureka Video**
Unit 9, Ironbridge Close
Great Central Way
London
NW10 0UF
Tel: 020 8451 0600
www.eurekavideo.co.uk

**Firefly Entertainment Ltd**
Suite 5, 3rd Floor
9 North Audley Street
London
W1K 6WF
Tel: 020 7659 0840
www.fireflyentertainment.co.uk

**Fremantle Home Entertainment**
1 Stephen Street
London
W1T 1AL
Tel: 020 7691 6000
www.fremantlemedia.com

**Granada International**
5th Floor, 35-38 Portman Square
London
W1H 0NU
Tel: 020 7486 6688
www.carltonvisual.com

**Hit Entertainment PLC**
5th Floor, Maple House
141-150 Tottenham Court Road
London
W1T 7NF
Tel: 020 7554 2500
Fax: 020 7388 9321
www.hitentertainment.com
Independent producer and distributor of high quality programmes for the world of television for kids and grown-ups alike.

**Lace International**
Lace House, 39-40 The Old Steine
Brighton, East Sussex
BN1 1NH
Tel: 012 7320 2220

**Manga Entertainment**
8 Kensington Park Road
London
W11 3BU
Tel: 020 7229 3000
www.manga.com

**Metrodome Distribution Ltd**
Fifth Floor, 33 Charlotte Street
London
W1T 1RR
Tel: 020 7153 4421
www.metrodomegroup.com

**MGM Home Entertainment**
5 New Road
Richmond, Surrey
TW9 2PR
Tel: 020 8939 9300
www.mgmuk.com
Home video distribution division of MGM Entertainment and Studios.

**Mosaic Home Entertainment**
19-24 Manasty Road, Orton Southgate
Peterborough, Cambridgeshire
PE2 6UP
Tel: 01733 363010
Fax: 017 3336 3011
mail@mosaic-entertainment.co.uk
www.mosaicentertainment.co.uk
Home video distribution.

**Paramount Home Entertainment**
UIP House, 45 Beadon Road
London
W6 0EG
Tel: 020 8741 9333
www.paramount.com
Home video distribution division of Paramount Pictures.

**Pathé Distribution Ltd**
Kent House, 14-17 Market Place
Great Titchfield Street
London
W1W 8AR
Tel: 020 7323 5151
www.pathe.co.uk

**Prism Leisure Corporation Plc**
1 Dundee Way, Mollison Avenue
Enfield, Middlesex
EN3 7SX
Tel: 020 8804 8100
www.prismleisure.com

**Revolver Entertainment**
10 Lambton Place
Notting Hill Gate
London, W11 2SH
Tel: 020 7243 4300
www.revolvergroup.com

**Sanctuary Visual Entertainment**
45-53 Sinclair Road
London
W14 0NS
Tel: 020 7602 6351
www.sanctuarygroup.com

**Telstar Video Entertainment**
Prospect Studios, Barnes High Street
London,
SW13 9LE
Tel: 020 8878 7888
www.telstar.co.uk

**Twentieth Century Fox Home Entertainment**
20th Century House, 31-32 Soho Square
London
W1D 3AP
Tel: 020 7437 7766
Fax: 020 7434 2170
www.fox.co.uk

**Universal Pictures Video**
1 Sussex Place
London
W6 9XS
Tel: 020 8910 5000

**Video Collection International**
76 Dean Street
London
W1D 3SQ
Tel: 020 7396 8888
www.vciplc.co.uk

**Warner Home Video**
Warner House, 98 Theobald's Road
London
WC1X 8WB
Tel: 020 7984 6400
www.warnerbros.co.uk

**Warner Vision UK (music videos)**
The Electric Lighting Stn, 45 Kensington Court
London
W8 5DA
Tel: 020 7938 5668
www.wmg.com

# Film Commissions

NB Most film commissions come under the jurisdiction of the relevant screen agency for that region.

**Bath Film Office**
Abbey Chambers, Abbey Church Yard
Bath
BA1 1LY
Tel: 01225 477 711
Fax: 01225 477 279
maggie_ainley@bathnes.gov.uk
www.visitbath.co.uk

**Isle of Man Film Commission**
Hamilton House, Peel Road
Douglas
Isle of Man
IM1 5EP
Tel: 016 2468 7173
Fax: 016 2468 7171
iofilm@dti.gov.im
www.filmmann.com

The Isle of Man Film and Television Fund offers equity investment for films and television productions that are shot at least in part on the island.

**Mid Wales Screen Commission**
6G The Science Park, Cefn Llan
Aberystwyth, Wales
SY23 3AH
Tel: 019 7061 7995
Fax: 019 7061 7942
enquiries@walesscreencommission.co.uk
www.walesscreencommission.co.uk

**North Wales Screen Commission**
Mentec, Deiniol Road, Bangor
Gwynedd, Wales
LL57 2UP
Tel: 012 4835 3769
Fax: 012 4835 2497

**Northern Ireland Film Television Commission (NIFTC)**
3rd Floor, Alfred House, Alfred Street
Belfast, Northern Ireland
BT2 8ED
Tel: 028 9023 2444
Fax: 028 9023 9918
info@niftc.co.uk
www.niftc.co.uk

**Scottish Screen**
249 West George Street, 2nd Floor
Glasgow, Scotland
G2 4QE
Tel: 014 1302 1700
Fax: 014 1302 1778
info@scottishscreen.com
www.scottishscreen.com

**South East Wales Screen Commission**
Sgrîn, The Bank, 10 Mount Stuart Square
Cardiff Bay
Cardiff, Wales
CF10 5EE
Tel: 029 2043 5385
Fax: 029 2043 5380
enquiries@walesscreencommission.co.uk
www.walesscreencommission.co.uk

**South West Scotland Screen Commission**
Gracefield Arts Centre, 28 Edinburgh Road
Dumfries
DG1 1JQ
Tel: 01387 263666
Fax: 01387 263666
screencom@dumgal.gov.uk

**South West Wales Screen Commission**
King's Head, Bridge Street, Llandeilo
Carmarthenshire, Wales
SA19 6BN
Tel: 015 5882 5000
Fax: 015 5882 5001
enquiries@walesscreencommission.co.uk
www.walesscreencommission.co.uk

**Wales Screen Commission**
6G The Science Park, Cefn Llan
Aberystwyth, Ceredigion
SY23 3AH
Tel: 019 7062 7186
Fax: 019 7062 6831
enquiries@walesscreencommission.co.uk
www.walesscreencommission.co.uk

## Film Festivals

**Edinburgh International Film Festival**
88 Lothian Road
Edinburgh, EH3 9BZ
Tel: 013 1228 4051
Fax: 013 1229 5501
info@edfilmfest.org.uk
www.edfilmfest.org.uk

**Raindance Film Festival**
81 Berwick Street
Londo,
W1F 8TW
Tel: 020 7287 3833
Fax: 020 7439 2243
info@raindance.co.uk
www.raindance.co.uk
Igniting and overseeing major shifts in the world of independent British films, providing a combination of innovative film training, a major film festival and the prestigious British Independent Film Awards.

**Sheffield International Documentary Film Festival**
The Workstation, 15 Paternoster Row
Sheffield
S1 2BX
Tel: 011 4276 5141
Fax: 011 4272 1849
info@sidf.co.uk
www.sidf.co.uk
Kathy Loizou

## Public funding

**Alt-W**
Leisure and Arts Department, Floor 13
Tayside House
Dundee, Scotland
DD1 3RA
Tel: 013 8243 3042
info@alt-w.com
www.alt-w.com

**Arts Council of England**
14 Great Peter Street
London
SW1P 3NQ
Tel: 020 7333 0100
Fax: 020 7973 6590
enquiries@artscouncil.org.uk
www.artscouncil.org.uk

**Arts Council of Northern Ireland**
MacNiece House, 77 Malone Road
Belfast, Northern Ireland
BT9 6AQ
Tel: 028 9038 5200
Fax: 028 9066 1715
reception@artscouncil-ni.org
www.artscouncil-ni.org

**Arts Council of Wales**
9 Museum Place
Cardiff, Wales
CF10 3NX
Tel: 029 2037 6500
Fax: 029 2022 1447
info@artswales.org.uk
www.artswales.org.uk

**Awards for All**
Ground Floor, St Nicholas Court
25-27 Castle Gate, Nottingham
NG1 7AR
Tel: 011 5934 9350
Fax: 011 5934 9355
enquiries.england@awardsforall.org.uk
www.awardsforall.org.uk

**Big Lottery Fund**
1 Plough Place
London
EC4A 1DE
Tel: 020 7211 1800
Fax: 020 7211 1750
enquiries@biglotteryfund.org.uk
www.biglotteryfund.org.uk

**Cineworks**
Glasgow Media Access Centre, Third Floor
34 Albion Street
Glasgow, Scotland
G11 1LH
Tel: 0141 553 2620
Fax: 0141 553 2660
info@cineworks.co.uk
www.cineworks.co.uk

**Cornwall Film**
Pydar House, Pydar Street
Truro, Cornwall
TR1 1EA
Tel: 018 7232 2886
Fax: 018 7232 2887
office@cornwallfilm.com
www.cornwallfilm.com

**Culture 2000**
Cultural Contact Point UK, EUCLID
85-89 Duke Street, Liverpool
L1 5AP
Tel: 015 1709 2564
Fax: 015 1709 8647
info@euclid.co.uk
www.culture2000.info

**EM Media**
35-37 St Mary's Gate
Nottingham, Nottinghamshire
NG1 1PU
Tel: 0115 934 9090
Fax: 0115 950 0988
info@em-media.org.uk
www.em-media.org.uk

**Film London**
20 Euston Centre, Regents Place
London
NW1 3JH
Tel: 020 7387 8787
Fax: 020 7387 8788
www.filmlondon.org.uk

**First Film Foundation**
9 Bourlet Close
London
W1P 7PJ
Tel: 020 7580 2111
info@firstfilm.co.uk
www.firstfilm.co.uk

**First Light**
Progress Works, Heath Mill Lane
Birmingham
B9 4AL
Tel: 012 1693 2091
Fax: 012 1693 2096
info@firstlightmovies.com
www.firstlightmovies.com

**Four Minute Wonders**
Studio 120, 96 Rose Street
Edinburgh, Scotland
EH2 4AT
www.4minutewonders.com

**Four Minute Wonders**
Greenmeadow Springs, Tongwynlais
Cardiff, Wales
CF15 7NE
Tel: 029 2069 4900
Fax: 029 2069 4999
www.4minutewonders.com

**Glasgow Film Office**
City Chambers, George Square
Glasgow, Scotland
G2 1DU
Tel: 014 1287 0424
Fax: 014 1287 0311
film.office@drs.glasgow.gov.uk
www.glasgowfilm.org.uk

**Greenwich Film Fund**
Studio 2B1, The Old Seager Distillery Brookmill Road
Greenwich, London
SE8 4JT
Tel: 020 8694 2211
Fax: 020 8694 2971
fund@greenwichfilms.demon.co.uk
www.greenwichfilms.co.uk

**Heritage Lottery Fund**
7 Holbein Place
London
SW1W 8NR
Tel: 020 7591 6000
Fax: 020 7591 6001
enquire@hlf.org.uk
www.hlf.org.uk

**The Jerwood Charitable Trust**
22 Fitzroy Square
London
W1T 6EN
Tel: 020 73886287
info@jerwood.org
www.jerwood.org.uk

**London Borough of Croydon**
Croydon Clocktower
Katharine Street, Croydon
CR9 1ET
Tel: 0208686 4433
Fax: 020 8253 1032
www.croydon.gov.uk/clocktower

**London Borough of Enfield**
Arts Unit Forty Hall
Forty Hill, Enfield
EN2 9HA
Tel: 020 8363 8196
Fax: 020 8367 9098
forty.hall@enfield.gov.uk
www.enfield.gov.uk
The Enfield Film Fund is run by Enfield Council and Film London.

**London Borough of Newham**
Regeneration & Partnerships Division, 330 Barking Road
London
E6 2RP
Tel: 020 8430 2793
www.newham.gov.uk/filmfund
The Newham Film Fund is run by Newham council and Film London.

**NESTA**
Fishmongers' Chambers,
110 Upper Thames Street
London
EC4R 3TW
Tel: 020 7645 9500
nesta@nesta.org.uk
www.nesta.org.uk

**North West Vision**
233 Tea Factory, 82 Wood Street
Liverpool
L1 4DQ
Tel: 015 1708 2967
Fax: 015 1708 2984
info@northwestvision.co.uk
www.northwestvision.co.uk

**The Prince's Trust**
18 Park Square East
London
NW1 4LH
Tel: 020 7543 1234
Fax: 020 7543 1200
webinfops@princes-trust.org.uk
www.princes-trust.co.uk

**Northern Film & Media**
Central Square, Forth Street
Newcastle
NE1 3PJ
Tel: 019 1269 9200
Fax: 019 1269 9213
info@northernmedia.org
www.northernmedia.org

**Scottish Arts Council**
12 Manor Place
Edinburgh, Scotland
EH3 7DD
Tel: 013 1226 6051
Fax: 013 1225 9833
help.desk@scottisharts.org.uk
www.scottisharts.org.uk

**Scottish Screen**
249 West George Street, 2nd Floor
Glasgow, Scotland
G2 4QE
Tel: 014 1302 1700
Fax: 014 1302 1778
info@scottishscreen.com
www.scottishscreen.com

**Screen South**
Folkestone Enterprise Centre
Shearway Road
Folkestone, Kent
CT19 4RH
Tel: 013 0329 8222
Fax: 013 0329 8227
info@screensouth.org
www.screensouth.org

**Screen Yorkshire**
Studio 22, 46 The Calls
Leeds, Yorkshire, LS2 7EY
Tel: 011 3294 4410
Fax: 011 3294 4989
info@screenyorkshire.co.uk
www.screenyorkshire.co.uk

**Sgrîn Cymru Wales**
The Bank, 10 Mount Square
Cardiff Bay
Cardiff, Wales, CF10 5EE
Tel: 02920 333 300
Fax: 029 20 333320
sgrin@sgrin.co.uk
www.sgrin.co.uk

**South West Screen**
St Bartholomews Court, Lewins Mead
Bristol , BS1 5BT
Tel: 0117 952 9977
Fax: 0117 952 9988
info@swscreen.co.uk
www.swscreen.co.uk

**Tower Hamlets and Hackney Film Fund**
Brady Centre, 192 Hanbury Street
London, E1 5HU
Tel: 020 7364 7920
Fax: 020 7364 7901
filmsoffice@towerhamlets.gov.uk

**UK Film Council**
10 Little Portland Street
London, W1W 7JG
Tel: 020 7861 7861
Fax: 020 7861 7862
info@ukfilmcouncil.org.uk
www.ukfilmcouncil.org.uk

**UnLtd**
123 Whitecross Street
London, EC1Y 8JJ
Tel: 020 7566 1100
Fax: 020 7566 1101
info@unltd.org.uk
www.unltd.org.uk

**London Borough of Wandsworth**
Arts Office, Room 224A, The Town Hall
Wandsworth High Street
London
SW18 2PU
Tel: 020 8871 8711
arts@wandsworth.gov.uk
www.wandsworth.gov.uk/arts

**The Wellcome Trust**
The Wellcome Building, 183 Euston Road
London
NW1 2BE
Tel: 020 7611 8888
contact@wellcome.ac.uk
www.wellcome.ac.uk

**City of Westminster Arts Council**
Room 70, Marylebone Library
Marylebone Road
London
NW1 5PS
Tel: 020 7641 1017
Fax: 020 7641 1018
cwac@ukonline.co.uk
www.cwac.org.uk

**West London Film Fund Awards**
Business Enterprise Centre, TEK House
11-13 Uxbridge Road
London
W12 8TB
Tel: 020 8746 0355
Fax: 020 8740 0493
www.focuswest.co.uk

## Government Agencies

**British Council**
Film & Television Department, 10 Spring Gardens
London
SW1A 2BN
Tel: 020 7389 3051
Fax: 020 7389 3175
filmandliterature@brtishcouncil.org
www.britfilms.com

The British Council is responsible for international educational and cultural relations, and supports the British Film Industry, by promoting British films through key national events and festivals.

**Department of Culture, Media and Sport (DCMS)**
2-4 Cockspur Street
London
SW1Y 5DH
Tel: 020 7211 6000
Fax: 020 7711 6249
enquiries@culture.gov.uk
www.culture.gov.uk

The DCMS is responsible for Government policy on the arts, sport, the National Lottery, tourism, libraries, museums and galleries, broadcasting, film, the music industry, press freedom and regulation, licensing, gambling and the historic environment. It aims to improve the quality of life for all through cultural and sporting activities, to support the pursuit of excellence and to champion the tourism, creative and leisure industries. The DCMS also works with other film-related bodies, such as the National Film and Television School (which it funds), the British Film Commission, and the British Film Institute.

**Department of Trade and Industry (DTI)**
DTI Enquiry Unit, 1 Victoria Street
London
SW1H 0ET
Tel: 020 7215 5000
dti.enquiries@dti.gsi.gov.uk
www.dti.gov.uk

The DTI helps people and companies become more productive by promoting enterprise, innovation and creativity. They champion UK business at home and abroad, invest heavily in world-class science and technology, and protect the rights of working people and consumers.

**Inland Revenue**
Film Industry Unit, Tyne Bridge Tower
Gateshead, Tyne and Wear
NE8 2DT
Tel: 019 1490 3662
Fax: 019 1490 3851
www.inlandrevenue.gov.uk

The Inland Revenue is responsible to the Treasury for the administration of tax-related matters, and acts a source of information for the public. Film-related tax and investment issues form part of its remit.

**Inland Revenue Savings, Pensions, Share Schemes (IR(SPSS))**
Technical Advice (VCT), St John's House
Merton Road, Bootle
L69 9BB
Tel: 015 14726154
www.inlandrevenue.gov.uk/spss

IR Savings, Pensions, Share Schemes is a business stream of the Inland Revenue. It is responsible for occupational and personal pensions, including approval and stakeholder pensions; personal savings schemes, including ISAs, the tax Deduction Scheme for Interest, Venture Capital Trusts (approval, accounts and reliefs) and continuing work on PEPs, TESSAs, MIRAS and Vocational Training Relief; Employee Share Schemes and equity remuneration; Audit work on banks, building societies and other financial intermediaries.

**Inland Revenue Small Company Enterprise Centre (SCEC)**
TIDO, Ty Glas
Llanishen
Cardiff, Wales
CF14 5ZG
Tel: 029 20327400
Fax: 029 20327398
enterprise.centre@ir.gsi.gov.uk
www.inlandrevenue.gov.uk

**Office of National Statistics**
The Library, Cardiff Road
Newport, South Wales
NP10 8XG
Tel: 0845 601 3034
Fax: 01633 652747
info@statistics.gov.uk
www.statistics.gov.uk

The official home of UK statistics, providing summaries and detailed data on Britain's national and local economy, population and society free of charge.

### Patent Office

The Patent Office, Concept House
Cardiff Road, Newport
South Wales
NP10 8QQ
Tel: 084 5950 0505
Fax: 016 3381 3600
enquiries@patent.gov.uk
www.patent.gov.uk

The Patent Ofiice handles the registration of patents and trademarks, as well as provide information to the public and clients through their web site, publications, free leaflets and their consultation service. Their aims are to stimulate innovation and enhance the international competitiveness of British Industry and commerce, offering customers an accessible, high quality, value for money system both national and international, for granting intellectual property rights.

### Small Firms Loan Guarantee Scheme (SFLGS)

Small Business Service, Kingsgate House
66-74 Victoria Street
London
SW1E 6SW
Tel: 084 5600 9006
gatewayenquiries@sbs.gsi.gov.uk

The Small Firms Loan Guarantee scheme (SFLG) is a UK-wide, Government backed scheme, and joint venture between the DTI and approved lenders. The scheme provides loans between £5000 and £100,000 for companies with a trading record of less than 2 years and this amount is increased to £250,000 for the older businesses. The DTI do not lend the money as they leave the commercial decision to the bankers. The loans are provided by the approved lenders who make all the commercial decisions about the loan application and SBS cannot intervene in that commercial process. Most business types are allowed including sole traders, Partnerships and Limited companies.

## industry Organisations

### British Academy of Film & Television Arts (BAFTA)

195 Piccadilly
London
W1J 9LN
Tel: 020 7734 0022
Fax: 020 7734 1792
www.bafta.org

BAFTA organises many events for its members from the film, television, interactive and children's entertainment industries. The most notable is the British Academy Film Awards presented each year in February. Members are invited to nominate films for the different categories; the shortlist is then voted on either by the voting members or a selected jury. Members must have at least three years experience in the industry contributing significantly within it. A current member with experience of the individual's work must also act as a referee.

### British Board of Film Classification (BBFC)

3 Soho Square
London
W1D 3HD
Tel: 020 7440 1570
Fax: 020 7287 0141
www.bbfc.co.uk

The British Board of Film Classification are responsible for viewing, and classifying, all films intended for theatrical and video/DVD release in the UK, under the Cinemas Act 1985, or the Video Recordings Act 1984, respectively. They may also ban a film or censor certain parts of it. The organisation is independent, funded by fees from those submitting films for classification.

### British Film Institute (BFI)

21 Stephen Street
London
W1T 1LN
Tel: 020 7255 1444
Fax: 020 7436 7950
www.bfi.org.uk

**British Independent Film Awards**
81 Berwick Street
London
W1F 8TW
Tel: 020 7287 3833
Fax: 020 7439 2243
info@bifa.org.uk
www.bifa.org.uk
Celebrates the excellence and achievement in independently funded British films, honours new talent and promotes British films and filmmaking across the world.

**British Kinematograph, Sound and Television Society (BKSTS)**
Pinewood Studios
Iver Heath, Buckinghamshire
SL0 0NH
Tel: 017 5365 6656
Fax: 017 5365 7016
info@bksts.com
www.bksts.com
The Society is dedicated to the promotion of excellence in these fields. Whilst remaining independent of all governmental and commercial organisations, it is active in fostering co-operation with other societies in the industry and in promoting its aims throughout the world. The BKSTS supports individuals involved in the creative or technological production of the moving image, by offering its members events, lectures, training, courses and information. Members range from students to retired practitioners. The BKSTS is funded by sponsors and annual member fees.

**Broadcasting Entertainment Cinematograph and Theatre Union (BECTU)**
373-377 Clapham Road
London,
SW9 9BT
Tel: 020 7346 0900
Fax: 020 7346 0901
info@bectu.org.uk
www.bectu.org.uk
BECTU represents the interests of its members, comprising permanently employed, freelance and contract workers within the screen, theatre, entertainment, leisure, media and related industries in the UK. BECTU is funded by annual membership fees, which vary depending on the membership type. Full membership can cost 1% of the individual's earnings with a ceiling of £400. Changes to this exist for payments by standing order, and introductory rates apply for new members in their first year, of either £120 for professionals or £30 for recent graduates.

**Directors Guild of Great Britain (DGGB)**
Acorn House, 314-320 Gray's Inn Road
London
WC1X 8DP
Tel: 020 7278 4343
Fax: 020 7278 4742
guild@dggb.co.uk
www.dggb.co.uk
The Guild represents directors in all media: film, television, theatre, radio, opera, commercials, corporate, multimedia and new technology. It is a trade union, offering help with contracts, a campaigning voice, policy to influence the future of the industry, and advice for members to meet and share their skills. The Director's Guild also lobbies important issues on behalf of its members.

**Equity**
London Office, Guild House
Upper St Martins Lane
London
WC2H 9EG
Tel: 020 7379 6000
Fax: 020 7379 7001
www.equity.org.uk
This trade union represents the rights of artists from the fields of arts and entertainment. Members receive an equity card, indicating their professional status, and can benefit from help and advice, a pension fund, and minimum pay and conditions negotiated for Equity members. Membership rates vary depending on whether the member is a young person (£20/year plus joining fee of £25), a student (£10), a long serving member (free), or full member (1% of annual earnings for those on a certain salary minimum and a

joining fee of £25). To receive membership, applicants must already be working professionally in the industry.

**The Guild of British Camera Technicians (GBCT)**
Panavision UK, Metropolitan Centre
Bristol Road, Greenford
UB6 8GD
Tel: 020 8813 1999
admin@gbct.org
www.gbct.org
The GBCT is a member association for individuals who work with motion picture cameras. This includes: directors of photography, camera operators, camera assistants, grips, gaffers, script supervisors, and stills photographers. Members benefit from training, products and services and a crew directory used by industry employers.

**Lux**
3rd Floor, 18-26 Shacklewell Lane
London
E8 2EZ
Tel: 020 7503 3980
Fax: 020 7503 1606
info@lux.org.uk
www.lux.org.uk
LUX is a registered charity for the promotion and support of artists' moving image work both in the UK and internationally.

**New Producer's Alliance (NPA)**
Suite 1.07 The Tea Building, 56 Shoreditch High Street
London
E1 6JJ
Tel: 020 7613 0440
Fax: 020 7729 1852
queries@npa.org.uk
www.npa.org.uk
The NPA is a charitable organisation set up to support independent new producers in the UK. Members benefit from a range of training, events, information and free and discounted services, including legal and financial telephone hot lines, and an online member's directory. NPA also lobbies important issues on behalf of its members, and offers information and advice about raising finance, copyright, and other services.

The NPA is funded by sponsors and minimal annual membership fees, which range from £75 to £675. Individuals and organisations within the industry are eligible to join, and members vary from students to established companies.

**Producers Alliance for Film and Television (PACT)**
45 Mortimer Street
London
W1W 8HJ
Tel: 020 7331 6000
Fax: 020 7331 6700
enquiries@pact.co.uk
www.pact.co.uk
PACT is a trade association for the independent film, television and media industries, representing the interests of its members to broadcasters, the government and the EU. Members range from production companies, financial companies, distribution companies and other related commercial services that can benefit from a range of resources, training, services, events, publications, and information. PACT is funded by annual membership fees and members must be a limited company. The fees vary from £825 per annum to £3970 per annum, depending on the company's annual turnover and field within the industry.

**Production Guild of Great Britain (PGGB)**
Pinewood Studios
Iver Heath, Buckinghamshire
SL0 0NH
Tel: 017 5365 1767
Fax: 017 5365 2803
lynne@productionguild.com
www.productionguild.com
The Production Guild is a membership association for senior management individuals in film and television. Membership guarantees that an individual has achieved a certain level of experience and expertise in their field, encouraging employers to use the

guild as a resource for personnel. The guild also offers some services to its members and lobbies important issues on behalf of the members. The PGGB is funded by annual membership fees, which range from £50 to £250, with an additional application fee.

### Professional Lighting and Sound Association (PLASA)

38 St Leonards Road
Eastbourne, East Sussex
BN21 3UT
Tel: 01323 410335
Fax: 01323 646905
membership@plasa.org
www.plasa.org

PLASA is a trade association for companies all over the globe, which trade with light, sound and audio-visual technologies. Member companies are from entertainment, presentation, architectural and communication industries. It was established to provide commercial benefits to a business community, whilst improving working practices and advancing levels of safety and training within the entertainment, presentation, installation and communications industries. The association is funded by annual membership fees, which range from £50, for an individual's membership, to £450 plus a £100 joining fee for full company membership.

### Rocliffe New Writing Forum

Rocliffe Ltd, PO Box 37344
London, N1 8YB
Tel: 07801 650 602
info@rocliffe.com
www.rocliffe.com

Rocliffe New Writing Forum is a platform for new writing and a networking event. Each forum has a guest co-chair from the industry giving feedback from a commercial perspective about the work performed. Past co-chairs have included Nik Powell, Michael Kuhn, Martha Coleman, and Ed King (see interview in Chapter 3 for more info)

### Screenwriters Workshop

Suffolk House
Whitfield Place off Whitfield Street
London
W1T 5JA
Tel: 0207 387 5511
screenoffice@tiscali.net
www.lsw.org.uk

The Screenwriters Workshop runs courses, workshops, events, a report service and script consultancies for writers and producers who wish to learn about screenwriting and develop a treatment or script to industry standard. It has a close working relationship with the New Producers Alliance, and one of its schemes is MATCH, which pairs a writer with a producer at an early stage of development.

### Script Factory

Wellbeck House, 66/67 Wells Street
London, W1T 3PY
Tel: 020 7323 1414
Fax: 020 7323 9464
general@scriptfactory.co.uk

The Script Factory supports screenwriters and script development through a number of schemes and projects across the UK and Europe. These include the Scene events, which take place at festivals such as London, Edinburgh, Berlin, Cannes and Rio, and the Masterclass programme that runs ahead of preview screenings in London. UK Film Council funded training covers script development and writing, with further services including script development, script registration and rehearsal room hire.

### Shooting People

www.shootingpeople.org

One of the web's largest and most popular filmmaking communities, Shooting People is run by filmmakers for filmmakers. It is 'a place for you to get what you need and share what you have' for anyone wanting to work in indie film - writers, directors, actors, producers, agents, cinematographers, animators, crew, editors, and people generally interested in the independent UK film industry.

As well as daily email bulletins that keep you connected with film people across the UK, SP runs events and screenings, interviews upcoming filmmakers, gets discounts for members and publishes books (including the fore-runner to this book, and a book on Documentary distribution and screenings).

## Law Firms

### Addleshaw Goddard

150 Aldersgate Street
London
EC1A 4EJ
Tel: 44 207 606 885
Fax: 44 207 606 4390
info@addleshawgoddard.com
www.addleshawgoddard.com

A leading UK law firm that is focused on delivering the highest quality legal advice and excellent client service with specialisation within the media and communications sector.

### Ashurst

Broadwalk House, 5 Appold Street
London
EC2A 2HA
Tel: 020 7638 1111
Fax: 020 7638 1112
enquiries@ashurst.com
www.ashurst.com

Ashurst is a leading international law firm advising corporates and financial institutions, with core businesses in M&A, corporate and structured finance.

### Bird & Bird

90 Fetter Lane
London
EC4A 1JP
Tel: 020 7415 6000
Fax: 020 7415 6111
www.twobirds.com

International sector focused full service law firm with a strong presence in the media sector.

### Davenport Lyons

30 Old Burlington Street
London
W1S 3NL
Tel: 020 7468 2600
Fax: 020 7437 8216
dl@davenportlyons.com
www.davenportlyons.com

A leading entertainment and media practice providing comprehensive legal services across a broad spectrum of market sectors including media in all its forms (film, TV, radio music, theatre, publishing and newspapers), advertising, sport and leisure, e-commerce and new media.

### Denton Wilde Sapte

Five Chancery Lane, Clifford's Inn
London
EC4A 1BU
Tel: 020 7242 1212
Fax: 020 7404 0087
info@dentonwildesapte.com
www.dentonwildesapte.com

A large film finance practice, representing leading UK and international banks and financial institutions, Hollywood studios and production companies. Providing advise on all aspects of film finance, including project finance, revolving credit facilities, syndicated loans, secured and equity lending and tax-based financing structures.

### Dorsey & Whitney LLP

21 Wilson Street
London
EC2M 2TD
Tel: 020 7588 0800
Fax: 020 7588 0555
www.dorsey.com

The Creative Industries practice group provides focused, seamless service to clients involved in the music, film, TV, video, DVD, fashion/luxury brands, advertising, publishing, sport, leisure, animation, computer games and technology sectors.

**Finers Stephens Innocent**
179 Great Portland Street
London
W1W 5LS
Tel: 020 7323 4000
Fax: 020 7580 7069
marketing@fsilaw.co.uk
www.fsilaw.co.uk
Leading law firm advising on all aspects of motion picture production, financing and distribution.

**Hammonds**
Lloyds Of London Office
Suite 688, One Lime Street
London
EC3M 7HA
Tel: 020 7327 3388
Fax: 020 7621 1217
enquiries@hammonds.com
www.hammonds.com
Providing a specialist pan European Media & Communication team, combining local information with an international perspective on all aspects of production, creation, protection, exploitation, finance, distribution, regulation or enforcement.

**Howard Kennedy**
Harcourt House, 19 Cavendish Square
London
W1A 2AW
Tel: 020 7636 1616
Fax: 020 7491 2899
enquiries@howardkennedy.com
www.howardkennedy.com
Howard Kennedy is a London-based law firm offering national and international clients a broad range of legal services, including all aspects of entertainment, media and sports law including film and television finance, production and distribution.

**Lee & Thompson**
Green Garden House, 15-22 St Christophers Place
London
W1U 1NL
Tel: 020 7935 4665
Fax: 020 7563 4949
mail@leeandthompson.com
www.leeandthompson.com
Lee & Thompson is a leading media and entertainment law firm, with experience in all areas of the industry, representing individual directors, producers and writers as well as major corporations.

**Marriott Harrison**
12 Great James Street
London
WC1 3DR
Tel: 020 7209 2000
Fax: 020 7209 2001
email@marriottharrison.co.uk
www.marriottharrison.co.uk
Marriott Harrison is a leading practice, specialising in film, television, music and new media. The firm is also active in advising theatre owners and production companies.

**Media Law Partnership**
33 Prospect Road
London
NW2 2JU
Tel: 020 7435 7127
Fax: 087 0130 7486
Offers experience in all aspects of the negotiation and drafting of agreements for film production, film financing and international co-productions.

**Olswang**
90 High Holborn
London
WC1V 6XX
Tel: 020 7067 3000
Fax: 020 7067 3999
olsmail@olswang.com
www.olswang.com
Olswang is a full-service law firm known for its groundbreaking work in the fields of media, communications, technology and property.

**Osbourne Clarke**
Hillgate House, 26 Old Bailey House
London
EC4M 7HW
Tel: 020 7809 1000
Fax: 020 7809 1005
www.osbourneclarke.com
One of the UK's more progressive commercial law firms, specialising in all aspects of media.

**Richards Butler**
Beaufort House, 15 St Botolph Street
London
EC3A 7EE
Tel: 020 7247 6555
Fax: 020 7247 5091
www.richardsbutler.com
Richards Butler provides expertise in contractual matters relating to film and television production, financing and distribution; on franchise bids for broadcasting and cable; on regulatory compliance; on all aspects of intellectual property, including rights clearances, character protection, and anti-piracy actions; on defamation and freedom of expression issues; on advertising and sales promotion law; and on competition matters affecting the media industries.

**Schillings**
Royalty House, 72-74 Dean Street
London
W1D 3TL
Tel: 020 7453 2500
Fax: 020 7453 2600
legal@schillings.co.uk
www.schillings.co.uk
Schillings is renowned for its media management and media intervention on behalf of clients and an in-depth knowledge and understanding of the various media industries in which it acts.

**Simkins Partnership**
45 - 51 Whitfield Street
London
W1T 4HB
Tel: 020 7907 3000
Fax: 020 7907 3111
info@simkins.com
www.simkins.com

**Simons Muirhead Burton**
50 Broadwick Street
London
W1F 7AG
Tel: 020 7734 4499
Fax: 020 7734 3263
mail@smab.co.uk
www.smab.co.uk
Law firm handling all aspects of film, television, video, theatre and radio agreements, including development, production and financing and other contractual work.

**SJ Berwin**
222 Gray's Inn Road
London
WC1X 8XF
Tel: 020 7533 2222
Fax: 020 7533 2000
info@sjberwin.com
www.sjberwin.com

## Private Funds

*(see Funding Organisation chapter for more info)*

**Aurelius**
8 Golden Square
London
W1F 9HY
Tel: 020 7287 6655
Fax: 020 7287 6294
info@aureliuscapital.com
www.aureliuscapital.com
One of the UK's leading facilitators of equity and tax-based financing for motion film productions. Offers gap finance and brokering, press and advertising finance, and a host of other services.

**Baker Street**
96 Baker Street
London
W1U 6TJ
Tel: 020 7487 3677
Fax: 020 7487 5667
enquiries@bakerstreetfinance.tv
www.bakerstreetfinance.tv
Baker Street Media Finance specialises in the co-production, financing and structuring of British feature films, and British qualifying international co-productions. Baker Street has established strong relationships with major production companies and studios as well as industry bodies such as Film Council, Scottish Screen, and the Australian Film Finance Corporation.

**Future Films Ltd**
25 Noel Street
London
W1F 8GX
Tel: 020 7434 6600
Fax: 020 7434 6633
www.futurefilmgroup.com
Offers an integrated package of film production finance including the structuring of international co-productions, which may also include the provisions of production services and state-of-the-art post production facilities.

**Grosvenor Park Media Limited**
53-54 Grosvenor Street
London
W1K 3HU
Tel: 020 7529 2500
Fax: 020 7529 2511
funding@grosvenorpark.com
www.grosvenorpark.com
Grosvenor Park is a leading provider of tax based film finance to producers around the world. With over 20 years of experience in film and television financing and international co-productions, Grosvenor Park has raised over $5 billion for over 400 film and television productions and manages investments on behalf of five thousand investors.

**Ingenious Film & Television Limited**
100 Pall Mall
London
SW1Y 5NQ
Tel: 020 7024 3600
Fax: 020 7024 3601
enquiries@ingeniousmedia.co.uk
www.ingeniousmedia.co.uk
A leading provider of project finance to British film, through sale & leaseback, equity investment and P&A support.

**Invicta Capital**
33 St James's Square
London
SW1Y 4JS
Tel: 020 7661 9376
Fax: 020 7661 9892
info@invictacapital.co.uk
www.invictacapital.co.uk
A film investor and tax/co-production advisor, and Invicta advises private clients and corporations on equity and tax efficient investments in film production and distribution. Through the provision of debt, equity and structured finance, Invicta has developed an influential position in the UK and US film industries.

**Matrix Film Finance LLP**
Gossard House, 7-8 Savile Road
London
W1S 3PE
Tel: 020 7292 0800
Fax: 020 7292 0801
enquiries@matrix-film-finance.co.uk
www.matrix-film-finance.co.uk

**Movision Entertainment Ltd**
Bridge Road Business Park, 4-5 Bridge Road
Haywards Heath, West Sussex
RH16 1TX
Tel: 014 4445 8252
Fax: 014 4445 8184
www.movision.co.uk
One of the UK's leading film financing and production companies.

**Park Caledonia Media Limited**
4 Park Gardens
Glasgow, Scotland
G3 7YE
Tel: 014 1332 9100
Fax: 014 1332 5641
www.parkcaledonia.biz

**Prescience Film Finance**
45 Wycombe End
Beaconsfield, Buckinghamshire
HP9 1LZ
Tel: 020 8354 7331
Fax: 014 9467 0740
www.presciencefilmfinance.co.uk
A dynamic funder of British, European and international feature films and television programming, working with leading producers through the Foresight limited liability partnerships and Studio Productions EIS offering.

**Random Harvest Limited**
Pinewood Studios
Iver Heath, Buckinghamshire
SL0 0NH
Tel: 017 5378 3900
Fax: 017 5363 0651
films@randomharvest.co.uk
www.randomharvestpictures.co.uk

A Production company and fund raising/fund management company, with a slate of 10 feature films and television programmes in development.

**Scion Films**
18 Soho Square
London
W1D 3QL
Tel: 020 7025 8003
Fax: 020 7025 8133
info@scionfilms.com
www.scionfilms.com

Co-produces and co-finances a small number of high quality feature films each year.

**ScottsAtlantic**
3 De Walden Court, 85 New Cavendish Street
London
W1W 6XD
Tel: 020 7307 9300
Fax: 020 7307 9292
info@scottsatlantic.com
www.scottsatlantic.com

Scotts Atlantic provides sale and leaseback funding for British Films. In addition it may provide mezzanine or equity finance dependent on a strict investment basis.

**UKFS**
7 Marlborough Place
Brighton, East Sussex
BN1 1UB
Tel: 012 7369 0285
Fax: 012 7367 9954
info@ukfs-online.co.uk

A worldwide network of production and finance companies that fund and make independent movies.

**Visionview Ltd**
3 Fitzhardinge Street
London
W1H 6EF
Tel: 020 7224 0234
Fax: 020 7486 7200
info@visionview.co.uk
www.visionview.co.uk

## Production Companies

(the below list is a slection of some of the UK's more active production companies - for a more complete list see Kays, Britfilms.com or The Knowledge)

**Aardman Animation**
Gas Ferry Road
Bristol, Somerset
BS1 6UN
Tel: 011 7984 8485
Fax: 011 7984 8486
www.aardman.com

**APT Films**
APT Films, 225a Brecknock Road
London, N19 5AA
Tel: 020 7284 1695
Fax: 020 7482 1587
admin@aptfilms.com
www.aptfilms.com

APT Films is dedicated to the development and production of innovative and commercially driven feature films which will attract audiences both nationally and internationally.

**Aria Films Limited**
6 Goldhurst Terrace
London
NW6 3HU
Tel: 020 7372 0282
Fax: 020 7624 6763
www.ariafilms.co.uk

Aria Films specialises in the financing, executive production and co-production of independently produced feature films, with a specific focus on complex international co-productions and access to subsidies and incentives to film production worldwide.

**BBC Films**
1 Mortimer Street, Room 101
London
W1T 3JA
Tel: 020 7765 0091
Fax: 020 7765 0194
www.bbc.co.uk/bbcfilms

BBC Films is the feature film-making arm of the BBC. It is firmly established at the forefront of British independent film-making and co-produces approximately eight films a year. Working in partnership with major international and UK distributors, including Miramax, PolyGram, Fox, Buena Vista, Pathé, Momentum and UIP, BBC Films aims to make strong British films with range and ambition. *(see funds chapter for more info)*

**Company Pictures**
Suffolk House, 1-8 Whitfield Place
London
W1T 5JU
Tel: 020 7380 3900
Fax: 020 7380 1166
enquiries@companypictures.co.uk
www.companypictures.co.uk

**Darlow Smithson Productions**
Highgate Business Centre, 33 Greenwood Place
London
NW5 1LB
Tel: 020 7482 7027
Fax: 020 7482 7039
mail@darlowsmithson.com
www.darlowsmithson.com

Darlow Smithson Productions is a multi-award winning company producing high quality factual programmes for broadcasters worldwide, with a focus on ambitious docudramas, series and documentaries for theatrical release. Their first feature, TOUCHING THE VOID, is the UK's most successful theatrical documentary ever.

**DNA Films**
First Floor, 15 Greek Street
London
W1D 4DP
Tel: 020 7292 8700
Fax: 020 7292 8701
www.dnafilms.com

DNA was one of the Lottery Franchises backed with funding from the UK Film Council. In September 2003 a new joint venture was created between DNA and Fox Searchlight to finance, produce and distribute British films worldwide and build a company with long term viability. DNA has around 10 projects in development at any time, taking two-to-three a year through into production with budgets generally under $15m. *(see funds chapter for more info)*

**Ecosse Films**
Brigade House, 8 Parsons Green
London
SW6 4TN
Tel: 020 7371 0290
Fax: 020 7736 3436
info@ecossefilms.com
www.ecossefilms.com

**Eon Productions**
Eon House, 138 Piccadilly
London
W1J 7NR
Tel: 020 7493 7953
Fax: 020 7408 1236
www.jamesbond.com

**The Film Consortium**
4th Floor, Portland House
Great Portland Street
London
W1W BQJ
Tel: 020 7612 0030
Fax: 020 7612 0031
contact@civiliancontent.com
www.civiliancontent.com

Financing, production and exploitation of UK film and TV rights. Owned by Civilian Content Plc and sister of The Works.

**FilmFour**
124 Horseferry Road
London
SW1P 2TX
Tel: 020 7306 8509
Fax: 020 7306 8638
www.channel4.com/films

The feature film division of Channel 4 Television.

*(see funds chapter for more info)*

### Fragile Films
95-97 Dean Street
London
W1N 3XX
Tel: 020 7287 6200
Fax: 020 7287 0069
fragile@fragilefilms.com
www.fragilefilms.com

### Future Films Ltd
25 Noel Street
London
W1F 8GX
Tel: 020 7434 6600
Fax: 020 7434 6633
www.futurefilmgroup.com

Offers an integrated package of film production finance including the structuring of international co-productions, which may also include the provisions of production services and state-of-the-art post production facilities.

### Gabriel Films
The Tower, 48 Cleveden Drive
Glasgow, Scotland
G12 0NU
Tel: 014 1357 4148
www.gabrielfilms.co.uk

### Goldcrest Films International
65-66 Dean Street
London
W1D 4PL
Tel: 020 7437 8696
Fax: 020 7437 4448
mailbox@goldcrest-films.com
www.goldcrest-films.com

An independent UK co-production company, involved in the funding, production and distribution of films with offices in London and the USA.

### Great British Films
3rd Floor, Hanover House, 118 Queens Road
Brighton, East Sussex
BN1 3XG
Tel: 012 73324122
Fax: 012 7332 7105
info@greatbritishfilms.com
www.greatbritishfilms.com

### Grosvenor Park Media Limited
53-54 Grosvenor Street
London
W1K 3HU
Tel: 020 7529 2500
Fax: 020 7529 2511
funding@grosvenorpark.com
www.grosvenorpark.com

Grosvenor Park is a leading provider of tax based film finance to producers around the world. With over 20 years of experience in film and television financing and international co-productions, Grosvenor Park has raised over $5 billion for over 400 film and television productions and manages investments on behalf of five thousand investors.

### Gruber Films
Office, 2 Sheraton Street
London
W1F 8BH
Tel: 087 0366 9313
Fax: 020 7851 4712
www.gruberfilms.com

Gruber Films had produced recent UK film successes, and development deals with Momentum Pictures, Film Council and MEDIA Plus.

### Impact Pictures
3 Percy Street
London,
W1T 1DE
Tel: 020 7636 7716
Fax: 020 7636 7814
production@impactpix.com

### Intandem Films Ltd
First Floor, 22 Soho Square
London
W1D 4NS
Tel: 020 7851 3800
Fax: 020 7851 3830
info@intandemfilms.com
www.intandemfilms.com

A feature film production company whose main focus is in executive production/ financing and international sales, marketing and distribution.

**International Movie Management**
Shepperton Studios
London, TW17 0QD
Tel: 019 3259 2061
Fax: 019 3256 9527
admin@moviemgt.com
www.moviemgt.com

**Jigsaw Film Limited**
10-11 St George's Mews
London, NW1 8XE
Tel: 020 7483 3556
Fax: 020 7586 8063
mail@srpltd.co.uk
Film development and production at all budget levels - with an emphasis on developing and producing children's and family material.

**Jim Henson Company Productions**
30 Oval Road
London, NW1 7DE
Tel: 020 7428 4000
Fax: 020 7428 4001
www.henson.com

**Little Bird Co**
9 Grafton Mews
London
W1P 5LG
Tel: 020 7380 3980
Fax: 020 7380 3981
info@littlebird.co.uk
www.littlebird.co.uk
Since Little Bird was established in 1982, the company has become one of Europe's leading independent film and television production companies, with offices in Dublin, London and Johannesburg.

**Number 9 Films**
First Floor
Linton House
24 Wells Street
W1T 3PH

**Passion Pictures**
3rd & 4th Floors, County House
33-34 Rathbone Place
London, W1T 1JN
Tel: 020 7323 9933
Fax: 020 7323 9030
info@passion-pictures.com
www.passion-pictures.com

**Pathé Entertainment**
Kent House, 14-17 Market Place
London
W1W 8AR
Tel: 020 7462 4406
Fax: 020 7436 1693
www.pathe.co.uk

**Pipedream Pictures**
15a Dean Road
London
NW2 5AB
info@pipedream-pictures.co.uk
www.pipedream-pictures.co.uk

**Portman Film**
21-25 St Anne's Court
London
W1F OBJ
Tel: 020 7494 8024
Fax: 020 7494 8046
sales@portmanfilm.com
www.portmanfilm.com
Worldwide sales, financing and marketing company which executive produces independent films and television.

**Qwerty Films**
5a Noel Street
London
W1F 8GE
Tel: 020 7292 3920
Fax: 020 7287 6860
Qwerty Films is a feature film production and development business and media consultancy. The team, Michael Kuhn, Malcolm Ritchie and Jill Tandy, were among the senior managers who established and ran PolyGram Filmed Entertainment, one of the few examples of a Europe-based worldwide studio built from scratch.

**Random Harvest Limited**
Pinewood Studios
Iver Heath, Buckinghamshire
SL0 0NH
Tel: 017 5378 3900
Fax: 017 5363 0651
films@randomharvest.co.uk
www.randomharvestpictures.co.uk
A Production company and fund raising/fund management company, with a slate of 10 projects in development.

**Recorded Picture Company**
24 Hanway Street
London
W1T 1UH
Tel: 020 7636 2251
Fax: 020 7636 2261
rpc@recordedpitcutre.com
www.recordedpicture.com

**Samuelson Productions**
13 Manette Street
London
W1D 4AW
Tel: 020 7439 4900
Fax: 020 7439 4901
samuelsonp@aol.com

**Sarah Radclyffe Productions Ltd**
10-11 St George's Mews
London
NW1 8XE
Tel: 020 7483 3556
Fax: 020 7586 8063
mail@srpltd.co.uk

Film development and production at all budget levels including co-productions (past co-productions with Australia, Germany, Norway and Ireland).

**Scala Productions**
4th Floor, Portland House
London
W1W 8QJ
Tel: 020 7612 0060
Fax: 020 7612 0031

**Scion Films**
18 Soho Square
London
W1D 3QL
Tel: 020 7025 8003
Fax: 020 7025 8133
info@scionfilms.com
www.scionfilms.com

Co-produces and co-finances a small number of high quality feature films each year and has a number of productions in pre-production and production at present.

**Slate Films**
91 Berwick Street
London, W1F 0NE
Tel: 020 7292 7388
Fax: 020 7292 6473
info@slatefilms.com
www.slatefilms.com

**Spice Factory Ltd**
14 Regent Hill
Brighton, East Sussex
BN1 3ED
Tel: 012 7373 9182
Fax: 012 7374 9122
info@spicefactory.co.uk

Finance and production of feature films intended for theatrical distribution.

**Studio of the North (SON)**
The Workstation, 15 Paternoster Row
Sheffield
S1 2BX
Tel: 011 4249 2204
Fax: 011 4249 2293
admin.ympa@workstation.org.uk
www.ympa.org.uk

An umbrella organisation providing finance and executive production services, working closely with a selected group of writers, producers and directors.

**Tartan Films Distribution**
Atlantic House, 5 Wardour Street
London
W1D 6PB
Tel: 020 7494 1400
Fax: 020 7439 1922
info@tartanfilms.com
www.tartanfilms.com

**Tiger Aspect Pictures**
5 Soho Square
London, W1V 5DE
Tel: 020 7434 0672
Fax: 020 7287 1448
general@tigeraspect.co.uk
www.tigeraspect.co.uk

**UKFS**
7 Marlborough Place
Brighton, East Sussex
BN1 1UB
Tel: 012 7369 0285
Fax: 012 7367 9954
info@ukfs-online.co.uk

A worldwide network of production and finance companies that fund and make independent movies.

**Vertigo Films**
The Big Room Studios, 77 Fortress Road
London
NW5 1AG
Tel: 020 7428 7555
Fax: 020 7485 9713
reception@vertigofilms.com
www.vertigofilms.com
Independent company formed by film producers.

**Visionview Ltd**
3 Fitzhardinge Street
London
W1H 6EF
Tel: 020 7224 0234
Fax: 020 7486 7200
info@visionview.co.uk
www.visionview.co.uk

**Warp Films**
Spectrum House, 32-34 Goron House Road
London, NW5 1LP
Tel: 020 7284 8366
info@warpfilms.com
www.warpfilms.com

**Working Title Films**
Oxford House, 76 Oxford Street
London, W1B 1BS
Tel: 020 7307 3000
www.workingtitlefilms.com
*(see funds chapter for more info)*

## Product Placement

**Brand Exposure Product Placement Ltd**
Studio 206, The Bon Marche Centre,
London, SW9 8BJ
Tel: 020 7924 9122
Fax: 020 7274 8616
www.brand-exposure.co.uk

**1st Place Product Props Ltd,**
The Old Bank, 30 High Street,
Cambridge, CB1 6HS
Tel: 01223 894949
Fax: 01223 894971

**Bellwood Media,**
The Trident Business Centre,
89 Bickersteth Road,
London, SW17 9SH
Tel: 020 8355 3451
Fax: 020 8682 248

**Contemporary Props Ltd,**
Pinewood Studios,
Pinewood Road, Iver,
Buckinghamshire,
SL0 0NH,
Tel: 01753 655766
Fax: 01753 655118

**Production Profiles Ltd,**
164 Waldegrave Road,
Strawberry Hill, Twickenham,
TW1 4TD
Tel: 020 8891 5194
Fax: 020 8404 2181

**Scenario (UK) Ltd**
Westfield, Westland Green,
Ware, Hertfordshire,
SG11 2AL
tel: 0870 0119567
fax: 01279 841459

## Professional Advice

**Aria Films Limited**
6 Goldhurst Terrace
London
NW6 3HU
Tel: 020 7372 0282
Fax: 020 7624 6763
www.ariafilms.co.uk
Aria Films specialises in the financing, executive production and co-production of independently produced feature films, with a specific focus on complex international co-productions and access to subsidies and incentives to film production worldwide.

**Baker Tilly**
2 Bloomsbury Street
London, WC1B 3ST
Tel: 020 7413 5100
Fax: 020 7413 5101
www.bakertilly.co.uk
Accounting and advising firm acting for independent film and TV producers providing advice on film and TV finance; acts for a number of the UK film funds.

**Curzon Capital**
34 Clarges Street
London
W1J 7EJ
Tel: 020 7355 2427
Fax: 020 7355 2428
www.curzoncapital.com
Curzon has a pool of knowledge and experience in dealing with the most complex of financial solutions, rendering them easily understandable and saleable. Recent successes have been in the promotion of the Movision film production partnerships for which over £50m was raised.

**Deloitte & Touche LLP**
Hill House, 1 Little New Street
London
EC4A 3TR
Tel: 020 7007 3336
Fax: 020 7007 3059
www.deloitte.co.uk

**Ernst & Young**
1 More London Place, 7 Rolls Buildings
London
SE1 2AF
Tel: 020 7951 3305
Fax: 020 7951 0708
tce@uk.ey.com
www.ey.com/uk

**HW Fisher and Company**
Acre House, 11-15 William Road
London
NW1 3ER
Tel: 020 7388 7000
Fax: 020 7380 4900
media@hwfisher.co.uk
www.hwfisher.co.uk
Accountancy firm with experience in the international film, television and media.

**Lerman & Co / Alfred Myers**
Suite 5, Stanmore Towers, 8-14 Church Road
Stanmore, Middlesex
HA7 4AW
Tel: 020 8954 5900
Fax: 020 8954 5772
enquiries@lermanandco.com
www.lermanandco.co
A leading firm of chartered accountants, offering advice and support for both business and personal affairs.

**Mansfields Associates**
66-68 Bell Lane
London
E1 7LA
Tel: 020 7377 1266
Fax: 020 7377 2080
ma@star.easynet.co.uk

**Studio of the North (SON)**
The Workstation, 15 Paternoster Row
Sheffield
S1 2BX
Tel: 011 4249 2204
Fax: 011 4249 2293
admin.ympa@workstation.org.uk
www.ympa.org.uk
An umbrella organisation providing finance and executive production services, working closely with a selected group of writers, producers and directors.

**WJB Chiltern**
3 Shelden Square
London
W2 6PS
Tel: 020 7339 9000
Fax: 020 7339 9017
www.wjbchiltern.com
A major tax and wealth management organisation, specialising in the media industry.

## Sales Agents

**Beyond Films**
22 Newman Street
London
W1T 1PH
Tel: 020 7636 9613
Fax: 020 7636 9614
films@beyond.com.au
www.beyond.com.au
A London based, Australian owned film sales company that seeks to represent quality, theatrical films from around the world with solid international appeal.

**Capitol Films**
23 Queensdale Place
London
W11 4SQ
Tel: 020 7471 6000
Fax: 020 7471 6012
films@capitolfilms.com
www.capitolfilms.com
One of Europe's largest leading international production, financing and sales companies

**Content International Film and Television Ltd**
19 Heddon Street
London
W1B 4BG
Tel: 020 78516500
www.contentinternational.com
Sales, finance, and production of feature films.

**Cori Film Distributors**
Hill House, 1 Little New Street
London
EC4A 3TR
Tel: 020 7493 7920
Fax: 020 7493 8088

**Civilian Content Plc**
4th Floor, Portland House
Great Portland Street
London
W1W BQJ
Tel: 020 7612 0030
Fax: 020 7612 0031
contact@civiliancontent.com
www.civiliancontent.com
Financing, production and exploitation of UK film and TV rights. Parent company of The Works.

**First Up Film International**
3 Shelden Square
London
W2 6PS
Tel: 020 7339 9000
Fax: 020 7339 9017
www.wjbchiltern.com
Offers services to producers that range from production finance to sponsorship, representing new feature films and packaged feature projects from a diverse group of international and UK producers.

**Goldcrest Films International**
65-66 Dean Street
London
W1D 4PL
Tel: 020 7437 8696
Fax: 020 7437 4448
mailbox@goldcrest-films.com
www.goldcrest-films.com
An independent UK co-production company, involved in the funding, production and distribution of films with offices in London and the USA.

**Hanway Films**
24 Hanway Street
London
W1T 1UH
Tel: 020 7290 0750
Fax: 020 7290 0751
info@hanwayfilms.com
www.hanwayfilms.com

**Icon Entertainment**
The Quadrangle, Fourth Floor
180 Wardour Street
London
W1F 8FX
Tel: 020 7494 8100
Fax: 020 7494 8151
www.icon-entertainment.co.uk
A film sales, finance and production company which has established itself as a leading supplier of theatrical feature films to the independent film market.

**Intandem Films Ltd**
First Floor, 22 Soho Square
London
W1D 4NS
Tel: 020 7851 3800
Fax: 020 7851 3830
info@intandemfilms.com
www.intandemfilms.com
A feature film production company whose main focus in executive production/financing and international sales, marketing and distribution.

**Intermedia Film Equities Ltd**
Unit 12 Enterprise House, 59-65 Upper Ground
London
SE1 9PQ
Tel: 020 7593 1630
Fax: 020 7593 1639
info@intermediafilm.com
www.intermedia.com

A division of Munich-based IM Internationalmedia AG, providing the development, financing and distribution of high-quality motion pictures thus covering the complete value chain. Offices also in Los Angeles, California.

**Moviehouse Entertainment**
9 Grafton Mews
London
W1T 5HZ
Tel: 020 7380 3999
Fax: 020 7380 3998
info@moviehouseent.com
www.moviehouseent.com

**Pathé Pictures International**
Kent House, 14-17 Market Place
London
W1W 8AR
Tel: 020 7323 5151
Fax: 020 7436 7891
international.sales@pathe-uk.com
www.pathe.co.uk

Handles international sales and marketing of films produced by Pathé in the UK as well as acquiring third party films for worldwide representation.

**Portman Film**
21-25 St Anne's Court
London
W1F OBJ
Tel: 020 7494 8024
Fax: 020 7494 8046
sales@portmanfilm.com
www.portmanfilm.com

Worldwide sales, financing and marketing company which executive produces independent films and television.

**Renaissance Films**
34/35 Berwick Street
London
W1F 8RP
Tel: 020 7287 5190
Fax: 020 7287 5191
info@renaissance-films.com
www.renaissance-films.com

Renaissance Films has evolved from a multi-award winning production company in the late 1980s to a leading international distribution, marketing and financing company over the past five years.

**The Works**
4th Floor, Portland House
Great Portland Street
London
W1W BQJ
Tel: 020 7612 1080
Fax: 020 7612 1081
www.theworkslimited.com

One of Europe's leading sales agents, and sister company to The Film Consortium.

**United Artists Films**
10 Stephen Mews
London
W1P 1PP
Tel: 020 7333 8877
Fax: 020 7333 8878

**Vine International Pictures**
VIP House, Greenacres, New Road Hill
Downe, Orpington, Kent
BR6 7JA
Tel: 016 8985 4123
Fax: 016 8985 0990
info@vine-international.co.uk
www.vine-international.co.uk

An independently owned sales company, established to finance and distribute quality, theatrically led feature films. Considered a boutique operation, specialising in all genres.

## Training Providers

### City Eye Media Centre

Swaythling Neighbourhood Centre
Rear 200 Burgess Road
Swaythling, Southampton
SO16 3AY
Tel: 023 8067 7167
admin@city-eye.co.uk
www.city-eye.co.uk

City Eye's aim is to create an artistic hub based around film and video production in the region. City Eye exists to help the community, arts organisations, individuals, emerging and establish talent. It has Charitable Status, and receives financial support from Southampton City Council, and Screen South the film and media agency for the South.

### Edinburgh Mediabase

25a Southwest Thistle Street Lane
Edinburgh, Scotland
EH2 1EW
Tel: 013 1220 0220
Fax: 013 1220 0220
info@edinburghmediabase.com
www.edinburghmediabase.com

Edinburgh Mediabase is a membership organisation that provides affordable access to training, facilities, exhibition, events, networking, information and advice.

### Film Education

21-22 Poland Street
London
W1F 8QQ
Tel: 020 7851 9450
Fax: 020 7439 3218
postbox@filmeducation.org
www.filmeducation.org

Since 1985, Film Education has been developing the range of its publications and services to respond to the growing importance of Media Education in the National Curriculum and to meet the increasing demand for current educational material on film and film making. In addition to providing free educational materials, Film Education organises training courses, conferences, workshops, seminars and events including National Schools Film Week.

### Lighthouse

9-12 Middle Street
Brighton, East Sussex
BN1 1AL
Tel: 012 7338 4222
Fax: 012 7338 4233
info@lighthouse.org.uk
www.lighthouse.org.uk

Lighthouse offers a variety of creative professional development opportunities for filmmakers, screenwriters and artists working with digital and moving image media, as well as free advice to filmmakers living in East or West Sussex who are applying to Screen South's Open Funds.

### National Film & Television School (NFTS)

Beaconsfield Studios, Station Road
Beaconsfield, Buckinghamshire
HP9 1LG
Tel: 014 9467 1234
Fax: 014 9467 4042
admin@nftsfilm-tv.ac.uk
www.nftsfilm-tv.ac.uk

The NFTS is unusual among film schools in being able to offer its students the experience of training in professional standard film and television studios and post-production facilities. Extensive facilities and equipment mean that students have guaranteed access to resources. A technical services team, professional electricians and carpenters/set builders are on hand to support both learning and productions.

### Raindance

81 Berwick Street
London
W1F 8TW
Tel: 020 7287 3833
Fax: 020 7439 2243
info@raindance.co.uk
www.raindance.co.uk

Igniting and overseeing major shifts in the world of independent British films, providing a combination of innovative film training, a major film festival and the prestigious British Independent Film Awards.

**Skillset**
Prospect House, 80-110 New Oxford Street
London
WC1A 1HB
Tel: 020 7520 5757
Fax: 020 7520 5758
info@skillset.org
www.skillset.org

Skillset is the Sector Skills Council for the Audiovisual Industries. Its role is to research and fill skills gaps to ensure the sustainability of the UK screen industries.

# International contacts

## Australia

**Arclight Films**
Bldg 22 (Box 40), Drive Avenue
Fox Studios, Australia Moore Park
Sydney, NSW 2021
Australia
Tel: +61 2 9955 8825
Fax: +61 2 8353 2437
info@arclightfilms.com
www.arclightfilms.com

Australian-based international sales company also involved in the co-production and finance, specialising in Australian and UK feature films for theatrical release

**Australian Film Commission**
Level 4, 150 William Street
Woolloomooloo
Sydney NSW 2011
Australia
Tel: +61 2 9321 6444
Fax: +61 2 9357 3672
marketing@afc.gov.au
www.afc.gov.au

**Australian Film Institute**
236 Dorcas Street
South Melbourne
Victoria, 3205
Australia
Tel: +61 3 9696 1844
Fax: +61 3 9696 7972
info@afi.org.au
www.afi.org.au

The AFI has promoted Australian film and television for over 45 years and is responsible for producing Australia's premier film and television awards, the annual AFI Awards. As a producer of the industry's night of nights, the AFI plays a central role in the way in which the Australian film industry is known and understood, both locally and internationally, and is crucial to the definition, business and culture of the Australian film, television and other moving image industries.

**Film Australia Limited**
101 Eton Road
Lindfield, NSW 2070
Australia
Tel: +61 2 9413 8777
Fax: +61 2 9416 5672
www.filmaust.com.au
Film Australia produces programs under the National Interest Program: a contract with the Australian Government to devise, produce, distribute and market productions that deal with matters of national interest or illustrate and interpret aspects of Australian life.

**Film Finance Corporation Australia Ltd (FFC)**
130 Elizabeth Street, Level 12
Sydney, NSW 2000
Australia
Tel: +61 2 9268 2555
Fax: +61 2 9264 8551
ffc@ffc.gov.au
www.fff.gov.au
Principal agency of the Australian government for funding the production of films and television programmes.

**Film Victoria**
7th Floor, 189 Flinders Lane
Melbourne, Victoria, 3000
Australia
Tel: +61 3 9660 3200
Fax: +61 3 9660 3201
www.film.vic.gov.au
Film Victoria is a cultural organisation that encourages and assists the development, production, exhibition and knowledge of film, television and new media. Funding is available for a variety of schemes, including development and production of feature films, short films and digital animation.

**First Australian Completion Bond Company Pty. Ltd**
24 Milverton Street
Moonee Ponds
Victoria 3039
Australia
Tel: +61 3 9372 7177
Fax: +61 3 9372 7133

**New South Wales Film and TV Office**
7/157 Liverpool Street
Sydney, NSW 2000
Australia
Tel: +61 2 9264 6400
Fax: +61 2 9264 4399
fto@fto.nsw.gov.au
www.fto.nsw.gov.au
New South Wales State government organisation of Australia that plays a critical development role in enhancing the film & television industry in NSW. Has a number of initiatives and programmes of assistance including production development and investment, a young filmmakers fund, a regional filming fund, and audience and industry development programmes.

**South Australian Film Corporation**
3 Butler Drive, Hendon Common
Hendon, 5014
Australia
Tel: +61 8 8348 9300
Fax: +61 8 8347 0385
safilm@safilm.com.au
www.safilm.com.au
Starting life as a production company in 1972, the SAFC is a statutory body established under the South Australian Film Corporation Act. It has helped to foster an internationally recognised industry that has produced hundreds of feature films, television dramas and documentaries.

## Belgium

**European Private Equity and Venture Capital Association (EVCA)**
EVCA Secretariat, Minervastraat 4
Zaventem
Brussels B-1930
Belgium
Tel: +32 2715 0020
Fax: +32 2725 0704
evca@evca.com
www.evca.com
The European Private Equity and Venture Capital Association (EVCA) is a non-profit-making representative body for the European

equity industry. It supports the industry in a number of ways including providing training, influencing public policy, research, publications, organising annual events and promoting high and consistent standards which it's members must follow. Their activities cover the whole range of private equity: venture capital (from seed and start-up to development capital), buyouts and buyins. With over 950 members in Europe, EVCA's role includes representing the interests of the industry to regulators and standard setters; developing professional standards; providing industry research; professional development and forums, facilitating interaction between its members and key industry participants including institutional investors, entrepreneurs, policymakers and academics.

**Flemish Audiovisual Fund**
Handelskaai 18/3
B-1000 Brussels
Belgium
Tel: +32 2 226 0630
Fax: +32 2 219 1936
info@vaf.be
www.vaf.be

The Flemish Audiovisual Fund annually receives a 12.5 (approx. £9) million grant of the Flemish government. A minimum of 78% of the annual budget goes to production support. Filmmakers can apply for support to fiction, documentary, animation and experimental media production. VAF makes a distinction between four types of support; scriptwriting support, development support, production support and support towards promotion.

**Wallonie Bruxelles Images**
18 Place E. Flagey
1050 Brussels
Belgium
Tel: +32 2 223 2304
Fax: +32 2 218 3424
wbimages@skynet.be
www.wbi.be

A source ofnformation on independent productions by the French-speaking Belgian community

## Brazil

**Agência de Cinema e Audiovisuel**
Avenida Rio Branco, 277 SI
102 - 20047-900
Rio De Janeiro
Brazil
Tel: +55 21 2210 1371
Fax: +55 21 2240 2791
xolotl@ism.com.br
www.cinemabrazil.com

## Canada

**British Columbia Film**
2225 West Broadway
Vancouver, British Columbia, V6K 2E4
Canada
Tel: +604 736 7997
Fax: +604 736 7290
bcf@bcfilm.bc.ca
www.bcfilm.bc.ca

Offers development and production financing to British Columbia filmmakers through a variety of funding programs and professional development to producers, writers and directors through marketing and skills assistance programs. A private, non-profit society that also administers the provincial tax credit program on behalf of the provincial government.

**Canadian Film and Television Production Association**
160 John Street, Fifth Floor
Toronto, Ontario,
M5V 2ES
Canada
Tel: +1 416 304 0280
Fax: +1 416 304 0499
dacosta@cftpa.ca
www.cftpa.ca

A non-profit trade association representing almost 400 film, television and interactive media companies across Canada; negotiates and manages labour agreements, and actively lobbies the federal and provincial governments on various policy areas including taxation, trade, copyright, broadcasting and film.

**Cassels Brock & Blackwell, LLP**
40 King Street, No. 2100
Toronto, M5H 3C2, Ontario
Canada
Tel: +1 416 869 5777
Fax: +1 416 640 3206
www.casselsbrock.com
Law firm with an entertainment practice of 15 lawyers specialising in film, television, music and sports.

**National Film Board of Canada**
Postal Box 6100, Centre-ville Station
Montreal, Quebec, H3C 3H5
Canada
Tel: +1 514 283 9000
Fax: +1 514 283 7564
www.nfb.ca
A public agency that produces and distributes films and other audiovisual works which reflect Canada to Canadians and the rest of the world. It is an exceptional fountain of creativity, which since its very beginnings has played a crucial role in Canadian and international filmmaking.

**New Brunswick Film**
16th Floor, Assumption Place, 770 Main Street
Moncton, New Brunswick, E1C 8R3
Canada
Tel: +1 506 869 6868
Fax: +1 506 869 6840
www.nbfilm.com
Film Commission and film development agency for province of New Brunswick, Canada. Provides information and advice on tax credits, finding investors and development loans.

**Newfoundland & Labrador Film Development Corporation**
189 Water Street, 2nd Floor
St John's, Newfoundland, A1C 1B4
Canada
Tel: +1 709 738 3456
Fax: +1 709 739 1680
info@newfilm.nf.net
www.newfilm.nf.net
Aims to fosters and promote the development and growth of the film and video industry in Newfoundland and Labrador, and to increase the national and international visibility of Newfoundland and Labrador as a location. NLFDC also provides production assistance in the form of an Equity Investment Program (EIP) and a Development Program, as well as information and advice on tax credits.

**Nova Scotia Film Development Corporation**
1724 Granville Street, 2nd Floor
Halifax, Nova Scotia, B3J 1X5
Canada
Tel: +1 902 424 7177
Fax: +1 902 424 0617
noviascotia.film@ns.sympatico.ca
www.film.ns.ca
Nova Scotia Film Development Corporation attempts to grow Nova Scotia's film, television and new media industries with partners by stimulating investment and employment and by promoting Nova Scotia's producers, productions, locations, skills and creativity in global markets.

**Ontario Media Development Corporation (OMDC)**
175 Bloor Street East, South Tower, No. 501
Toronto, Ontario, M4W 3R8
Canada
Tel: +1 416 314 6858
Fax: +1 416 314 2495
www.omdc.on.ca
The OMDC is an agency to stimulate the growth of Ontario's film, television, book and magazine publishing, sound recording and digital media industries. OMDC has a series of funding and programs available for business development, as well as information and advice on investment and tax credits.

**Telefilm Canada**
360 rue Saint-Jacques, Suite 700
Montreal, Quebec, H2Y 4AD
Canada
Tel: +1 514 283 6363
Fax: +1 514 283 3317
info@telefilm.gc.ca
www.telefilm.gc.ca

A Federal cultural agency dedicated to the development and promotion of the Canadian film, television, new media and music industries. Telefilm offers a range of film funding schemes, for screenwriting, development, production and marketing.

**Toronto Film & Television Office**
Main Floor, Rotunda North
Toronto City Hall, 100 Queen Street W
Toronto, Quebec, M5H 2N2
Canada
Tel: +1 416 392 7570
Fax: +1 416 392 0675
filmtoronto@toronto.ca
www.toronto.ca/tfto
The Toronto Film and Television Office are extremely knowledgeable about all aspects of filming and are available to guide filmmakers through any part of the permitting process.

## Czech Republic

### Audiovisual Producers' Association
Národní 28, 110 00 Praha 1
Czech Republic
Tel: +420 221 105 302
Fax: +420 221 105 303
apa@iol.cz
www.asociaceproducentu.cz
Audiovisual Producers' Association (APA) was founded in 1994. It associates producers and production companies both in the sphere of the Czech film, film service and promotion. The main activity of the Association is the protection and promotion of producers' interests, dealing with professional associations, protective authors' organisations and bodies of the state administration.

**Czech Film Centre**
Národní 28, 110 00 Praha 1
Czech Republic
Tel: +420 221 105 321
Fax: +420 221 105 303
info@filmcenter.cz or newsletter@filmcenter.cz
www.filmcenter.cz
The Czech film center (CFC) has been established as an office whose main aim is to enhance systematically the visibility of Czech film worldwide. The CFC and its activities are financed by APA - Audiovisual Producers´ Association and from public funds.

**Ministry of Culture**
Ministerstvo Kultury, Maltézské nám?stí 471/1
118 11 Praha 1 - Malá Strana
Czech Republic
Tel: +420 257 085 111
Fax: +420 224 318 155
posta@mkcr.cz
www.mkcr.cz
The Ministry of Culture is a central governmental agency for art and cultural heritage, handling issues concerning regulations in the sphere of radio and television broadcasting, and production and trade in the sphere of culture.

## Denmark

**Danish Film Institute**
Gothersgade 55
Copenhagen, 1123
Denmark
Tel: +45 3374 3400
Fax: +45 3374 3435
dfi@dfi.dk
www.dfi.dk
The Danish Film Institute is the national agency responsible for supporting and encouraging film and cinema culture and for conserving these in the national interest. The Institute's operations extend from participation in the development and production of feature films, shorts and documentaries, over distribution and marketing, to managing the national film archive and the cinematheque.

**Filmkontakt Nord**
Vognmagergade 10, 1st floor
DK-1120 Copenhagen K
Denmark
Tel: +45 3311 5152
Fax: +45 3311 2152
mail@filmkontakt.com
www.filmkontakt.dk
Filmkontakt Nord offers a range of services and events designed to stimulate and

facilitate Nordic and international production and distribution collaboration.

# France

### Alsace Cultural Agency

1 Espace Gilbert Estève
BP 90025, 67601 Sélestat
Cedex, France
Tel: +33 3 88 58 87 58
Fax: +33 3 88 58 87 50
agence@culture-alsace.org
www.culture-alsace.org

The Alsace Cultural Agency provides free support to audiovisual and cinema crews wishing to shoot in Alsace. Its services include giving assistance on location, administration and logistic processes and local suppliers.

### Centre National De La Cinematographie (CNC)

12 rue de Lubeck
75784 Paris, Cedex 16
France
Tel: +33 1 44 34 37 80
Fax: +33 1 44 34 36 59
www.cnc.fr

A government institution, under the auspices of the Ministry of Culture. Its areas of concern are the economics of cinema and the audio-visual industries; film regulation; the promotion of the cinema industries, and the production of cinema heritage. Offers financial assistance in all aspects of French cinema (production, exhibition, distribution, etc).

### Commission National du Film

33, rue des Jeûneurs
75002 Paris
France
Tel: +33 1 53 83 98 98
Fax: +33 1 53 83 98 99
film@filmfrance.net
www.filmfrance.net

Film France is the first stop for foreign production companies and individuals preparing to film in France. A network of 34 local film commissions throughout the country offers free information on locations, crews, labour rates and facilities.

### Eurimages

Conseil de l'Europe
Strasbourg, F-67075
Cedex, France
Tel: +33 3 88 41 36 77
Fax: +33 3 88 41 27 60
eurimages@coe.int
www.coe.int/eurimages

Eurimages is the Council of Europe fund for the co-production, distribution and exhibition of European cinematographic works. It aims to promote the European film industry by encouraging the production and distribution of films and fostering co-operation between professionals. Since it was set up, Eurimages has supported the co-production of more than one thousand full-length feature films and documentaries.

### Rhone-Alpes Film Commission

24 Rue Emile Decorps
69100 Villeurbanne
France
Tel: +33 4 7298 0798
Fax: +33 4 7298 0799
sergetachon@comfilm-rhones-aples.fr
www.rhone-alpes-cinema.fr

In addition to the national funds, some of the departments and regions of France offer film funding which international co-productions may be eligible to benefit from such as the Rhone Alps Film Commissions, if the film is shot in their region.

# Germany

### Bavarian Film & Television Fund

Sonnenstraße 21
80331 Munich
Germany
Tel: +49 89 544602 0
Fax: +49 89 544602 21
filmfoerderung@fff-bayern.de
www.fff-bayern.de

Annually the Bavarian Film and Television Fund (FFF) made available a total of approx. E32 (approx. £22) Million for screenplay, production, distribution and sales, as well as theatre funding. Financial support can be requested at each stage of the production process starting with script funding to packaging, production of theatrical and TV-movies, as well as exhibition. At least 150% of the production support must be spent in Bavaria, and feature films can be supported with up to  1.6 (approx. £1.1) million as long as the producer or co-producer is based in Germany. Foreign producers can only access FFF funding by submitting an application through a local partner. The distribution of the funds is based on the criteria mentioned in the Guidelines (accessible via the website). Applications for Film funding must be submitted by 1st of July.

**Bundesamtes für Wirtschaft und Ausfuhrkontrolle (BAFA)**
Post fach 5171
65726, Eschborn
Germany
Tel: +49 6196 404 401
Fax: +49 6196 404 422
www.bawi.de

**European Film Market**
Potsdamer Str. 5
Berlin, 10785
Germany
Tel: +49 30 25 92 06 66
Fax: +49 30 25 92 06 99
info@film.region-stuttgart.de
www.film.region-stuttgart.de
Organiser of the Berlin International Film Festival.

**Film & Entertainment VIP Medienfonds GmbH**
Bavariafilmstrasse 2
82031, Grunwald, Munich
Germany
Tel: +49 89 74 73 43 43
Fax: +49 89 74 73 43 44
www.vip-muenchen.de
A media fund and production company, placing funds with a volume of 100 Million Euros, it has co-produced international TV and feature films.

**Film Commission Region Stuttgart**
Breitscheidstr.4
Stuttgart, 70174
Germany
Tel: +49 71 12 59 44 30
Fax: +49 71 12 59 44 333
info@mfg.de
www.mfg.de/film
Actively supports the search for locations and filming permits, artistic and technical professional, young talent, producers and other service providers in the Stuttgart region.

**FOCUS Germany**
Tel: +49 211 930 500
Fax: +49 211 93050 85
info@focusgermany.de
www.focusgermany.de
FOCUS Germany is a coordinating service for film professionals seeking information and professional guidance regarding Germany's broad range of funding and production possibilities. Established in 1990 as an umbrella organisation for the major German film funding institutions, it was launched at a time when regional funding in Germany was becoming increasingly important on the national an international production scene. FOCUS Germany supplies the necessary contacts for an efficient co-production with Germany including every aspect of production from location research to post production.

**German Federal Film Board**
Große Präsidentenstraße 9
10178 Berlin
Germany
Tel: +49 30 27577 414
Fax: +49 30 27577 444
presse@ffa.de
www.ffa.de
For foreign producers to access the national funding available from the German Federal Film Board, they must be part of a German co-production, though the production need not take place in the country. The FFA has an annual budget of around  70 (approx. £48) million at its disposal. Funding is available for the production and distribution of feature

films and short films, and project funding can amount as a rule to 250,000 (approx. £171k), and up to 1m (approx. £680k) in individual cases.

### Hamburg Film Fund

Friedensallee 14-16
D - 22765 Hamburg
Germany
Tel: +49 40 398 37 0
Fax: +49 40 398 37 10
www.ffhh.de

FilmFörderung Hamburg, who part financed *Bend It Like Beckham*, is a company that supports film and TV production in Hamburg, through funding, film commission, services and events. Their previous annual budgets have been up to E9.5m (approx. £6.5m), current details of which can be found on their website.

### Medienboard Berlin-Brandenburg GmbH

August-Bebel-Str. 26-53
Potsdam-Babelsberg, 14482
Germany
Tel: +49 331 743 870
Fax: +49 331 743 87 99
info@medienboard.de
www.filmboard.de

Medienboard Berlin-Brandenburg GmbH is the central access point for all players in the region's media industry. The board is a joint venture of the two states in the area of film promotion and location development. Medienboard's film promotion supports films and film-related projects in the categories of script development, project development, package promotion, production, distribution and sales, and other activities.

## Hungary

### Hungarian Film

Budapest 1015
Szabó Ilonka 63/c
Hungary
Tel: +36 1 225 30 69
Fax: +36 1 214 48 51
info@szamak.film.hu
www.hungarianfilm.com

Providing a detailed listing of feature and TV films shot on location in Hungary during the past decade. Features a comprehensive website offering a film industry registry, a job forum, a location database and gallery and international references of the Hungarian film industry.

### Hungarian Film Commission

www.filmlocationpecs.com

The Hungarian Film Commission was set up in 1998 within the framework of the Motion Picture Public Foundation of Hungary with the support of the Ministry of National Cultural Heritage in order to provide location services and promote Hungary as a film location.

### Magyar Filmunio

H-1068 Budapest
Városligeti fasor 38
Hungary
Tel: +361 351 7696
Fax: +361 352 8789
mmk2@axelero.hu
www.filmunio.hu

Magyar Filmunió was established in 1992 by the Motion Picture Public Foundation of Hungary to promote awareness of Hungarian film-making at an international level within the circle of professionals as well as the wider public. The annual Hungarian feature film, short, documentary and animation production is offered for selection and is nominated by Magyar Filmunió at international film festivals.

# Iceland

### Film In Iceland

Skolavordustigur 11
101, Reykjavik
Iceland
Tel: +354 561 5200
Fax: +354 561 5205
info@filminiceland.org
www.filminiceland.org

Film in Iceland is a project set up to promote film production in Iceland. The project is run by the Invest In Iceland Agency, an agency of the Ministry of Industry and Commerce.

### Icelandic Film Centre

Túngata 14
101 Reykjavik
Iceland
Tel: +354 562 3580
Fax: +354 562 7171
info@icelandicfilmcentre.is
www.icelandicfilmcentre.is

Public organisation allocating funds for the development and production of features, shorts, TV live action, and documentaries. Involved in promotion of Icelandic films abroad and promoting the general development of film culture in Iceland.

# Ireland

### Allied Irish Bank

Bankcentre, Ballsbridge
Dublin, 4, Ireland
Tel: +353 1660 0311

### Anglo Irish Bank

Stephen Court, 18/21 St. Stephen's Green
Dublin, 2, Ireland
Tel: +353 1 616 2000
Fax: +353 1 616 2488
www.angloirishbank.ie

Anglo Irish Bank has been actively involved in providing financing for film production in Ireland since 1990. The Bank raises Section 481 financing for Irish based producers and for international production companies who produce films on location in Ireland. Anglo Irish Bank also provides cash flow production facilities by discounting pre-sales contracts provided by international distributors.

### Bank of Ireland

Lower Baggot Street
Dublin, 2, Ireland
www.bankofireland.ie

### Irish Film Board

Rockfort House, St Augustine Street
Galway, Ireland
Tel: +353 91 561398
Fax: +353 91 561405
info@filmboard.ie
www.filmboard.ie

Ireland's National Film funding agency funding feature films, documentaries, short films, and animation. The Film Board provides both development and production funding for feature length projects, and also runs a wide range of short film schemes.

### Irish Film Institute

6, Eustace Street, Temple Bar
Dublin, Ireland
Tel: +353 1 679 5744
Fax: +353 1 677 8755
ifi@irishfilm.ie
www.irishfilm.ie

The national body with responsibility for the promotion of film culture in Ireland. Major activities include film distribution and exhibition; responsible for the Irish Film Archive, an extensive Education and Outreach programme, as well as publishing activities.

# Italy

### Italian Film Commission

www.filminginitaly.com

The Italian Film Commission (IFC) is a division of the Italian Trade Commission (ITC) and operates as the promotional office for the Italian Entertainment Industry. The IFC provides information and assistance to the audiovisual industry by showcasing, promoting and assisting with Italian locations, facilities and Italian crews - above and below the line. Their role is also as a liaison between the Italian film community, its services and products and the global industry, has helped increase productions in Italy.

**Ministry of Culture - Cinema Office**
via della Ferratella in Laterano, 51
00184 - Roma
Italy
Tel: +39 067 7321
segreteria@cinema.beniculturali.it
www.cinema.beniculturali.it

## Luxembourg

**Film Fund Luxembourg**
5, rue Large
1917, Luxembourg
Tel: +352 47 82 165
Fax: +352 22 09 63
info@filmfund.etat.lu
www.filmfund.lu

The Film Fund of the Grand-Duchy of Luxembourg exists to promote and to encourage the development of the country's audiovisual production sector, and to administer film-making incentive and assistance schemes.

**Media Desk Luxembourg**
5, rue Large
1917, Luxembourg
Tel: +352 47 82 178
Fax: +352 46 74 95
mail@mediadesk.etat.lu
www.mediadesk.lu

Information office of the Media Programme of the European Union.

## Mexico

**National Film Commission**
Av. División del Norte # 2462 5to. Piso
Col. Portales C.P., 03300 D.F
Mexico
Tel: +1 525 688 7813
Fax: +1 525 688 7027
conafilm@conafilm.org.mx
www.conafilm.org.mx

With the cooperation of the Federal Government, the States Governments and the public and private organizations and institutions, the National Film Commission - Mexico, and its network of State Film Commissions head the over-all efforts to promote the production of films, TV programs and commercials in Mexico and to give assistance to all companies and producers interested in developing their projects.

## The Netherlands

**Dutch Film Fund**
Jan Luykenstraat 2
1071 CM Amsterdam
The Netherlands
Tel: +31 20 570 7676
Fax: +31 20 570 7689
info@filmfund.nl
www.hollandfilm.nl

Holland Film, affiliated with the Dutch Film Fund, is the official marketing & promotion agency for Dutch film abroad. The organisation, financed from public funds and some private sponsors, offers a wide variety of services to Dutch filmmakers and producers to enhance the perception of Dutch filmmaking worldwide. It acts as a consultant when Dutch films are presented at international film festivals and film markets, and it provides the international film circuit with information on current activities within the Dutch film industry.

**Film Investors Netherlands (FINE BV)**
Sarphatikade 12
Amsterdam, 1017 WV
The Netherlands
Tel: +31 20 530 4700
Fax: +31 20 530 4701
info@fine.nl
www.fine.nl

FINE BV acts as an intermediary between producers and potential investors, seeking venture capital for film projects through a network of financial institutions such as banks.

**Fintage House**
Stationsweg 32
Leiden, 2312 AV
The Netherlands
Tel: +31 71 565 9999
Fax: +31 71 565 9960
entertainment.assets@fintagehouse.com
www.fintagehouse.com
Subsidiary of Fintage House, a globally operating boutique entertainment company, services of which include: international licensing and distribution, collection account management and music publishing and secondary rights collection.

## New Zealand

**Film New Zealand**
PO Box 24142
Wellington, New Zealand
Tel: +64 4 385 0766
Fax: +64 4 384 5840
info@filmnz.org.nz
www.filmnz.com
Film New Zealand's role is to provide information, introductions and support to filmmakers both internationally and locally, including help with the production environment, regional film offices, diverse locations, state-of-the-art facilities, experienced crews, and guidelines about shooting and who can help make projects happen.

**New Zealand Film**
PO Box 11 546
Wellington, New Zealand
Tel: +64 4 382 7680
Fax: +64 4 384 9719
mail@nzfilm.co.nz
www.nzfilm.co.nz
New Zealand Film provides financial assistance for New Zealand feature film projects and New Zealand filmmakers, by way of loan or equity financing. They commit up to 8% of their annual budget to feature film development financing, and up to 60% to feature film production financing. Development decisions are made by either the senior staff group (up to $15,000 per project) or the Development Committee (up to $75,000 cumulative per projects). The Film Commission Board makes decisions involving financing beyond $75,000 for either advanced project development or for production financing.

## Norway

**Norwegian Film Commission**
Georgernes Verft 12
Bergen, N-5011
Norway
Tel: +47 55 56 43 43
Fax: +47 55 56 43 48
post@norwegianfilm.com
www.norwegianfilm.com
An autonomous, national foundation whose purpose is to encourage production of international films in Norway.

**Norwegian Film Fund**
Postbox 752, Sentrum
Oslo, NO-0106
Norway
Tel: +47 22 47 80 40
Fax: +47 22 47 80 41
post@filmfondet.no
www.filmfondet.no
A civil executive body under the auspices of the Royal Ministry for Cultural Affairs, it administers all nation support for film production in Norway.

## Puerto Rico

**Puerto Rico Film Commission**
PO Box 362350
San Juan, 00936-2350
Puerto Rico
Tel: +1 787 758 4747
Fax: +1 787 756 5706
www.puertoricofilm.com/english

## South Africa

### South African Film Finance Corporation

Glenmain Bldg, 1st Floor
359 A Main Road, Sea Point
Cape Town, 8005
South Africa
Tel: +27 21 434 2851
Fax: +27 21 434 1229
info@theimaginarium.com
www.theimaginarium.com

The Imaginarium provides financing of feature films in Southern Africa and executive production services. Funding is secured through the South African Film Finance Corporation (SAFFCO). SAFFCO is South Africa's leading film finance company, with unparalleled expertise in the structuring of complex financial, legal and multi-country co-productions. SAFFCO secures financing in a variety of forms, including equity, gap, tax incentives and facilities deals.

## Spain

### Filmoteca Espanol

Magdalena 10
28012 Madrid
Spain
Tel: +34 91 467 26 00
Fax: +34 91 467 26 11
filmoteca@filmoteca.mcu.es
www.mcu.es

## Sweden

### Swedish Film Commission

PO Box 27183,
S-102 52 Stockholm
Sweden
Tel: +46 8 665 11 00
Fax: +46 8 666 37 48
info@swedenfilmcommission.com
www.swedenfilmcommission.com

Sweden Film Commission is the national commission marketing Sweden as an excellent location for shooting commercials, feature films and television. The unit co-ordinates the regional film commissions and facilitates contacts with the local technical infrastructure. Sweden Film Commission is a first stop for information, support, and local assistance.

### Swedish Film Institute

Box 27 126
Stockholm, 102 52
Sweden
Tel: +46 8 665 11 00
Fax: +46 86 663 698
uof@sfi.se
www.sfi.se

The Swedish Film Institute aims to promote, support and develop Swedish cinema in its cultural and broader contexts; it allocates grants for the production, support and of films at an international level. The Film Institute's funds are used for production support for Swedish films, support for the distribution and public screening of films throughout Sweden and support for cultural activities relating to cinema.

## USA

### Academy of Motion Picture Arts and Sciences (AMPAS)

Academy Foundation, 8949 Wilshire Boulevard
Beverly Hills, California, 90211
USA
Tel: + 1 310 247 3000
Fax: +1 310 859 9351
ampas@oscars.org
www.oscars.org

The Academy of Motion Picture Arts and Sciences, a professional honorary organization of over 6,000 motion picture professionals, was founded to advance the arts and sciences of motion pictures; fostering cooperation among creative leaders for cultural, educational and technological progress; recognising outstanding achievements; cooperate on technical research and improvement of methods and equipment; providing a common forum and meeting ground for various branches and crafts; representing the viewpoint of actual creators of the motion picture; and foster educational activities between the professional community and the public-at-large.

**Association of Film Commissioners International (AFCI)**
314 North Main Street
Helena, Montana, 50601
USA
Tel: +1 406 495 8040
Fax: +1 406 495 8039
info@afci.org
www.afci.org
AFCI is the official professional organization for film commissioners who assist film, television and video production throughout the world. It is a non-profit educational association whose members serve as city, county, state, regional, provincial or national film commissioners for their respective governmental jurisdictions.

**Candide Media Works, Inc**
27 West 24th Street, Suite 202
New York, New York, 10010, USA
Tel: +1 212 647 0400
Fax: +1 212 647 8255
help@tensecondfilms.com
www.tensecondfilms.com

**Cinema Management Group LLC**
9056 Santa Monica Boulevard, Suite 204
West Hollywood, California, 90069
USA
Tel: +1 310 788 9959
Fax: +1 310 300 2220
www.cinemamanagementgroup.com
Acquires, co-finances, licenses and distributes new quality feature films to the international market place in all media.

**Cinetic Media**
555 West 25th Street, Fourth Floor
New York, New York, 10001, USA
Tel: +1 212 204 7979
Fax: +1 212 204 7980
office@cineticmedia.com
www.cineticmedia.com
Secures financing and US distribution for high profile film-makes, producers and international sales companies.

**Entertainment Business Group (EBG)**
155 Granada Street, Suite L
Camarillo, California, 93010
USA
Tel: +1 805 383 2766
Fax: +1 805 383 3766
www.ebgroup.net
Provides business services to the entertainment industry, possessing relationships with a number of successful filmmakers, studios, international distributors and entertainment banks. Film project planning that includes development and production funding, as well as global, all media and ancillary rights liquidation.

**Independent Feature Project (IFP)**
104 West 29th Street, 12th Floor
New York, New York, 10001
USA
Tel: +1 212 465 8200
Fax: +1 212 465 8525
ifpny@ifp.org
www.ifp.org
IFP is a not-for-profit service organisation that provides services to independent filmmakers of varying levels of experience, offering invaluable assistance, information and access to the world of independent film.

**Nicholl Fellowships**
Academy of Motion Picture Arts and Sciences
1313 North Vine Street
Los Angeles, California, 90028
USA
Tel: +1 310 247 3059
nicholl@oscars.org
www.oscars.org

# Films and intellectual property

By Justin Kelly

*The contents of this section are provided for information purposes only. When dealing with intellectual property rights the advice of a practising solicitor should be sought.*

## WHAT IS FILM?

'Film' is an ambiguous term in that it may denote:

- the celluloid used for the projection of moving images;
- a planned production constituting a cinematographic work; or
- a recording on any medium from which a moving image may, by any means, be produced.

For the purposes of this article, the use of the word 'film' denotes a recording on any medium from which a moving image may, by any means, be produced and shall include the sound track accompanying the film[1]. In this sense the film is to be distinguished from the cinematographic work portrayed by use of the film in projection.

The law relating to a film should be considered in the context of the relevant jurisdiction (i.e. which courts would decide on the interpretation of the law) and choice of law (i.e. which law the courts apply). For example, if so dictated by the terms of a contract, it is possible for the courts of England and Wales to apply U.S. law. This chapter will focus on European law as interpreted by the courts of England and Wales (and implemented through national statutes and statutory instruments). If the claimant is not an E.C. national, or if first publication occurred outside of the E.C., then rules on nationality and place of publication may have an effect on the rights of those claiming film protection[2].

## WHAT IS INTELLECTUAL PROPERTY?

Intellectual Property ("IP") is a generic term used to describe rights resulting from intellectual activity in the industrial, scientific, literary and artistic fields. IP includes:

- copyright, related rights and moral rights;
- trade marks and domain names;
- database rights;
- design rights; and
- patents.

# Copyright

Copyright protects expressions rather than ideas or procedures. For example, someone may have an idea for a film but only once they express the idea in some tangible form (e.g. writing or filming) might copyright arise. Furthermore, such copyright will not be in the bare idea but in the elaborated concept (e.g. in plot, presentation features etc.). A work must be original to qualify for copyright protection i.e. it must not have been copied from another work. Generally, the author is the first owner of copyright in a work.

Copyright is a generic English word used to cover the rights granted to authors and others involved in the film. In other European countries the rights granted may be author's rights, personality rights and related rights (i.e. separate rights in the cinematographic work on the one hand and for performances and the recording on the other). Although there are provisions harmonising E.U. law in this area there are still differences between the national laws of E.U. Members.

## OWNERSHIP OF COPYRIGHT

Ownership of copyright is a matter for legislation in the country where protection is claimed[3]. In the U.K., the producer and the principal director of a film are the initial owners of the copyright in the recording of the film[4]. For these purposes, a producer means the person by whom the arrangements necessary for the making of the film are undertaken[5]. However, any copyright work produced in the course of employment belongs to the employer[6]. Therefore, if the director is employed by the producer, the copyright in the director's contribution will belong to the producer and the producer will be the sole copyright owner.

In the case of a literary, dramatic, musical or artistic work which is computer generated, e.g. an animation, the author is the person by whom the arrangements necessary for the creation of the work are undertaken[7].

In order to avoid confusion and give notice of protection, copyright material should be accompanied by the standard notice "© [Name of copyright owner] [year of first publication]".

Such notice is not, however, a condition of copyright protection.

## GRANTED RIGHTS

Copyright in a work is infringed by a person who, without the permission of the copyright owner, does, or authorises another to do, any of the acts restricted by copyright[8]. The following acts are restricted by copyright[9]:

- to reproduce/copy the work;

Something is considered a copy if it is substantially the same as the original. Substantiality is judged on the basis of quantity and/or quality. For example, someone may take only a few notes of a song but if they are the crucial hooks of the song then substantial copying may be held to have taken place. Copying includes the making of transient copies or copies incidental to some other use of the work[10]. Furthermore, a copy may be an indirect copy. The taking of a plot of a novel or play (e.g. the characters and context change but the essential plot remains the same) is likely to constitute copying of the work[11].

Copying of a film includes making a photograph of the whole or a substantial part of any image forming part of the film[12].

- To issue the work to the public;

- to rent or lend the work to the public;
- to perform, show or play the work in public;
- to communicate the work to the public;

Communication may be by wire or wireless means, including the making available to the public of the work in such a way that members of the public may access the work from a place and at a time individually chosen by them. This may be called the 'on demand availability right' and includes communication over the internet.

- To make an adaptation/derivation of the work (including a translation) or to do any of the above acts in relation to an adaptation/derivation.

The following acts may constitute secondary infringement of copyright[13]:

- importing infringing copies;
- possessing or dealing with infringing copies;
- providing means for making infringing copies;
- permitting the use of premises for an infringing performance; and
- providing apparatus for infringing performances.

Amongst other things, an article is an infringing copy if its making constituted an infringement of the copyright in the work in question[14].

The main difference between acts restricted by copyright and acts constituting secondary infringement is that, to be liable for the later, the defendant must have had some form or knowledge that the relevant material was infringing copyright.

## DURATION OF COPYRIGHT

In the U.K., copyright generally expires 70 years after the death of the author. Copyright in a film expires 70 years from the end of the calendar year in which the death occurs of the last to die of the following persons:

1. director;
2. author of the screenplay[15];
3. author of the dialogue; or
4. composer of music specifically created for the film[16].

## REGISTRATION OF COPYRIGHT

In the E.U., it is not necessary to register a copyright work to benefit from protection.

There are copyright registration services for the E.U. territory but such registration, or posting a work to your self, is not required for protection although it may help in providing evidence in court[17]. In the U.S. registration is required in order to benefit from certain procedural rights in infringement actions[18].

## EXCEPTIONS TO COPYRIGHT

In the E.U., there is no harmonised system for copyright exceptions and limitations. The recent Information Society Directive effectively gave Internet Service Providers basic immunity when people use their systems to infringe copyright but otherwise each E.U. country can have different exceptions and limitations. However such exceptions and limitations must come within one of those listed in the Directive (there are over 20 of these) and in addition must:

1. be only in special cases;
2. not conflict with the normal exploitation of the subject matter (e.g. a film); and
3. not unreasonably prejudice the legitimate interests of the rights holder (e.g. a film producer).

1-3 above are known as the "3 step test".

In the U.K., there are, amongst others, the following defences to copyright infringement:

- in relation to literary, dramatic, musical or artistic works, copyright as not infringed by fair dealing for the purposes of:
    - o non-commercial research[19]; or
    - o private study[20].

Note that this does not apply to films, broadcasts, cable programmes and sound recordings.

- In relation to any work, copyright is not infringed by fair dealing for the purposes of criticism and review (if accompanied by a sufficient acknowledgement and provided the work has been made available to the public)[21].
- In relation to any work (other than a photograph), copyright is not infringed by fair dealing for the purposes reporting current events (if accompanied by a sufficient acknowledgement)[22].
- In relation to any work, copyright is not infringed by its incidental inclusion in an artistic work, sound recording, film or broadcast. However, a musical work or words spoken, or sung, with music shall not be regarded as incidentally included in another work if it is deliberately included.
- In relation to buildings, sculptures and works of artistic craftsmanship permanently situated in a public place, copyright in such works is not infringed by making a:
    - o graphic work representing it;
    - o photograph or film of it; or
    - o broadcast of a visual image of it.
- There are also substantial complex provisions regarding use by persons with disabilities, education, libraries, computer programs and time shifting.

The burden of proof generally falls on the defendant to prove that they, on the balance of probabilities, come within the exceptions.

## Moral Rights

Moral rights exist along side copyright, are non-economic in nature and may include:

- the identification right (also known as the paternity right); this includes the right of an author or director to have his or her identity brought to the attention of anyone seeing or hearing the work or to have a work published anonymously or pseudonymously[23]. For example, a screen writer who sells a script may have the right to have his or her name or pseudonym associated with the script. A film director may only exercise a claimed moral right when the film is shown in public, communicated to the public or copies of it have been distributed to the public[24]. To be enforced, the identification right must be asserted (by written notice, as provided in the CDP Act 1988) generally or in relation to a specific work[25]. The right does not apply to anything done when the employer is the copyright owner by virtue of the employer/employee copyright ownership provisions (see above)[26].

- The integrity right; this is the right not to have a work subjected to derogatory treatment, i.e. distorting, mutilating or otherwise prejudicing the honour or reputation of the author or director[27]. For example, a director may object to a producer adding pornographic scenes to the director's cut. However, when the employer is the copyright owner (due to the employer/employee relationship), the integrity right does not apply to anything done to the work with the authority of the copyright owner, provided there is a sufficient disclaimer, unless the author or director:
    - o is identified at the time of the relevant act; or
    - o has previously been identified in or on the published copies of the work[28].
- The right not to be falsely attributed as the author of a literary, dramatic, musical or artistic work or director of a film[29].
- A commissioner of a film made for non-commercial purposes also has the right to prevent such commissioned works being issued or distributed to the public (despite the fact that, unless agreed to the contrary, the copyright in the work vests in the commissioned author)[30].

Moral rights may not be assigned but they may be waived in writing signed by the person giving up the right[31].

The identification right, non-derogatory treatment right and right of privacy in certain private photos last for as long as copyright lasts in the relevant work. The false attribution right lasts for 20 years after a person's death[32].

Producers of films do not generally have any moral rights in relation to their films (they do in Germany).

## PRESUMPTION OF TRANSFER OF THE RENTAL RIGHT FOR FILM PRODUCTION AGREEMENTS AND RIGHT TO EQUITABLE REMUNERATION

Where an agreement concerning film production is concluded between an author and a film producer, there is a statutory presumption that the author, unless the agreement provides to the contrary, transfers to the film producer the right to rent the film[33]. For these purposes an author is any author of a literary, dramatic, musical or artistic work (such as a script, play, score or film poster)[34]. However, this presumption of rental right transfer does not apply to an author whose work is specifically created for use in a film[35].

When there is a transfer of an author's or director's rental rights in a sound recording or film to the producer, due to the above presumption or otherwise, the author or director retains a right to equitable remuneration for the rental (e.g. payment)[36]. This right may not be assigned (except to a collecting society) nor excluded by agreement[37]. The amount payable is to be agreed between the parties or decided by the Copyright Tribunal[38].

## PERFORMERS' RIGHTS

In the U.K. (which is a common law system), copyright is granted to authors of original works, producers of sound recordings and films, broadcasters and publishers. Performers have separate rights. In the civil law system of the countries of continental Europe and other countries, a distinction is made between "author's right" (granted to authors of original works) and "related (or neighbouring) rights" (granted to film and sound recording producers, broadcasters and performers).

In the E.C., performers have the following exclusive related rights:

1. right to make a recording of the whole or any substantial part of a qualifying performance directly from the live performance[39];
2. right to broadcast live, or include in a cable programme service, the whole or any substantial part of a qualifying performance[40];
3. right to make a recording of the whole or any substantial part of a qualifying performance directly from a broadcast of, or cable programme including, the live performance[41];
4. right to make a copy (the reproduction right), directly or indirectly, of a recording of the whole or any substantial part of a qualifying performance[42];
5. right to distribute the original or copies of the recording of their performance[43];
6. right to authorise or prohibit the rental and lending of originals and copies of fixations of a performance[44]; and
7. right to make available to the public a recording of the whole or any substantial part of a qualifying performance by electronic transmission in such a way that members of the public may access the recording from a place and at a time individually chosen by them ('making available right')[45].

The above rights expire 50 years after the performance or, if during that 50 years a recording of the performance is released, 50 years after the date of such release[46].

When a performer concludes a contract with a film producer, the performer shall be presumed, subject to contractual clause to the contrary, to have transferred the rental right. However, in such a case, the performer shall retain the right to obtain an equitable remuneration for the rental[47]. An agreement is of no effect to the extent that it purports to exclude or restrict a performer's right to equitable remuneration under these provisions.

The World Intellectual Property Organisation's Performances and Phonograms Treaty provides that, in relation to live aural performances or performances fixed in recordings, performers have moral rights to be identified as the performer (except where omission is dictated by the manner of the use of the performance e.g. it might be unrealistic to grant such a right to every performer in an orchestra) and to object to any distortion, mutilation or other modification of the performance that would prejudice his or her reputation[48]. These moral rights last at least until the expiry of the economic rights. However, since it has not yet ratified the Treaty (it is envisaged that eventually there will be a simultaneous ratification by all E.C. Member States), the U.K. has not yet implement these provisions.

## EXCEPTIONS TO PERFORMERS' RIGHTS

The following acts may be done notwithstanding the existence of performer's rights:

1. fair dealing for the purpose of criticism or review provided that the performance or recording has been made available to the public;
2. fair dealing for the purpose of reporting current events;
3. incidental inclusion of a performance or recording in a sound recording, film or broadcast;
4. copying a recording of a performance in the course of non-commercial instruction in the making of films or film sound tracks; and
5. certain restricted uses by libraries[49].

## FILM PRODUCER RELATED RIGHTS

In the E.U., in addition to a producer potentially having copyright in a film (by way of transfer from the authors of the film or otherwise), a producer may have the following exclusive related rights in a film:

1. right to rent and/or lend the original and/or copies of a film[50];
2. right to distribute the original and/or copies of a film[51];
3. right to reproduce a film directly or indirectly, temporarily or permanently by any means and in any form, in whole or in part[52]; and
4. right to make available on demand the original and/or copies of a film[53].

Film producer related rights expire 50 years after the first fixation of the film (i.e. the date when a record is made, in any medium, from which a moving image may be produced). However, if the film is lawfully published (i.e. made available to the public) during this period the related rights expire 50 years from the date of the first such publication[54].

In light of the above, when dealing with a film, amongst other things, it is important to consider:

- copyright in lyrics and music (symbolised as a ©);
- related rights of performers and producers of music (symbolised as a "P" in a circle);
- producer's (and possibly the director's) copyright in the film;
- moral rights (of the director and performers);
- trade mark rights.

## DEALINGS WITH COPYRIGHT AND PERFORMERS' RIGHTS

Copyright and related rights may be transferred via a number of means including assignments and licences. An assignment is a transfer in ownership whereas a licence is a permission to do something which is otherwise the exclusive right of the copyright owner.

A copyright licence may be partial in that the copyright owner may licence another person to do one or more acts restricted by copyright for a certain length of time (within the term of copyright) within a certain geographical area. For example, a copyright licence may provide that the licensee is exclusively licensed to play a copy of a film for one week in three specific cinemas or to exclusively make copies of a film and distribute them throughout France for 15 years.

An exclusive licence means a licence in writing signed by the copyright owner authorising the licensee to the exclusion of all others, including the person granting the licence, to exercise a right which would otherwise be exercisable exclusively by the copyright owner[55]. With such a licence, if the copyright owner were to do any act licensed to the licensee, the licensee would arguably have an action against the copyright owner for breach of contract.

## MUSICAL/ARTISTIC WORKS AND COLLECTING SOCIETIES

Music and/or lyrics which are featured in a film may be pre-existing musical works or works specially commissioned for the film. In both cases, the producer should obtain a 'synchronisation' licence to record (or 'dub') the music (and lyrics) onto the soundtrack. If a composer has an exclusive publishing contract the publisher will need to be made a party to such agreement.

The producer will also need to obtain 'mechanical' rights i.e. to be allowed to make and distribute copies of the music/lyrics (e.g. on to DVDs). Furthermore, the producer must ensure that he or she has the right to perform such a work in public (i.e. in addition to making a sound recording of the work). As can be seen form the aforesaid, the producer must 'drill down' to ensure that he or she has documentary proof that all those who have contributed to the music/ lyrics have given their appropriate consent for all the things which the producer wants to do with the relevant work. If relevant, the producer should be particularly careful to ensure he or she has the necessary rights to issue a 'soundtrack album'.

Artistic works may deliberately appear in a film for example due to them being part of the set or wardrobe. In such cases, the producer should ensure an appropriate assignment or licence is in place with those who contribute such works. Generally, a producer does not need copyright clearance to incidentally include artistic works or sound recordings (such as buildings, paintings, sculptures and radio) in a film[56]. However, if a copyright work is prominently or deliberately featured then copyright clearance may be needed.

Useful contacts for clearing content include:

- **Authors Licensing and Collecting Society** (www.alcs.co.uk)
  The Authors Licensing and Collecting Society handles photocopying, lending and some recording and retransmission rights for authors in the U.K..
- **British Equity Collecting Society Ltd**. (www.equitycollecting.org.uk)
  BECS' main objective is to collect, distribute and administer performers' remuneration e.g. due to the rental or re-transmission of a film incorporating their performance.
- **Broadcasting, Entertainment, Cinematograph and Theatre Union**
  BECTU is the independent union representing U.K. workers in the broadcasting, film, theatre, entertainment, leisure, interactive media and related industries
- **Compact Collections Ltd** (www.cla.co.uk/)
  Compact Collections Ltd. collects secondary television royalties for film and television content owners regarding, amongst other things, private copying, cable re-transmission and the showing of films by televised broadcast in public places. It does not collect royalties regarding exercise of U.K. rights.
- **Copyright Licensing Agency** (www.cla.co.uk/)
  The CLA represents authors and publishers in the U.K. regarding the copying of

published literary, dramatic, musical and artistic works using photocopiers and other methods of multiple copying such as scanning.

- **Directors and Producers Rights Society** (www.dprs.org)
  The DPRS represents U.K. directors and collects and distributes money due to them for the exploitation of their work.
- **Directors' Guild of Great Britain** (www.dggb.co.uk)
  The DGGB represents directors in film, television, theatre, radio, opera, commercials, corporate, multimedia and new technology industries.
- **Mechanical Copyright Protection Society** (MCPS) and **Performing Rights Society (PRS) alliance** (www.mcps-prs-alliance.co.uk/)
  The MCPS collects and distributes royalties based on the "mechanical" copyright in musical works i.e. the right to make sound bearing copies of musical works, to issue such copies to the public, to import such copies and to authorise any of the aforesaid. The PRS collects licence fees for the public performance, broadcast and cable transmission of musical works (such as those included in films). Ideally, the producer will ensure that a composer is contractually bound to procure rights for the producer or from PRS.
- **Performing Artists' Media Rights Association Ltd**. (www.pamra.org.uk)
  PAMRA represents featured and non-featured performers across all genres of music and is the largest performers' collecting society in the UK.
- **Phonographic Performance Ltd**. (www.ppluk.com)
  PPL represents record companies and the performers who have contributed to the recordings. It collects income generated from the broadcast of commercially released recordings from broadcasters and public performance venues.
- **Video Performance Ltd**. (www.vpluk.com)
  VPL is the collecting society to grant licences to users of music videos, e.g. broadcasters, film/documentary makers, video jukebox system suppliers.
- **Musicians' Union** (www.musiciansunion.org.uk)
- **British Phonographic Industry Ltd**. (www.bpi.co.uk)
  The BPI is the British record industry's trade association
- **FastTrack Digital Copyright Network** (www.fasttrackdcn.net/)
  FastTrack is a new global alliance of music copyright societies.
- **Audio Network Plc** (www.fasttrackdcn.net/)
  Audio Network owns the rights to an archive of music and sound effects which it supplies to the international film, television and media markets.

## COPYLEFT

Copyleft is based on copyright. Based on copyright, an owner can licence the use of copyright material under conditions that ensure that everyone has the right to use, modify and redistribute the material *or any material derived from it.* Anyone who redistributes the content, with or without changes, must pass along the freedom to further copy and change it. Copyleft is designed to guarantee that every user has freedom to use the content and not the freedom to restrict other users[57]. Despite the altruistic motives, copyleft licences could be considered to be against the interests of authors because, amongst other things, they are irrevocable and last for the whole term of the copyright.

*See further www.creativecommons.org www.gnu.org www.craphound.com/msftdrm.txt*

## DIGITAL MEDIA AND THE INTERNET

The advent of digital technology and the internet has substantially changed the landscape in which copyright laws operates. There are new types of works such as software, CD-ROMS, DVDs and web sites. Such digital media may contain text, still and/or moving images and sound (including music). Consequently a wide rage of rights holders may have copyright, related rights, moral rights, design rights and/or database rights in such works. Furthermore, the effect of new means of reproduction and communication means content can be rapidly disseminated without substantial expense, deterioration or scarcity. These new factors have strained the balance between the protection of the rights owner and the interests of society for there to be access to information and new product development.

## ANTI-CIRCUMVENTION PROVISIONS

Content protected by copyright and/or related rights may have access and copy control technologies applied to them together with digital rights management information. It is a civil and criminal offence to circumvent, or attempt or circumvent, these technologies including dealing with circumvention technologies and services. This includes such activity otherwise than in the course of business to the extent that it prejudicially affects the rights owner[58].

## T.V. FORMAT RIGHTS

In the U.K., there is no statutory format right. However, the courts are gradually beginning to protect rights in formats under the umbrella of copyright, confidentiality and trade mark law. The more written detail about the format the greater the chance of protecting it. In order to best protect format rights, the owner should:

1. record, in as much detail as possible, what the format is, such as:
    a. the title;
    b. sample scripts;
    c. the principal characters, names, details of character, suitable candidates to play them;
    d. the set and settings;
    e. principal stage properties;
    f. the role of the presenter;
    g. intended catch phrases;
    h. the role of any participating professionals;
    i. the role of any participating members of the public;
    j. the role and type of any celebrities; and
    k. the order in which different parts or sections of the programmes are to run.

2. Keep a detailed, written record of the development process including who contributed what to the project, the date of such contribution and their status in doing so. Ensure that ownership of such contributions is documents e.g. through employment contracts, licenses and/or assignments. These records should be supported by backed up digital records and hard copy records of e-mails, meeting notes, telephone attendance notes, faxes, design documents, contracts etc.
3. Develop ideas as much as possible before showing it to anyone. Before you show it to anyone, as them to sign a confidentiality agreement or at least make it clear that the information is confidential (mark it as such) and is not to be used without your permission.
4. Register the title of the format as a trade mark and domain name.
5. Develop 2D drawings and/or 3D models and/or a pilot.
6. If any licensee adds an element to your format they should be contractually obligated to licence that element back to you.
7. Sign exclusive agreements with the people who have the relevant know-how.
8. Consider registration with organisations such as the Format Recognition and Protaction Association. (www.frapa.org) or with a reputable law firm.

## Trade Marks

A trade mark means any sign capable of being represented graphically which is capable of distinguishing goods or services of one undertaking from those of another; i.e. it is an indication that goods or services come from a particular origin[59]. A trade mark may include names, designs, letters, numerals, shapes or packaging. Trade mark rights are territorial and may be unregistered or registered[60].

Generally, the more a mark is used the more possible it is that unregistered trade mark rights will begin to accrue. Unregistered trade mark rights (also known as rights in 'passing off') enable the owner to stop another party from using a similar mark, and possible receive damages, provided the owner can prove the following:

1. goodwill in the mark; i.e. that there are consumers who are drawn to buy the product on the basis of the mark;
2. misrepresentation; i.e. that another party is misrepresenting itself as being the owner of the mark;
3. damage; i.e. that the owner of the mark has suffered damage due to the misrepresentation.

A trade mark may be registered provided it can overcome absolute and relative grounds for refusal. The absolute grounds include:

1. trade marks which are devoid of any distinctive character (although distinctiveness may be gained through use in the market)[61];
2. trade marks which consist exclusively of signs which may serve to designate the kind, quality, intended purpose, value, geographical origin, time of production or other

characteristics of goods or services e.g. "Film Maker Production Company Ltd." for a production company or "London Films" for a London film company[62].

The relative grounds include:

1. the applied for mark is identical to a mark previously registered and the relevant goods or services of the applied for mark are identical to the goods or services for which the earlier mark is registered[63];
2. the applied for mark is similar to a mark previously registered and the relevant goods or services of the applied for mark are similar to the goods or services for which the earlier mark is registered AND there exists a likelihood of confusion on the part of the public[64].
3. the applied for mark is similar to a mark that has a reputation (i.e. 'goodwill' as in unregistered trade mark rights) and its use would take unfair advantage of, or be detrimental to, the distinctive character or repute of the earlier mark[65].

A UK trade mark registration last for 10 years from the date of registration and may be renewed indefinitely[66]. A trade mark owner may also apply for a European Community Trade Mark ("CTM") registration[67] and/or for registrations in other countries around the world as part of the Madrid Protocol[68].

Registering a company name at Companies House does not entitle the registrant to trade mark rights in that name. Notice of unregistered trade mark rights is given by attaching the "TM" symbol after the mark. If a mark is registered the "®" symbol may be attached. Attaching the "®" symbol to an unregistered mark is a criminal offence[69]. A registered trade mark is personal property that may be licensed or assigned and such transactions should be registered at the trade mark registry[70].

Merchandising rights will invariably involve the use of names and features of characters which may be trade marked. In addition, merchandising may involve copyright in costumes, sets, artwork and drawings thereof.

The protection of titles is best suited to actions in unregistered and/or registered trade mark law. Copyright is less appropriate due to its requirements as to originality and substantiality.

## Domain names

Registering a domain name does not necessarily give the owner trade mark rights in the name. However, the more the domain name is used the more goodwill is likely to be generated in the name. The domain name system is governed by the Internet Corporation for Assigned Names and Numbers (www.icann.org) and the UK registry for domain names is Nominet UK (www.nic.uk).

When there is a dispute about ownership of a domain name it will be settled according to the alternative dispute resolution system of the relevant registry. These generally require the complainant to prove, on the balance of probabilities, that:

1. it has rights in respect of a name or mark which is identical or similar to the domain name in question; and
2. the domain name was registered in a manner which, at the time of registration, took unfair advantage of, or was unfairly detrimental to, the complainant's rights; or

3. the domain name has been used in a manner which has taken unfair advantage of, or was unfairly detrimental to, the complainant's rights.

On the basis of a dispute resolution decision, a registry has the power to transfer, cancel or suspend a domain name registration.

## Database rights

A database is a collection of independent works which are arranged in a systematic or methodical way and are individually accessible by electronic or other means. The rights included in a database may include:

1. Copyright in the individual entries of the database (e.g. each film in an archive).
2. Copyright in the database itself if the selection or arrangement of the contents of the database is the product of the author's original intellectual protection (e.g. a selection of films representing the seasons of the year).
3. '*Sui generis*' database rights if there has been a qualitatively and/or quantitatively substantial investment in either the obtaining, verification or presentation of the contents of the database (e.g. a compilation of scenes or films)[71]. The requisite investment refers to the resources used to:
   a. ensure the reliability of information contained in a database; and/or
   b. monitor the accuracy of materials collected when a database is created and during its operation.

It does not refer to the resources used for verification during the stage of creation of materials which are subsequently collected in a database[72].

The *sui generis* database right is without prejudice to the rights in 1 and 2 above.

The requirement for systematic or methodical arrangement and individual accessibility means that a recording of an audiovisual, cinematographic, literary or musical work as such does not generally fall within the scope of database protection. Furthermore, a compilation of musical performances on a CD does not come within the scope of copyright (because as a compilation it does not meet the conditions of protection) or sui generis database rights (because it does not represent a substantial enough investment)[73]. However, it might be argued that a DVD with individually accessible chapters could constitute a database.

## Design rights

Design rights generally relate to any aspect of the shape or configuration (whether internal or external) of the whole or part of an article. They may include an icon on a desk top computer or the user interface of a software program. Design right do not include surface decoration or anything considered to be common place in the design field in question at the time of creation (i.e. the design must be original). Design rights may be unregistered or registered[74].

## Patents

Patents generally relate to inventions, i.e. how things work, how they are made or what they are made of. To be patentable an invention must be new, inventive, capable of industrial application and not excluded by being any of the following:

- a discovery;
- a scientific theory or mathematical method;
- an aesthetic creation such as a literary, dramatic or artistic work;
- a scheme or method for performing a mental act, playing a game or doing business; or
- the presentation of information, or a computer program[75].



*With the kind assistance of Professor Adrian Sterling, Queens Intellectual Property Research Institute, University of London, author of World Copyright Law" Sterling, J.A.L., (2nd edition 2005) Sweet & Maxwell Ltd."*
*(although any inaccuracies or omissions remain those of the author)."*

*Justin Kelly qualified as a solicitor in September 2000. Since June 2004, he has been working as an independent film producer with projects in the UK and Eastern Europe. He can be contacted at justinkelly@london.com.*

### Footnotes

[1] Section 5B Copyright, Designs and Patents Act (CDPA) 1988; for further information on U. K. law see "Copinger and Skone James on Copyright" (15th edition 2005) and on national, regional and international law see "World Copyright Law" Sterling, J.A.L., (2nd edition 2005).

[2] Section 153 ff CDPA 1988

[3] Art. 14bis(2)(a) of the Berne Convention

[4] Section 9(2)(ab) CDPA 1988

[5] Section 178 CDPA 1988

[6] Section 11(2) CDPA 1988

[7] Section 9(3) CDPA 1988

[8] Section 16(2) CDPA 1988

[9] Section 16 ff CDPA 1988 and articles 2-4 of the Directive 2001/29/EC of the European Parliament and the Council of 22 May 2001 on the harmonisation of certain aspects of copyright and related rights in the information society ("Information Society Directive")

[10] Section 17(6) CDPA 1988

[11] Holland v Vivian van Damm Productions Ltd [1936-1945] MacG CC 69

[12] Section 17(4) CDPA 1988

[13] Sections 22-26 CDPA 1988

[14] Section 27 CDPA 1988

[15] There is some uncertainty as to the exact distinction between the screenplay and the dialogue. It has been suggested that the 'screenplay' is the script including the dialogue and scene directions (see "Copinger and Skone James on Copyright" (15th edition 2005) at 27-184 foot note 5).

[16] Section 13B CDPA 1988 and article 1 Council Directive 93/98/EEC of 29 October 1993 harmonising the term of protection of copyright and certain related rights ("Term Directive")

[17] For example see www.copyrightservice.co.uk, www.scriptfactory.co.uk, www.publaw.com and www.wgaeast.org

18 See further www.copyright.gov/register

[19] Section 29(1) CDPA 1988

[20] Section 29(1C) CDPA 1988

[21] Section 30(1) CDPA 1988

[22] Section 30(2) CDPA 1988; no acknowledgement is required in connection with the reporting of current events by means of a sound recording, film or broadcast where this would be impossible for reasons of practicality or otherwise (section 30(3) CDPA 1988).

[23] Section 77 CDPA 1988

[24] Section 77(6) CDPA 1988

[25] Section 78 CDPA 1988

[26] Section 79(3) CDPA 1988 and see section 11(2) CDPA 1988

[27] Section 80 CDPA 1988; in France the Court of Appeal held that the colourisation of a black and white film could infringe the integrity right (Turner Entertainment v Heirs to the Estate of John Huston, Court of Appeal of Versailles, Revue Internationale des droits d'auteur No. 164 April 1995 at p. 389.

[28] Section 82 CDPA 1988

[29] Section 84 CDPA 1988

[30] Section 85 CDPA 1988

[31] Section 87 and 94 CDPA 1988

[32] Section 86 CDPA 1988

[33] Section 93A(1) CDPA 1988

[34] Section 93A(2) CDPA 1988

[35] Section 93A(3) CDPA 1988

[36] Section 93B CDPA 1988

[37] Sections 93B(2) and (5) CDPA 1988

[38] Sections 93B(4) and 93C CDPA 1988

[39] Article 6 of E.C. Rental/Lending and Related Rights Directive and section 182(1)(a) CDPA 1988

[40] Section 182(1)(b) CDPA 1988

[41] Section 182(1)(c) CDPA 1988

[42] Section 182A CDPA 1988

[43] Article 9 Council Directive 92/100/EEC of 19 November 1992 on rental right and lending right and on certain rights related to copyright in the field of intellectual property ("Rental/ Lending and Related Rights Directive") and section 182B CDPA 1988

[44] Articles 1 and 2 Rental/Lending and Related Rights Directive, s.182C CDPA 1988

[45] Article 8 Rental/Lending and Related Rights Directive and section 182CA CDPA 1988 This is more limited than the communication right granted to authors

[46] Article 3(1) Term Directive

[47] Articles 2 and 4 Rental/Lending and Related Rights Directive and section 191F and 191G CDPA 1988

[48] Article 5 WIPO Performance and Phonogram Treaty

[49] Sections 189 CDPA 1988

[50] Article 2 Rental/Lending and Related Rights Directive

[51] Article 9 Rental/Lending and Related Rights Directive

[52] Article 2 Information Society Directive

[53] Article 3 Information Society Directive

[54] Article 3(3) Term Directive

[55] Section 92 CDPA 1988

[56] Section 31 and 62 CDPA 1988

[57] Sections 296ZA-304 CDPA 1988

[58] Section 1(1) Trade Mark Acts 1994

[59] See further the UK trade mark registry at http://www.patent.gov.uk/tm/ and the Institute of Trade Marks Attorneys at www.itma.org.uk.
60 Section 3(1)(b) Trade Marks Act 1994

[61] Section 3(1)(c) Trade Marks Act 1994

[62] Section 5(1) Trade Marks Act 1994

[63] Section 5(2) Trade Marks Act 1994

[64] Section 5(3)(a) Trade Marks Act 1994

[65] Section 42 Trade Marks Act 1994

[66] See further www.oami.eu.int
67 See further www.wipo.org
68 Section 95 Trade Marks Act 1994
69 Sections 22-31 Trade Marks Act 1994
70 See further Directive 96/9/EC of the European Parliament and of the Council of 11 March 1996 on the legal protection of databases ("Database Directive") and sections 3A, 50D and 296B of the CDPA 1988.
71 British Horseracing Board and others v William Hill Organisation [2001] EWCA (Civ) 1268; Case 2003/02; [2004] All ER (D) 146
72 Recital 19 Database Directive
73 Section 213 ff. CDPA 1988 and http:// www.patent.gov.uk/design/index.htm
74 For further informaiton see Patents Act 1977 and http://www.patent.gov.uk/patent/ index.htm.

# Recoupment schedule

Below is a simple form of Recoupment Schedule which might be used where the financing has been fairly straightforward on a 70% equity basis, the remaining 30% comprising a gap loan, some soft money, and deferments. Applying the Six Tenths rule of thumb, this gives the equity financiers 42% of Net Profits (six tenths of 70%). The creative Net Profit participations stated are, of course, completely arbitrary, as the actual figures will be subject to negotiation with the relevant contributors. Naturally, in cases where more of the budget has been financed through deferments (particularly on lower budget films), the Producer will have a much lager share of Net Profit, and will be expected to distribute more amongst the cast and crew.

The capitalised terms will be defined in the Collection Account Management Agreement ("CAMA") to which the Recoupment Schedule is appended. These definitions should reflect those used in the Interparty Agreement, Sales Agency Agreement, Commissioning Agreement, etc.

**A couple of points to note:**

Where a bank has discounted a pre-sale, the Distributor will occasionally be instructed or permitted to pay the MG balance into the Collection Account upon delivery (rather than directly to the bank). In these circumstances, provision in the Recoupment Schedule needs to be made for those amounts to be paid from the Collection Account straight to the Bank with little or no deduction.

Also, in cases where it is agreed that receipts from certain countries (often called "collateral territories") are allocated exclusively to repay a specific financier, rather than mixed with other receipts and distributed generally from the "pot", a separate "waterfall" has to be drawn up specifically for the receipts from those collateral territories. Sometimes, therefore, a Recoupment Schedule has a number of waterfalls, but to keep things simple, we have included just one for all world receipts.

## SAMPLE RECOUPMENT SCHEDULE

All Gross Receipts derived from the exploitation of the Film shall be paid directly by all Distributors into the Collection Account [details]. The Collection Agent shall allocate and pay such Gross Receipts in accordance with the terms of the Collection Account Management Agreement in the following order:

1) The Collection Agency Fee to the Collection Agent; thereafter
2) The Non-Deferred Sales Commissions to the Sales Agent; thereafter
3) The Sales Expenses to the Sales Agent; thereafter
4) The Deferred Director's Fee to the Director; thereafter
5) The Gap Loan Amount to the Bank; thereafter
6) The Deferred Sales Commission to Sales Agent; thereafter
7) Repayment on a *parri passu* basis of Investment A to Financier A, Investment B to Financier B and Investment C to Financier C; thereafter
8) Repayment of any Completion Bond Production Contributions made by the Completion Guarantor under the Completion Guaranty, as notified by the Completion Guarantor to the Collection Agent in writing, to the Completion Guarantor; thereafter

(9) The Deferred Producer's Fee to the Producer; thereafter

(10) All further Gross Receipts (less the Sales Commission) shall be deemed "Net Profits" and shall be paid on a parri passu basis in accordance with the following Net Profit Schedule:

| BENEFICIARY | PERCENTAGE OF 100% |
|---|---|
| Investor A | 20 |
| Investor B | 14 |
| Investor C | 8 |
| Producer | 30 |
| Director | 5 |
| Actor A | 5 |
| Actor B | 2.5 |
| Actor C | 2.5 |
| Writer A | 2 |
| Writer B | 2 |
| Cinematographer | 1.5 |
| Composer | 1.5 |
| Production designer | 1 |
| Costume Designer | 1 |
| Other cast & Crew | 4 |
| **Total** | **100** |

# Forming a company

Before almost any financier will give you any money, you need to be a registered company with a dedicated business bank account. Incorporating as a limited company is a relatively straightforward process, but the subsequent associated workload should not be underestimated. Limited companies offer their shareholders limited liability in case the company goes bankrupt – that is, when the company is set up, each of its shareholders guarantees a minimum amount of capital that s/he will provide to cover the company if it is wound up with outstanding debts.

But in return for providing this protection to its owners, a limited company has a number of obligations: it needs to submit annual accounts to Companies House as well as an annual return; and submit accounts and a tax return to the Inland Revenue. If its turnover is above £350,000 the company accounts must be audited. If the company pays you as a director, – or pays anyone else who isn't a legitimate freelancer – it will need to be registered as an employer with the Inland Revenue, which means it will have to deduct National Insurance and tax from wages via the Pay As You Earn scheme (PAYE). Furthermore, once its annual turnover passes £58,000, (or before, if you wish to claim back VAT receipts), you will need to register with HM Customs & Excise for VAT, submitting quarterly returns.

Ideally you will engage an accountant to look after these responsibilities, but many new companies attempt to do much of the bookkeeping and filing themselves, which is a sizeable administrative workload, particularly if you're learning as you go along. There is the constant pressure that failure to deliver accurate accounts and forms at the right time in the right state can lead to an inspection, a fine, or even a prison sentence. An overview of the various possible business structures written by Michael Lerman, of accountants Lerman and Co (www.lermanandco.com) is set out below.

## SOLE TRADER

**Overview.** The basic method of setting up a business. Limited reporting requirements and easy to establish.

**Advantages.** Easy to setup; limited reporting requirements; good use of loss relief.

**Disadvantages.** Liabilities are personal; higher tax rates on large profits.

**How to register.** Only requirement is to register with the Inland Revenue within 30 days (£100 fine if later!).

**Records to keep.** Full accounting records and receipts for all transactions. All records need to be kept for 6 years.

**Year end responsibilities.** Other than the requirement of third parties (e.g. banks, etc) accounts must be prepared for inclusion into the sole-traders' Self Assessment tax return.

**How to pay yourself.** Free to draw cash at will. Tax is only paid based on profits/losses as per the annual accounts.

**Tax rate(s).** Income tax rates, from 0% to 40%. National Insurance rates are 8% on profits and £2.10 per week.

## PARTNERSHIP

**Overview.** An entity which is useful when many people wish to trade together and share profits.

**Advantages.** Same as self-employment except for many joint owners.

**Disadvantages.** As above, plus the fact that when a partner leaves or joins, the partnership ceases and restarts; causing legal and taxation consequences. Also, each partner will be individually liable for the debts of the whole partnership, even if incurred by other partners.

**How to register.** As above, although a partnership agreement is thoroughly recommended.

**Records to keep.** As above.

**Year end responsibilities.** As above. The partners' share of profits are included in their own Self Assessment Tax Returns, and they pay tax on their individual proportion of the partnership profit. The partnership does not pay tax itself, although it does submit a tax return of its own.

**How to pay yourself.** As above, subject to the agreement of the other partners!

**Tax rate(s).** As above (for each partner individually).

## LIMITED LIABILITY PARTNERSHIP ("LLP")

**Overview.** A partnership except with limited liability for the partners.

**Advantages.** The partners are limited in terms of their liability for the business debts.

**Disadvantages.** The LLP is treated as a company for reporting and in terms of the responsibilities of the partners to the outside world.

**How to register.** The LLP is "incorporated" at companies house for a fee. A partnership agreement is required, but does not have to be filed at companies house.

**Records to keep.** As above. In addition, certain information is submitted to companies house on an annual basis relating to partners and the LLP's address. Details of mortgages and other such items must also be communicated to companies house.

**Year end responsibilities.** Annual accounts, in statutory format, are submitted to companies house within strict deadlines.

**How to pay yourself.** As partnership above.

**Tax rate(s).** As above (for each partner individually).

## LIMITED COMPANY

**Overview.** A limited company is treated as a separate legal entity from its owners. Thus its business belongs to, and is operated by, the company. In turn, the company belongs to its shareholders. Its affairs are controlled by directors, who are appointed by (and may be the same people as) the shareholders.

**Advantages.** Limited liability for its shareholders due to the legal separation of the business from its owners. Often percieved by outside parties as having a certain amount of credibility over and above a self-employment or partnership.

**Disadvantages.** Costly, more time-consuming than self-employment or partnerships. Also, the legal responsibilities of its directors are fairly onerous.

**How to register.** Company "incorporated" through, and registered at, Companies House for a fee. Its constitution (the rules by which it can carry on business), known as the "memorandum and articles of association" are filed at companies house.

**Records to keep.** As for LLPs.

**Year end responsibilities.** Annual accounts, in statutory format, are submitted to Companies House within strict deadlines. Accounts, together with a corporation tax self assessment return must be submitted to the Inland Revenue.

**How to pay yourself.** The shareholder of a company is entitled to receive dividends based on after tax profits (ie. income less expenses) made by the company. Dividends, on which income tax is payable, are not wages and therefore do not attract national insurance. For those employed in the business, including directors, salaries can be drawn. Salaries attract income tax, national insurance and the company pays am employers' national insurance surcharge on top.

**Tax rate(s).** Companies pay corporation tax on profits, rather than income tax on earnings. The rates start at 0%, rising to 19%/23.75% and finally a top rate of 30%.

## MUTUAL SOCIETY/CO-OP

**Overview.** An entity where the objects are for the benfit of all the members. Not usually useful for profit-making businesses, such as film production, where there are people wanting to own the business.

**Advantages.** Often treated by the Inland Revenue as non-profit making and therefore do not pay tax on surpluses, so long as they are re-invested into the business.

**Disadvantages.** No scope for taking out profits.

**How to register.** This depends on what type of underlying entity. Normally a company with no share capital.

**Records to keep.** According to the type of underlying entity.

**Year end responsibilities.** According to the type of underlying entity.

**How to pay yourself.** N/A.

**Tax rate(s).** Not usually taxable.

## PUBLIC LIMITED COMPANY ("PLC")

**Overview.** This is a limited company of a minimum size that is permitted by its constitution to raise money for investment from the public.

**Advantages.** Ability to raise capital from outside sources and to be listed on the stock exchange or other public markets.

**Disadvantages.** Highly regulated, especially if listed. Shorter and more reporting requirements. More public exposure.

**How to register.** As for Limited company.

**Records to keep.** As for Limited company.

**Year end responsibilities.** As for Limited company, except the submission time limits are shorter and penalties are higher. For publically quoted (ie. listed) companies, there are also stock-exchange and other regulatory requirements to meet.

**How to pay yourself.** As for Limited company. Although, having independent shareholders, the freedom of the owner to decide on remuneration policy is limited.

**Tax rate(s).** As Ltd companies

## DIY Incorporation

A solicitor will charge around £200 to set-up a limited company; by following the guide below you can do it yourself for just over £40. That said, this is not legal advice, and if you have any doubts or queries you should contact a solicitor, accountant, and/or Companies House.

1. Check that the name of your company is available by ringing Company's House on 0870 3333636 or searching their website at www.companieshouse.gov.uk. Also check that your "trading" name (often – but not always - the same as the company name) is unique within your field (the film business) by searching industry directories, the internet, phonebooks, etc. Decide upon company directors, registered offices and appoint a company secretary.
2. Download form 10 and form 12 from the Companies' House website. Download form 10cs if you have more than two directors. Download or order the relevant guidance notes which includes Company Formation - code GBF1, Company Names - code GBF2, Business Names - code GBF3, Director's and Secretaries Guide - code GBA1
3. Fill in the forms on your computer and print out. Get the company directors and secretary to sign form 10 (and 10cs if necessary).
4. Buy a copy of Memorandums and Articles for company formation, for about £6 from a legal stationer such as Oyez. Oyez is based in London, but can mail the Articles if you purchase them via 0870 7377370 or at www.oyezformslink.co.uk.
5. Fill in the Memorandums and Articles and get all directors and the company secretary to sign it with a witness (the witness can be anyone).
6. Take form 12 to a solicitor and sign it in front of them. Get their signature on the form. Most solicitors charge £7 or so per signature. Photocopy each form for your records.
7. Post form 10, form 10cs (if used), form 12 and the Memorandum and Articles, with a cheque for £20 to Companies House. This is supposed to take 5-6 working days to process upon receipt.

# Glossary of financing agreements

| AGREEMENT NAME | ABBRV. | PARTIES | MAIN PURPOSE |
|---|---|---|---|
| Artist's Agreement | n/a | (1) Producer<br>(2) Lead Artist | For Artist's services and contribution. Similar agreements exist for the Director, Composer, Heads of Departments, etc |
| Charge/ Secrurity | n/a | (1) Bank / Chargee<br>(2) Copyright owner | Similar to a mortgage. Gives the bank or chargee a right to take possession of the asset (usually part of the copyright) if certain conditions in this or other agreements are not met. |
| Collection [Agent's Management] Agreement | CAMA | (1) Collection Agent<br>(2) Sales Agent<br>(3) Producer<br>(4) All Financiers<br>(5) All Profit Participants<br>(6) Completion Guarantor | Provides for the distribution by the Collection Agent of income as it comes into the "pot", based upon the terms of the Recoupment Schedule. Covers recoupment of production finance and distribution of Net Profits. |
| Commissioning [Producer] Agreement | CPA | (1) Commissioning Producer<br>(2) Production Company | Commissioning Producer (CP), in order for it to obtain necessary tax breaks, engages and pays Production Company to make the Film on CP's behalf,. Production Company may be a single purpose vehicle or a production services company. Similar to PFD. |

| Completion Agreement | n/a | (1) Completion Guarantor<br>(2) Producer | Gives rights to Completion Guarantor rights (including take-over rights) over the production of the Film in order to make sure it is completed on time and on budget. |
|---|---|---|---|
| Completion Guaranty | Bond | (1) Completion Guarantor<br>(2) All Financiers | Guarantees to the financiers that the Film will be completed on time and on budget, or they get their money back. |
| Distribution Agreement | n/a | (1) Producer<br>(2) Distributor | Arranged by the Sales Agent, who will sometimes sign on behalf of the Producer. Grants territorial rights to local distributors. |
| Facility Agreement | n/a | (1) Financier<br>(2) Producer | Confirms the terms of a financing facility, usually provided by a bank. |
| Interparty Agreement | IPA | (1) All financiers<br>(2) Producer<br>(3) Completion Guarantor<br>(4) Collection Agent<br>(5) Sales Agent<br>(6) Production Services Company (if any) | Overrides all other agreements. Ensures that all financiers make their money available at the same time. Expresses the respective rights and obligations of all parties that are not expressed elsewhere. Sets out the definitive Recoupment Schedule (copied on the CAMA). |
| Laboratory Access Agreement | LAA or "Lab Letter" | (1) Laboratory<br>(2) Sales Agent<br>(3) Producer<br>(4) Distributor (sometimes) | Sometimes combined with LPA. Ensures that the laboratory provides access as necessary to Sales Agent / Distributors in order for them to make necessary distribution copies of the film at the lab. |

| | | | |
|---|---|---|---|
| Laboratory Pledgeholder Agreement | LPA | (1) Laboratory<br><br>(2) Production Services Company<br><br>(3) Producer<br><br>(4) Sales Agent<br><br>(5) All Financiers<br><br>(6) Completion Guarantor | Ensures that the Laboratory (at which the film is made / stored / copied) holds the materials on behalf of the Producer, Financiers (etc), and doesn't try to lay claim or prevent access to any of the materials. |
| Letter of Credit | L/C | From a Bank | Guarantee from a bank that if its client does not pay up when due, the bank will pay instead. The recipient of the L/C is often another bank (eg when discounting a distributor's MG on a pre-sale). |
| Non-disturbance Letter | n/a | From Producer to Distributor | Confirms that if, for some reason, the SAA (through which the Distributor was granted rights by the Sales Agent) is terminated prematurely, the Producer (copyright owner) will not prevent the Distributor from continuing to exploit the film under the Distribution Agreement it entered into with the Sales Agent |
| Notice of Availability | NoA | From Sales Agent to Distributor | Informs a Distributor that the film elements are ready to be delivered in accordance with the Delivery Schedule. Clock starts ticking for Distributor to check quality and pay balance of MG. |

| Production, Finance and Distribution Agreement | PFD | (1) Financier(s)<br>(2) Producer | Provides for the Producer to produce the Film and grant the financier(s) distribution rights in return for the financiers providing the production funds. Similar to a CPA. Not necessarily used where there is a thorough IPA and a CPA. |
|---|---|---|---|
| Sales Agency Agreement<br>(or, sometimes, International Distribution Agreement) | SAA<br>(or IDA) | (1) Producer<br>(2) Sales Agent | Appoints Sales Agent to sell film on behalf of Producer (the copyright owner). Has an agreed form Distribution Agreement attached to the back. |
| Sale & Leaseback Agreements | n/a | (1) Producer<br>(2) All Financiers<br>(3) Sale & Leaseback Company | Set of agreements to effect the sale & leaseback transaction, including a Purchase Agreement, Lease Agreement, Charge, Releases, etc |

# Sample delivery schedule

Below is a sample Delivery Schedule, reproduced with kind courtesy of International Delivery Film and Television Limited ("ID Films"). Naturally, in practice, each Delivery Schedule will be different, depending on a number of factors. The size of the budget obviously has an impact on what might be made available, as the items generally have to be paid for by the Producer from the production funds (although, in some cases, the proceeds of the MG will have to be used under certain distribution deals). The entity to which the materials are being delivered will also have its own requirements, and will not pay for the film until these are met.

The Delivery Schedule on the back of the Sales Agency Agreement should contain the aggregate of everything that any of the Sales Agent's buyers (Distributors) are likely to need, so that it has all the necessary materials to deliver on to them. As for the Distributors themselves, some have greater requirements than others. German buyers, for example, have higher technical requirements than most, and American (especially Studio) Distributors usually insist on an inordinate amount of paperwork. The Completion Guarantor will usually agree to bond most of the essential elements on the Sales Agent's Delivery Schedule, but not all; paperwork and publicity materials usually being the first casualties. For any one film, therefore, there may be a number of conflicting Delivery Schedules, and care must be taken in ensuring that the underlying agreements provide for who must pay for what in the event of a discrepancy.

One last point relates to "**Access**" as opposed to "**Delivery**". Sometimes the recipient is entitled to receive actual hard copies of the materials, and sometimes it is given the right to attend the laboratory at which the masters are stored in order to make its own copies (again, on whom the relevant costs fall can be a major issue). If all copies are made at the Producer's own lab, s/he will have a little more control over the number of copies in existence. It is also cheaper for the Producer if s/he doesn't have to pay and deliver the copies around the world him/herself.

## Sample Delivery Schedule

### A FEATURE ELEMENTS

1 **Laboratory Access to 35mm fully cut and assembled Original (or Output) Negative of Feature**, complete with Main and End Titles.

2 **35mm Combined Stereo Answer Print** of Feature from Original (or Output) Negative, fully corrected and approved by Producer, complete with Main and End Titles.

3 **35mm Feature Interpositive**, fully timed, complete with Main and End Titles.

4 **2 x 35mm Feature Internegatives**, fully timed, complete with Main and End Titles.

**** NOTE FOR ITEMS 3 & 4 – If feature has subtitles inherent in reels then textless reels will have to be supplied for domestic and international use ****

5 **2 x 35mm Feature Optical Sound Track Negatives**, fully cut with Main and End Titles, edited, scored and assembled, synchronised with picture negative elements.

6 **2 x 35 Combined Check Print From I/Negatives**, full timed, complete with Main and End Titles.

7 **35mm Magnetic 2-Track Stereo Print Master (SVA)** of Feature and MO Disk if Digital.

8 **35mm Magnetic 6-Track 5.1 Print Master Digital Version of Feature** (L/LS/R/RS/C/Sub).

9 **35mm Magnetic Stereo International Music & Effects Track of Feature**, fully fitted with full 4+2 configuration (L/C/R/S/Clean Dialogue/Additional Material).

10 **35mm Magnetic Stereo International 6-Track Digital SRD Music & Effects Track** (L/LS/R/RS/C/Sub) of Feature, fully filled, with full 6-Track Digital configuration.

11 **35mm Magnetic Stereo 6-Track D/M/E of Feature** (Stereo Dialogue, Stereo Music, Stereo Effects).

**** ITEMS 7-11 ABOVE CAN BE DELIVERED ON DA88 At 24 FPS, 25 EBU, 48 KHz. However, if items 7-11 are delivered on DA88, then item 7a and 10a shown below must also be delivered.* ***

7a DAT 2-Track Final Mix at 25 FPS, 25 EBU, 48 KH

10a DAT 2-Track Music & Effects Track at 25 FPS, 25 EBU, 48 Khz

12 **Full QC (Quality Check)** of above Sound Elements (items 7-11).

13 **35mm Interpositive and Internegative of Textless Backgrounds of Main and End Titles**, and any captions or subtitles contained in the picture – to include all optical fades and dissolves, to length of title sequence.

13a **35mm Check Print** from above internegative.

14 **Access to Television Version of the Film**, if created by the Producer as well as access to the Negative and Positive Print of all available alternative takes, cover shots, looped dialogue lines and other material not used in the final version of the Film.

15 **Electronic Press Kit** or other documentary material if created, access to and loan of master elements as well as delivery of the EPK on a Digital Video Tape format.

16 **Digital Audio Tape of all Master Music** specifically recorded for the Film.

17 **1 x High Def Master** 4 x 3 Pan and Scan Full Frame Video Master of Feature.

17a **1 x Digi Beta PAL** 4 x 3 Pan and Scan Full Frame Video Master of Feature.

17b **1 x Digi Beta NTSC** 4 x 3 Pan and Scan Full Frame Video Master of Feature.

18 **1 x High Def Master** 16 x 9 Full Height Anamorphic Video Master of Feature.

18a **1 x Digi Beta PAL** 16 x 9 Full Height Anamorphic Video Master of Feature.

18b **1 x Digi Beta NTSC** 16 x 9 Full Height Anamorphic Video Master of Feature.

19 **1 x High Def Master** 16 x 9 Original Ratio (ie Letterbox 1.85:1 or 1:2.35) Video Master of Feature.

19a **1 x Digi Beta PAL** 16 x 9 Original Ratio (ie Letterbox 1.85:1 or 1:2.35) Video Master of Feature.

19b **1 x Digi Beta NTSC** 16 x 9 Original Ratio (ie Letterbox 1.85:1 or 1:2.35) Video Master of Feature.

*** *ITEMS 17-19b TO HAVE TEXTLESS BACKGROUNDS ADDED AT THE END OF THE FEATURE AND AUDIO FINAL MIX ON 1&2 AND M/E ON 3&4* ***

*** *IF THE FILM IS MASTERED ONTO HIGH DEF, THEN WE WILL REQUIRE COPIES AS PER ITEMS*

*17-19b, IF NOT AN AGREED DELIVERABLE THEN DIGI BETAS AS PER 17a-19b WITH ACCESS TO ORIGINAL HIGH DEFS IF CREATED ****

20 **DA88 5.1 Print Master** conformed to Video Master.

21 **DA88 5.1 M&E** conformed to Video Master.

22 **Full QC (Quality Check)** by video house to approve above Masters.

23 **Full Dialogue Continuity and Spotting List of Feature** including all spotting information. Both hard copy and on disc.

## B PUBLICITY / DOCUMENTATION

**Detailed Synopsis** (minimum 500 words). Also to be delivered on disc.

**Credit List of full Cast and Technical Personnel**. Also to be delivered on disc.

**Production Notes, Biographies and Filmographies** of Principal Cast, Producer, Director and Writer, and descriptions or locations used. Copies of all available Press Clippings, Press Kits, Books, Synopses, Flyers and other Publicity Material. (Also to be delivered on disc)

**Black and White Stills and Original Negatives** of Stills maximum of 250 10"x8". (These are also to be delivered on CD – and are to include full contact sheets detailing each image)

**35mm Original Colour Transparencies** maximum of 250. (These are also to be delivered on CD – and are to include full contact sheets detailing each image)

*Note: All Stills and Transparencies to have been taken during production and to be titled and captioned with all persons appearing, to be identified and to be supplied together with written clearances from any party featured who has any Stills Approval Rights.*

**Key Art** if created by the Producer, a first generation Dupe Transparency of the Key Art created for the One-Sheet. (this must also be delivered on CD).

**Final Billing Blocks for Posters, Video Packaging, Paid Advertising and Trailers**, approved by all parties, as well as camera-ready Black and White Stats of all the Logos required by the Producer to be included in the Billing Block (this must also be delivered on CD, with separate files for the fonts and logos included as well as the text itself).

**Notarised copy of the E&O Certificate**.

**Credit Statement** of both the contractual Screen Credits and the Paid Advertising Credits applicable to the Film. The Statement should include each credit in one column and a summary of the credit obligation in the adjacent column, including form, placement, type size and exclusions. If there is no obligation to accord a certain credit which has been accorded on screen or is included in your Billing Block, the "obligation" should be stated as "Producer's Discretion". Also to be delivered on disc.

**Statement of Restrictions**, a statement listing all dubbing, cutting and other restrictions applicable to the Film. Also to be delivered on disc.

**Music Cue Sheets** stating for each composition in the Film the Title, the Composers, Publishers, Copyright Owners, Performers, Usage, Performing Rights Society, as well as in the film footage and running time. Also to be delivered on disc.

**Original notarised Chain of Title Report**

**Full copy of all Chain of Title agreements**

**Final Certified Cost Statement**

**MPAA Rating Certificate** (if applicable).

**Certificate of Nationality** – 5 original, signed copies to be supplied.

**Certificate of Origin** – 5 original, signed copies to be supplied.

**Cast/Talent/Personnel Agreements**, access to copies of fully executed agreements for the Writer, Director, Producer, Composer and Principal Cast members, as well as Other Cast members, Talent and Personnel whose names are accorded Paid Advertising Credit.

**Final Certified Cost Statement,** prepared by either a certified public accounting firm or the production company auditor, setting forth the final actual negative cost of the Film.

**Dolby License**, if applicable, a copy of the executed Licence Agreement in full force and effect between the Producer and Dolby Laboratories Inc. in connection with the Film.

**Editor's Script Notes**, a copy of the final shooting script marked with Slate and Take numbers used in photographing each script scene, indicating the portion of each script scene covered by each Slate and Take number with notations as to camera movements used, if requested.

**Editor's Code Book**, a copy of the Code Book bearing identification of Slate and Take numbers of each scene by cutting print code numbers, if requested.

**Music Licenses**, copies of fully executed synchronisation and master use Licenses for each item of licenses music in the Film, fully executed agreements for each Composer of Underscoring, and evidence of payments under such agreements.

## C TRAILER PICTURE AND SOUND ELEMENTS

1. **35mm Fully Timed Action Internegative** of Trailer.
2. **35mm Optical Sound Track Negative** of Trailer, fully edited, scored and assembled, synchronised with Trailer Picture element.
3. **35mm Check Print of Trailer**, fully graded and in sync.
4. **35mm Master Timed Interpositive** of Trailer.
5. **35mm Textless Internegative and Interpositive of Trailer,** if applicable.
6. **35mm 4-Track Magnetic Master of Sound Track** of Trailer which will contain separate Music, Effects and Dialogue (N/D/M/E), plus 4-Track Stereo (L/C/R/S) and 6-Track Digital M&E if mixed digitally.
7. **35mm Stereo 2-Track SVA Magnetic Master** of Sound Track to Trailer & MO Disc if Digital.
8. **Full Dialogue Continuity List** of Trailer including all spotting information.

*** *ITEMS 6 & 7 CAN BE DELIVERED ON DA88 AT 24 FPS, 25 EBU, 48 KHz*

# UK film statistics

| TOP 20 UK FILMS RELEASED IN THE UK IN 2004 | | | | |
|---|---|---|---|---|
| | **Title** | **Country of origin** | **Box office gross (£m)** | **Distributor** |
| 1 | Harry Potter and the Prisoner of Azkaban | UK/USA | 46.08 | Warner Bros |
| 2 | Bridget Jones: The Edge of Reason | UK/USA | 36 | UIP |
| 3 | Troy | UK/USA/Mal | 18 | Warner Bros |
| 4 | *Phantom of the Opera | UK/USA | 8.9 | Entertainment |
| 5 | Wimbledon | UK/USA | 7.17 | UIP |
| 6 | King Arthur | UK/USA/Ire | 7.07 | Buena Vista |
| 7 | Shaun of the Dead | UK | 6.69 | UIP |
| 8 | Thunderbirds | UK/USA | 5.43 | UIP |
| 9 | Bride and Prejudice | UK/USA | 5.17 | Pathé |
| 10 | Alien Vs. Predator | UK/Cze/Can/Ger | 5.15 | 20th Fox |
| 11 | Alfie | UK/USA | 4.71 | UIP |
| 12 | Layer Cake | UK | 4.45 | Sony Pictures |
| 13 | Around the World in 80 days | UK/USA/Ger/Ire | 4.15 | Entertainment |
| 14 | Girl with a Pearl Earring | UK/Lux | 3.84 | Pathé |
| 15 | *Finding Neverland | UK/USA | 3.54 | Buena Vista |
| 16 | Ladies in Lavender | UK | 3.16 | Entertainment |
| 17 | Resident Evil: Apocalypse | UK/Ger/Fra/Can | 1.97 | Sony Pictures |
| 18 | Tooth | UK | 1.68 | Redbus |
| 19 | 5 Children & It | UK | 1.57 | Pathé |
| 20 | Man About Dog | UK/Ire 1.45 | Redbus | |
| *Source: Nielsen EDI, RSU analysis* | | | | |

| BOX OFFICE RESULTS FOR THE TOP 20 FILMS RELEASED IN THE UK IN 2004 | | | | | | |
|---|---|---|---|---|---|---|
| | **Title** | **Country of origin** | **Box office gross (£m)** | **Number of opening cinemas** | **Opening weekend gross (£m)** | **Dist.** |
| 1 | Shrek 2 | USA | 48.1 | 512 | 16.22 | UIP |
| 2 | Harry Potter and the Prisoner of Azkaban | UK/USA | 46.08 | 535 | 23.88 | Warner Bros |
| 3 | Bridget Jones: The Edge of Reason | UK/USA | 36 | 504 | 10.44 | UIP |
| 4 | *The Incredibles | USA | 32.04 | **494 | **9.75 | Buena Vista |
| 5 | Spider-Man 2 | USA | 26.72 | 504 | 8.77 | Sony Pictures |
| 6 | The Day After Tomorrow | USA | 25.21 | 429 7.32 | 20th Fox | |
| 7 | Shark Tale | USA | 22.82 | 504 7.55 | UIP | |
| 8 | Troy | UK/USA/ Mal | 18 | **504 | **6.02 | Warner Bros |
| 9 | I, Robot | USA | 17.98 | 447 | 4.75 | 20th Fox |
| 10 | Scooby-Doo Too | USA | 16.49 | 489 | 3.55 | Warner Bros |
| 11 | Van Helsing | USA | 15.15 | 458 | 5.43 | UIP |
| 12 | *Lemony Snicket's A Series of Unfortunate Events | USA | 13.11 | 452 | 2.21 | UIP |
| 13 | Starsky & Hutch | USA | 12.6 | 81 | 0.41 | Buena Vista |
| 14 | The Last Samurai | USA/Jap/ NZ | 11.9 | 430 | 2.72 | Warner Bros |
| 15 | The Bourne Supremacy | USA/Ger | 11.56 | 418 | 2.72 | UIP |
| 16 | The Passion of the Christ | USA | 11.08 | 46 | 0.23 | Icon |
| 17 | School of Rock | USA/Ger | 10.50 | 376 | 2.74 | UIP |
| 18 | The Village | USA | 10.31 | 433 | 2.95 | Buena Vista |
| 19 | Lost in Translation | USA/Jap | 10.06 | 96 | 0.8 | Mntm |
| 20 | Dodge Ball: A True Underdog Story | USA | 10.03 | 315 | 2.2 | 20th Fox |
| *Source: Nielson EDI* | | | | | | |

# UK films on British TV

| NUMBER OF RECENT UK FILMS AS A PERCENTAGE OF TOTAL FILMS BROADCAST IN 2004 | | | |
|---|---|---|---|
| **Channel** | **2003** | **2004** | **% change** |
| BBC1 | 4.6 | 6.2 | 34.8 |
| BBC2 | 3.3 | 9.6 | 190.9 |
| ITV1 | 3.9 | 3.3 | -15.4 |
| Channel 4 | 2.6 | 6.5 | 150 |
| Five | 0.5 | 0.4 | -20 |
| Total | 2.8 | 5.3 | 89.3 |
| *Source: DGA Metrics, BARB* | | | |

| NUMBER OF RECENT (MADE WITHIN THE LAST 8 YEARS) UK FILMS BROADCAST IN 2004 | | | |
|---|---|---|---|
| *Channel* | *2003* | *2004* | *% change* |
| BBC1 | 20 | 27 | 35 |
| BBC2 | 15 | 48 | 220 |
| ITV1 | 12 | 9 | -25 |
| Channel 4 | 15 | 33 | 120 |
| Five | 3 | 2 | -33.3 |
| Total | 65 | 119 | 83.1 |
| Source: DGA Metrics, BARB | | | |

# UK production

| SIZE DISTRIBUTION OF BUDGETS, DOMESTIC UK FEATURES, 2004 | | | |
|---|---|---|---|
| **Budget band (£m)** | **Number** | **Total Budget in band (£m)** | **% of total budget** |
| £10-£30m | 3 | 44.9 | 38.2 |
| £5 – 10m | 4 | 23.2 | 19.7 |
| £2 – 5m | 10 | 34.3 | 29.1 |
| £0.5 – 2m | 10 | 15.3 | 13 |
| Under £0.5m | not monitored | | |
| Total | 27 | 117.8 | 100 |
| *Source: UK Film Council International, RSU analysis.* | | | |

# UK Film Council Development Fund slate awards

**UK Film Council Development Fund slate awards 2003 - 2005**

| | | |
|---|---|---|
| Company Pictures | £ 160,000 | 1/12/05 |
| Capitol Films | £ 400,000 | 12/8/04 |
| Darlow Smithson | £ 250,000 | 12/8/04 |
| Jupiter | £ 400,000 | 12/8/04 |
| Number 9 Films Ltd | £ 400,000 | 12/8/04 |
| Pathe Pictures Limited | £ 350,000 | 12/8/04 |
| Scarlet Films | £ 300,000 | 12/8/04 |
| Fox Phillips | £ 80,000 | 8/18/04 |
| Ecosse Films | £ 250,000 | 7/21/04 |
| Riverchild Films | £ 32,500 | 3/31/04 |
| October Films Ltd | £ 90,000 | 3/31/04 |
| Riverchild Films | £ 65,000 | 3/31/04 |
| Ruby Films | £ 255,000 | 3/31/04 |
| Tall Stories | £ 100,000 | 3/31/04 |
| NFTS | £ 12,000 | 3/31/04 |
| Riverchild Films | £ 65,000 | 3/31/04 |
| Gruber Films | £ 100,000 | 3/31/04 |
| Fragile Films | £ 200,000 | 3/24/04 |
| Tall Stories | £ 50,000 | 3/17/04 |
| Recorded Picture Company | £150,000 | 3/17/04 |
| CFF Enterprises | £ 100,000 | 11/5/03 |
| Passion Pictures | £ 100,000 | 11/5/03 |
| Qwerty Films (formerly Kuhn & Co) | £ 250,000 | 11/5/03 |
| Autonomous | £ 125,000 | 11/5/03 |
| Archer Street/Tigerlily | £ 73,750 | 6/18/03 |
| Fox Phillips | £ 120,000 | 6/4/03 |
| Impact Pictures | £ 108,500 | 3/26/03 |
| Company Pictures | £ 130,000 | 3/19/03 |
| Ecosse Films | £ 250,000 | 3/19/03 |
| Fragile Films | £ 200,000 | 3/19/03 |
| Mission Pictures | £ 250,000 | 3/19/03 |
| Ruby Films | £ 70,000 | 3/19/03 |
| *Source: UK Film Council* | | |

# Further Reading

## FILMMAKING

"Independent Feature Film Production" by Gregory Goodell ((St Martin's Griffin)

"The Beginning Filmmaker's Guide to a Successful First Film" by Renee Harman, James Lawrence and Jim Lawrence (contributor) (Walker & Co)

"The Guerilla Filmmakers Handbook and the Film Producers Toolkit" by Chris Jones & Genevieve Jolliffe (Continuum)

"Media Law" by Rhonda Baker (Routledge Press / Blueprint Press)

"Hollywood Dealmaking - negotiating talent agreements" by Dina Appleton & Daniel Yankelevits (Allworth Press)

## SHORT FILMS

"How To Make Great Short Feature Films: The Making Of Ghosthunter " by Ian Lewis (Focal Press)

"In Short: A guide to Short Filmmaking in the Digital Age" by Eileen Elsey and Andrew Kelly (BFI Publishing)

"Making the Winning Short: How to Write, Direct, Edit and Produce a Short Film" by Edmond Levy (Henry Holt)

## CAREER AND TRAINING

"Lights, Camera, Action! Career in Film, Television and Video 2nd Revised Edition" by Josephine Langham (BFI Publishing)

"Listing of Short Courses in Media and Multimedia" by Lavina Orton (BFI Publishing)

## REFERENCE

"BFI Film Handbook" edited by Eddie Dyja (BFI Publishing)

"Kays Production Manual" (Kay Media)

"The Knowledge" (Miller Freeman Information Services)

"The Writer's and Artist's Yearbook" by A C Black (A & C Black)

"The PACT directory of independent producers" (PACT)

"Ernst & Young Guide to International Film Production" (Ernst & Young LLP)

## FUNDING

"The Film Finance Handbook" edited by Mike Downey (The Media Business School)

"The Art of the Deal" by Dorothy Viljoen (PACT)

"Filmmakers & Financing, Business Plans for Independents" by Louise Levison (Focal Press)

## OTHER PUBLICATIONS

"A Guide to Help for Small Business" a free booklet from the Department of Trade & Industry

"A Filmmakers Guide to Distribution & Exhibition" (BFI) free to download from www.bfi.org.uk

"Directory of UK Co-producers 2003-2004" (British Council) free to download from www.britfilms.com

"The Media Business File" by the Media Business School, updated three times a year

# Useful websites

## INTELLECTUAL PROPERTY ISSUES

World Intellectual Property Organisation: www.wipo.int

UK legislation: www.legislation.hmso.gov.uk

UK patent, trade mark and design office: www.patent.gov.uk

UK company information: www.companieshouse.gov.uk

European legislation: www.europa.eu.int/eur-lex/en

European trade mark and design office: www.oami.eu.int

US patent and trade mark office: www.uspto.gov

Internet Corporation for Assigned Names and Numbers (ICANN): www.icann.org

http://www.legalzoom.com/law_library/copyrights/resources_copyright.html

## INDUSTRY NEWS

Africa Film and TV, www.africafilmtv.com, African trade journal, focused on African screen industry within International market

Box Office, www.boxoff.com, North American trade journal

Film Journal, www.filmjournal.com, American trade journal with international outlook

Hollywood Reporter, www.hollywoodreporter.com, Hollywood trade journal with an international news section

Le Film Francais, www.lefilmfrancais.com, French trade journal, focused mainly on French and European screen news

Screen Digest, www.screendigest.com, International trade journal for screen business news, research, reference and statistics

Screen Finance, www.informamedia.com, International trade journal about screen finance news and issues

Screen International, www.screendaily.com, English International trade journal with offices around the globe

Variety, www.variety.com, Hollywood-focused screen trade journal

Indiewire, www.indiewire.com, US independent film news

## MACGREGOR'S LOW BDUGET SITES

Alternative Hollywoodunhollywood.com/

Low Budget Tips

www.exposure.co.uk/

Sony DV Cameras

www.sonybiz.net/

Pinnacle Editing Systems

www.pinnaclesys.com/

Low Budget Scriptwriting Tips

www.online-communicator.com/scriptip.html

SoYouWannaMakeLowBudgetMovies

www.soyouwanna.com/site/syws/makemovie/makemovie.html

Low Budget Horror Film Society

lbhfs.proboards18.com/

No Budget FX

www.angelfire.com/movies/nobudgetsfx/nobudgetsfx.html

Special FX

www.matthawkins.co.uk/index.php?module=PostWrap&page=static_pages/special_fx.htm&resize=1

Horror Makeup

www.geocities.com/Hollywood/Lot/9373/SCREAM/scream.html

Society of Make Up Artists

www.sapsema.org/

www.vfx.co.nz/

Get the Film Look On Video

www.creativecow.net/articles/graham_doug/film_look/

DIY Photographic Filters

medfmt.8k.com/bronfilters.html#homemade

Video-Film Transfer

www.moviemaker.com/issues/38/38_dv.htm

"I am going to make my movie now..

www.dvmoviemaking.com/Part1.html

Ready, Aim, Shoot..

www.dvmoviemaking.com/Part2.html

Making A Movie On Your Desktop

www.dvmoviemaking.com/Part3.html

Movie's Finished! Now What?

www.dvmoviemaking.com/Part4.html

Matt Hawkins' Low Budget Movie Guide

Thrae Guide to No Budget Moviemaking

www.thrae.com/nbmm/guide/

Guerilla Filmmaking 101

www.proletariatpictures.com/r-101.html

Learning From Low Budgets

www.nextwavefilms.com/ulbp/learning.html

Ultra Low Budget Production

www.nextwavefilms.com/ulbp/index.html

Not Forgetting.

**Shooting People**
shootingpeople.org

**Wideshot**
shootingpeople.org/wideshot

**Netribution**
www.netribution.co.uk

## AROUND THE WORLD

### Argentina

AVH www.avh.com.ar
Gativideo www.gativideo.com.ar
LK-Tel www.lk-tel.com.ar
UIP www.argenuip.com.ar

### Australia

ACCC www.accc.gov.au
Australian Film Commission www.afc.gov.au
Beyond International www.beyond.com.au
CEASA www.geko.net.au/-ceasa
Cinemedia www.cinemedia.com.au
Disney www.disney.com.au
Film Australia www.filmaust.com.au
Fox Movies www.foxmovies.com.au
Greater Union www.greaterunion.com.au
Hoyts www.hoyts.com.au
Palace Cinemas www.palace.net.au

SAWA www.sawa.com
Screen Network Australia www.sna.net.au
SPAA www.spaa.org.au
Val Morgan www.valmorgan.com.au
Village Roadshow www.villageroadshow.com.au

**Austria**

Austrian Film Institute www.filminstitut.at
BMWF www.bmwfgv.at
Buena Vista www.buenavista.at
Cine Tirol Filmförderung www.cinetirol.com
Cinemaxx www.cinemaxx.at
Constantin Film www.constantinfilm.at
Europlex www.europlex.at
Filmladen www.filmladen.at
Filmfonds Wien www.filmfonds-wien.at
Infoscreen www.infoscreen.at
Metropol www.metropol-kino.at

**Belgium**

Cinergie www.cinergie.be
CSA www.csa.cfwb.be
Kinepolis group www.kinepolis.be
RMB www.rmb.be
Vlaams Audiovisueel Fonds www.vaf.be
Wallimage www.wallimage.be

**Brazil**

ACNielsen www.acnielsen.com.br
Cinemark www.cinemark.com.br
Disney www.disneycom.br
Fox www.foxfilm.com.br
Jornal do Video www.jornaldovideo.com.br
MPAA www.mpaa.org/mpa-al
Promocine www.promocine.com.br
UIP www.uip.com.br
Warner Bros. Brazil www.warnerbros.com.br

**Canada**

Alliance Atlantis www.allianceatlantis.com
Cinemas Guzzo, www.cinemasguzzo.com
Cineplex Odeon www.cineplexodeon.com
CSC www.csc.ca
Empire Theatres www.empiretheatres.com
Famous Players www.famousplayers.com
Imax www.imax.com
Lions Gate www.lionsgate-ent.com
NFB www.nfb.ca
RDS Data www.rdsdata.com
Statistics Canada www.statcan.ca

**China**

China Film www.chinafilm.com
China Shinco www.china-shinco.com
Shanghai Paradise www.paradise.com.cn

Czech Republic
Barrandov www.barrandov.cz
Bontonfilm www.bonton.cz
Falcon www.falcon.cz

**Denmark**

Danish Film Institute www.dfi.dk
Danish Novelle Film www.novellefilm.dk
Metronome www.metronome.dk
Ministry of Culture www.kum.dk
Scanbox www.scanbox.dk
Videoclub www.videoclub.dk

**Finalnd**

Centre for the Promotion of Audiovisual Culture in Finland www.kopiosto.fi/avek
Suomen Elokuvasäätiö www.ses.fi

**France**

Agence Culturelle d'Alsace www.culture-alsace.org/accueil.php
Allocine www.allocine.fr
Aquitaine Image Cinéma www.aquitaine-image-cinema.fr
Atelier de Production Centre Val de Loire www.apcvl.com
Bac Films www.bacfilms.com
CCRAV www.ccrav.com
Centre National du Cinema www.cnc.fr
Cinefil www.cinefil.com
Circuit A www.circuita.com
Columbia TriStar www.columbiatristar.fr
Communauté Urbaine de Strasbourg www.strasbourg-film.com
CSA www.csa.fr

Diaphana www.diaphana.fr
DVD France www.dvdfr.com
EAO www.obs.coe.int
Gaumont www.gaumont.fr
INA www.ina.fr
Le Film Francais www.lefilmfrancais.com
Media France www.mediafrance.org
Mediavision www.mediavision.fr
MK2 www.mk2.com
National Film Commission of France www.filmfrance.com
Pathe www.pathe.fr
Premiere www.premiere.fr
Rhône-Alpes Cinéma www.rhone-alpes-cinema.fr
Région Ile de Franc www.iledefrance.fr/conseil/action_cinema.asp
Théâtre et Cinéma en Île-de-France www.thecif.org
Unifrance www.unifrance.org
USPA www.uspa.fr

## Germany

ACNielsen www.acnielsen.de
Betafilm www.KirchGruppe.de
Blickpunkt www.cinebiz.de
Bremer Innovationsagentur www.bia-bremen.de
Buena Vista International www.movie.de
Cinecitta www.cinecitta.de
Cinema online www.cinema.de
Cinemaxx www.cinemaxx.com
Cinemedia www.cinemedia.de
Columbia TriStar www.columbiatristar.de
Constantin www.constantinfilm.de
Deutsches institut fur filmkunde www.filminstitut.de
FilmFernsehFonds Bayernwww.fff-bayern.de
Filmboard Berlin-Brandenburg www.filmboard.de
Filmbuero Bremen e.V. www.filmbuero-bremen.de
Filmbüro NW e.V www.filmbuero-nw.de
Filmförderung Hamburg GmbH www.filmfoerderung-hamburg.de
Filmförderungsanstalt www.ffa.de
Filmstiftung Nord-Rhein Westfalen GmbH www.filmstiftung.de
Fox Germany www.foxfilm.de
FSK www.fsk.de
GEMA www.gema.de
GVU www.gvu.de
HDF www.kino-hdf.de
Hessische Filmförderung www.hessische-filmfoerderung.de
Helkon www.helkon.de
Intertainment www.intertainment.de
jugendfilm www.jugendfilm.de
Kieft & Kieft www.cinestar.de
Kinopolis www.kinopolis.de
Kinowelt www.kinowelt.de
Kirch Group www.kirchgruppe.de
Kulturelle Filmförderung Mecklenburg-Vorpommern www.Film-MV.de
Kulturelle Filmförderung Sachsen www.smwk.de/index-js.html
Kulturelle Filmförderung Schleswig-Holstein e.V www.filmbuero-sh.de
MFG www.film.mfg.de
Mitteldeutsche Medienförderung GmbH www.mdm-foerderung.de
Moviedata www.moviedata.de
MSH www.m-s-h.org
Nordmedia www.nord-media.de
Omniplex www.omniplex.de
Saarland Medien GmbH www.Saarlandmedien.de
Senator Film www.senatorfilm.de
SPIO www.spio.de
Stiftung Kuratorium Junger Deutscher Film www.kuratorium-junger-film.de
TOBIS www.tobis.de
UCI www.filmab.de
UFA cinemas www.ufakino.de
UIP www.uip.de
Warner Village www.villagekinos.de
Wegra www.wegra.de

## Greece

Greek Film Centre www.gfc.gr

## Hong Kong

ACNielsen www.acnielsen.com.hk
Broadway Cinemas www.cinema.com.hk
Chinastar www.chinastarcom.hk
Golden Harvest www.goldenharvest.com
Media Asia Group www.mediaasia.com
Mei Ah www.meiah.com
UA Cinemas www.cityline.com.hk

## Hungary

Budapest Film www.budapestfilm.hu
Cineplex Odeon www.cineplexodeon.hu
Flamex www.flamex.hu
Intercom www.intercom.hu
MMA www.mma.hu
MOKEP www.mokep.hu

## India

Multi Media Frontiers www.multimediafrontiers.com
NFDC www.nfdcindia.com
Zee TV www.zeetelevision.com

## Ireland

Bord Scannan na hEireannwww.filmboard.ie
Dept. of Arts, Sport and Tourism www.arts-sport-tourism.gov.ie
Irish Film & TV Network www.iftn.ie

## Italy

20th Century Fox www.20thfox.it
ACNielsen www.acnielsen.it
AGCM www.agcm.it
AGCOM www.agcom.it
ANICA www.anica.it
Cecchi Gori www.cecchigori.com
Cinema 5 www.cinema5.it
Columbia TriStar www.columbiatristar.it
Direzione Generale per il Cinema www.spettacolo.beniculturali.it/cinema/cinema.htm
Film Auto www.filmauro.it
Filmexport Group www.filmexport.it
Intrafilms www.intrafilms.it
Istituto Luce www.luce.it
Lucky Red www.luckyred.it
Media Salles www.mediasalles.it
Medusa Film www.medusa.it
Rai www.raitrade.it
Warner Bros. www.warnerbros.it

## Japan

Daiei www.daiei.tokuma.com
Fox www.foxjapan.com
TOEI www.toei.co.jp
Toho www.toho.co.jp
Shochiku wwA,.shochiku.co.jp
Sony www.sonyco.jp
Warner Mycal www.mycal.co.jp
Luxembourg National Film Production Fund www.filmfund.lu

## Mexico

Canacine www.canacine.org.mx
Cinemark de mexicowww.cinemark.com.mx
Cinemex www.cinemex.com.mx
Fox www.foxmexico.com
Ramirez cinemas www.cinepolis,com.mx

## The Netherlands

Audiovisuele Federatie Nederland www.afn.nl
AV-SCENE www.scene.nl
Commissariaat voor de Media www.cvdm.nl
Disney www.disney.nl
The Dutch Co-production Fund for Broadcasting Companieswww.cobofonds.nl
Dutch film fund www.filmfand.nl
Het Rotterdams Fonds voor de Film en Audiovisuele Media/ www.rff.rotterdam.nl
Holland Film www.hollandfilm.nl
Hubert Bals Fund www.filmfestivalrotterdam.com
Jan Vrijman Fund www.idfa.nl
Minerva www.minervagroep.nl
NBF www.nbf.nl
Nederlands Fonds voor de Film www.filmfund.nl
RCV www.rcv.nl

## Poland

Imperial www.imperial.com.pl

ITI www.iticinema.com.pl
Multikino www.multikino.com.pl
Statistical Office www.stat.gov.pl/english/
Syrena Entertainment www.syrena.com

**Portugal**

Instituto do Cinema, www.icam.pt

**Russia**

Gemini Film www.geminifilm.ru
Goskino www.goskino.ru
Media Most www.mediamost.ru

**Singapore**

ACNielsen www.acnielsen.com.sg
Cathay Organisation www.cathaycom.sg
Golden Village www.goldenvillage.com.sg
Mediatech www.mediatech.com.sg
Min. of Information & the Arts www.mita.gov.sg
Shaw Organisation www.shawcom.sg
Singapore Film Commission www.sfc.org.sg

**South Africa**

Cinemark www.cinemark.co.za
Primedia www.primedia.co.za
Ster-Kinekor www.sterkinekorcom

**South Korea**

CJ Golden Village www.cgvco.kr
Daewoo www.daewoo.co.kr
Hyundai www.hbs.co.kr
J-Com www.jcom.co.kr
KOFIC www.kofic.or.kr
Min. of Culture & Tourism www.mct.go.kr
Pusan International Film Festival www.piffor.kr
Seoul Cinema www.seoulcinema.com

**Spain**

ACEC vwww.acec.es
Alta Films www.altafilms.es
CINESA www.cinesa.es
FAPAE www.cinespain.com
Golem www.golem.es
ICAA www.cinespain.com/ICAA
Lauren Films www.laurenfilms.es
Movierecord www.movierecord.com
Madrid Film Promotion Office www.comadrid.es
Sogepaq www.sogepaq.es
Yelmo Cineplex www.yelmocineplex.es

**Sweden**

BVI www.bionytt.com
Disney www.disneyse
Film i Dalarna www.filmidalarna.se
Film i Skaane www.filmiskane.nu
Film i Sydöst www.kalmar.regionforbund.se/kultur/film
Film i Väst www.filmivast.se
FHR www.fhrse
Fox Film www.foxfilm.se
Göteborg Film Festival Filmfund www.filmfestival.org/html/eng/filmfonder.html
Metronome www..metronome.se
Nordic-Baltic Film Fund www.bmc.dk/guidelines.htm
Nordisk Film- & TV Fond www.nftf.net
Sandrew www.sandrews.se
SF Media www.sf-media.com
Statistiska Centralbyran www.scb.se
Svensk Filmindustri www.sfse
Svenska Filminstitutet www.sfi.se
UIP www.uip.se

**Switzerland**

Filmnet www.filmnet.ch
Fox www.fox.ch
Metrocine vwww.metrocine.ch

**USA**

AFI www.afionline.org
AFMA www.afma.com
AMC www.amctheatres.com
AMPAS www.ampas.org
Buena Vista www.movies.com
Carmike www.carmike.com
Castle Rock www.castle-rock.com
Cinema Screen Media www.cinemamedia.com

Cinemark www.cinemark.com
Cinemark International
www.cinemarkinternational.com
Columbia TriStar www.spe.sony.com
Digital Theater Systems www.dtstech.com
Disney www.disney.com
Dolby www.dolby.com/movies
EDI www.entdata.com
Edwards Cinemaswww.edwardscinemas.com
Electronic Industries Alliance www.eia.org
FCC www.fcc.gov
Fine Line www.flf.com
Fox www.fox.com
Fox Searchlight www.foxsearchlight.com
General Cinemas www.generalcinemas.com
Hoyts www.hoyts.com
IMAX www.imax.com
Loews Cineplex www.loewscineplex.com
MGM www.mgm.com
Miramax www.miramax.com
MPA www.mpaa.org
National Amusements
www.nationalamusements.com
National Cinema Network www.ncninc.com
New Line www.newline.com
Paramount www.paramount.com
Pixar www.pixar.com
PolyGram www.polygram.com
Regal Theaters www.regaltheaters.com
Rentrak www.rentrak.com
Rysher www.rysher.com
Screenvision Cinema Network
www.screenvision.com
SDDS www.sdds.com
Sony www.sony.com
Sony Pictures www.sonypictures.com
THX www.thx.com
Technicolor www.technicolor.com
UIP www.uipcorp.com
United Artists Theatre Circuitwww.uatc.com
Universal www.universalstudios.com
Video Software Dealers Association
www.vsda.orgom
Warner Bros. www.warnerbros.com